Edwin Forrest

Polyglot Press Alger Series

Life of Edwin Forrest.

Volume II.

Horatio Alger, Jr.

Polyglot
Press

Philadelphia

THIS IS A POLYGLOT PRESS ALGER EDITION

Published in the United States by Polyglot Press, Inc.
A member of Polyglot Press Alliance
Philadelphia • Barcelona • Beijing • Cairo • Mexico DF • Moscow •
Rio de Janeiro • Toronto • Trivandrum • London • Sydney • Tel Aviv
Copyright ©2002 by Polyglot Press, Inc.

Life of Edwin Forrest.
Volume Two.
By Horatio Alger, Jr., Trade Paperback.
ISBN: 1-4115-0017-2.

This book is printed on acid-free paper. Designed for readability
using Adobe Minion type family.

Library of Congress

Cataloging-in-Publication Data

1. Alger, Horatio, 1832-1899 • 2. Authors, American-19th century •
3. Literature • 4. American Writers • 5. Fiction

First edition—1877, Philadelphia: J.B. Lippincott & Co.
Co-author with cousin, William Rounsville Alger.

Composition by Polyglot Press, Inc. Philadelphia, PA www.polyglotpress.com

Polyglot Mission Statement

Polyglot Press brings hard-to-find books and manuscripts back into print, making previously scarce and rare literary and historical information available to scholars, modern libraries and the general public at affordable prices.

Polyglot digitally restores (recovers, edits and proofs); custom typesets; and republishes comprehensive collections by well known authors in a high-legibility optical font. Each title is simultaneously printed in paperback, hardcover, library, collectors and large print editions.

Polyglot also digitally restores the covers, frontispieces and illustrations accompanying the original and reprint editions of these works, selecting the most representative examples available from public and private collections.

Polyglot Literary Collections feature sixteenth to nineteenth century Northern European, North American and Australasian novelists and historians writing in English; and Mediterranean and Latin American novelists and historians writing in Spanish, Portuguese, French and Italian—with selected titles also available in translation.

Polyglot Historical Collections highlight scholarship on Mediterranean culture from late antiquity through the Renaissance.

Care is taken to insure that the complete originally published work is present, including author prefaces and dedications.

On each credits page, Polyglot catalogs the original publisher and publication dates; serialization publishers and dates; and available illustrator information.

Polyglot also includes, as faithfully as possible, original author introductions and dedications as well as appendices with a comprehensive list of published works.

Polyglot will augment each literary collection with previously publish-ed and unpublished short stories, poetry and essays as acquired.

To make this possible, Polyglot relies on special grants, numerous volunteers and cooperating institutions worldwide.

Polyglot staff, friends and contributors join libraries and museums dedicated to this important tradition, from the ancient Libraries at Alexandria and Cordoba to the great collections of today.

Polyglot welcomes inquiries from cooperating author societies about reissuing comprehensive collections of currently out of print titles.

David Scott, Publisher

Acknowledgements

In appreciation of those who made the
Polyglot Press Horatio Alger Series possible:

Horatio Alger Society
Robert G. Huber, President
Carol Nackenoff, Past President
Robert E. Kasper, Executive Director
Murray D. Levin, Past Treasurer

Northern Illinois University
Arthur P. Young, Dean of Libraries

Free Library of Philadelphia
Mary Wood Fischer, Chief, Collection Development Office

Polyglot Horatio Alger books are available in
Paperback, Hard Cover, Large Print
and Collector's Editions.

Beginning in 2004 Polyglot Press will offer a range of fine art reproductions, posters, as well as note, greeting and playing cards based on the original cover art and illustrations from the Horatio Alger, Jr. collection.

***

Polyglot Press titles are available in Large Print.

***

Polyglot Press collections include rare as well as scarce titles.

For a complete list of authors, titles, special offers, discounts and future products visit

www.polyglotpress.com.

Introduction

HORATIO ALGER, JR.

Most Americans easily recognize a typical "Horatio Alger hero" as someone who rises from humble beginnings to success and prosperity through hard work, perseverance, and pluck. But few can identify Horatio Alger as a real person in spite of being the most widely read author of juvenile literature during the latter part of the nineteenth century.

Horatio Alger, Jr. was born on January 13, 1832, in Chelsea (now Revere) Massachusetts, the oldest of five children. His father, Reverend Horatio Alger, Sr., was a Unitarian minister and his mother, Olive (Fenno) Alger, was from a prominent local business family. His early schooling was conducted at home but was constantly interrupted by his father's other activities, which included teaching, farming and politics. Despite these interruptions, Alger was a voracious reader and was well versed in Latin and algebra by the age of ten. In December 1844, after business reversals and bankruptcy, Alger's father moved the family to Marlborough, Massachusetts where Horatio entered Gates Academy. He finished his preparatory studies in 1847 and entered Harvard the following year. He graduated in 1852 near the top of his class and was elected to the prestigious academic society, Phi Beta Kappa.

During the next five years Alger held several positions including teacher, headmaster, editor and writer. It was during this time that Alger published his first book, *Bertha's Christmas Vision* (1856) and a year later, *Nothing To Do*, an anonymously published volume of satirical poetry.

In 1857, Alger entered the Harvard Divinity School to prepare for the ministry. After graduating in 1860, he embarked on a nine-month tour of Europe and wrote travel narratives for the *New York Sun*. Upon his return to the United States, he continued to write short stories and poetry but found it increasingly difficult to support himself despite regularly supplying the pulpit at several churches.

Alger was drafted for service in the Army of the Potomac commanded by General George Meade in July 1863. However, two weeks later at his preinduction physical, Alger was exempted because of severe myopia and failure to meet the minimum height requirement. Unable to serve as a soldier in the Union Army, Alger wrote dozens of war ballads and poems for *Harper's Weekly* and other magazines.

In November 1864, just as Alger published his third book, *Frank's Campaign*, he accepted the ministerial position at the First Unitarian Church and Society of Brewster, Massachusetts. He continued to submit short stories and poetry to various publications and also completed three more books during the next two years. In March of 1866, Alger left the ministry and moved to New York City to write full-time.

Shortly after his arrival in New York City, Alger visited the Newsboys' Lodging House operated by Charles Loring Brace, a social worker and philanthropist, who founded the Children's Aid Society in 1853. It was here, among the vagrant street urchins – newsboys, bootblacks and homeless boys – that Alger gleaned material for his eighth book, titled *Ragged Dick; or, Street Life in New York*. Published in May 1868, it was an immediate success and propelled Alger from obscurity to literary prominence.

Alger completed the **Ragged Dick Series** with five other volumes, all depicting New York street life from the viewpoint of abandoned or orphaned runaways, beggars and messenger boys. His early training as a classical scholar and his linguistic skills gave Alger a unique perspective regarding the colloquialisms of his young heroes and his ability to manifest them was unequaled. Sales of the **Ragged Dick Series** were respectable and Alger's publisher requested more stories, which he churned out with punctual alacrity, including the **Brave and Bold, Luck and Pluck** and the **Tattered Tom Series**.

Alger also took a stab at several nonfiction juvenile biographies including the lives of James Garfield, Abraham Lincoln, and Daniel Webster. His boys' life of Garfield, titled *From Canal Boy to President*, was available less than three weeks after Garfield died in September 1881, and enjoyed exceptional sales. He also collaborated with his cousin, William Rounseville Alger, on the official biography of Edwin Forrest, the infamous theatrical actor.

In order to supplement his well-worn depiction of city life, Alger embarked on three trips out West, in 1877, 1878 and 1890, to gather new material. These trips produced *Joe's Luck, Digging for Gold* and the four-volume **Pacific Series**. Some critics argued that Alger's stories were overly didactic and formulaic, constantly rehashing the "strive and succeed" premise to inspire his young audience. Whether his works possessed literary merit is debatable – whether boys (and girls) liked them is not.

During his life, Alger wrote more than 100 books and scores of short stories and articles. In fact, his output was so prolific that he used at least six pen names since many of his serial stories appeared concurrently in the same publication. Although most of Alger's books were geared for juvenile audiences, he did make several attempts at writing for adults, albeit with less than satisfactory results.

His most notable non-juvenile book appeared in 1875, titled *Grand'ther Baldwin's Thanksgiving*, a slim volume of poetry and ballads all previously published in various periodicals. It was generally well received and proved that Alger was, on occasion, able to successfully deviate from his usual juvenile fare. Much of Alger's verse was patterned after Henry Wadsworth Longfellow, best known for his long narrative poems on historical subjects. Alger became acquainted with Longfellow during his early Harvard years when Longfellow was a professor there.

Despite declining sales during the last few years of his life, Alger was able to earn a modest living from writing and from occasional tutoring assignments from wealthy New York families. After a long illness, Alger died on July 18, 1899, at the home of his sister in Natick,

Massachusetts. It wasn't until after his death, however, that his books were sold by the millions in cheap ten-cent editions and paperbacks.

Social historians have often disagreed on Horatio Alger's place in history. Some regard him simply as the author of popular children's stories while others opine that he was the prophet of business success and the embodiment of the American Dream. The concept of self-help, upward mobility and economic prosperity is, more or less, a twentieth-century interpretation of Alger's literature.

In his stories, Alger preached respectability, honesty and integrity, not material possessions or great wealth. He disdained the idle rich and was disturbed by the growing chasm between the poor and the affluent. In fact, the villains in Alger's stories were almost always rich bankers, lawyers and country squires ready to foreclose on the mortgage of the hero's widowed mother.

Today it is generally accepted that the "rags to riches" success myth has been erroneously attributed to Horatio Alger, but he still remains a cultural phenomenon because of his effect on American principles and values. Perhaps Henry Steele Commager and Samuel Eliot Morison stated it best in their book *The Growth of the American Republic* that Alger probably had exerted more influence on the national character than any other writer except perhaps Mark Twain.

More than a century after his death, Horatio Alger endures as author and metaphor, a legacy achieved by very few of his contemporaries.

Robert E. Kasper
Executive Director
Horatio Alger Society
Richmond, Virginia

Table of Contents

Life of Edwin Forrest.

Volume II.

Chapter XIV.
Newspaper Estimates—Elements of the Dramatic Art, and its True Standard of Criticism

The newspaper in some countries has been a crime and in others a luxury. In all civilized countries it has now become a necessity. With us it is a duty. It is often corrupted and degraded into a nuisance. It ought to be cleansed and exalted into a pure benefaction, a circulating medium of intelligence and good will alone. Certainly it is far from being that at the present time. It is true that our newspapers are an invaluable and indispensable protection against all other tyrannies and social abuses; and their fierce vanity, self-interest, and hostile watchfulness of one another keep their common arrogance and encroachments pretty well in check. If they were of one mind and interest we should be helplessly in their power. From the great evils which so seriously alloy the immense benefits of the press, Forrest suffered much in the latter half of his life. The abuse he met irritated his temper, and left a chronic resentment in his mind. Two specimens of this abuse will show something of the nettling wrongs he encountered.

A Philadelphia newspaper stigmatized him in the most offensive terms as a drunkard. Now it was a moral glory of Forrest that, despite the temptations to which his professional career exposed him, he was never intoxicated in his life. The newspaper in question, threatened with a libel suit, withdrew its words with an abject apology,—a poor satisfaction for the pain and injury it had inflicted.

The other instance was on occasion of the driving of Macready from the stage of the Astor Place Opera House. A New York newspaper, in language of studied insolence, called Forrest the instigator and author of the outrage. "Mr. Forrest succeeded last night in doing what even his bad acting and unmanly conduct never did before: he inflicted a thorough and lasting disgrace upon the American character." "To revenge himself on Mr. Macready he packed the house and paid rowdies for driving decent people away." "With his peculiar tastes he will probably enjoy the infamy and deem it a triumph." Forrest, instead of cowhiding the writer of this atrocious slander,—as some men of his high-spirited nature would have done,—sent a letter, through his legal friend Theodore Sedgwick, demanding immediate retraction and apology. The editor assented to the request, confessing that he had spoken with no knowledge of facts to justify him!

From the time of his first appearance on the stage, Forrest was a careful reader of the criticisms on his performances. He generally read them, too, with a just mind, discriminating the valuable from the worthless, quick to adopt a useful hint, indignant or contemptuous towards unfairness and imbecility. There were three classes of persons whose comments on his performances gave him pleasure and instruction. He paid earnest attention to their remarks, and was always generous in expressing his sense of indebtedness to them.

The first class consisted of those who had a personal friendship for him, combined with a strong taste for the drama, and who studied and criticised his efforts in a sympathetic spirit for the purpose of encouraging him and aiding him to improve. Such men as Duane and Chandler and Swift in Philadelphia, Dawson in Cincinnati, Holley at Louisville, Canonge in New Orleans, Leggett and Lawson in New York, and Oakes in Boston, gave him the full benefit of their varied knowledge of human nature, literary art, and dramatic expression. Their censure was unhesitating, their questionings frank, their praise unstinted. Among these friendly critics the name of James Hunter, of Albany, one of the editors of "The Daily Advertiser," in the important period of young Forrest's engagement there, deserves to be remembered. He was one of the best critics of that day. He used to sit close to the stage and watch the actor with the keenest scrutiny, not allowing the smallest particular to escape his notice. Then at the end of the play he would in a private interview submit to his protégé the results of his observation, carefully pointing out every fault and indicating the remedy. He lived to see the favorite, who profited so well from his instructions, reach the proudest pitch of success and fame. When Mr. Hunter died, Forrest interrupted an engagement he was filling in a distant city in order to attend the funeral, and followed the remains of his old benefactor to the tomb as one of the chief mourners.

The second class of commenters on the playing of Forrest from whose judgments he received satisfaction and help was composed of that portion of the writers of dramatic criticism for the press who were comparatively competent to the task they undertook. They were men who were neither his friends nor his foes, but impartial judges, who knew what they were writing about and who recorded their honest thoughts in an honorable spirit and a good style. Among the many thousands of articles written on the acting of Forrest during the fifty years of his career there are hundreds written in excellent style, revealing competent knowledge, insight, and sympathy, and marked by an unexceptionable moral tone. They suggest doubts, administer blame, and express admiration, not from caprice or prejudice, but from principle, and with lights and shades varying in accordance with the facts of the case and the truth of the subject. These articles have an interest and a value in the highest degree creditable to their authors, and they go far to redeem the dramatic criticism of our national press from the severe condemnation justly provoked by the greater portion of it. Did space allow, it would be a pleasure to cite full specimens of this better class of dramatic critiques from the collected portfolios left behind him by the departed actor. Enough that he profoundly appreciated them, and that in various directions they did good service in their day.

The third class whose words concerning his performances Forrest gladly heeded were men who simply gave truthful reports of the impressions made on themselves, not professing to sit in judgment or to dogmatize, but honestly declaring what they felt and what they thought. Free from prejudices and perversities, fair average representatives of human nature in its ordinary degrees of power and culture, their experiences under his impersonations, ingenuously expressed, were always interesting and instructive, throwing light on many secrets of cause and effect, on many points of conventional falsity and of natural sincerity, in histrionic portrayals. Often while the newspaper writer who pretends to know the most about the dramatic art is so full of conceit and biases that his verdict on any particular representation has neither weight nor justice, the instincts of the bright-minded and warm-hearted boy or girl, the native intelligence and sympathy of the unsophisticated man or woman, whose soul is all open to the living truth of things, are almost infallible. Nobody knew this better than our tragedian, or was readier to act on it.

The light and joy he drew from these three sets of critics found a heavy counterpoise in the unjust estimates, perverse, exaggerated, malignant, or absurd, of which he was constantly made the subject by five classes of censors. The first were his personal enemies. Among the meaner fry of men who came in contact with him, a multitude hated him from jealousy and envy, from resentment of his independent and uncompromising ways, his refusal to grant them his intimacy or to serve their purposes. They sought to gratify their animosity by backbiting at his reputation, and especially by trying to destroy his professional rank. Year after year they made the columns of many a newspaper groan and reek under the load of their abuse, ranging from envenomed invective to grotesque ridicule. For example, a jocose foe said, in parody of the great Moslem proclamation, "There is but one Bowery, and Hellitisplit is its profit." And a serious foe said, "Mr. Forrest is an injury to the stage. He is a false leader, an oppression, a bad model, and a corrupter of the popular taste." A great part of the hostile criticism he suffered may be traced to bitter personal enmity, which had but slight regard to truth or fairness in its attacks on him, whether as man or as player.

The next class of assailants of Forrest in his professional repute were not his personal enemies, but were the tools of the various cliques, cabals, or social castes who had an antipathy for him and for the party to which he belonged. The English interest was especially active and bitter against him after his quarrel with Macready. Some of these writers were wilfully corrupt in their attitude and consciously false in their written estimates. They expressed neither their own feelings nor their own convictions, but merely the passion and policy of their employers. For example, at the time of the death of the tragedian a well-known editor confessed to a friend that some twenty years previously, when he was a reporter, his employer sent him to the theatre to see Forrest play, and with explicit directions to write the severest condemnation he could of the actor. He went accordingly, and made notes for a savage satirical article, although at the moment of his making these notes the tears were streaming down his cheeks, so sincere and so powerful was the representation which he was, against his conscience, preparing to abuse. Much dishonorable work of this kind has been done, and still is done, by men disgracefully connected with the press.

Another set of critics who assailed the acting of Forrest were those whose tastes were repelled by his realistic method and robust energy. He was too vehemently genuine, his art not far enough removed from material reality, to suit their fancy. They demanded a style more graceful, delicate, and free. Under the impulse of their resentful prejudices they overlooked his great merits, depreciated everything he did, angrily denied him his just rank, magnified every fault beyond measure, and maliciously caricatured him. A volume might be filled with articles purely of this description, proceeding from writers whose want of native manliness unfitted them for appreciating the magnificent manliness of his impersonations, and whose offended fastidiousness expressed itself in terms which were an offence to justice.

The fourth class of abusers of Forrest were men who had an instinctive repugnance for the imposing grandeur of the types of character he represented, for the self-sufficing, autocratic power and stateliness of his impersonations. Mean and envious spirits dislike to look up to those higher and stronger than themselves. Those who either never had any romance and reverence or have been disenchanted, feel an especial enmity or incompetent contempt for every one whose character and bearing appeal to those qualities. This disinclination to admire, this wish to look on equals or inferiors alone, is the special vice of a democracy. Demagogues, whether in politics or in letters, are men of torpid imaginations and dry hearts,—slow to worship, quick to sneer. The style of man enacted by Forrest, full of an imperial personality, overswaying all who come near, massive in will, ponderous in movement, volcanic in passion, majestic in poise, was hateful to the cynical critic the petty proportions of whose soul were revealed and rebuked in its presence. He seized the weapon of ridicule to revenge himself on the actor whose grander portrayals angered him instead of aweing or shaming or delighting him. There seems to be among us in America a growing dislike for the contemplation on the stage of the grandest heroism and power, and an increasing fondness for seeing specimens of commonplace or inferiority promotive of amusement. Already in his life Forrest was a sufferer by this degradation of popular taste, and were he now to appear in our theatres he would feel it still more.

The fifth and largest class of writers who assumed to criticise the acting of Forrest was made up of persons professionally connected with the press, whose blundering or extravagant estimates arose rather from their ignorance and utter incompetency for the task they undertook than from a spirit of antipathy or partisanship. The censures and laudations in these notices were the cause of an immense amount of varied mortification, amusement, vexation, and anger, as they came under his eyes. No small portion of the criticisms in the American newspapers on actors, singers, lecturers, and other public characters have been written, and still continue to be written, by uneducated and inexperienced young men scarcely out of their teens, serving an apprenticeship in the art and trade of journalism. With low aims and views, slight literary culture, superficial knowledge of life, a vile contempt for sentiment, a cynical estimate of human nature, equally ready to extol and to denounce for pay, these writers are the nuisance and the scandal of their craft. Were their articles accompanied by their names they would be destitute of weight or mischief; but, published with apparent editorial sanction, they often assume a pernicious importance.

The art of a people expresses the character and aspiration of a people and reacts to develop them. To sit in judgment on it is a high and sacred office, for which none but the most intelligent, refined, and honorable are fit. The praise and blame given to artists play on the living sensibilities of that most sensitive class whose careers are a vital index of the moral state of the community. Yet this momentous office is frequently entrusted to beardless youths, whose chief experience is in dissipation, and who unblushingly sell their pens to the highest bidder. A severe article exposing this abuse appeared in the "Round Table" in 1864, written by the editor, and entitled "Dramatic Critics in New York." Forrest put it in one of his scrap-books with the endorsement, "How true this is!" Mr. Sedley said, "What dramatic criticism in New York has been the public well know. Its low, egotistic, unfair, malicious character, its blind partialities and undying hates, its brazen ignorance and insulting familiarity, have given it wide notoriety and brought upon it equally wide contempt."

There is no art which more needs to be criticised than that of criticism itself, because there is none which requires in its votary such varied knowledge and cultivation, and such integrity of mind and purity of motive; because, furthermore, no other art is exposed to such subtle temptations of prejudice and vanity. The critic, in assuming to be a judge, is no exception to other writers. Like them he reveals and betrays himself in what he writes. In dissecting others he lays his own soul bare. In consciously judging them he pronounces unconscious judgment on himself,—in the tenderness or the insensibility, the generosity and candor or the meanness and spite, the knowledge and beauty or the ignorance and foulness, which he expresses. The pen of a base, vindictive critic is a stiletto, a fang, or an anal gland. The pen of a competent and genial critic is the wand of an intellectual Midas turning everything it touches to gold. For such a critic has the true standard of judgment in his knowledge, and, whatever the merit or demerit of the work he estimates, as he points out its conformity with that standard or its departure from it his lucid illustration is always full of instruction and help.

But the great majority of those journalists who presume to print their estimates of histrionic performances are profoundly ignorant of the elements of the dramatic art. Thus, having no knowledge of the real standard of judgment by which all impersonations should be tested, they cannot fairly criticise the artists who appear before them for a verdict. Instead of criticising or even justly describing them they victimize them. They use them as the stalking-horses of their own presumption or caprice, prejudice or interest. Unable to write with intelligent candor on the subject which they profess to treat, they employ it only as a text whereon to append whatever they think they can make effective in displaying their own abilities or amusing their readers. The unfittedness of such critics for their task is sufficiently proved by the chief attributes of their writing, namely, prejudice, absurd extravagance, reckless caprice, ridiculous assumption of superiority, violent efforts to lug in every irrelevant matter which they can in any way associate with the topic to enhance the effect they wish to produce regardless of justice or propriety.

A few specimens of these various kinds of criticism will be found full of curious interest and suggestiveness, while they will illustrate something of what the proud and sensitive nature of Forrest had to undergo at the hands of his admirers and his contemners.

One enthusiastic worshipper, in the year 1826, overflowed in the following style: "In the Iron Chest, on Thursday evening last, Mr. Forrest established a name and a fame which, should he die to-morrow, would give him a niche in the temple of renown to endure uncrumbled in the decay of ages!" Another one wrote thus: "In his Richard, Macbeth, Lear, and Othello, Mr. Forrest displays abilities and accomplishments which, for power and finish, we do not believe have ever been at all approached by any other actor that ever stepped upon the stage. The range of his delicate and varied by-play and the terrific energy of his explosions of naked passion leave the very greatest of his predecessors far in the rear and deep in the shade!" Such slopping eulogy defeats its own purpose. For want of discrimination its exaggerations are unmeaning and powerless. To be thus bedaubed and plastered with praise mortifies the actor, and injures him with the judicious, though springing from a generous sensibility and most kindly meant. This style of praise, however, is quite exceptional. The general run of critics have altogether too much knowingness and vanity for it. Their cue is to depreciate and detract, to satirize and belittle, so as either directly or indirectly to imply the superiority of their own knowledge and taste. Your ordinary critic is nothing if not superior to the artist he assumes to estimate. The publicity and admiration enjoyed by the performer seem to taunt the critic with his own obscurity and neglect, and he seeks an ignoble gratification in denying the merit of what he really envies. This base animus of the baser members of a properly high and useful literary guild betrays itself in many ways. For example, one of this sort, sneering at the idea of applauding the genius of an actor, characterized dramatists as "the class of men who administer in the most humiliating of all forms to the amusement of a large and mixed assembly." It needs no more than his own words to place Pecksniff before us in full life.

Through the whole dramatic life of Forrest one class of his assailants were found accusing him of tameness and dulness, while another class blamed him for extravagant energy and frenzied earnestness. Both classes spoke from personal bias or capricious whim, instead of judging by a fixed standard of truth and discerning where reserve and quietness were appropriate and where explosive vehemence was natural. One critic, in 1831, says, "He wants passion and force. He has no sincerity of feeling, no spontaneous and climacteric force. He often counterfeits well,—for the stage,—but nature is not there." At the same time the critic attached to another journal wrote, "Mr. Forrest's greatest fault is lack of self-control and repose. His feelings are so intense and mighty that they break through all bounds. With added years, no doubt, he will grow more reserved and artistic." Thirty years later the same blunt contradiction, the same blind caprice or prejudice, are found in the two extracts that follow:

"For nearly three months the heavy tragedian has weighed like an incubus on the public, which now, that the oppression of this theatrical nightmare is removed, breathes freely. We part with Mr. Forrest without regret; he has taken his leave, and, as that slight acquaintance of his, William Shakspeare, remarks, he could 'take nothing we would more willingly part withal.' Those only who, like ourselves, have constantly attended his performances, have a true knowledge of their tedium and dulness. The occasional visitor may bear with Mr. Forrest for a night or two, but *we* are really nauseated. The stupid, solemn, melancholy evenings we have passed in watching his stupid, solemn, and melancholy personations will always be remembered with disgust. Nothing but a sense of duty compelled us to submit to this ineffable bore."

"Mr. Forrest belongs to the robustious school of tragedy,—that class who 'split the ears of the groundlings,'—and his eminent example has ruined the American stage. He is a dramatic tornado, and plucks up the author's words by the roots and hurls them at the heads of the audience. He mistakes rant for earnestness, frenzy for vigor. The modulations of his voice are unnatural, and his pauses painful. A man in a furious passion does not measure his words like a pedagogue declaiming before his school, but speaks rapidly and fiercely, without taking time to hiss like a locomotive blowing off steam. Mr. Forrest was not so in his prime; and he has probably borrowed the habit from some antiquated actor who has been afflicted with asthma."

There is no candid criticism in such effusions of obvious prepossession and satire. They show no reference to a fixed standard, no sincere devotion to the interests of truth and art; but a desire to awaken laughter, a purpose to make the player appear ridiculous and the writer appear witty. The same may be said of the following examples, wherein amusing or malignant ridicule takes the place of fair and intelligent judgment. Such writers care not what their victims suffer, or what justice suffers, so long as they can succeed in gaining attention and raising a laugh. They feel with the English critic who excoriated Payne for his Macbeth, "No matter if the labor we delight in physics Payne, it *pays* us."

First. "Mr. Forrest's personation of the Broker of Bogota is feeble and uninteresting. Contrasted with his *Othello*, it has the advantage which the Stupid has over the Outrageous. *Febro* may be compared to one of those intolerable bores who prose and prose, with sublime contempt of all that is interesting, for hours. *Othello* is like one of those social torments who destroy your peace of mind with incessant and furious attacks. The bore is the negative of Good; his opposite is the affirmative of Evil."

Second. "We can account for the popularity which Forrest enjoys as the greatest master of the Epigastric School of Acting on no other hypothesis than that of the innate depravity of human taste. Like the vicious propensity in mankind to chew tobacco and drink whisky, the majority of men have a depraved appetite for this false and outrageous caricature of human nature which Mr. Forrest calls acting. Our strictures apply in a lesser degree to the stage delineations of all tragedians. They are all false, and Forrest is only a little more so. His particular excellence seems to lie in his extraordinary power of pumping up rage from his epigastrium, and expectorating it upon his audience, through the interstices of his set teeth. Other tragedians equal him in their facial contortions, and in the power of converting their chests into an immense bellows Violently worked. His great rival, McKean Buchanan, excels Mr. Forrest in this department of high art, but fails in the epigastric power. Mr. Forrest may well claim to stand at the head of the Epigastric School. He does not underestimate the value of epilepsy in delineation, and 'chaws,' tears, rends, and foams at the mouth quite as artistically as the best of his rivals; but he especially cultivates his epigastrium. We do not want Mr. Forrest to die soon. But when he *does* pass away, we have a physiological and anatomical curiosity which we would be pleased to have gratified at the expense of a *post mortem* on the great tragedian. We have a grave suspicion that, deep down in his stomach, beneath the liver and other less important viscera, he has concealed additional vocal apparatus, by means of which he is enabled to produce those diabolical *tremolo* sounds which have so often thrilled and chilled his auditors. But in our opinion, with its two great exponents, Edwin Forrest and McKean Buchanan, the Epigastric and Epileptic School of Acting will pass away."

Third. "We thought to have dropped Mr. Edwin Forrest as a subject of newspaper remark; but several of his friends, or persons who think themselves such, are very anxious that we should do him justice, as an actor, though that is just what they ought to fear for him. We will take his performance as Richard. In this part, in the first place, his gait is very bad, awkward, and ungraceful. Richard may, possibly, have halted a little, but he did not roll like a sailor just ashore from a three years' cruise. A king does not walk so. Then, his features are totally devoid of expression; he can contort, but he can throw neither meaning nor feeling into them. When he attempts to look love, anger, hate, or fear, he resembles one of the ghouls and afrites in Harper's new illustrated edition of the Arabian Nights. He wins Lady Anne with a smile that would frighten a fiend, and that varies not a single line from that with which he evinces his satisfaction at the prospect of gaining the crown, and his contempt for the weakness of his enemies. A more outrageous and hideous contortion still expresses his rage at Buckingham's importunity, and at the reproaches of his mother. When he awakes in the tent-scene, he keeps his jaws at their utmost possible distension for about two minutes, and presents no bad emblem of an anaconda about to engorge a buffalo; one might fling in a pound of butter without greasing a tooth. At the same time, his whole frame writhes and shakes like a frog subjected to the action of a galvanic battery. We have seen folks frightened and convulsed before now, but we never saw one of them retain his senses in a convulsion. We like a deep, manly, powerful voice; but we dislike to hear it strained to the screech of a damned soul in hell-torment, like Mr. Forrest's when he calls on his drums to strike up and his men to charge. Often he displays his tremendous physical energies where there is not the least occasion for them, and as often does he repress them where they are needed. For instance, Richard ought to work himself into a passion before he slays King Henry. Mr.

Forrest kills him as coolly and as quietly as a butcher sticks a pig or knocks down a calf, and he repulses Buckingham with the voice and action of a raving maniac. But Mr. Forrest is not to blame for his face; which is as nature moulded it, neither because he has but three notes to his voice, nor because the only inflections he is capable of are their exaltation and depression. But he need not aggravate the slight deformity of Richard more than Shakspeare did, who greatly exaggerated it himself. Nor do we blame him for raving, ranting, roaring, and bellowing to houses who never applaud him but when he commits some gross outrage upon good taste and propriety. He adapts his goods to his market, and he does wisely."

As a contrast and offset to the foregoing specimens of self-display disguised as criticism of another, it is but fair to cite a few extracts from different writers who had really something appropriate to say on the subject they were treating, and who said it with exemplary directness and impartiality:

"As a reader Mr. Forrest has, in our opinion, few equals. Believing him to be the most overrated actor on the stage, we are yet not blind to his merit, but are glad to speak of the least of his excellences, and only wish they were more numerous. Let us take his inherent faults for granted, and consider his reading at the best. Does he fail in the first essential,—intelligibility? On the contrary, he enunciates a thought with such clearness that the meaning cannot be mistaken. Does he fail to give the rhythm and the rhetoric of verse? On the contrary, verse in his utterance retains its melody and music, and the high-sounding eloquence of words its majesty. He subtly marks the changes of reflection, and keeps the leading idea emphatic and distinct. There stands the *thought* at least, no matter if the *feeling* is a thousand miles away. He has carved the statue correctly, though he wants the power of the ancient sculptor to give the cold marble life. This he cannot do by ' emphasizing every word,' in the unnatural way of which our correspondent accuses him. Analyze one of his well-read sentences, and mark how the strong word and the strong sound fall together; then listen to most of the actors that surround him, and notice with what amusing vehemence they shout their 'ands' and ' ifs' and 'buts.'

They begin every sentence with a stentorian cry that dwindles into an exhausted whisper."

"As regards Forrest, we are often amused to hear people, who have vainly refused for years to recognize his great histrionic abilities, wonder how it is that he invariably attracts crowded houses whenever he performs. We do not know any actor of his rank who has been so scurrilously abused and to so little purpose. The most elaborate pretences at criticism are always poured out on his devoted head, and if the power of the press could have written a man down he surely would have been long since; for he has few special champions among acknowledged critics, a fact which shows how deep is the feeling against him among particular classes. We must candidly confess to have never been biased by profound admiration of Forrest's acting, and yet we must also admit that after having calmly, patiently, and attentively watched some entire performances of his, we were convinced that he really possessed far greater powers of mind than any of the critics ever had given him credit for. His style is apt to be uneven, and men of his mould of intellect cannot always enact the same parts with the same good taste. But of his superb elocution,—of the noble idea of latent force and suppressed passion which his whole manner embodies,—of the perfection of manly dignity and physical development which have never had a better representative on the stage than in his person, —of the marvellous voice, so musical in its sound, and so happily adjusted in its modulations to increase the expression of a sentence,—there ought, in our judgment, to be no abatement of that admiration so long and so justly accorded to him. If all the critics in the country were with one Voice to deny the existence of these things, their fiat would be powerless against the evidence of men's senses. We admit that he has no subtlety of intellect, no finely-drawn perceptions of delicate shades of human character. What he does is the result of the action of a very strong mind, capable of being directed in a particular channel with resistless energy; but this is the very class of minds out of which have arisen some of the greatest men in the world's annals. When Forrest performs an engagement people go to see him who know all his defects, but they go because it is the only acting of the highest class they have the opportunity of seeing, and it is so far above the rivalry of such actors as have been here during the last decade as to admit of no comparison."

"It is said when Canova was finishing a choice marble that his friends were very anxious to see the work on exhibition, but the great artist restrained their impatience, and proposed to gratify their desire at the end of a given term. At the expiration of the time, his friends assembled eagerly, and, in tones of disappointment, exclaimed,' What have you been doing? You have been idle; you have done nothing to your piece.' To which he replied, 'On the contrary, my chisel has been exceedingly busy; I have subdued this muscle, I have brought out this feature, enlivened this expression, polished my marble.' 'Oh, but,' said they, 'these are mere trifles!' 'They may be,' he said, 'but trifles make up the sum of perfection. The Virginius of Mr. Forrest revived this anecdote of Canova. as well as remembrances of his early performances. The difference in the two cases, however, is that it is not the artist now, but his friends that see the perfection. Virginius has long been identified with Mr. Forrest's fame; but, great as the lustre may be which his surpassing self-possession, noble and balanced bearing, rich, copious, and manly elocution, and deft, minute, and relative action have heretofore thrown upon this character, it has now been still more varied and beautified by the mellow tints that shadow and relieve the local splendor of salient features. It is indeed a masterpiece of acting and the 'top of admiration.' It is difficult to perceive any point of improvement that could give it more truth, in its lifelike resemblance, as a copy of fiction; and we are sure, after the ribaldry which of late years has degraded the boards, that there is not a single lover of the drama who saw this enactment who does not feel grateful to Mr. Edwin Forrest for his manly reassertion of the dignity of the stage."

"We are disposed to admit the greatest liberty possible to the theatrical critic employed upon the daily press, but we cannot help alluding to the disgracefully savage bitterness of the writer in one of our weekly cotemporaries as equally damaging to his employer's reputation and his own. Mr. Forrest has now passed that period of his life in which he might have been injured by the malevolence of the individual. In the mass, criticism bows before his assured superiority, and it is simply a petty spite which dares persistently to deny his claims to genius of the highest order. He is no longer a man respecting whose position in the history of the American stage there can be any dispute. He stands completely alone. We are induced this week to make this remark from having freshly seen him in '*Othello*' and '*Macbeth*.' Can any observer who remembers his interpretation of the first of these characters, some twenty years since, or his rendering of the last one, but four years ago, and is disposed to examine them fairly, with reference to his present reading and acting of either part, deny this? If he does so, we can but feel that he is alike ungifted with the talent to recognize and the honesty to admit the wide difference which exists between them. His '*Othello*' is now a most coherent and perfect whole. Where is the artist who can infuse a more perfect and thorough spirit of love than he does in that scene where he meets *Desdemona* again in Cyprus, after having quitted her in Venice? Where is the one who grows under the heat of *Iago's* viperous tongue into a more sublimely savage delineation of jealousy than he does in the subsequent acts? Is not his

'I love thee, Cassio,
But never more be officer of mine,'

one of the most perfect bits of natural feeling that has ever been uttered upon the stage? Friendship, anger, pity, and justice are all struggling within him, and shape the sorrow of the words that strip his lieutenant of the office which he considers him no longer worthy to retain. It may be observed that in alluding to these points we have not marked any of those more obvious beauties which have for many years been acknowledged in his representation of this character. These are settled excellencies in the estimation of all who love the tragic stage. Certain lines have been stereotyped to us by the genius of those who have embodied this greatest of Shaksperian characters; but for those who will reverently observe his impersonation, there are hitherto hidden points developed by Forrest which justify us in laughing at those whose resolute hatred of the artist blinds them to his excellence, and to the wonderful finish in the histrionic portraits which he offers them. We have good artists amongst us, but we certainly have none who can for a moment be fairly compared with him; and therefore is it that we say the man who constantly undervalues him simply marks himself as notoriously incapable of balancing the critical scales."

The next extract is taken from a long article by the well-known scholar and author, Dr. R. Shelton Mackenzie:

"We once heard a great author say, 'Scurrility is the shadow of Fame, and as often precedes as follows it.' That author was Bulwer, and his remark has the weight of an aphorism. With respect to Mr. Edwin Forrest, it is singular that he has been assailed in his native town by scurrility at an advanced period of his brilliant career, and at a time when his powers have ripened into something very close to perfection.

"Unless the actuating principle of the writer be a merely malignant dislike of the man, it seems almost impossible to us that any critic, possessed of the ordinary intelligence current among the more respectable members of the fraternity, can refuse or be so morally blind as not to see the wide difference existing between the Forrest of the present time and the Forrest who was admitted by the public to be the greatest American actor some twenty years ago. At that time he was wonderful,—wonderful by his intensity, his dashing power, his superb manhood, his fine voice, and his noble presence. This made him a great artist. He might have many faults, but these were obliterated from the mind of the spectator by his many and dazzling merits, which were even the more striking from the comparative blemishes with which they were mingled.

"The artistic career of Edwin Forrest has now, however, made a great stride in advance. He has polished, refined, and completed his style. It was said of Garrick, who was several years older than Forrest when he retired from the stage, that in his latter seasons he acted better than ever, and the fact that he never, even when a master in the art, ceased to be a student, explained the cause. The same may be said, and even with more truth, of Edwin Forrest. There is no living actor half so studious as himself. His mind, always under thorough self-cultivation, has matured in later years, and the effects are apparent. He is so near perfection as an actor that it is impossible to be so attracted by his excellencies now as we might have been when contrast made them more palpable.

"Fully to appreciate the various power of Mr. Forrest cannot be done by examining him in any single character. We have therefore waited until his engagement is nearly completed, and have carefully studied him in eleven different characters,—*Richelieu, Damon, Richard III, Hamlet, Othello, Virginius, Macbeth, Lucius Junius Brutus, Febro, Jack Cade,* and *Lear.* Of these, perhaps, his Lear, his Othello, his Macbeth, his Richelieu, and his Damon are the greatest; but there is comparatively so little difference in excellence between his Hamlet and his Othello, his Virginius and his Damon, that he might reasonably except to us for noting that difference, which, after all, is in some measure the result of a purely physical variation in the bodily means at his disposal for each special embodiment.

"The almost even excellence, in so many of his great parts, to which Edwin Forrest has attained, contains in itself a strong assertion of his right not only to the first place in the histrionic annals of the last few years, but registers a positive claim to the highest position, as an artist, in all histrionic history to which the slightest degree of faith can be attached. To be at the same time a great Hamlet and a great Othello, even granting a difference in the excellence of the two parts, argues that the actor possesses to a larger extent than common that intellectual adaptability without which it would be impossible for him to represent two such widely different men. Slightly deranged, a philosophic dreamer, without the capability of sustained action, energetic only by immediate impulse, the Danish Prince differs widely from the passionate, powerful, one-purposed, and sublimely simple nature of the Moor. In grasping these two opposite characters as completely as Edwin Forrest has done, he has displayed an intellectual strength of the highest order, approaching very nearly to that subtlety of intelligence which is but rarely coupled with genius, but which, when coupled with it, makes it a genius of the highest order.

"This subtlety of intelligence he develops in his wonderful rendering of Richard, as widely opposed a character to both or either of the others as could well be presented to us. For the physical nature of Richard he has preferred Horace Walpole's 'Historic Doubts' to Shakspeare's delineation of the man, but in portraying him intellectually Edwin Forrest has simply depended on himself. He paints Richard with strong and vigorous execution, as a crafty and cruel hypocrite, with a positively unequalled subtlety of touch, rendering his hypocrisy frank and pleasant to the outside observer and coloring it with a comedy of which he offers no example in *Othello* and but a vague suspicion in *Hamlet*. His love-scene with Lady Anne is a marvellous piece of acting, which excerpts from the character as a worthy pendant to the mad scene in *Lear*. It was probably much more easily, although more recently, perfected by him than the latter, inasmuch as the last named was the result of careful and minute study, while the former is simply an effort of pure cultured genius which is as positively real as stage simulation ever can be. But this difference in character of the three extends even to those points in which Richard touches upon the two others. Richard is a man of strong passion as well as Othello. He is a philosopher as well as Hamlet. But passion is suppressed in Richard under the vest of his craft. It is addressed to other objects than Othello yearns for. It is bold and crafty. Othello is brave and honest. This is wonderfully discriminated by Mr. Forrest The philosophy of Hamlet is reflective and uncertain, colored by study and lunacy. That of Richard is worldly and practical, subjected by him to his immediate ambition. Here Mr. Forrest, as an artist, is truly admirable. In Hamlet his philosophy is impulsively given to the audience. In Richard it is reasoned out and calculated with.

"Let us look at Macbeth, reaching, as Richard does, at the Crown. Most of our modern actors vary the two but little in their manner, without following the line of difference made between them by the great dramatist. This difference was in the intellectual strength of their natures. Richard is the tool of nobody. Macbeth is but a plaster in the fingers of his wife. How exquisitely does Mr. Forrest mark out the two natures! You trace Macbeth's indecision of purpose in his very manner. His entrance in the first scene is characterized by it. The breaking off from his friends,—his return to himself when addressed by them,—his interjectional reveries,—his uncertainty of action, are all as they are given to us by Shakspeare, but scarcely such as we might have expected a man of Mr. Forrest's physical temperament to embody. In Richard the ambition is positive. He does not reason of the acts which he commits. Hence here the artist's actions are positive. When he commits or orders one of these deeds which tend to secure his desires or objects, it is done at once. The positive decision of the man is translated by the actor, whether it be in the passionate command or the sneering jest, by the calculated impulse of the man."

Here is a part of an elaborate attack written by a relentless enemy and persecutor, quite remarkable for the untempered way in which it mixes truth and misrepresentation, justice and wrong:

"Mr. Forrest is now an actor who depends almost entirely on his voice as a medium of expression. He throws all his force into his reading; elocution is intended to compensate for everything,—for facial expression, for suitable action, for muscular vigor, and often, indeed, for true feeling and appreciation. By his impressive reading he frequently gains applause when in reality he deserves condemnation. There are whole scenes in his *Lear* unredeemed by one spark of feeling, the poverty of which he attempts to hide under a superficial gloss of elocutionary charlatanism. His fine voice aids him in this attempt; for that he has a noble voice, of great power,—whose tones are often commanding, and sometimes would be tender if they were inspired by any sincere feeling,—no one who has heard him can doubt. Take away this voice and Mr. Forrest is a nonentity, for *he cannot act*, and his face has no variety of expression. We know that, instead of using this fine element of success well, he has abused it; for his mannerisms of tone are perpetual, and disfigure every lengthy passage he reads. His voice has too great a burden to bear.

"This is one reason why he is so very monotonous. Another and a deeper reason is that the man himself is nothing but a monotone. No man on the stage has a more strongly marked individuality than Mr. Forrest; once seen, he cannot be easily forgotten, nor can his performances ever be confused in memory with those of others. Yet this individuality is a prison-house to him; he cannot escape from it. He is forced, in spite of himself, to play every character in exactly the same way. He develops Spartacus by the identical methods he employs in *Hamlet*; his Lear and his Claude Melnotte are made impressive, not by different styles. He has but one style. He is Edwin Forrest in everything; and, worse than this, he seems to care nothing for the best character he plays in comparison with his own success. Egotism is a marked peculiarity of his acting; he seems to say to the audience, not, How fine is this character! how great was the author!' but ever, 'How finely I play it! am I not the greatest actor you ever saw?'

"Of course this strong personality is sometimes to Mr. Forrest an advantage. There are *rôles* which are adapted to his powers, —such as Virginius, Damon, and Spartacus. These he plays well because they do not require of him the transcendent power of genius,—the imagination which enables a man to penetrate the motives of a being foreign to himself, and to re-create in his own living nature the beauty and the passion of a dream. These he plays well because he finds in them something of himself. And even in Shaksperian characters, which are alien to his nature, he occasionally meets a passage which he *can* feel, and which he therefore expresses; and these moments of earnestness, occurring suddenly in the midst of long scenes of artificiality and dulness, are like flashes of lightning in a black midnight: while they last they are bright, but when they are gone they make the darkness deeper."

The two brief notices that succeed appeared at the same time and in the same city in two opposed newspapers. The contrast is amusing, and it is easy to see how little impartial critical judgment went to the composition of either of them, as well as how bewildering they must have been to the reader who was seeking from the judgment of the press to form a dispassionate opinion on the merits of the actor:

"Having within the present year closely criticised Edwin Forrest's performances during a long engagement, we do not intend to bore our readers with repetitions of what we have said. Mr. Forrest will go through his, programme like a machine, and like most machines it may be discovered that his powers have suffered somewhat by wear and tear. He has long since passed the point of improvement. Fully settled in his own conceit that his personations are the most wonderful that the world ever saw, his only care will be to heighten defects which, he considers beauties, and to dwell with increased tenderness upon each fault. There are some mothers who give their hearts to their puny, deformed, and bad-tempered children, to the neglect of others who are handsome, gentle, and intelligent Mr. Forrest is an admirer of this policy. He slights his better qualities in acting, and dandles his absurdities with more than just parental fondness. His faults are inveterate; his beauties daily grow homely. It would be supererogation to expose at length those vices and stage tricks which have already been freely cauterized."

"During the week Mr. Forrest has been performing the characters of Richelieu, Damon, Richard, and Hamlet. At each representation the invariable compliment of a crowded house has been paid him. With the advance of every year this actor seems to grow greater. The intellectuality of his acting becomes more and more apparent. The experience of years is now devoted to his art; a lifetime is concentrated upon the development of his transcendent genius. Mr. Forrest has shaped the colossal block of crude genius into wonderful statues of natural and lovely proportions. No intelligent praise can be extravagant which extols, the exceeding beauty of the conceptions of this wonderful artist. We can scarcely think of Mr. Forrest's fame as otherwise than increasing. It throws around his name a luminous halo, whose brightness and extent the progress of years will only intensify and enlarge."

One more specimen will suffice. It is from the pen of an anonymous English critic:

"If Forrest is not in a paroxysm, he is a mere wicker idol; huge to the eye, but *full of emptiness,*—a gigantic vacuum. His distortions of character are monstrous; the athletic, muscular vigor of his Lear is a positive libel upon consistency and truth. Spartacus was made for him, and he for Spartacus; the athlete is everlastingly present in all his personations. His ravings in Othello, in Macbeth, and in Richard the Third are orgasms of vigorous commonplace.

"When Mr. Forrest represents terror, his knees shake, his hands vibrate, his chest heaves, his throat swells, and his muscles project as if he were under the influence of a galvanic battery or his whole frame put in motion by a machine. He always appears anxious to show the toughness of his sinews, the cast-iron capabilities of his body, and the prodigious muscularity of his legs, which really haunt the spectator's eyes like huge, grim-looking spectres, appearing too monstrous for realities, as they certainly are for the dignified grace of tragedy. He delights to represent physical agony with the most revolting exaggerations. When he dies, he likes that the audience should hear the rattles in his throat, and will, no doubt, some day have a bladder of pig's blood concealed under his doublet, that, when stabbed, the tragic crimson may stream upon the stage, and thus give him the opportunity of representing death, in the words of his admirers, *to the life.*

"Perhaps no stronger test of Mr. Forrest's want of intellectual power as an actor can be given than his slow, drawling, whining mode of delivering the speech to the senate, in the play of Othello. No schoolboy could do it worse, and though in the more energetic scenes there is a certain mechanical skill and seeming reality of passion, yet the charm which this might be calculated to produce is lost by the closeness of resemblance to a well-remembered original. It is almost frightfully vigorous, and though there are some touches of true energy, this is much too boisterous, coarse, and unrelieved by those delicate inflections which so eloquently express true feeling to obtain for it that meed of praise only due to the efforts of original genius. There is much art and much skill in Mr. Forrest's acting; but its grand defect is the general absence of truth."

The medley of praise and abuse, the hodge-podge of incongruous opinions, seen in the foregoing illustrations of newspaper criticism, arose far less from any contradiction of excellences and faults in the acting of Forrest than from the prejudices and ignorance of the writers. A large proportion of those writers were obstinately prepossessed or corruptly interested, and few of them had any distinct appreciation of the constituent elements of the dramatic art. Destitute of the true standard of criticism, the final canon of authority, their judgments were at the mercy of impulse and chance influences.

But Forrest was no solitary, though he was an extreme sufferer in this respect. The greatest of his predecessors, all the most gifted and famous actors and actresses, have had to undergo the same pitiless ordeal. Those concerning whose illustrious preeminence there can be no question whatever have borne the same shower of detraction, insult, and ridicule, the same pelting of cynical badinage. The restless vanity, presumptuous conceit, and *blasé* omniscience of the common order of critics have spared none of the conspicuous dramatic artists. And if any one infer from the abuse and depreciation rained on Forrest that he must have been guilty of the worst faults, he may draw the like conclusion from the like premises in relation to every celebrated name in the history of the stage.

The bigoted opposition and belittling estimates met by Talma in his bold and resolute effort to displace the conventional inanity and stilted bombast of the French stage with truth and nature are a matter of notorious record. Some of his sapient critics thought they were administering a caustic censure when they uttered the unwitting compliment, extorted by their surprise at his severe costume and grand attitudes, "Why, he looks exactly like a Roman statue just stepped out of the antique." The biographers of Garrick give abundant evidence of the misrepresentation, ridicule, and manifold censure with which his enemies and rivals and their venal tools pursued and vexed him. He even stooped to buy them off, and sometimes counteracted their malice with his own anonymous pen. Horace Walpole wrote, "I have seen the acting of Garrick, and can say that I see nothing wonderful in it." His small stature, his starts and pauses, were, in especial, maliciously animadverted on. Mossop was sneered at as "a distiller of syllables," Macklin for the prominent "lines, or rather cordage, of his face," and Quin for the "mechanic regularity and swollen pomp of his declamation." George Steevens wrote a bitter satire, utterly unjust and unprovoked, on Mrs. Siddons. She and her brother, John Philip Kemble, were stigmatized as icebergs and pompous pretenders, and were repeatedly hissed and insulted on the stage. Before her marriage, while Siddons was playing at the Haymarket, a critic, trying to put her down, wrote to Hayley, the manager, "Miss Kemble, though patronized by a number of clamorous friends, will prove only a piece of beautiful imbecility." In 1807 a leading London newspaper said of George Frederick Cooke, "His delivery of Lear is just what it is in Richard: in its subdued passages, little and mean; in its more prominent efforts, rugged, rumbling, and staccato, resembling rather a watchman's rattle than any other object in art or nature."

William Robson, in his "Old Play-Goer," says of Edmund Kean, "His person and carriage are mean and contemptible, his judgment poor, his pathos weak, his passion extravagant and unnatural;" and then sums up his estimate of the immortal histrionist in these remarkable words: "He is nothing but a little vixenish black girl in short petticoats!" On the first appearance of Kean in Philadelphia some critics there, who were great admirers of Cooke, called him "a quack, a mountebank, a vulgar impostor." William B. Wood said of Kean, when he had just finished a rehearsal and gone out, "He is a mere mummer." Joseph Jefferson, great-grandfather of the Joseph Jefferson of Rip Van Winkle fame,—a beautiful and noble old man, afterwards characterized by Forrest in loving memory as "one of the purest men that ever lived, sad, sweet, lofty, thoughtful, generous,"—overheard the remark, and replied, with a quiet indignation in his tone, "Ah, Wood, you would give all the riches you ever dreamed of amassing in this world to be another just such a mummer." The "London Spectator," in 1836, said, "Bunn in his drowning desperation catches at any straw. He has just put forward Booth, the shadow and foil of Kean in by-gone days. Booth's Richard seems to have been a wretched failure." At the same time another English journal used the following expressive language, in which the writer evidently does justice to himself whatever he endeavors to do to the actors he names: "Since the retirement of Young and the death of Kean, the very name of tragedy has passed away from us. We have had to submit to the presumptuous and uninspired feelings of Mr. Bell-wether Kemble, or to the melodramatic jerks and pumpings of Mr. Macready."

An American critic wrote thus of the Nancy Sykes of Charlotte Cushman: "Miss Cushman's performance is of the Anatomical Museum style. Her effects are thrilling and vulgar. Her poses are awkward, and her pictures unfinished and coarse in outline. She has an unpleasantly pre-raphaelite death scene, and is dragged off, stiff and stark, when all the characters express their internal satisfaction at the circumstance by smiling, shaking hands, and joining in a feeble chorus. The secret of her attraction is vigor. The masses like vigor. If they can have a little art with it, very well. But vigor they must have." Of late it has been the fashion to extol Miss Cushman as the queenly mistress of all the dignities and refinements of the dramatic profession; but the foregoing notice is exactly of a piece with the treatment visited upon Forrest for many years by the vulgar coteries of criticism, whose aim was not justice and usefulness but effect upon the prejudiced and the careless. Even the quiet and gentlemanly Edwin Booth has been as unsparingly assailed as he has been lavishly praised. An insidious article on him, entitled "The Machine-Actor," called him a "self-acting dramatic machine warranted;" and while admitting, with great generosity, that "he was not wholly destitute of dramatic ability," attributed his success and reputation chiefly to extraneous conditions, in especial the shrewdness of "his managing agent, who judiciously prepared his houses for him, and pecuniarily and personally appreciated the power of the press and conciliated the critics." The two following notices of Mr. Booth's Melnotte—the first obviously by a critic who had, the second by one who had not, been "conciliated"— are quite as absurd in their contradiction as those so often composed on Forrest:

"On Monday evening last we enjoyed the first opportunity of seeing Mr. Edwin Booth in the character of Claude Melnotte, in the 'Lady of Lyons.' Our impressions of Mr. Booth in the part may be briefly summed up in saying that he is one of the very best Claudes we have ever seen,—scholarly, sustained, and forcibly reticent at all points,—

not so youthful in his make-up as to suggest the enthusiastic boy of Bulwer's drama, but in all other regards the very ideal of the character. His marvellously melodious voice sounds to peculiar advantage in the rich prose-poetry of the more sentimental passages, and in the passages of sterner interest the latent strength of the tragedian comes nobly into play. Booth's Claude is an unqualified success, and its first rendering was witnessed by an audience brilliant in number and intelligence and markedly enthusiastic in their reception of the best points."

"Mr. Booth's Claude Melnotte was a failure. It was neither serious nor sentimental, comic nor tragic. The best that can be said of it is that it came near being an effective burlesque. When he first came on to the stage, I almost thought it was his intention to make it so. His carriage and general make-up were those of one of Teniers' Dutch boors, even to the extent of yellow hair combed straight down the forehead and clipped square across from temple to temple. His action consisted mainly in a series of shrugs. I don't remember a natural movement of body or expression of countenance, from the beginning of the piece to the end; nor a natural tone of voice."

Still later we have seen different representatives of the press, both in America and in England, alternately describing the wonderful Othello of Salvini as "the electrifying impersonation of a demi-god" and as "an exhibition of disgusting brutality."

The class of examples of which these are a few specimens show how little worthy the ordinary newspaper dramatic criticism is to be considered authoritative. No branch of journalism, allowing for notable individual exceptions, is more incompetent or more corrupt, because no other set of writers have so difficult a task or are so beset by vicious influences. Their vanity, prejudice, and interest worked upon, their sympathies appealed to by the artist and his friends, their antipathies by his rivals and foes, harassed and hurried with work, moved by promises of money and patronage, no wonder they often turn from the exactions of conscientious labor and study to something so much easier. The unsophisticated portion of the public, who are too much influenced by what they read in the papers, and who fancy that applause is a good proof of merit and censure a sure evidence of fault, ought to know how full of fraud and injustice the world of histrionic ambition and criticism is, and to learn to give little weight to verdicts not ascertained to come from competent and honest judges. The husband of Madame Linguet, a favorite actress at the Italian Theatre in Paris, hired a party to hiss every other actress, but to applaud her to the echo. A ludicrous mistake let out the secret. Linguet told his men one night to hiss the first actress who appeared and applaud the second. The play was changed, and in the substituted piece Madame Linguet came forward first, and was overpowered with hisses. Sir John Hill asked Peg Woffington if she had seen in the paper his praise of her performance the previous evening in the part of Calista. She thanked him for his kindness, but added that the play was changed and she had acted the character of Lady Townley. In a New York paper, in 1863, this notice appeared: "Mr. Forrest repeated, by special request, his great character of Spartacus last evening, before one of the most brilliant and enthusiastic audiences of the season. His acting was grand throughout, and at the end of the last act he received a perfect ovation from the audience." Appended to this, in his own handwriting, pasted in one of his scrap-books, were found these words: "Mr. Forrest on the night above referred to was in Philadelphia, and did not act at all, having been called home by the death of his sister."

After going over the mass of ignorant, capricious, and contradictory criticism bestowed on Forrest,—criticism destitute of fundamental principles or ultimate insight,—the reader may well feel at a loss to know how he is to regulate his judgment upon the subject and form a just estimate of the actor and his performances. The critics, instead of aiding, bewilder him, because themselves appear to be wildly adrift. To work our way through the chaos it is necessary for us to understand distinctly what the dramatic art is in its nature and object, and what are the materials and methods with which it aims to accomplish its purpose. The answers to these inquiries will clear away confusion, lay bare the elements of the art, and put us in possession of those laws of expression which constitute the only final standard for justly criticising the efforts of the player.

Considered in its full scope, the drama is *the practical science of human nature exemplified in the revelation of its varieties of character and conduct.* It aims to uncover and illustrate man in the secret springs of his action and suffering and destiny, by representing the whole range and diversity of his experience in living evolution. The drama is the reflection of human life in the idealizing mirror of art. In what does this reflection consist? In the correct exhibition of the different modes of behavior that belong to the different types of humanity in the various exigencies of their fortunes. The critic, therefore, in order to be able to say whether histrionic performances are true or false, consistent or inconsistent, noble or base, refined or vulgar, artistically elaborated and complete or absurdly exaggerated and defective, must understand the contents of human nature in all its grades of development, and know how the representatives of those grades naturally deport themselves under given conditions of inward consciousness and of exterior situation. That is to say, a man to be thoroughly equipped for the task of dramatic criticism must have mastered these three provinces of knowledge; first, the characters of men in their vast variety; second, the modes of manifestation whereby those characters reveal their inward states through outward signs; third, the manner in which those characters and those modes of manifestation are affected by changes of consciousness or of situation, how they are modified by the reflex play of their own experience.

Every man has three types of character, in all of which he must be studied before he can be adequately represented. First he has his inherited constitutional or temperamental character, his fixed native character, in which the collective experience and qualities of his progenitors are consolidated, stamped, and transmitted. Next he has his peculiar fugitive or passional character, which is the modification of his stable average character under the influence of exciting impulses, temporary exaltations of instinct or sentiment. And then he has his acquired habitual character, gradually formed in him by the moulding power of his occupation and associations, as expressed in the familiar proverb, "Habit is a second nature." The first type reveals his ancestral or organic rank, what he is in the fatal line of his parentage. The second shows his moral or personal rank, what he has become through his own experience and discipline, self-indulgence and self-denial. The third betrays his social rank, what he has been made by his employment and caste. The original estimate or value assigned to the man by nature is indicated in his constitutional form, the geometrical proportions and dynamic furnishing of his organs, his physical and mental make-up. The estimate he puts on himself, in himself and in his relations with others, his egotistical value, is seen in the transitive modifications of his form by movements made under the stimulus of passions. The conventional estimate or social value awarded him is suggested through the permanent modifications wrought in his organs and bearing by his customary actions and relations with his fellows. Thus the triple type of character possessed by every man is to be studied by means of an analysis of the forms of his organs in repose and of his movements in passion or habit.

The classes of constitutional character are as numerous as the human temperaments which mark the great vernacular distinctions of our nature according to the preponderant development of some portion of the organism. There is the osseous temperament, in which the bones and ligaments are most developed; the lymphatic temperament, in which the adipose and mucous membrane preponderate; the sanguine temperament, in which the heart and arteries give the chief emphasis; the melancholic temperament, in which the liver and the veins oversway; the executive temperament, in which the capillaries and the nerves take the lead; the mental temperament, in which the brain is enthroned; the visceral temperament, in which the vital appetites reign; the spiritual temperament, in which there is a fine harmony of the whole. The enumeration might be greatly varied and extended, but this is enough for our purpose. Each head of the classification denotes a distinct style of character, distinguished by definite modes of manifesting itself, the principal sign of every character, the key-note from which all its expressions are modulated, being the quality and rate of movement or the *nervous rhythm* of the organism in which it is embodied.

Besides the vernacular classes of character ranged under their leading temperaments, there are almost innumerable dialect varieties arising from these, as modified both by the steady influence of chronic conditions of life, historic, national, local, or clique, and by fitful and eccentric individual combinations of faculty and impulse. For instance, how many types of barbarian character there are,—such as the garrulous, laughing, sensual Negro, the taciturn, solemn, abstinent Indian, the fat and frigid Esquimaux, the Hottentot, the Patagonian, the New Zealander, —all differing widely in stature, feature, gesture, disposition, costume, creed, speech, while agreeing in the fundamentals of a common nature. Among civilized nations the diversity of characters is still greater. It would require an almost endless recital of particulars to describe the differences of the Chinaman, the Japanese, the Egyptian, the Persian, the Arab, the Hindu, the Italian, the Spaniard, the German, the Russian, the Frenchman, the Englishman, the American. And then what a maze of attributes, each one at the same time clear in its sharpness or its profundity, qualify and discriminate the various orders, castes, and groups of society!—the Brahmin, the Sudra, the king, the slave, the soldier, the doctor, the lawyer, the priest, the teacher, the shop-keeper, the porter, the detective, the legislator, the hangman, the scientist, and the philosopher. Every professional pursuit, social position, mechanical employment, physical culture, spiritual belief or aptitude, has its peculiar badge of dress, look, posture, motion, in which it reveals its secrets; and the pettifogger or the jurisconsult, the prophet or the necromancer, the Quaker and the Shaker, the Calvinist and the Catholic, the tailor, the gymnast, the gambler, the bully, the hero, the poet, and the saint, stand unveiled before us. How the habitual life reveals itself in the bearing is clearly seen in the sailor when he leaves his tossing ship for the solid shore. His sensation of the strange firmness of the earth makes him tread in a sort of heavy-light way,— half wagoner, half dancing-master. There is always this appearance of lightness of foot and heavy upper works in a sailor, his shoulders rolling, his feet touching and going.

To know how consistently to construct an ideal character of any one of these kinds, at any given height or depth in the historic gamut of humanity, and to be able to embody and enact it with the harmonious truth of nature, is the task of the consummate actor. And to be qualified to catalogue all these attributes of human being and manifestation with accuracy, recognizing every fitness, detecting every incongruity, is the business of the dramatic critic. Who of our ordinary newspaper writers is competent to the work? Yet the youngest and crudest of them never hesitates to pronounce a snap judgment on the most renowned tragedians as if his magisterial "we" were the very ipse dixit of Pythagoras!

Still further, the task of the actor and of the critic is made yet more complicated and difficult by the varied modifications of all the classes of character indicated above under the influence of specific passion. The great dramatic passions, which may be subdivided into many more, are love, hatred, joy, grief, jealousy, wonder, pity, scorn, anger, and fear. To obtain a fine perception and a ready and exact command of the relations of the apparatus of expression to all these passions in their different degrees as manifesting different styles of character, to know for each phase of excitement or depression the precise adjustment of the limbs, chest, and head, of intense or slackened muscles, of compressed or reposeful lips, of dilated or contracted nostrils, of pensive or glaring or fiery or supplicating eyes, of deprecating or threatening mien, of firm or vacillating posture, is an accomplishment as rare as it is arduous. All this is capable of reduction by study and practice to an exact science, and then of development into a perfect art. For every passion has its natural law of expression, and all these laws are related and consistent in an honest and earnest character, incoherent only in a discordant or hypocritical character. There is an art to find the mind's construction in the face. The spirit shines and speaks in the flesh. And a learned eye looks quite through the seemings of men to their genuine being and states. This is indeed the very business of the dramatic art,—to read the truths of human nature through all its attempted disguises, and expose them for instruction. How minute the detail, how keen the perception, how subtle and alert the power of adaptation requisite for this, may be illustrated by a single example. Suppose a criminal character is to be played. He may be of a timid, suspicious, furtive type, or careless, jovial, and rollicking, or brazen and defiant, or sullen and gloomy, yet be a criminal in all. He may be portrayed in the stage of excitement under the interest of plot and pursuit, or in success and triumph, or in defeat and wrath, or in the shame and terror of detection, or in final remorse and despair. There is scarcely any end to the possibilities of variety, yet verisimilitude must be kept up and nature not violated.

But we have as yet hardly hinted at the richness of the elements of the dramatic art and the scope of the knowledge and skill necessary for applying them. The aim of the dramatic art being the revelation of the characters and experiences of men, the question arises, By what means is this revelation effected? The inner states of man are revealed through outer signs. Every distinct set of outer signs through which inner states are made known constitutes a dramatic language. Now, there are no less than nine of these sets of signs or dramatic languages of human nature.

The first language is forms. When we look on an eagle, a mouse, a horse, a tiger, a worm, a turtle, an alligator, a rattlesnake, their very forms reveal their natures and dispositions and habits. In their shapes and proportions we read their history. So with man. His generic nature, his specific inheritance, his individual peculiarities are signalized in his form and physiognomy with an accuracy and particularity proportioned to the interpreting power of the spectator. The truth is all there for the competent gazer. The actor modifies his form and features by artifice and will to correspond with what should be the form of the person whose character he impersonates. And costume, with its varieties of outline and color, constitutes a secondary province artificially added to the natural language of form.

The second language is attitudes. Attitudes are living modifications of shape, or the fluencies of form. There are, for example, nine elementary attitudes of the feet, of the hands, of the toes, of the head, which may be combined in an exhaustless series. Every one of these attitudes has its natural meaning and value. All emotions strong enough to pronounce themselves find expression in appropriate attitudes or significant changes of the form in itself and in its relations to others. He who has the key for interpreting the reactions of human nature on the agencies that affect it, easily reads in the outer signs of attitude the inner states of defiance, doubt, exaltation, prostration, nonchalance, respect, fear, misery, or supplication, and so on.

The third language is automatic movements, which are unconscious escapes of character, unpurposed motions through which the states of the mover are betrayed, sometimes with surprising clearness and force. For instance, how often impatience, vexation, or restrained anger, breaks out in a nervous tapping of the foot or the finger! What can be more legible than the fidgety manner of one in embarrassment? And the degree and kind of the embarrassment, together with the personal grade and social position and culture of the subject, will be revealed in the peculiar nature of the fidgeting. There is a whole class of these automatic movements, such as trembling, nodding, shaking the head, biting the lips, lolling the tongue, the shiver of the flesh, the quiver of the mouth or eyelids, the shudder of the bones, and they compose a rich primordial language of revelation, perfectly intelligible and common to universal humanity.

The fourth language is gestures. This is the language so marvellously flexible, copious, and powerful among many barbarous peoples. It was carried to such a pitch of perfection by the mimes of ancient Rome, that Roscius and Cicero had a contest to decide which could express a given idea in the most clear and varied manner, the actor by gestures, or the orator by words. Gestures are a purposed system of bodily motions, both spontaneous and deliberate, intended as preparatory, auxiliary, or substitutional for the expressions by speech. There is hardly any state of consciousness which cannot be revealed more vividly by pantomime than is possible in mere verbal terms. As fixed attitudes are inflected form, and automatic movements inflected attitude, so pantomimic gestures are systematically inflected motion. The wealth of meaning and power in gesticulation depends on the richness, freedom, and harmony of the character and organism. The beauty or deformity, nobleness or baseness, of its pictures are determined by the zones of the body from which the gestures start, the direction and elevation at which they terminate, their rate of moving, and the nature and proportions of the figures, segments of which their lines and curves describe. Music has no clearer rhythm, melody, and harmony to the ear than inflected gesture has to the eye. The first law of gesture is, that it follows the look or the eye, and precedes the sound or the voice. The second law is, that its velocity is precisely proportional to the mass moved. The third and profoundest law, first formulated by Delsarte, is that efferent or outward lines of movement reveal the sensitive life or vital nature of the man; that afferent or inward lines reveal the percipient and reflective life or mental nature; and that immanent or curved lines, blended of the other two, reveal the affectional life or moral nature.

The fifth language is what is called facial expression. It consists of muscular contractions and relaxations, dilatations and diminutions, the fixing or the flitting of nervous lights and shades over the organism. Its changes are not motions of masses of the body, but visible modifications of parts of its periphery, as in smiles, frowns, tears. The girding up or letting down of the sinews, the tightening or loosening or horripilating creep of the skin, changes of color, as in paleness and blushing, and all the innumerable alterations of look and meaning in the brows, the eyes, the nose, the mouth, the chin, come under this head. The delicacy, power, and comprehensiveness of this language are inexhaustible. So numerous and infinitely adjustable, for instance, are the nerves of the mouth, that Swedenborg asserts that no spoken language is necessary for the illuminated, every state of the soul being instantly understood from the modulation of the lips alone.

The sixth language is inarticulate noises, the first undigested rudiments of the voice. All our organic and emotional states, when they are keen enough to seek expression, and we are under no restraint, distinguish and reveal themselves in crude noises, each one the appropriate effect of a corresponding cause. We breathe aloud, whistle, gasp, sigh, choke, whimper, sob, groan, grunt, sneeze, snore, snort, sip, hiss, smack, sniff, gulp, gurgle, gag, wheeze, cough, hawk, spit, hiccup, and give the death-rattle. These and kindred noises take us back to the rawest elemental experiences, and express them to universal apprehension in the most unmistakable manner. The states of the organism in its various sensations, the forms its affected parts assume under different stimuli, are as dies which strike the sounds then made into audible coins or medals revelatory of their faces. This is the broadest and vulgarest language of unrefined vernacular man. The lower the style of acting the larger part this will play in it. From the representation of high characters it is more and more strained out and sublimated away, the other languages quite superseding it.

The seventh language is inflected tones, vocalized and modulated breath. The mere tones of the sounding apparatus of the voice, in the variety of their quality, pitch, and cadence, reveal the emotional nature of man through the whole range of his feelings, both in kind and degree. The moan of pain, the howl of anguish, the yell of rage, the shriek of despair, the wail of sorrow, the ringing laugh of joy, the ecstatic and smothering murmur of love, the penetrative tremor of pathos, the solemn monotone of sublimity, and the dissolving whisper of wonder and adoration,—these are some of the great family of inflected sounds in which the emotions of the human heart are reflected and echoed to the recognition of the sympathetic auditor.

The eighth language is articulated words, the final medium of the intellect. Vocal sounds articulated in verbal forms are the pure vehicle of the thoughts of the head, and the inflected tones with which they are expressed convey the accompanying comments of the heart upon those thoughts. What a man thinks goes out on his articulate words, but what he feels is taught in the purity or harshness of the tones, the pitch, rate, emphasis, direction and length of slide with which the words are enunciated. The word reveals the intellectual state; the tone, the sensitive state; the inflection, the moral state. The character of a man is nowhere so concentratedly revealed as in his voice. In its clang-tints all the colors and shades of his being are mingled and symbolized. But it requires a commensurate wisdom, sensibility, trained skill and impartiality to interpret what it implies. Yet one fact remains sure: give a man a completely developed and freed voice, and there is nothing in his experience which he cannot suggest by it.

Nothing can be clearer or more impressive than the revelation of characters by the voice: the stutter and splutter of the frightened dolt, the mincing lisp of the fop, the broad and hearty blast of the strong and good-natured boor, the clarion note of the leader, the syrupy and sickening sweetness of the goody, the nasal and mechanical whine of the pious hypocrite, the muddy and raucous vocality of vice and disease, the crystal clarity and precision of honest health and refinement. Cooke spoke with two voices, one harsh and severe, one mild and caressing. His greatest effects were produced by a rapid transition from one of these to the other. He used the first to convince or to command, the second to soothe or to betray.

Actions speak louder than words; and the ninth language is deeds, the completest single expression of the whole man. The thoughts, affections, designs, expose and execute themselves in rounded revelation and fulfilment in a deed. When a hungry man sits down to a banquet and satisfies his appetite, when one knocks down his angered opponent or opens the window and calls a policeman, when one gives his friend the title-deed of an estate, everything is clear, there is no need of explanatory comment. The sowing of a seed, the building of a house, the painting of a picture, the writing of a book or letter, any intentional act, is in its substance and form the most solid manifestation of its performer. In truth, the deeds of every man, in their material and moral physiognomy, betray what he has been, demonstrate what he is, and prophesy what he will become. They are a language in which his purposes materialize themselves and set up mirrors of his history. Deeds are, above all, the special dramatic language, because the dramatic art seeks to unveil human nature by a representation of it not in description, but in living action.

These nine languages, or sets of outer signs for revealing inner states, are all sustained and pervaded by a system of invisible motions or molecular vibrations in the brain and the other nerve-centres. The consensus of these hidden motions, in connection at the subjective pole with the essence of our personality, at the objective pole with other personalities and all the forces of the kosmos, presides over our bodily and spiritual evolution; and all that outwardly appears of our character and experience is but a partial manifestation of its working. From the differing nature, extent, and combination of these occult vibrations in the secret nerve-centres originate the characteristic peculiarities of individuals. It may not be said that all the substances and forms of life and consciousness *consist in* modes of motion, but undoubtedly every vital or conscious state of embodied man is *accompanied by* appropriate kinds and rates of organic undulations or pulses of force, and is revealed through these if revealed at all. The forms and measures of these molecular vibrations in the nerve-centres and fibres,—whether they are rectilinear, spherical, circular, elliptical, or spiral,—the width of their gamut, with the slowness and swiftness of the beats in their extremes,—and the complexity and harmony of their co-operation,—determine the quality and scale of the man. The signals of these concealed things exhibited through the nine languages of his organism mysteriously hint the kinds and degrees of his power, and announce the scope and rank of his being. This is the real secret of what is vulgarly called animal magnetism. One person communicates his vibrations to another, either by direct contact, or through ideal signs intuitively recognized and which discharge their contents in the apprehending soul, just as a musical string takes up the vibrations of another one in tune with it. He whose organism is richest in differentiated centres and most perfect in their co-ordinated action, having the exactest equilibrium in rest and the freest play in exercise, having the amplest supply of force at command and the most consummate grace or economy in expending it, is naturally the king of all other men. He is closest to nature and God, fullest of a reconciled self-possession and surrender to the universal. He is indeed a divine magnetic battery. The beauty and grandeur of his bearing bewitch and dominate those who look on him, because suggestive of the subtlety and power of the modes of motion vibrating within him. The unlimited automatic intelligence associated with these interior motions can impart its messages not only through the confessed languages enumerated above, but also, as it seems, immediately, thus enveloping our whole race with an unbroken mental atmosphere alive and electric with intercommunication.

The variety of human characters, in their secret self-hood and in their social play,—the variety of languages through which they express themselves and their states, all based on that infinitely fine system of molecular motions in the nerve-centres where the individual and the universal meet and blend and react in volitional or reflex manifestation,—the variety of modes and degrees in which characters are modified under the influence of passion within or society and custom without,—the variety of changes in the adaptation of expression to character, perpetually altering with the altering situations,—such are the elements of the dramatic art. What cannot be said can be sung; what cannot be sung can be looked; what cannot be looked can be gesticulated; what cannot be gesticulated can be danced; what cannot be danced can be sat or stood,—and be understood. The knowledge of these elements properly formulated and systematized composes the true standard of dramatic criticism.

It is obvious enough how few of the actors and critics of the day possess this knowledge. Without it the player has to depend on intuition, inspiration, instinct, happy or unhappy luck, laborious guess-work, and servile imitation. He has not the safe guidance of fundamental principles. Without it the critic is at the mercy of every bias and caprice. Now, one of the greatest causes of error and injustice in acting and in the criticism of acting is the difficulty of determining exactly how a given character in given circumstances will deport and deliver himself. With what specific combinations of the nine dramatic languages of human nature, in what relative prominence or subtlety, used with what degrees of reserve or explosiveness, will he reveal his inner states through outer signs? Here the differences and the chances for truthful skill are innumerable; for every particular in expression will be modified by every particular in the character of the person represented. What is perfectly natural and within limits for one would be false or extravagant for another. The taciturnity of an iron pride, the demonstrativeness of a restless vanity, the abundance of unpurposed movements and unvocalized sounds characteristic of boorishness and vulgarity, the careful repression of automatic language by the man of finished culture, are illustrations.

And then the degree of harmony in the different modes of expression by which a given person reveals himself is a point of profound delicacy for actor and critic. In a type of ideal perfection every signal of thought or feeling, of being or purpose, will denote precisely what it is intended to denote and nothing else, and all the simultaneous signals will agree with one another. But real characters, so far as they fall short of perfection, are inconsistent in their expressions, continually indefinite, superfluous or defective, often flatly contradictory. Multitudes of characters are so undeveloped or so ill developed that they fall into attitudes without fitness or direct significance, employ gestures vaguely or unmeaningly, and are so insincere or little in earnest that their postures, looks, motions, and voices carry opposite meanings and thus belie one another. It requires no superficial art to be able instantly to detect every incongruity of this sort, to assign it to its just cause, and to decide whether the fault arises from conscious falsity in the character or from some incompetency of the physical organism to reflect the states of its spiritual occupant. For instance, in sarcastic speech the meaning of the tone contradicts the meaning of the words. The articulation is of the head, but the tone is of the heart. So when the voice is ever so soft and wheedling, if the language of the eyes and the fingers is ferocious, he is a fool who trusts the voice. In like manner the revelations in form and attitude are deeper and more massive than those of gesture. But in order that all the expressions of the soul through the body should be marked by truth and agreement, it is necessary that the soul should be completely sincere and unembarrassed and that the body should be completely free and flexible to reflect its passing states. No character furnishes these conditions perfectly, and therefore every character will betray more or less inconsistency in its manifestations. Still, every pronounced character has a general unity of design and coloring in its type which must be kept prevailingly in view.

The one thing to be demanded of every actor is that he shall conceive his part with distinctness and represent it coherently. No actor can be considered meritorious who has not a full and vivid conception of his rôle and does not present a consistent living picture of it. But, this essential condition met, there may be much truth and great merit in many different conceptions and renderings of the same rôle. Then the degree of intellectuality, nobleness, beauty, and charm, or of raw passion and material power, in any stated performance is a fair subject for critical discussion, and will depend on the quality of the actor. But the critic should be as large and generous as God and nature in his standard, and not set up a factitious limit of puling feebleness and refuse to pardon anything that goes beyond it. He must remember that a great deal ought to be pardoned to honest and genuine genius when it electrifyingly exhibits to the crowd of tame and commonplace natures a character whose scale of power is incomparably grander than their own. It is ever one of the most imposing and benign elements in the mission of the stage to show to average men, through magnificent examples of depth of passion, force of will, strength of muscle, compass of voice, and organic play of revelation, how much wider than they had known is the gamut of humanity, how much more intense and exquisite its love, how much more blasting its wrath, more awful its sorrow, more hideous its crime and revenge, more godlike its saintliness and heroism.

It is not to be pretended that Forrest had ever made the systematic analysis of the dramatic art sketched above. But when it was submitted to him he instantly appreciated it with enthusiasm; for he was experimentally familiar with all the rudiments of it. He was all his life an earnest student of human nature, in literature, in social intercourse, in his own consciousness, and in the critical practice of his profession. In fixing his rank as an actor the only question is how far he had the ability to represent in action what he unquestionably had the ability to appreciate in conception. While some of his admirers have eulogized him as the greatest tragedian that ever lived, some of his detractors have denounced him as one of the worst. The truth, of course, lies between these extremes. His excellences were of the most distinguished kind, but the limitations of his excellence were obvious to the judicious and sometimes repulsive to the fastidious.

To be the complete and incomparable actor which the partisans of Forrest claim him to have been requires some conditions plainly wanting in him. The perfect player must have a detached, imaginative, mercurial, yet impassioned mind, free from chronic biases and prejudices, lodged in a rich, symmetrical body as full of elastic grace as of commanding power. The spirit must be freely attuned to the whole range of humanity, and the articulations and muscles of the frame so liberated and co-operative as to furnish an instrument obviously responsive to all the play of thought and emotion. Now, Forrest, after his early manhood, under the rigorous athletic training he gave himself, was a ponderous Hercules, magnificent indeed, but incapable of the more airy and delicate qualities, the fascination of free grace and spontaneous variety. He lacked the lightning-like suppleness of Garrick and of Kean. His rugged and imposing physique, handsome and serviceable as it was, wanted the varying flexibility of the diviner forms of beauty, and so put rigid limitations on him. The same was true mentally; for while his intellect was keen, clear, broad, and vigorous, and his heart warm and faithful, and his passion deep and intense, yet his seated antipathies were as strong as his artistic sympathies, and shut him up in scorn and hostility from whole classes of character. Both physically and spiritually he was moulded in the fixed ways of the general type of characters which his own predominant qualities caused him to affect. These were grand characters, glorious in attributes, sublime in manifestation, but in spite of all his art many of their traits were in common, and there was something of monotony in the histrionic cortege, electrifying as their scale of heroism and strength was. Could he but have mastered in tragedy the spirituelle and free as he did the sombre and tenacious, he had been perfect.

The same defect here admitted for his form and mind, it must be confessed applied to his facial expression, gesture, and voice. As in attitude he could express with immense energy everything slow and tremendous in purpose or swift and resistless in execution, while the more subtile and fleeting moods were baffled of a vent, so in look and motion and tone he could give most vivid and sustained revelation to all the great cardinal emotions of the human breast, the elemental characteristics of our nature, but could not so well expose the more elusive sentiments and delicate activities. As in his tone and limbs so in his face and voice, the heavy style of gymnastic culture had fixed itself in certain rigid moulds or lines, which could not break up in endless forms accordant with endless moods, melting into one another, all underlaid by that living unity which it is the end of a true aesthetic gymnastic to produce. On occasion of his first professional visit to London an English journal well said,—

"Mr. Forrest is in person most remarkable for symmetrical but somewhat Herculean proportions. He might take the Farnese club and stand a perfect model to painter or sculptor. His neck is also as a pillar of strength, and his head is finely set on. His features are marked, but by no means of a classic caste, nor are they well suited for histrionic effect. Abundantly indicative of energy, they have not breadth of character, or beauty, or variety of expression. Under strong excitement they cut or contrast into sharp angularities, which cannot harmonize with the grand in passion."

Even the marvellous voice of Forrest—celebrated as it was for power, tenderness, and manly sincerity—was prevailingly too dark or too crashing. He articulated a certain range of thoughts and intoned a certain range of feelings with superb correctness and force. Still, his voice wanted a clarity and a bolted solidity corresponding with its sombreness and its smashing violence. That is to say, while it wonderfully expressed the ordinary contents of understanding and passion, it relatively failed in delivering the contents of intellectualized imagination and sentiment. His voice was astonishing in volume of power, tearing fury of articulation, long-drawn cadences of solemnity and affectional sweetness, but it was deficient in light graceful play, brilliancy, concentrated and echoing sonority. For the absolute perfection often claimed in its behalf its crashing gutturality needed supplementing with that Italian quality of transparent, round, elastic, ringing precision which delivers the words on the silent air like crystal balls on black velvet.

The everlasting refrain in the cry of the weak or snarling critics of Forrest was that he overdid everything,—striding, screeching, howling, tearing passions to tatters, disregarding the sacred bounds of propriety. That there was an apparent modicum of justice in this charge must be admitted. And yet when all the truth is seen the admission makes but a very small abatement from his merit. There is a comparatively raw elemental language of human nature, such as is seen in the sneer, the growl, the hiss, the grinding of the teeth, muscular contortion, which is progressively restrained, sifted out and left behind with the advance of polished dignity and refinement. In his impersonations Forrest unquestionably retained more of this than is tolerated by the standard of courtly fashion. His democratic soul despised courtly fashion and paid its homage only at the shrine of native universal manhood. But, on the other hand, it is unquestionable that these vigorous expressions were perfectly in accordance with truth and nature as represented in men of such exceptional strength and intensity as he and the types of character he best loved to portray. He gave extraordinarily vigorous expression to an extraordinarily wide gamut of passion because he sincerely felt it, and thus nature informed his art with it. He did not in cold blood overstep truth for effect, but he earnestly set forth the truth as he conceived and felt it. With the mould and furnishing given by his physique and soul for the great roles he essayed, efforts were easy and moderate which pale and feeble spindlings might well find extravagant or shocking. The fault clearly is more theirs than his. Power, sincerity, earnestness, are always respectable except to the envious. His total career is proof enough how profound and conscientious and popularly effective his sincerity, earnestness, and power were. But he must needs run the scathing gauntlet which all bold originality has to run. It is the same in all the arts. Nine-tenths of the current criticism is worthless and contemptible, because ignorant or corrupt. Beethoven was ridiculed as a madman and a bungler, Rossini sneered at as a shallow trickster, Bellini, Donizetti, and Verdi denounced as impostors, and Wagner systematically scouted as an insufferable charlatan. As Lewes says, "The effort to create a new form is deprecated, and a patient hearing denied. Repeat the old forms, and the critics denounce the want of originality. Present new forms, and the critics, deprived of their standards, denounce the heresy. It remains with the public to discover real genius in the artist, and it does so by its genuine response to his work."

In reply to the accusation of overdoing a character by excessive force of demonstration, Forrest might fairly have asked his critics, Overdone for whom? For Boythorn or for Skimpole? For Coriolanus or for Launcelot Gobbo? For Spartacus or for a dry-goods clerk? The precision with which he conceived each of his leading characters, the patience with which he elaborated all its elements into a consistent unity, the thoroughness with which he assimilated it into his soul and identified himself with it, and the unfaltering coherency and bold relief with which he enacted it, carefully observing every condition of perspective and light and shade and relative emphasis, placed his chief roles among the most complete specimens of the dramatic art in their way. And they forced from his own generation the almost universal acknowledgment of his solitary pre-eminence on the American stage. An anonymous writer justly said of him in 1855, "An actor of the most positive qualities, decisive in discrimination, pronounced in every attitude and phase, his embodiments have sharp and stern definition. Therefore they challenge with double force the most searching criticism, and invite while they defy the sneers of less bold and more artificial schools. His delineations are not mere cartoons, where the faults, like the virtues, are elusive and shadowy. They are pictures finished with unmistakable color, sharp expression of form, and a single, unerring meaning. Their simplicity is such that if not grand they would be shallow commonplace: just as it is but a step from Doric majesty to unrelieved and squat ugliness. A modern school of actors is perplexing itself to get rid of demonstration on the stage, to avoid scrupulously what is called 'a scene,' to express passion by silent and gentlemanly bitterness, to reduce all emotion to bloodless and suppressed propriety. Love is to be made a morbid gnawing; anger clipped as close as hypocrisy; jealousy corrode, but never bubble; joy be trim and well behaved; and madness violent only at rare intervals. Not of such stuff as this are made the Virginius, the Lear, the Metamora, and the Hamlet of Forrest. It is not in his nature to polish passion until, like a sentence too much refined, it loses all that is striking and natural. His anger is not conveyed off like electricity by invisible agents. His moods are construed in his audience by instinct, not by analysis. The moment he touches an emotional key a major chord is struck that rings out clear and piercing and brings back an echo equally distinct."

The "London Times" said of the Metamora of Forrest, "It is a most accurate delineation of Indian character. There is the awkward bluntness that even approaches the comic and raises a laugh when it defies; and there is, rising from behind this, the awful sense of right that makes the Indian respected as a wronged man. The dull deportment which petrifies the figurative language that flows lazily from the lips, and the hurricane of passion that rages beneath it, are the two elements of the character, and the manner in which they are combined by Mr. Forrest renders his Metamora a most remarkable performance." In contrast with the foregoing fairness of statement the following specimen of base and insolent ridicule is a literary curiosity:

"The *Metamora* of Mr. Forrest is as much like a gorilla as an Indian, and in fact more like a dignified monkey than a man. It has not the face of a man, nor the voice nor the gait of a man. Du Chaillu's description of the gorilla would apply equally well to Forrest's *Metamora*. We are told by that celebrated traveller that upon the approach of an enemy this ferocious baboon, standing upright on his hind legs, his eyes dilated, his teeth gritting and grinding, gives vent to divers snorts and grunts, and then, beating his breast fiercely with his hands till it sounds like a muffled drum, utters a loud roar. What a singular coincidence! The similarity need scarcely be pointed out. Substitute the words 'great tragedian' for 'ferocious baboon,' omit the word ' hind,' and you have as accurate a description of Mr. Forrest in *Metamora* as any reasonable man could wish. The snorting, gritting, and especially the beating of the breast and roaring, are so familiar to us, that we could almost imagine that the tragedian and the traveller have met."

One more example of the kind of "criticism" too common in the American press will suffice:

"Can any man or woman who has paid a dollar to see Mr. Forrest in any of his great characters recall any evidence in real life to substantiate his assertions that such bellowing is natural? Did anybody ever see anybody that looked as Mr. Forrest looks when he pretends to be representing the passions of rage, hate, remorse? If Mr. Forrest 'holds the mirror up to nature,' he first carefully scrawls over the face certain hideous etchings, with only a small portion of surface here and there left open for reflection. His Othello is a creature to be kicked, instead of feared or loved, if met with in actual life. Is it credible that any one was ever actually moved or interested in witnessing one of this actor's tedious and absurd performances?"

Ample reply to these brutal inquiries is afforded by the rapt silence, the copious tears, and the all-shaking plaudits of the unprecedented crowds, drawn for so long a series of years in every part of the country by the magnetic impersonations which have secured him the first illustrious place in the history of his country's stage. But two or three individual anecdotes possess interest enough to warrant their preservation here.

While he was enacting the part of Iago to the Othello of Edmund Kean in Albany one night, a stalwart canal-boatman was seated in the pit, so near the stage that he rested his elbow on it close to the footlights. Iago, in the scene where he had wrought so fearfully on the jealousy of the Moor, crossed the stage near the boatman, and, as he passed, the man looked savagely at him and hissed through his teeth while grinding them together, "You damned lying scoundrel, I would like to get hold of you after this show is over and wring your infernal neck!" When they met in the dressing-room, Kean generously said to Forrest, "Young man, if my acting to-night had received as high a compliment as that brawny fellow in the pit bestowed on yours I should feel very proud. You made the mimic show real to him, and I will tell you your acting merited the criticism."

Mr. Rees recalls among his interesting reminiscences an incident of which he was a witness in New Orleans. Forrest was delivering the curse in Lear with his wonted fierce and overwhelming vehemence. Mr. Rees heard a strange sound proceeding from some one beside him, and, turning, found, to his alarm, an elderly gentleman with his eyes fixed, his mouth open, and a deathly paleness overspreading his face. Seizing him by the shoulders and giving him a sudden jerk, he caused a reaction of the blood. The gentleman gasped, heaved a deep sigh, and gazed around like one awaking from a troubled sleep. The awful curse so awfully uttered, which had taken away his breath, seemed still ringing in his ears. "One moment more and I should have been a dead man," he said. And, looking towards the vacant stage, he asked, "Is that terrible old man gone?"

Hazlitt tells the traditional story that once when Garrick was acting Lear the crown of straw which he wore was discomposed or fell off, which happening to any common actor would have caused a burst of laughter; but with him not the slightest notice was taken of the accident, but the attention of the audience remained riveted. The same thing actually befell Forrest, and gave the most astonishing proof of his absorbed earnestness and magnetizing power. It was in the old Broadway Theatre, near Anthony Street. He was performing Lear, with Barry, Davidge, Conway, Whiting, Madame Ponisi, Mrs. Abbott, and other favorites in the cast. In the last scene of the second act, when depicting the frenzy of the aged monarch, whose brain, maddened by injuries, was reeling on its throne, in the excitement of the moment Forrest tore the wig of whitened hair from his head and hurled it some twenty feet towards the footlights. The wig thus removed, there was revealed to the audience a head of glossy raven locks, forming a singular contrast to the hoary beard still fastened by a white cord to the actor's chin. Not the least embarrassment resulted either to actor or to spectators. Amidst the vast assembly not a titter was heard, scarce a smile discerned. Enchained, entranced by the power of the player, two thousand breathless spectators gazed with bedimmed eyes oh the mimic scene. Nor made he any pause or hesitation. Still did that superb voice, so rich and grand in melody and compass, speak forth in anguish and wrath the indignant denunciation of the outraged king and father, making every heart tremble with his tones. One of the actors on the stage at the time, in describing the event more than twenty years afterwards, said that as he recalled the effect produced by

Forrest in that scene on the house, and on the players about him, it seemed something superhuman.

In the tragedy of Cleopatra, by Marmontel, an asp had been made so natural that it seemed alive. As it approached the queen its eyes sparkled like fire, and it began to hiss. At the close of the scene one asked a critic who sat by him how he liked the play. He replied, "I am of the same opinion as the asp." This is the case with the average sort of critic, whose commonplace inferiority of soul seeks to revenge itself, whose vanity or complacency seeks to exalt itself, by a demeaning estimate of every artist of whom he writes. But, fortunately, there are numerous instances of a nobler style, men equally just and generous, who in all their judgments hold individual prejudices in abeyance, and, actuated solely by public spirit and love of truth and of art, follow the guidance not of whim or interest, but of general principles, as exemplified in the great fixed types of character and modified in their dialect variations. One writer of this kind has admirably said,—

"Every actor has some particular excellence, which stamps his style in everything he does. This in Forrest is the ever visible manliness of spirit, and love of equality and liberty, which place his Damon, Spartacus, Brutus, and all characters of a like nature so far above the reach of other actors. He is always the *true man*, casting defiance in the face of tyranny; his hand always open to the grasp of a friend, resolute, generous, and faithful. This spirit is something which every true heart, be its owner rich or poor, learned or unlearned, will always acknowledge and worship as the noblest attribute of man; and here is the real secret of Forrest's success. The unlettered cannot but admire him for this feature, while to those who can appreciate artistic finish and detail, his acting must be an inexhaustible source of pleasure. After he has gone the stage will feel his worth. Who has not wept over the last act of Brutus? Who has not felt his 'seated heart knock at his ribs' while listening to the tragedian's astonishing delivery in the third act of Damon and Pythias? Who that has ever heard him exclaim in the last act of the Gladiator, 'There are no gods in heaven!' can accuse him of being coarse or vulgar? Indeed, it may be said of his acting in many characters (as a Shaksperian commentator has said of Lear), 'The genius of antiquity bows before it, and moderns gaze upon it with awe."

The strong proclivity of professional artists to jealousy is as proverbial as the tendency of the critic to attack and belittle. Forrest suffered much from both. His imperious independence, not less than his great success, provoked it, and he was maligned, spattered, and backbitten sufficiently from the stage as well as from the office. If in this respect he was an exception, it was merely in degree. The mortified and envious actors of Drury Lane discussing Kean in the greenroom, one of them sneeringly remarked, "They say he is a good harlequin."

"Yes," retorted honest Jack Bannister, "an extraordinary one; for he has leaped over all your heads." But the other side of this view was also true, and Forrest numbered his most enthusiastic admirers in the dramatic profession itself in all its ranks. They paid him many tributes from first to last, on which he justly set the highest value. For when the player is intelligent and candid, his special experience makes him the most competent critic of a player. The extent to which the peculiar style of Forrest took effect in producing imitators, conscious and unconscious,—who often, it is true, unhappily, copied his least praiseworthy points,—was a vast and unquestionable testimonial to his original power. And in here leaving the subject of criticism, it is enough, passing ever the recorded praises of his genius by many leading American actors, to set down the deliberate estimate of James E. Murdock, himself a player of uncommon merit, as well as a man of refined scholarly culture. Some one had made a degrading allusion to Forrest, when Murdock replied, "Never had I been able to find a fitting illustration of the massive and powerful acting of Forrest until, on a visit to Rome some years ago, I stood before the mighty works of Michael Angelo,—his Last Judgment, his gigantic Moses. Call it exaggerated if you will. But there it is, beautiful in symmetry, impressive in proportions, sublime in majesty. Such was Edwin Forrest when representing the chosen characters of Shakspeare." The illustration was as exact as the spirit that prompted it was generous. It indicates precisely the central attribute of the subject. For the powerful and reposeful port, the elemental poise and swing of the colossal figures of Angelo, reveal just what the histrionic pose and bearing of Forrest revealed, namely, the preponderance in him of the universal over the individual, the working of the forces of nature rather than the straining of his will. This is what makes a personality memorable, for it is contagious on others, and so invisibly descends the ages.

Chapter XV.
Personal and Domestic Life—Fonthill Castle—Jealousy—Divorce—Lawsuits—Tragedies of Love in Human Life and in the Dramatic Art

Forrest was now in his forty-fourth year, as magnificent a specimen of manhood perhaps as there was on the continent. His strength, vitality, fulness of functional power, and confronting fearlessness of soul before the course of nature and the faces of men, were so complete as to give him a chronic sense of complacency and luxury in the mere feeling of existence endowed with so much ability to do whatever he wished to do.

Despite a few annoying drawbacks his cup of outward prosperity too was full. It is true his fancy had been somewhat disenchanted and his temper embittered by experiences of meanness, ingratitude, and worthlessness, the envy and rancor of rivals, the shallowness and malignity of the multitude, and especially by a lasting soreness created in his heart from his late English trip and its unhappy sequel. It is also true that this evil influence had been negatively increased by the loss of the wise and benign restraint and inspiration given him during their lives by the devoted friendship of Leggett and the guardian love of his mother. Still, he had an earnest, democratic sympathy with the masses of men and a deep pride in their admiration. His popularity was unbounded. His rank in his art was acknowledged on the part of his professional brethren by his election as the first President of the Dramatic Fund Association, a society to whose exchequer he contributed the proceeds of an annual benefit for many years. He had fought his way with strenuous vigor through many hardships of orphanage, poverty, defective education, and a fearful furnace of temptations. And his reputation in every respect was without stain or shadow. This was certified by all sorts of public testimonials, the offers of political office and honor, the studied eulogies of the most cultivated and eloquent civilians, the smiling favors of the loveliest women in the land, the shouts of the crowd, and the golden filling of his coffers. His large earnings were invested with rare sagacity, his sound financial judgment and skill always enabling him to reap a good harvest wherever he tilled his fortune. He was at this time already worth two or three hundred thousand dollars. And this, in an age of Mammon, is a pledge to society of high deserts and a hostage for good behavior.

But above all he was signally blessed in his married life, the point in a character like his by far the most central and vital of all; The first ten years of his state of wedlock had indeed been happy beyond the ordinary portion of mortals. It was a well-mated match, he a noble statue of strength, she a melting picture of beauty, mutually proud and fond of each other, his native honesty and imperious will met by her polished refinement and conciliatory sweetness. Beyond all doubt he deeply and passionately loved her. And well he might, for his nature was one greatly endowed in all points for impassioned love, and she was in person, disposition, and accomplishments equally adapted to awaken it. "She was perfection," said one, in allusion to her bridal landing in America; "the most beautiful vision I ever saw." After the death of Forrest she herself said, "The first ten years of our married life were a season of contentment and happiness, scarcely ruffled by so much as a summer flaw; then bickering began, followed by deeper misunderstanding, and the fatal result drew on, which I have always deplored." Yet even in these halcyon years, too short and too few, there was one thing wanting to finished household felicity. This one want was children, the eternal charm of the passing ages of humanity. Of the four pathetic creatures born to them, but one lived, and that only for a few months. Abandoning the hope of heirs to his name and fortune, and foreseeing that his estate was destined to be a large one, Forrest, with the long anticipation characteristic of a reflective mind, bethought him what disposal he had best make of his acquisitions when he should be forced to relinquish them in death. He settled upon a purpose combining elements of romance, beneficence, and imposing permanence, which showed him possessed of qualities above the vulgar average of men.

He bought an extensive tract of land on the banks of the Hudson, about sixteen miles from New York, on a site commanding one of the most enchanting prospects in the world. Here he proposed to erect a building to be called Fonthill Castle, somewhat after the fashion of the old ruined structures on the banks of the Rhine, whose beauty should gratify his taste, whose conveniences should secure his household comfort, whose historic and poetic suggestiveness should please his countrymen passing up and down the river, and whose final object should be an enduring memorial of his love for his profession and of his compassion for its less fortunate members. The building of a house is an epoch of great interest in the lives of many men. This was especially so in the life of Forrest. In a chiselled orifice of the cornerstone of Fonthill Castle he placed specimens of the American coinage, a copy of Shakspeare, and the following paper,—marred only by its betrayal of that prejudice against foreigners which was so unworthy of his own nature and of his nationality:

"In building this house, I am impelled by no vain desire to occupy a grand mansion for the gratification of self-love; but my object is to build a desirable, spacious, and comfortable abode for myself and my wife, to serve us during our natural lives, and at our death to endow the building with a sufficient yearly income, so that a certain number of decayed or superannuated actors and actresses of American birth (*all foreigners to be strictly excluded*) may inhabit the mansion and enjoy the grounds thereunto belonging, so long as they live; and at the death of any one of the actors or actresses inhabiting the premises, his or her place to be supplied by another from the theatrical profession, who, from age or infirmity, may be found unable to obtain a livelihood upon the stage. The rules and regulations by which this institution is to be governed will, at some future day, be framed by

"Edwin Forrest."

To this charity he meant to devote his whole property forever. As the estate grew in value an American Dramatic School was to be added to it, lectures delivered, practical training imparted, and native histrionic authors encouraged. It was estimated that in fifty years the rich acres surrounding the Castle would be a part of New York, and that the rise of value would make the bequest at last one of the noblest known in any age.

Fonthill Castle was built of gray silicious granite of extraordinary hardness and fine grain, hammer-dressed and pointed with gray cement. The building consists of six octagon towers clumped together, the battlements of some notched with embrasures, the others capped with corniced coping. The highest tower rises about seventy feet from the base, the centre tower, the main tower, the library tower, the drawing-room tower, and the dining-room tower being of proportioned heights. The basement contains the kitchen, cellar, and store-rooms. On the next floor are the parlor, banquet-hall, study, boudoir, and library The centre tower comprises a hall or rotunda, and above this a picture-gallery lighted from the dome. The upper rooms are divided into chambers for guests and apartments for servants. The staircase tower has a spiral staircase of granite inserted in a solid brick column, rising from the basement to the top of the tower, with landings on each floor leading to the chief apartments. The architectural design was understood to be chiefly the work of Mrs. Forrest, with modifications by him. It combined the Norman and Gothic styles, softened in detail so as to embrace some of the luxuries of modern improvements. For instance, the drawing-room and banqueting-room are lighted with deep, square, bay-windows, while those of the upper chambers and of the boudoir are of the Gothic order. In other portions of the edifice are to be seen the rounded windows of the Norman period, with their solid stone mullions dividing the compartments again into pointed Gothic. Loop-holes and buttresses give the structure the military air of a fortified castle. There are two entrances, one on the water side, one on the land side. From the summit of the staircase tower one sees up the river as far as Sing Sing and down to Staten Island. On the opposite shore frowns the wall of the Palisades. On the north lie Yonkers, Hastings, Nyack, the lovely inlet of Tappan Zee, and the cottages of Piermont, glistening like white shells on the distant beach.

During the progress of the building Forrest had improvised a rude residence on the grounds, which he constantly visited, growing ever more deeply attached to the place and to his enterprise. In this romantic spot, one Fourth of July, he gathered his neighbors and friends, to the number of some two or three hundreds, and held a celebration,—reading the Declaration of Independence and delivering an oration, followed by the distributing of refreshments under waving flags and amidst booming guns. It was a brilliant and joyous affair,—a sort of initial, and, as it proved, farewell, dedication of the scene with commingled. Friendly and patriotic associations. For in its opening stages of suspicion and distress the domestic tragedy had already begun which was destined to make the enchantments of Fonthill so painful to him that he would withdraw from it forever, sell it to a Catholic sisterhood for a conventual school, and take up his final abode in the city of his birth.

In the spring of 1848 Forrest was fulfilling a professional engagement in Cincinnati, and his wife was with him. One day, on entering his room at the hotel unexpectedly, he saw Mrs. Forrest standing between the knees of George W. Jamieson, an actor of low moral character, whose hands were upon her person. Jamieson at once left the room. Forrest was greatly excited, but the protestations of his wife soothed his angry suspicion, and he overlooked the affair as a mere matter of indiscreetness of manners. Still, the incident was not wholly forgotten. And some months later, after their return home, certain trifling circumstances came under his observation which again made him feel uneasy. On opening a drawer in which his wife kept her papers, he found, addressed to her, the following letter, worn and rumpled, and in the handwriting of this Jamieson:

"And now, sweetest Consuelo, our brief dream is over; and such a dream! Have we not known real bliss? Have we not realized what poets love to set up as an ideal state, giving full license to their imagination, scarcely believing in its reality? Have we not experienced the truth that ecstasy is not a fiction? I have and, as I will not permit myself to doubt you, am certain you have. And oh! what an additional delight to think,—no, to know, that I have made some hours happy to you! Yes, and that remembrance of me may lighten the heavy time of many an hour to come. Yes, our little dream of great account is over; reality stares us in the face. Let us peruse its features. Look with me and read as I do, and you will find our dream is 'not all a dream.' Can reality take from us, when she separates and exiles us from each other,—can she divide our souls, our spirits? Can slander's tongue or rumor's trumpet summon us to a parley with ourselves, where, to doubt each other, we should hold a council? *No! no!* a doubt of thee can no more find harbor in my brain than the opened rose shall cease to be the humbird's harbor. And as my heart and soul are in your possession, examine them, and you will find no text from which to discourse a doubt of *me*. But you have told me (and oh! what music did your words create upon my grateful ear) that you would *not doubt me*. With these considerations, dearest, our separation, though painful, will not be unendurable; and if a sombre hour should intrude itself upon you, banish it by knowing there is one who is whispering to himself, Consuelo.

"There is another potent reason why you should be happy,— that is, having been the means of another's happiness; for I *am* happy, and, with you to remember and the blissful anticipation of seeing you again, shall remain so. I wish I could tell you my happiness. I cannot. No words have been yet invented that could convey an idea of the depth of that passion, composed of pride, admiration, awe, gratitude, veneration, and love, without being earthy, that I feel for you.

"Be happy, dearest; write to me and tell me you are happy. Think of the time when we shall meet again; believe that I shall do my utmost to be worthy of your love; and now God bless you a thousand times, my own, my heart's altar.

"I would say more, but must stow away my shreds and tinsel patches. Ugh! how hideous they look after thinking of you!

'Adieu! adieu! and when thou'rt gone,
My joy shall be made up alone
Of calling back, with fancy's charm,
Those halcyon hours when in my arm
Clasped Consuelo.
'Adieu! adieu! be thine each joy
That earth can yield without alloy,
Shall be the earnest constant prayer
Of him who in his heart shall wear
But Consuelo.
'Adieu! adieu! when next we meet,
Will not all sadness then retreat,
And yield the conquered time to bliss,
And seal the triumph with a kiss?
Say, Consuelo."

On reading this missive, as might well be supposed, Forrest was struck to the heart with surprise, grief, and rage. To one of his ample experience of the world it seemed to leave no doubt of an utter lapse from the marriage-vow on the part of its recipient. He was heard rapidly pacing the floor of his library until long after midnight, when his wife arrived from a party and a violent scene of accusation and denial occurred. He wrote an oath, couched in the most stringent and solemn terms, which she signed, swearing that she was innocent of any criminal infringement of her marital obligations. He was quieted, but not satisfied. On questioning the servants as to the scenes and course of conduct in his house during his absences, and employing such other methods of inquiry as did not involve publicity, he learned a variety of facts which confirmed his fear and resulted in a fixed belief that his wife had been unfaithful to him. Many a jealous husband has entertained a similar belief on insufficient and on erroneous grounds. He, too, may have done so. All that justice requires to be affirmed here is the assertion that he was himself firmly convinced, whether on adequate or inadequate evidence, that he had been grossly wronged, and he acted on that conviction in good faith. The pretence that he had tired of his marriage, longed to be free, and devised false charges in order to compass his purpose, is a pure slander, without truth or reason. And as to the theory of the distinguished counsel against him, namely, that he found himself by the building of Fonthill Castle involved in a financial ruin that would disgrace him and change its name to Forrest's Folly, and so, as the easiest way out, he deliberately "determined to have a quarrel with his wife for some private cause not to be explained, and then to assign the breaking up of his family as the reason for relinquishing his rural residence,"—it is not only the flimsiest of fancies, but a perfect absurdity in face of the facts, and an infamous outrage on the helpless memory of the dead. Could a woman of the mind, spirit, position, and with the friends of Mrs. Forrest be expected meekly to submit to such a fiendish sacrifice? How does such a thought seem in the light of the first letters of the parties in the controversy? The supposition, too, is inconceivably contradictory to the character of Forrest, who, however rough, violent, or furious he may sometimes have been, was not a man of cruel injustice or selfish malignity, was never a sneaking liar and hypocrite. Furthermore, no financial difficulty existed; since the fortune of Forrest at that time was about three hundred thousand dollars, and his direct earnings from his professional labor some thirty thousand a year. Fonthill cost him all told less than a hundred thousand, and on separating from his wife, in addition to carrying the load of Fonthill for six years longer, the residence which he purchased and occupied in Philadelphia was worth nearly as much more, and, besides paying out over two hundred thousand dollars in his divorce lawsuits, his wealth was steadily swelling all the time.

After the intense personal hostility and indomitable professional zeal and persistency with which Charles O'Conor pushed the cause of his fair client, in eight years securing five repetitions of judgment, heaping up the expenses for the defendant, as he says, "with the peculiar effect of compound interest," he should not have penned so unfounded and terrible an accusation. The man who could sacrifice the honor and happiness of his wife with the motive and in the manner O'Conor attributes to Forrest must be the most loathsome of scoundrels. But in the very paper in which the great illustrious lawyer presents this theory he says, "Mr. Forrest possessed great talents, and, unless his conduct in that controversy be made a subject of censure, he has no blemish on his name." The innocence of Mrs. Forrest is publicly accredited, and is not here impugned. But history abundantly shows that her husband's affirmation of her guilt does not prove him to have been a wilful monster. His suspicion was naturally aroused, and, though it may have been mistaken, naturally culminated, under the circumstances accompanying its course, in an assured conviction of its justice.

In his proud, sensitive, and tenacious mind, recoiling with all its fibres from the fancied wrong and shame, the poison of the Consuelo letter worked like a deadly drug, burning and mining all within. By day or by night he could not forget it. The full experience of jealousy, as so many poor wretches in every age have felt it, gnawed and tore him. He who had so often enacted the passion now had to suffer it in its dire reality. For more than a year he kept his dark secret in silence, not saying a word even to his dearest friends, secluding himself much of the time, brooding morbidly over his pent-up misery. Now he learned to probe in their deepest significance the words of his great Master,—

"But oh, what damned minutes tells he o'er

Who dotes yet doubts, suspects yet strongly loves!"

The evidence of the love he had for his wife and of the agony his jealousy caused him is abundant. His letters to her are tender and effusive. Such extracts as these are a specimen of them: "I am quite tired of this wandering, and every hour I wish myself again with you. God bless you, my dearest Kate, and believe me wholly yours."

"This is a warm, bright, beautiful day, and I am sitting at an open window in the Eutaw House; and while I write there is above me a clear, blue, cloudless sky,—just such a day as I yearn to have with you at Fonthill."

"I saw Mr. Mackay to-day. He spoke of you in terms of unmitigated praise, and said you were every way worthy of my most devoted affection. Of course he made conquest of my whole heart. I do love to hear you praised, and value it most highly when, as in the present instance, it is the spontaneous offering of the candid and the good."

"Your two letters have been received, and I thank you, my dearest Kate, for your kind attentions in writing to me so often. Indeed, your messages are always welcome."

"I seem quite lonely without you, and even in this short absence have often wished you were here. But the three weeks *will* pass away, and then we shall see each other again." Many witnesses in the trial testified to the happy domestic life of the couple, their devoted attentions and confiding tenderness up to the time of their dissension. And that the change which then occurred was as secretly painful as it was publicly marked is beyond doubt. He appeared no longer on the stage, but shunned society, even shrank from his friends, wore a gloomy and absorbed air, and brooded in solitude. The following verses—as unjust as they are severe, for jealousy is always more or less insane, a morbid fixture displacing the freedom of the mind—reflecting his feelings were found after his death, in his handwriting, copied into one of his scrap-books at the date of the divorce trial:

Away from my heart, for thy spirit is vain
As the meanest of insects that flutter in air;
I have broken the bonds of our union in twain,
For the spots of deceit and of falsehood are there.
The woman who still in the day-dawn of youth
Can hold out her hand to the kisses of all,
Whose tongue is polluted by guile and untruth,
Doth justify man when he breaks from her thrall.
But think not I hate thee; my heart is too high
To prey on the spoil of so abject a foe;
I deem thee unworthy a curse or a sigh,

For pity too base, and for vengeance too low.
Then away, unregretted, unhonored thy name,
In my moments of scorn recollected alone,—
Soon others shall wake to behold thee the same
As I have beheld thee, and thou shall be known.

When at last he spoke reservedly on the subject to his confidential friend, he said he had begun life a very poor boy had struggled hard to reach a pinnacle, and it now seemed severe to be struck down from all his happiness by one individual, and that one the woman whom he had loved the most of all on earth. And when the listener to whom he spoke replied with praises of the physical and spiritual beauty of Mrs. Forrest, he exclaimed, "She now looks ugly to me: her face is black and hideous." This friend, Lawson, wrote these words at the time: "I am persuaded that both parties are still warmly attached to one another. He, judging by his looks, has suffered deeply, and has grown ten years older during the last few months. She is not less affected."

At length a natural but unfortunate incident carried their alienation to the point of a violent and final rupture. In indignant reply to some cutting remarks on her sister, Mrs. Forrest inconsiderately said to her husband, "It is a lie!" If there was one point on which he had always been proudly scrupulous, as every friend would testify, it was that of being a man of the uttermost straightforward veracity, whatever might betide. The words, "It is a lie!" fell into his irascible blood like drops of molten iron. He restrained himself, and said, "If a man had said that to me he should die. I cannot live with a woman who says it." From that moment separation was inevitable and irrevocable.

A little later they agreed to part, mutually pledging themselves not to allow the cause to be made known. Before leaving his house she asked him to give her a copy of the works of Shakspeare as a memento of him. He did so, writing in it, "Mrs. Edwin Forrest, from Edwin Forrest," a sad alteration from the inscription uniformly made in the books he had before presented to her, "From her lover and husband, Edwin Forrest." Taking her in a carriage, with a large portrait of himself at the most glorious height of his physical life, he accompanied her to the house of her generous friends, Parke and Fanny Godwin, whose steadfast fidelity had caused them to offer her an asylum in this trying hour. Parting from each other silently at that hospitable door, the gulf of pain between them was henceforth without a bridge. Slow months passed on, various causes of irritation still at work, when the following letter, which explains itself, was written:

"I am compelled to address you, by reports and rumors that reach me from every side, and which a due respect for my own character compels me not to disregard. You cannot forget that before we parted you obtained from me a solemn pledge that I would say nothing of the guilty cause; the guilt alone on your part, not on mine, which led to our separation; you cannot forget that, at the same time, you also pledged yourself to a like silence, a silence that I supposed you would be glad to have preserved; but I understand from various sources, and in ways that cannot deceive me, that you have repeatedly disregarded that promise, and are constantly assigning false reasons for our separation, and making statements in regard to it intended and calculated to exonerate yourself and to throw the whole blame on me, and necessarily to alienate from me the respect and attachment of the friends I have left to me. Is this a fitting return for the kindness I have ever shown you? Is this your gratitude to one who, though aware of your guilt and most deeply wronged, has endeavored to shield you from the scorn and contempt of the world? The evidence of your guilt, you know, is in my possession; I took that evidence from among your papers, and I have your own acknowledgment by whom it was written, and that the infamous letter was addressed to you. You know, as well as I do, that the cause of my leaving you was the conviction of your infidelity. I have said enough to make the object of this letter apparent; I am content that the past shall remain in silence, but I do not intend, nor will I permit, that either you, or any one connected with you, shall ascribe our separation to my misconduct.

"I desire you, therefore, to let me know at once, whether you have by your own assertions, or by sanctioning those of others, endeavored to throw, the blame of our miserable position on me. My future conduct will depend on your reply.

"Once yours,
"Edwin Forrest."

To this the writer received immediate response:

"I hasten to answer the letter Mr. Stevens has just left with me, with the utmost alacrity, as it affords me, at least, the melancholy satisfaction of correcting misstatements, and of assuring you that the various rumors and reports which have reached you are false.

"You say that you have been told that I am 'constantly assigning false reasons for our separation, and making statements in regard to it intended and calculated to exonerate myself and throw the whole blame on you;' this I beg most distinctly to state is utterly untrue.

"I have, when asked the cause of our sad differences, invariably replied that was a matter only known to ourselves, and which would never be explained, and I neither acknowledge the right of the world, nor our most intimate friends, to question our conduct in this affair.

"You say, 'I desire you, therefore; to let me know at once, whether you have by your own assertions, or by sanctioning those of others, endeavored to throw the blame of our miserable position on me.' I most solemnly assert that I have never done so, directly or indirectly, nor has any one connected with me ever made such assertions with my knowledge, nor have I ever permitted any one to speak of you in my presence with censure or disrespect. I am glad you have enabled me to reply directly to yourself concerning this, as it must be evident to you that we are both in a position to be misrepresented to each other; but I cannot help adding that the tone of your letter wounds me deeply: a few months ago you would not have written thus. But in this neither do I blame you, but those who have for their own motives poisoned your mind against me; this is surely an unnecessary addition to my sufferings, but while I suffer I feel the strong conviction that some day, perhaps one so distant that it may no longer be possible for us to meet on this earth, your own naturally noble and just mind will do me justice, and that you will believe in the affection which, for twelve years, has never swerved from you. I cannot, nor would I, subscribe myself other than,

"Yours now and ever,
"Catharine N. Forrest."

The above letter was succeeded five days later by another:

"In replying to the letter I received from you on Monday last, I confined myself to an answer to the questions you therein ask me; for inasmuch as you said you were content that the past should remain in silence, and as I was myself unwilling to revive any subject of dispute between us, I passed over the harsh and new accusations contained in your letter; but on reading and weighing it carefully, as I have done since, I fear that my silence would be construed into an implied assent to those accusations. After your repeated assurances to me prior to our separation, and to others since then, of your conviction that there had been nothing criminal on my part, I am pained that you should have been persuaded to use such language to me. You know as well as I do that there has been nothing in my conduct to justify those gross and unexpected charges, and I cannot think why you should now seem to consider a foolish and anonymous letter as an evidence of guilt, never before having thought so, unless you have ulterior views, and seek to found some grounds on this for divorce. If this be your object, it could be more easily, not to say more generously, obtained. I repeatedly told you that if a divorce would make you happy, I was willing to go out of this State with you to obtain it, and that at any future time my promise to this effect would hold good. You said such was not your wish, and that we needed no court of law to decide our future position for us. From the time you proposed our separation, I used no remonstrance, save to implore you to weigh the matter seriously, and be sure, before you decided, that such a step would make you happy; you said it would, and to conduce as much as lay in my power to that happiness, was my only aim and employment until the day you took me from my home. Of my own desolate and prospectless future I scarcely dared to think or speak to you, but once you said that if any one dared to cast an imputation on me? not consistent with honor, I should call on you to defend me. That you should, therefore, now write and speak as you do, I can only impute to your yielding to the suggestions of those who, under the garb of friendship, are daring to interfere between us; but it is not in their power to know whether your happiness will be insured by endeavoring to work my utter ruin. I cannot believe it, and implore you, Edwin, for God's sake, to trust to your own better judgment; and, as I am certain that your heart will tell you I could not seek to injure you, so likewise I am sure your future will not be brighter if you succeed in crushing me more completely, in casting disgrace upon one who has known no higher pride than the right of calling herself your wife.

"Catharine N. Forrest."

To this Forrest replied thus:

"I answer your letter dated the 29th and received by me on the 31st ult., solely to prevent my silence being misunderstood. Mr. Godwin has told me that the tardy reply to the most material part of mine of the 24th was sent by his advice. I should indeed think from its whole tone and character that it was written under instructions. I do not desire to use harsh epithets or severe language to you; it can do no good. But you compel me to say that all the important parts of yours are utterly untrue. It is utterly untrue that the accusations I now bring against you are 'new.' It is utterly untrue that since the discovery of that infamous letter, which you callously call ' foolish,' I have ever, in any way, expressed my belief of your freedom from guilt. I could not have done so, and you know that I have not done it. But I cannot carry on a correspondence of this kind; I have no desire to injure or to crush you; the fatal wrong has been done to me, and I only wish to put a final termination to a state of things which has destroyed my peace of mind, and which is wearing out my life.

"Edwin Forrest."

The next step in the tragedy was the filing of an application for divorce by Forrest in Philadelphia, instantly counterchecked by a similar application on the part of Mrs. Forrest in New York. He was led to his suit because, in his own words, "unwilling to submit to calumnies industriously circulated by my enemies that, I had unmanfully wronged an innocent woman, the only choice open to me was either to assert my rectitude before the tribunals of my country or endure throughout life a weight of reproach which I trust my entire life proves undeserved." Her obvious motive in the counter-suit was the instinctive impulse and the deliberate determination to protect herself from remediless disgrace and utter social ostracism. No woman with her spirit, and with the host of friends which she had in the most honored walk of the community, could willingly accept the fearful penalty of letting such a case go by default, whether she were innocent or guilty. To those who held her innocent, as the best people did, her attitude appealed to every chivalrous sentiment of admiration and sympathy; but to him who believed her guilty, as her husband did, it presented every motive to aggravate anger and resentment. The inevitable consequences resulted, and a prolonged struggle ensued, which was a desperate fight for moral existence. The miserable details need not be specified. As the combat thickened, the deeper grew the passions on each side, and the more damaging the charges and alleged disclosures. The hostile championship likewise became intenser and wider. The trial, with the incrimination of adultery and the recrimination of the same offence, began in December, 1851, and reached through six weeks. No trial of the kind in this country had ever awakened so eager and extended an interest. The evidence and arguments were minutely reproduced in the press, sold by wholesale in every corner of the land, and devoured by unnumbered thousands with every sort of scandalous gossip and comment. The completed report of the trial fills two enormous volumes of more than twelve hundred pages each. The lady gained much for her cause by her strict propriety of language, her elegant deportment, the unequalled ability and passionate zeal of her counsel, and the exalted character of her large circle of influential and unfaltering friends. The man lost as much for his cause by the partisan prejudices against him, by the imprudences of his more reckless friends, and especially by the repelling violence and coarseness of expression and demeanor to which in his exasperated state he was too often tempted. Abundant examples have already been furnished in these pages of his scholarly taste, intellectual dignity, moral refinement and strength. Justice to the truth requires the frank admission that there was also in him a rude and harsh element, a streak of uncivilized bluntness or barbaric honesty of impulse, shocking to people of conventional politeness. These people did him injustice by chiefly seeing this cruder feature in his character, for it was quite a subordinate part of his genuine nature. But it is only fair to give specimens of the level to which it not unfrequently sank him in social appearance. In his eyes observance of external seemings was nothing in comparison with sincerity to internal realities. After his separation, but before his divorce, meeting his wife in the street, she said he kept her there walking up and down for over two hours in a pouring rain, hearing and replying to him, neither of them having an umbrella. At this same period watching one night to see who entered or left his house, in which his wife was still residing, though alone, a man named Raymond came out. The following intelligible dialogue immediately took place, as sworn to in court by Raymond himself. "Why are you sneaking away like a guilty man?"

"Edwin Forrest, you have waylaid me by night with a bludgeon. You want a pretence for attacking me, and I shall not give it you."

"Bludgeon! I don't want a bludgeon to kill you. Damn you, I can choke you to death with my hands. But you are not the man I am after now. If I catch that damned villain I'll rip his liver out. I'll cut his damned throat at the door. You may go this time, damn you. But I have marked you, all of you, and I'll have vengeance." This style of speech, as laughable as it is repulsive, and which really marked not at all the extent but merely the limitation of his culture, greatly injured him, alloying alike his worth, his peace, and his success. In one instance alone, however, did his violence of temper carry him beyond discourteous and furious speech to illegal action. Meeting in Central Park Mr. N. P. Willis, whom he regarded as one of the chief fomenters of his domestic trouble, he inflicted severe personal chastisement on him. The sufferer prosecuted his assailant, and secured a verdict with damages of one dollar. Forrest brought a suit against Willis for libel, and gained a verdict with five hundred dollars damages.

In the divorce case a somewhat unexpected judgment was decreed against Forrest, acquitting his wife and condemning him to pay costs and three thousand dollars a year for alimony. He appealed, and was defeated, with an added thousand dollars a year alimony. Five times he appealed, carrying his case from court to court, and every time was baffled and thrown. And it actually was not until 1868, after eighteen years of unrelenting litigation, —years filled with irritation, acrimony, and every species of annoyance, settling in many instances into a lodged hatred,—that he finally abandoned further resistance and paid over the full award. Sixty-four thousand dollars came to Mrs. Forrest, of which sum the various expenses swallowed fifty-nine thousand, leaving the pittance of five thousand,—an edifying example of the beauty of legal controversies.

The writer is unwilling in any way to enter between the now long and forever separated disputants or to go behind the rendering of the court. The defendant is dead, and only requires for justice's sake the assertion that he believed himself to have been wronged, and that he acted on that belief with the unforgivingness belonging to him. The plaintiff has suffered fearfully enough for any imprudence or error, was believed by her intimate and most honored friends to be innocent, was vindicated by a jury after a most searching trial, and is now living in modest and blameless retirement. She has a right to the benefit of her acquittal, and shall be left unassailed to that unseen Tribunal which alone is as just and merciful as it is infallible.

The verdict of the jury was hailed with acclamations by one party, with amazement and derision by the other. Rumors and charges of perjury, fraud, and corruption were rife, and many a character suffered badly, while the end left the contestants pretty much where the beginning found them, with the exception of the bad passion, costs, and anguish that lay between. They had been hoisted into a public pillory in the face of the whole country, subjected to all kinds of odious remarks, the very sanctities of their being defiled and profaned by the miscellaneous gawking and commenting of the prurient crowd. Besides all this long strain on his feelings and huge drain on his purse, Forrest had the angry grief of seeing large numbers of his most cherished friends fall away from him to the side of his antagonist, never to be spoken to again. And then he had the mortification of defeat amidst the cheers and jeers of his foes, who combined to honor the victorious lawyer to whom at every step he owed his repulses with a brilliant banquet and a service of plate, including a massive silver pitcher bearing the inscription, "From God the conquering champion cometh!" He was just the kind of man to feel these things most keenly. No wonder the unsuccessful warfare and its shameful close stung his pride, envenomed his resentment, darkened his life, and left on him rather a permanent wound than a scar. But, sure of the rightfulness of his cause, his self-respect and his faith in ultimate justice for the iniquity he felt had been done him enabled him to bear up with defiant fortitude. And he was far from being unsustained without, numerous as were the familiar associates who deserted him. Whenever he appeared in public the same enthusiastic multitudes as of old greeted him with an even wilder admiration. Many a voice and pen were lifted to defend and applaud him, while many attacked him. The tributes in the newspapers more than equalled the denunciations. Two examples in verse will show the estimate of him and his cause formed by close acquaintances:

TO EDWIN FORREST.
Thou noble and unflinching one,
Who stoodst the test so firm and true;
Doubt not, though clouds may hide the sun,
The eye of truth shall pierce them through.
Heed not the sneer and heartless mirth
Of those whose black hearts cannot know
The sterling honesty and worth
Of him at whom they aim the blow.
Thy peace is wrecked—thy heart is riven—
By her so late thy joy and pride,
And thou a homeless wanderer driven
Upon the world's tumultuous tide.
Yet doubt not, for amid the throng
There's many a heart beats warm and high
For him who cannot brook a wrong,
Whose noble soul disdains a lie.
Then hail, Columbia's gifted son,
Pride of our glorious Drama, hail!

Thou deeply wronged and injured one,
Let not thy hope or courage fail.
Though perjury seek thy name to blight,
And venomed tongues with envy rail,
The truth, in all its lustre bright,
'Gainst heartless fops shall yet prevail.
M. C.
TO EDWIN FORREST.
May I, in this gay masquerade of thought,
When crowds will seek thee,
With gay devices curiously wrought,
And love-words greet thee,
Bestow the offering of an earnest soul,
Though it be vain
As to Niagara's eternal roll
The drops of summer rain!
A thought of thee dwells ever in my heart
And haunts my brain,
And tears unbidden to mine eyelids start
Whene'er I hear thy name.
Yet 'tis no love-thought,—no impassioned dream
Of wild unrest
Quickening my pulses when with earnest beam
Thine eyes upon me rest.
But something deeper, holier far than this,—
A mournful thought
Of all the sorrow and the loneliness
With which thy life is fraught,—
Of thy great, noble heart, so rudely torn
From the deep trust of years,—
Of the proud laurels which thy brow has worn,
Dim with the rust of tears;
Of wrongs and treachery in the princely home
Thy genius earned;
Thy hearth made desolate, thy pathway lone,

Thy heart's deep worship spurned;
Thy manly prayer for justice coldly met
With mocking jeers,
The seal of exile on thy forehead set
For all thy coming years.
Most deeply injured! yet unshaken still
Amid the storm,
Thy soul leans calmly on its own high will
And waits the coming morn.
And all pure hearts are with thee, and beat high
To know at last
The world will scan thee with unbiassed eye,
Revoking all the past.
Celia.

A fortnight after the close of the trial, Forrest began a new engagement at the Broadway Theatre.

One of the leading journals of the day said, "The return of Mr. Forrest to the stage, from which he has been so long self-exiled, will form the most interesting feature in the dramatic season. There have been many, though we have not been of the number, who have thought he would never reappear on the boards after the unwarrantable treatment he received at the hands of the maliciously and ignorantly prejudiced. Mr. Forrest, however, has justly relied upon the spirit of fair play which characterizes the American people. Let all men be fairly judged before they are condemned, and especially those who, like him, have long and manfully withstood such a 'downright violence and storm of fortune' as would have overwhelmed most men, and whose careers have added to the lustre of their country's history. We believe that he will never have cause to say, like Wolsey,—

'I shall fall
Like a bright exhalation in the evening,
And no man see me more!'
but that he who has so long

'Trod the ways of glory,
And sounded all the depths and shoals of honor,
Will find a way, out of his wreck, to rise in.'
"All men have their faults, and envy makes those of the great as prominent as possible.
'Men's evil manners live in brass; their virtues
We write in water.'

"Much to their ignominy, the assailants of Forrest have never given him credit for those high-minded and disinterested acts of generosity which those who know him best can never recall without admiration, and which, when his history is written, will leave little comfort to his maligners, professional or otherwise. We wish for him a delighted welcome back to the stage, and a complete deliverance from the toils in which his enemies have sought to destroy him."

The house was packed to its extremest capacity, and hundreds clamored in the streets. An inscription was hung across the parquet, "This is the people's verdict!" As he entered on his ever favorite roll of Damon, the audience rose en masse, and greeted him with waving hats, handkerchiefs, and scarfs, and long, deafening plaudits, which shook the building from dome to foundation. In matchless solidity of port he stood before the frenzied tempest of humanity, and bowed his acknowledgments slowly, as when Zeus nods and all Olympus shakes. A shower of bouquets entwined with small American flags fell at his feet. He addressed the assembly thus, constantly interrupted with cheers:

"Ladies and Gentlemen,—After the unparalleled verdict which you have rendered me here to-night, you will not doubt that I consider this the proudest moment of my life. And yet it is a moment not unmingled with sadness. Instinctively I ask myself the question, Why is this vast assemblage here to-night, composed as it is of the intelligent, the high-minded, the right-minded, and last, though not least, the beautiful of the Empire City? Is it because a favorite actor appears in a favorite character? No, the actor and the performances are as familiar to you as household words. Why, then, this unusual ferment? It is because you have come to express your irrepressible sympathy for one whom you know to be a deeply-injured man. Nay, more, you are here with a higher and a holier purpose,—to vindicate the principle of even-handed justice. I do not propose to examine the proceedings of the late unhappy trial; those proceedings are now before you, and before the world, and you can judge as rightly of them as I can. I have no desire to instruct you in the verdict you shall render. The issue of that trial will yet be before the court, and I shall patiently await the judgment of that court, be it what it may. In the mean while I submit my cause to you; my cause, did I say?—no, not 'my' cause alone, but yours, the cause of every man in this community, the cause of every human being, the cause of every honest wife, the cause of every virtuous woman, the cause of every one who cherishes a home and the pure spirit which should abide there. Ladies and gentlemen, I submit my cause to a tribunal uncorrupt and incorruptible; I submit it to the sober second-thought of the people. A little while since, and I thought my pathway of life was filled with thorns; you have this night strewed it with roses (looking at the bouquets at his feet). Their perfume is gratifying to the senses, and I am grateful for your beautiful and fragrant offering."

The success of the entire engagement was unprecedentedly brilliant. Called before the curtain at the close of the final performance, he said,—

"Ladies and Gentlemen,—This is the sixty-ninth night of an engagement which, take it all in all, has, I believe, no parallel in the history of the stage. It is without parallel in its duration, it is without parallel in the amount of its labors, and it is without parallel in its success. For sixty-nine almost successive nights, in despite of a season more inclement than any I ever remember, the tide of popular favor has flowed, like the Pontic Sea, without feeling a retiring ebb. For sixty-nine nights I have been called, by your acclamations, to the spot where I now stand to receive the generous plaudits of your hands, and I may say hands with hearts in them. No popular assembly, in my opinion, utters the public voice with more freedom and with more truth than the assembly usually convened within the walls of a theatre. If this be so, I have reason to be greatly proud of the demonstration which for twelve successive weeks has greeted me here. Such a demonstration any man ought to be proud of. Such a demonstration eloquently vindicates the thought of the great poet:

'Sweet are the uses of adversity,
Which, like the toad, though ugly and venomous,
Wears yet a precious jewel in his head.'

Such a demonstration speaks more eloquently to the heart than any words. Such a demonstration contains in it an unmistakable moral. Such a demonstration vindicates me more than a thousand verdicts, for it springs from those who make and unmake judges."

But despite the flattering applause of the multitude, added to the support of his own conscience, and notwithstanding his abounding health and strength and enhancing riches, from the date of his separation and desire for divorce the dominant tone of the life of Forrest was changed. His demeanor had a more forbidding aspect, his disposition a sterner tinge, his faith in human nature less genial expansion, his joy in existence less spontaneous exuberance. The circle of his friends was greatly contracted, a certain irritable soreness was fixed in his sensibility, he shrank more strongly than ever from miscellaneous society, and seemed to be more asserting or protecting himself cloaked in an appearance of reserve and gloom. In fact, the excitement and suffering he had gone through in connection with his domestic unhappiness gave his whole nature a fearful wrench, and deposited some permanent settlings of acridity and suspicion. The world of human life never again wore to him the smiling aspect it had so often worn before. His sense of justice had been wounded, his heart cut, his confidence thrown back, and his rebelling will was constrained to resist and to defy.

And why all this strife and pain? Why all this bitter unyielding opposition and writhing agony under what was and is and will be? Wherefore not quietly accept the inevitable with magnanimous gentleness and wisdom, and, without anger or fuss or regret, conform his conduct to the best conditions for serenity of soul and wholesomeness of heart, in contentment with self and charity for all? Why not rather have suppressed wrath, avoided dispute, foregone retaliation, parted in peace if part they must, and, each uncomplained of and uninterfered with by the other, passed freely on in the strangely-checkered pathways of the world, to test the good of life and the mystery of death and the everlasting divineness of Providence? How much more auspicious such a course would have been than to be so convulsed with tormenting passions and strike to and fro in furious contention! Yes, why did they not either forgive and forget and renew their loving covenant, or else silently divide in kindness and liberty without one hostile deed or thought? Thus they would have consulted their truest dignity and interest. But, alas! in these infinitely delicate, inflammable, and explosive affairs of sentiment, dignity and interest are usually trampled contemptuously under foot by passion.

Every one acts and reacts in accordance with his style and grade of character, his degrees of loyalty or enslavement to the different standards of action prevailing around him. A man held fast in a certain low or mediocre stage of spiritual evolution will naturally conduct himself in any trying emergency in a very different manner from one who has reached a transcendent height of emancipation, spontaneity, and nobleness. And there were two clear reasons why Forrest, in this most critical passage of his life, did not behave purely in the best and grandest way, but with a mixture of the vulgar method and the better one. First, he had not attained that degree of self-detachment which would make it possible for him to act under exciting circumstances calmly in the light of universal principles. He could not disentangle the prejudiced fibres of his consciousness from the personality long and closely associated with his own so as to treat her with impartiality and wisdom, regarding her as an independent personality rather than as a merged part of his own. He must still continue related to her by personal passion of some kind, when one passion died an opposite one springing up in its place. And, secondly, he could not in this matter free himself, although in many other matters he did remarkably free himself, from the tyranny of what is called public opinion. He had in this instance an extreme sensitiveness as to what would be thought of him and said of him in case his conduct openly deviated much from the average social usage. Thus his personal passions, mixed up in his imagination with every reference to the woman he had adored but now abominated, incapacitated him from acting consistently throughout with disinterested delicacy and forbearance, though these qualities were not wanting in the earlier stages of the difficulty before he had become so far inflamed and committed.

Speculation is often easy and practice hard. One may lightly hold as a theory that which when brought home in private experience gives a terrible shock and is repelled with horror and loathing. Both Forrest and his wife had reflected much on what is now attracting so much attention under the title of the Social question. They both entertained bold, enlightened views on the subject, as clearly appears from a remarkable letter written from Chicago, in 1848, by Mrs. Forrest in reply to one from James Lawson. A comprehensive extract, followed by a few suggestions on the general lessons of the subject, particularly as connected with the dramatic art, shall close this unwelcome yet indispensable chapter of the biography.

"It is impossible, my dear friend, that the wonderful change, which has taken place in men's minds within the last ten years can have escaped the notice of so acute an observer as you are; and if you have read the works which the great men of Europe have given us within that time, you have found they all tend to illustrate the great principle of progress, and to show at the same time that for man to attain the high position for which he is by nature fitted, woman must keep pace with him. Man cannot be free if woman be a slave. You say, 'The rights of woman, whether as maid or wife, and all those notions, I utterly abhor.' I do not quite understand what you here mean by the rights of woman. You cannot mean that she has none. The poorest and most abject thing of earth has some rights. But if you mean the right to outrage the laws of nature, by running out of her own sphere and seeking to place herself in a position for which she is unfitted, then I perfectly agree with you. At the same time, woman has as high a mission to perform in this world as man has; and he never can hold his place in the ranks of progression and improvement who seeks to degrade woman to a mere domestic animal. Nature intended her for his companion, and him for hers; and without the respect which places her socially and intellectually on the same platform, his love for her personally is an insult.

"Again, you say, 'A man loves her as much for her very dependence on him as for her beauty or loveliness.' (Intellect snugly put out of the question.) This remark from you astonished me so much that I submitted the question at once to Forrest, who instantly agreed with me that for once our good friend was decidedly wrong. (Pardon the heresy, I only say for once.) What! do you value the love of a woman who only clings to you because she cannot do without your support? Why, this is what in nursery days we used to call 'cupboard love,' and value accordingly. Depend upon it, as a general rule, there would be fewer family jars if each were pecuniarily independent of the other. With regard to mutual confidence, I perfectly agree with you that it should exist; but for this there must be mutual sympathy; the relative position of man and wife must be that of companions,—not mastery on one side and dependence on the other. Again, you say, 'A wife, if she blame her husband for seeking after new fancies, should examine her own heart, and see if she find not in some measure justification for him.' Truly, my dear friend, I think so too (when we do agree, our unanimity is wonderful); and if after that self-examination she finds the fault is hers, she should amend it; but if she finds on reflection that her whole course has been one of devotion and affection for him, she must even let matters take their course, and rest assured, if he be a man of appreciative mind, his affection for her will return. This is rather a degrading position; but a true woman has pride in self-sacrifice. In any case, I do not think a woman should blame a man for indulging in fancies. I think we discussed this once before, and that I then said, as I do now, that he is to blame when these fancies are degrading, or for an unworthy object; the last words I mean not to apply morally, but intellectually. A sensible woman, who loves her husband in the true spirit of love, without selfishness, desires to see him happy, and rejoices in his elevation. She would grieve that he should give the world cause to talk, or in any way risk the loss of that respect due to both himself and her; but she would infinitely rather that he should indulge ' new fancies' (I quote you) than lead an unhappy life of self-denial and

unrest, feeling each day the weight of his chains become more
irksome, making him in fact a living lie. This is what society demands
of us. In our present state we cannot openly brave its laws; but it is a
despotism which cannot exist forever; and in the mean time those
whose minds soar above common prejudice can, if such be united, do
much to make their present state endurable. It is a fearful thing to
think of the numbers who, after a brief acquaintance, during which
they can form no estimate of each other's characters, swear solemnly
to love each other while they 'on this earth do dwell.' Men and women
boldly make this vow, as though they could by the magic of these few
words enchain forever every feeling and passion of their nature. It is
absurd. No man can do so; and society, as though it had made a
compact with the devil to make man commit more sins than his nature
would otherwise prompt, says, 'Now you are fairly in the trap, seek to
get out, and we cast you off forever,—you and your helpless children.'
Man never was made to endure even such a yoke as unwise
governments have sought to lay on him; how much more galling, then,
must be that which seeks to bind the noblest feelings and affections of
his nature, and makes him—

'So, with one chained friend, perhaps a jealous foe,

The dreariest and the longest journey go.'

"That there is any necessity to insure, by any means, a woman's
happiness, is a proposition you do not seem to have entertained while
writing your letter of May 24th; but perhaps we are supposed to be
happy under all circumstances."

There is for man and woman on this earth one supreme happiness,
one contenting fulfilment of destiny, whether there are more or not. It
is a pure, calm, holy, and impassioned love, joining them in one life,
filling both soul and body with a peaceful and rapturous harmony,
glorifying the scenery of nature by its reflection, making the current of
daily experience a stream of prophetic bliss, revealing to them
authentic glimpses of God in each other, and opening eternity to their
faith with mystic suggestions of worlds bygone and worlds to come,
lives already led and forgotten and lives yet to be welcomed. This is the
one absolute blessing, without whose appeasing and sufficing seal the

human creature pines for he knows not what, and dies unsatisfied, no matter how much else is granted him. Any one to whom this divine fortune falls, and whose conscience, instead of wearing it proudly as a crown of glory in the sight of God, shrinks with it guiltily before the sight of men, is a contemptible coward, unworthy of the boon, and sure to forfeit it. As the most original thinker, the boldest diver into the mysteries of our nature, America has produced, expresses it,—

"The sense of the world is short,
Long and various the report,
To love and be beloved.
Men and gods have not outlearned it,
And how oft soe'er they've turned it,
'Tis not to be improved."

Thousands, enslaved by the conventional, distracted by the external, absorbed in the trivial, may be ignorant of the incomparable importance of the truth here expressed, care nothing about it, and give themselves up to selfish ambitions and contemptible materialities. This must be so, since the blind cannot see; and even the seeing eye sees in an object only what it brings the means of seeing; and the marvellous heights and depths of experience are fatally locked from the inexperienced. Nevertheless, the truth above affirmed survives its overlooking by the unworthy, and every man and woman gifted with profound insight and sensibility knows it and feels it beyond everything else. The great multitudes of society also have at least dim glimpses of it, strange presentiments of it, blind intuitions awakening a strong and incessant curiosity in that direction. This is the secret cause of the universal interest felt in the subject of love and in every instance of its transcendent experience or exemplification. One of the most central functions of art—whether written romance, painting, sculpture, music, or the drama—is directly or indirectly to celebrate this truth by giving it concentrated and relieved expression, and thus inciting the contemplators to aspire after their own highest bliss. To those whose emotions are rich and quick enough to interpret them, what are the finest songs of the composers but sighings for the fulfilment of affection, or raptures in its fruition, or wailings over its loss? With what unrivalled power Rubens, in his fearful pictures of love and war, has uncovered to the competent spectator the horrible tragedy all through history of the intimate association of lust and murder, libidinous passion and death! And pre-eminently the stage, in all its forms,—tragic, comic, and operatic,—has ever found, and always will find, its most fascinating employment and crowning mission in the open display—published to those who have the keys to read it, veiled from all who have not—of the varied bewitchments, evasions, agonies, and ecstasies of the passion of love between the sexes. That is the most effective actor or actress whose gamut of emotional being and experience, real and ideal, is greatest, and whose training gives completest command of the apparatus of expression, making the organism a living series of revelations, setting before the audience in visible play, in the most precise and intense manner, the working of love, in all its kinds and degrees, through the language of its occult signals. The competent actor shows to the competent gazer the exact rank and quality of the love actuating him by the adjustment of his behavior to it,—every look and tone, every changing rate and quality in the rhythm of his motions, every part of his body which leads or dominates in his bearing, whether head, shoulder, chest, elbow, hand, abdomen, hip, knee, or foot, having its determinate significance. Thus people are taught to discern grades of character through styles of manners, inspired to admire the noble and loathe the base at the same time that they are deepened in their own desires for the divine prizes of beauty and joy.

The most wholesome and triumphant art of the stage has always taught in its personifying revelation that the highest blessedness of human life is the perfect attunement of the natures of man and woman in a perfect love around which nature thrills and over which God smiles. No diviner lesson ever has been or ever will be taught on this earth. All other fruitions here are but preliminaries to this, all sacrifices penances for its failure, all diseases and crimes the fruit of its violation.

In contrast with this glorious proper fulfilment of affection, wherever we look on the history of our race we find six great chronic tragedies which dramatic art has portrayed perhaps even more fully than it has the positive triumph itself.

First, is the tragedy of the indifferent heart which neither receives nor gives nor possesses love. Thin and sour natures, frivolous, dry, cynical, or hard and arrogant,—the enchanted charms and mysteries of nature and humanity have no existence for them. They sit aloof and sneer, or plot and struggle and get money and win office, or eat and drink and joke and sleep and perish,—the amazing horrors and the entrancing delights of experience equally sealed books to them. They may attain incidental trifles, but, with their poor, shrivelled, loveless hearts, not attaining that for which man most was made, to the sorrowing gaze of nobler natures their earthly lot is a tragedy.

Secondly, is the pathetic tragedy of being loved without the power to return it Coquetry, which has strewn its way everywhere with ravaged and trampled prizes, reverses this, and without sympathy or principle seeks to elicit and attract affection merely to pamper vanity and gratify an obscene love of power; and this too is a tragedy, but one of a fiendish import. The other is a sad and painful experience, yet with something of an angelic touch in it. It seems to hint at a great dislocation somewhere in the past of our race, causing this plaintive discord of conjoined but jarring souls, whose incongruous rhythms can never blend though in juxtaposition, like an ill-matched span whose paces will not coincide but still hobble and interfere. To be the recipient of a great absorbing love which one is absolutely unable to reciprocate is to any one of generous sympathies a keen sorrow. Sometimes too it is a sharp and wearing annoyance. And yet it is not infrequent, both out of wedlock and in it. There are limits alike of adaptation and of misadaptation to awaken love; and we can never have any more love than we awaken or give any more than is awakened in us. There are fatalities in these relations wholly beyond the reach of the will. When two persons are married whose characters, culture, and fitnesses place them on such different levels that they can meet only by a laborious ascent on one side or a distasteful descent on the other, where the ideal life of one is constantly hurt and baffled and flung in on itself from every attempt at genial fellowship, any high degree of love is hopeless. The conjunction is a yoke, not a partnership. Respect, gratitude, pity, service, almost every quality except love, may be earned. But love comes, if it come at all, spontaneously, in answer to the native signals which evoke it. In vain do we strive to love one not suited to us nor fitted for us; and a sensitive spirit forced to receive the affectionate manifestations of such a one is often sorely tried when seemingly bound to appear blessed.

The same considerations apply with double weight and poignancy to the third and larger class of tragedies of affection, namely, those who love where they are not acceptable and cannot win a return. Piteous indeed is the lot, touching the sight, of one humbly offering his worship, patiently continuing every tender care and service at a shrine which, despite every effort to change or disguise its insuperable repugnance, must still feel repugnant. And then, furthermore, there is the anguish of the homage welcomed at first and toyed with, but soon betrayed and cast away. The pangs of jilted love are proverbial, and the experience is one of the commonest as it is one of the cruellest in the world. Broken hearts, blasted lives, early deaths, terrible struggles of injured pride and sacred sentiment to conceal themselves and hold bravely up, caused by failures to secure the hand of the one devotedly beloved but idly entreated, are much more numerous than is imagined by the superficial humdrum world. They are in reality so numerous that if they were all known everybody not familiar with the poetic side and shyer recesses of human nature would be astonished. This forms a heavy item in the big statistics of human woe.

The examples contained under the head of the fourth tragedy are the experiences of those who are full of rich affections but find no congenial person on whom to bestow them or from whom to obtain a return. Accordingly, their real passions find only ideal vents in fervent longings and dreams, in music, prayer, and faith, or embodiment in industry and beneficence. Their unfulfilled affection thus either fortifies their being with the culture and good works it prompts, or opens an imaginative world into which they exhale away in romantic desires. A noble woman whose rare wealth and effusiveness of soul had not been happily bestowed, once said, with a sigh, to Thackeray, when they had been conversing of the extremes in the character of the great Swift, "I would gladly have suffered his brutality to have had his tenderness." The remark pierces us with a keen and wide pain expanding to brood in pity over the vast tragedy of humanity pining unsatisfied in every age. Yes, exhalations of sinless and ardent desire, yearnings of beautiful and baffled passion, are wasted in the air, sufficient, if they were legitimately appropriated, to make the whole world a heaven. Ah, let us trust that they are not wasted after all, but that they enter into the air to make it warmer and sweeter for the breathing of the happier generations to come, when the earth shall be purely peopled with children begotten by pairs all whose rhythms correspond, and who love the individuality of self in one another not less because they love the universality of God in one another more.

The fifth tragedy in the history of human affection consists of the instances of those who have been blessed with an adequate love rounded and fulfilled on both sides, but who have ceased to possess it longer, except in its results. They have in some cases outgrown and wearied of their objects, in others been outgrown and wearied of, in others still been parted by death. These examples likewise are tragic each in its way, but less melancholy on the whole than the others. These have had fruition, have, once at least, lived. The memory is divine. If they are worthy, it enriches and sanctifies their characters, and, in its treasures of influence, remains to be transferred from its exclusive concentration on one and freely poured forth on humanity, nature, and God. It then prepares its possessor for that immortal future of which it is itself an upholding prophecy. And so every deep and tender nature must feel with the poet that it is better to have loved and lost than never to have loved at all.

But the sixth tragedy of love is the most lacerating and merciless of the whole, and that is the tragedy of jealousy. This dire passion played the most ravaging part in the domestic life of Forrest, and his enactment of it in the rôle of Othello held the highest rank in his professional career. It has also exercised a most extensive and awful sway in the entire history of the human race up to this moment. The relative place and function of the dramatic and lyric stage cannot be appreciated without a full appreciation of this hydra passion, the green-eyed monster that makes the meat it feeds on.

Even of its victims few clearly understand the ingredients and essence of jealousy. In the catalogue of the passions it is the impurest, the insanest, and the most murderous. Every composition whose elements blend in harmony is pure. Earth is pure and honey is pure, but a mixture of earth and honey is impure. So in moral subjects. Loyalty is pure, being consonantly composed of reverence and obedience; conscious disloyalty is impure, being inconsonantly composed of a perception of rightful authority and rebellious resistance to it. Now, no other passion is composed of such an intense and incongruous combination of intense opposites as jealousy. In it love and hate, esteem and scorn, trust and suspicion, hope and fear, joy and pain, swiftly alternate or discordantly mix and conflict. It is these meeting shocks of contradictory polarities repulsing or penetrating one another in the soul, rending and exploding in every direction in the consciousness of its victim, that make jealousy the maddest and most slaughterous because it is the most violently impure passion known to man. In every one of its forms, when strong enough, it is a begetter of murders, has been ever since the devil first peered on Adam and Eve embracing in Paradise, and will be until it is abolished by slowly-advancing disinterestedness. It is an appalling fact that the murders of wives by jealous husbands are tenfold greater in number than any other single class of murders. When we add to these the husbands murdered by their wives, and the despatched paramours on both sides, the wild and deadly raging of jealousy may be recognized in something of its frightful fury.

The cause of the greater prevalence of murder between the married is not far to seek. It is the weariness of an over-close and continual intimacy, with the wearing and goading irritations it engenders. It is the tyrannical assertion of the possession of one by the other as something owned and to be governed. This provokes the rebellious and revengeful instincts of a personality aching to be free; and the aggravated and ruminating desire is finally so nourished and stung as to burst into frenzied performance. And those ill-starred couples one of whose members violently destroys the life of the other are insignificant in number when compared with those who are slowly and stealthily murdered without the explicit consciousness of either party, by the gnawing shock and fret of discordant nerves, the steady grinding out of the very springs and sockets of the faculties by repressive contempt and hate and fear. A proud, sensitive woman may go into the presence of her husband an angel, and leave it a fiend, her *amour-propre* having been wounded in its sacredest part and filled with irrepressible resentment. Persons of genius, of absorbing devotion to an aim, are either more unhappy in wedlock or else more exquisitely blessed and blessing than others. They live largely in an ideal realm, on a ticklish level of self-respect, a height of consciousness vital to them. Socrates, Cicero, Dante, Milton, Chateaubriand, Byron, Bulwer, Kean, Talma, Thackeray, Dickens, are examples. A collision jars the statue off its pedestal. A tone of contempt or a look of indifference cuts like a dagger, tears the spiritual tissues of selfhood,—and the invisible blood of the soul follows, draining faith, love, life itself, away. The one vast secret of pleasing and living happily with high sensitive natures is sympathetic and deferential attention. Where this is not given, and there is sorrow and chafing, an intercourse which is ever a slow moral murder, and often inflamed into a swift physical murder, that liberty of divorce should be granted for which the chaste and noble Milton so long ago made his plea. Society should cease to say, Whom man has joined together let not God put asunder!

Having seen what the constituent elements of jealousy are, it now remains to probe its essence. What is jealousy in its substance and action? It is the appropriation of one person by another as a piece of property, and a spontaneous resentment and resistance to any assertion of its personality on its own part. The jealous man virtually says, "She belongs to me and not to herself. If she dares to alienate herself from me or give anything to anybody besides me, I will kill her." The jealous woman says, "He is mine, and if he leaves me or smiles on another I will stab him and poison her." This is the fell passion in its fiercest extreme of selfishness.

Viewed in another light it is less dreadful, though just as narrow and selfish. The lover has assimilated the beloved as a portion of his own being. His life seems bound up in her and dependent on her. Her withdrawal is a loss so impoverishing to his imagination that it threatens death. He feels that the dissolution of their unity will tear him asunder. Then jealousy is his instinct of self-preservation, rising in grief, pain and anger to repel or revenge an attack on the dearest part of his life. Still, in this form as in the previous it implies the subdual and suppression of one personality by another, and is the sure signal of a crude character and an imperfect development. The rich, generous nature, detached from himself, full of free affection, living directly on objects according to their worth, ready to react on every action according to its intrinsic claim, is not jealous. Liberty and magnanimity at home and abroad are the marks of the fully-ripened man. He knows his own personal sovereignty and abundant resources as a child of God and an heir of the universe, and frankly allows the equal personal sovereignty of each of his fellow-creatures. He claims and grants no imposition of will or slavish subserviency, but seeks only spontaneous companionship in affection. Mechanical conformity and hypocrisy can be compelled. Love, veiled in its divinity, conies and goes as it lists, and is everywhere the most authentic envoy of the Creator. Jealousy is mental slavery, spiritual poverty, the ravenous Cry of affectional starvation, the blind, fallacious, desperate, murderous struggle of a frightened and famishing selfhood.

The conduct dictated by such a passion must be of the worst kind. It begins with a mean espionage and ends with a maniacal violence. Its relentless cruelty compels its objects to have recourse to the most unprincipled methods to avert its suspicion and avoid its wrath, sinking self-respect and honorable frankness in hypocrisy and fraud. Why is the word or even the oath of any man or woman in regard to a question of chastity or fidelity to the marriage vow almost universally considered perfectly worthless? It is because the penalties of dereliction on the part of woman are so intolerable, so much worse than death, that to secure escape from them the social conscience justifies means which the social code condemns. Accordingly, we see the highest personages, the greatest dignitaries and popular favorites, go into court and openly perjure themselves, while society cries bravo! The woman is so fearfully imperilled that for her rescue the fashionable standard of honor sustains deliberate perjury, the debauching of religious conscience on the very shrine of public authority.

This wicked social exculpation of the male and immolation of the female is a lingering accompaniment of the historic evolution of man, the survival in human civilization of the selfish instincts which in the lower ranks of the animal kingdom cause the stronger to drive away the weaker and monopolize the weakest. Among the most potent and fearless beasts the male, seeing any other male sportively inclined, is seized with a frenzy to kill him and appropriate the object. Animal man has the same instinct, and it has smeared the entire course of history with broad trails of blood and victimized womanhood by the double weapons of force and fear. The spectacle of the harem of one man with a thousand imprisoned women guarded by eunuchs tells the whole story. But surely when human beings, no longer remaining mere instinctive animals, become free personalities, lords of thought and sentiment, each with a separate individual responsibility distinctly conscious and immortal, they should govern themselves by spontaneous choice from within and not be coerced by an artificial terror applied from without.

The method in history of giving the strongest males possession of the females is no doubt the mode in which nature selects and exalts her breeds. But as society refines it will be seen that the strength of brute instinct, the strength of position, the strength of money, the strength of every artificial advantage, should be put aside in favor of the diviner strength of genius, goodness, beauty, moral and physical completeness of harmony. Freedom would secure this as compulsion prevents it. Man is destined to outgrow the destructive monopolizing passion of jealousy native to his animality. This is shown by his capacity for chivalry, which is a self-abnegating identification of his personality with the personalities of others, not merely freeing them from his will, but aiding them to secure their own happiness in their own way.

The effort to suppress free choice by the use of terror has been tried terribly enough and long enough. It has always proved an utter failure, viewed on any large scale. Has the awful penalty affixed to any deviation from the prescribed legal method of sexual relations wholly prevented such deviation? It has often led to concealment and duplicity,—two lives carried on at once, a life of demure conformity in public, a life of passionate fulfilment in secret. The well-understood sacrifice of truth to appearance has ever served to inflame the mistrust and swell the vengeance of the jealous. The only real remedy will be found in perfect truth, frankness, and justice. In regard to the personal autonomy of the affections, woman should be raised to the same status and be tried by the same code as man. That code should not be as now the legacy of the brutish and despotic past, but the achievement of a scientific morality, those laws of universal order which express the will of the Creator, the collective harmony of Nature. Since the unions of the sexes are of all grades and qualities, all degrees of impurity and beastliness or of purity and sacredness, the parties to them cannot be justly judged by a single rigid rule of external technicality, and ought not to be sealed with one unvarying approval of respectable or branded with one monotonous stigma of illicit. They should be judged by the varying facts in the case as they are in the sight of God; and when those facts are not known in their true merits there is no competency or right to judge the man or the woman at all. The present judgments of society unquestionably ought in many cases to be reversed. For example, it is to be said that the women who consort with men they loathe, and against their will breed children infected with ferocious passions and diseased tendencies, no matter how regularly they are married or how proud their social position, should be condemned or rescued. Also it is to be said that persons filled with a true and divine love, whether sanctioned or unsanctioned by conventional usages, claim to be left to the inherent moral reactions of their acts, and to the unprejudiced judgments of the competent. This central truth, compromise whom it may, and encompassed with delicacies and with difficulties as it may be, is to be firmly maintained, although Pecksniff and Grundy shriek at it until the whole continent quivers.

The distinction of love and freedom from lust and license is obvious, and the unleashing of the. latter in the disguise of the former cannot be too vehemently deprecated. But that a man or a woman may cherish in the wedded state an impure and detestable passion, or outside of it know a heavenly one, is a truth which can be denied only by a character of odious vulgarity. The rank and worth of a love are to be estimated by its moral and religious quality in the sight of God and its natural influence on character. To estimate it otherwise, as is usually done, is to violate morality and religion with conventionality, and in place of nature, sincerity and truth install arbitrary artifice, hypocrisy and falsehood. The grand desiderata in all relationships of affection are, first, the observance of open truth and honor, second, the recognition of their varying grades of intrinsic nobleness and charm or intrinsic foulness and criminality, and the treatment of the parties to them accordingly. Meanwhile, the frank and clear discussion of the subject is imperatively needed. The double system hitherto in vogue of at once enforcing ignorance and stimulating prurience by banishing the subject from confessed attention and study into the two regions of shamefacedness and obscenity has wrought immeasurable evil. For the sexual passion, morbidly excited by nearly all the influences of society, and then mercilessly repressed by public opinion, has a morbid development which breaks out in those monstrous forms of vice which are the open sores of civilization. Take away the inflaming lures of mystery and denial—shed the clear, cold light of scientific knowledge on the facts of the case and the principles properly regulative of conduct—and the passion will gradually become moderate and wholesome. Science has brought region after region of human life under the light and guidance of its benign methods. The region of the personal affections in society and the procreation of posterity, being most obstinately held by passions and prejudices, longest resists the application of impartial, fearless study to the usages imposed by traditional authority. The consistent doing of this will be one of the greatest steps ever taken. It will break the historic superstition that the conjunction of a pair married in seeming by a priest is necessarily holier than that of a pair married in reality by God, destroy the stupid prejudice which makes in the affectional relations of the sexes only the one discrimination that they are in or out of wedlock, and remove the cruel social ban which renders it impossible for straight-forward sincerity of affection and honesty of speech to escape the dishonor which double-facedness of passion and duplicity of word and deed so easily shoulder aside. And when this is done, much will have been done to inaugurate the better era for which the expectation of mankind waits.

The principal reason why the married so frequently experience satiety and weariness, and the consequent sting of a foreign hunger provocative of the wandering which gives occasion for jealousy, is that in their long and close familiarity the partners come to feel that they have seen all through and all around each other, have exhausted each other of all fresh charm, piquancy, and interest. The genuine remedy for this, the only really adequate and enduring remedy, is the recognition in each other of the infinite mystery of all conscious being, a free personality on endless probation and destined for immortal adventures. Then each will be to the other—what every human being intrinsically is—a concentrated epitome of the Kosmos and an explicit revelation of God. There is no revelation of the free conscious God except in the free conscious creature, and in every such being there is one. Let a pair be worthy to see and feel this truth, and there can be no exhaustion of their mutual interest, because before their reverential observation there can be no end to the surprises of the infinite in the finite. Then the sweetness, the wonder, the varying lure of love will never wither and die into indifference, nor roil and perturb into jealousy and madness.

No doubt to many these views will seem a transcendental romance, a delusive dream. Not every one has the nature finely touched to fine issues capable of living in the ether of these ideal heights. But there *are* on the earth holy and entranced souls who live there. It is obvious enough how absurdly inapplicable all this class of considerations must be to the basest kinds of persons, those who, like brutes, wallow in styes of sensuality, or, like devils, surrender themselves to the tyranny of the lowest passions. Such must needs be relegated to an inferior standard. Those whose consciences are coarser and lower than the code of society may most properly be held in subjection by its laws. But those whose consciences are purer and higher than the current social code, the nobler natures who sincerely aspire to the fulfilment of their destiny as children of God, should be a law unto themselves. They will not be tyrants over or spies upon one another. Full of self-respect and mutual respect, owning the indefeasible sovereignty of each personality in the offices of its individual being, they will pass and repass shrouded in transparent royalty, exacting no subjection, making no inquiries.

And now this long and central chapter in the life of Forrest, with the essential lessons it has for others, may be ended by a brief statement of the moral scale of degrees in the conduct of different men under the provoking conditions of jealousy.

One man detects the woman to whom he is legally united, but whom he hates and loathes, in criminal relations with another. He takes an axe, chops them in pieces, then sets the house on fire, and, cutting his own throat, falls into the flames. In other cases his insane fury satiates itself with a single victim, the man or the woman, as caprice dictates. This is crazy ferocity, making its subject first a maniac, then a tiger, then a devil. Has not humanity by its smothered approval too long kept the diabolical horror of this style of behavior recrudescent?

Another mournful and shocking form of this tragedy there is. And it is a form repeated far more frequently in its essential features than ever comes to the open light of day. A man of a sombre, vivid, and proud nature, possessed with a passion so absorbing that it sways his being with tidal power, awakens to the fact that the love he thought all his own has wandered elsewhere. His heart stands still and his brain reels. His love is too true and deep to change. To injure her is as impossible as to restrain himself. He says not a word, makes not a sign, but his sad, dark purpose is fixed. He leaves directions that no questions be asked, no public notice taken of him or of his fate further than the most modest funeral, and that a plain stone be reared over him with the single word, *Infelicissimus*. Then a pistol-ball in his heart closes the throbbing of an agony too great to be borne. The suicide is the pathetic slave of his passion. Surely for such there must be a sequel in some choicer world, where the tangled plot will be cleared up and the soul not be thus helplessly self-entangled.

In the third case, a husband, receiving proof of the infidelity of his honored and trusted wife, in a furious revulsion of scorn and detestation thrusts her into the street, proclaims her offence everywhere, and seeks release and redress in a public court. This is one form of the average of social feeling and conduct in such a case. It is the common spirit of revenge cloaked in justice. It may not be thought base, but it cannot be called noble.

In still another example the jealous man is now enraged and now distressed with conflicting impulses to revenge and to pardon. First he storms and threatens, then he weeps and entreats; now, he strides up and down, tearing his hair, crying and sobbing; and now he rushes out and confides his misery, begging for sympathy and counsel. And whether he condones or dismisses the offender depends on her own policy. This course, ruled by no principle, is a mess of incoherent impulse, raw and childish, a manner of proceeding of which, although it is so common, any grown-up and well-conditioned man should be ashamed.

In the next instance we see the man, on learning his misfortune in losing the exclusive affection of her whom alone he has loved, staggered by the blow, smitten to the heart with grief, flung upon himself in recoiling anguish. But, to shield her from disgrace, and to avoid shame to himself and scandal to the public, he keeps the secret sacredly; ending, however, all marriage intimacy, their lives henceforth a mere contiguity of ice and gloom until death. This is another expression of the average level of men and style of social feeling, not lower, not much higher, than might be expected.

A greatly superior example, finer and braver, comparatively rare, perhaps, yet with a larger list of performers than many would suppose, is where the fault is frankly confessed and freely forgiven, just as other faults are, or the deed justified and accepted on the ground of an integral affection and an approving conscience willing with courageous openness to take every consequence. There is valor, dignity, consistency, force of character in this. It is impossible for persons of low animal instincts or where there is treachery and lying.

But the highest degree of chivalry under such circumstances is that exemplified by the man who, cleansed from the foul and cruel usages of the past, freed from the taints of the tyrannical masculine selfhood, does what man has so rarely done, but what multitudes of women have often done. He shows a love so pure and exalted that it subordinates his selfhood and blends his happiness in that of the beloved object. For her well-being he is willing to stand aside and yield up every claim. Is such generosity beyond the limit of human nature? It may be beyond the limit of *historic* human nature, trailing the penalties of the past. It is not beyond the limit of *prophetic* human nature, carrying the purposes of God.

No doubt some barrier at present is necessary; and society has a right to give the law, from insight, but not from despotism. Monogamic union is the true relation, and its vow should not be broken by either party. But if it is broken the social penalty should be the same for man as for woman. In such case the parties should either condone or separate without furious controversy or personal revenge. Truth and fitness should be set above conventionality and prejudice, and frankness remove hypocrisy. Such alone is the teaching of this chapter, which invokes the pure, steady light of science to shine on the facts of sex, cleanse foulness out, and bring the code of society into unison with the code of God.

Chapter XVI.
Professional Character—Relations with Other Players—The Future of the Drama

One of the most striking traits in the character of Forrest was a profound respect for his profession and a scrupulous observance of the duties it imposed. His conscientiousness in studying his parts, in being punctual in rehearsal and at performance, in holding all considerations of convenience or pleasure sternly subordinate to the conditions for the best fulfilment of his rôle, were worthy of exact imitation. Before beginning a season he went into training, carefully regulating his habits in diet and in hours of exercise and sleep; and during an engagement he always exerted a good deal of self-denial in the nursing and husbanding of his powers. He strove also to improve in his renderings not only by an earnest, direct study of the part, and by a careful attention to critical suggestions from every quarter, but likewise by keeping his faculties alert during his own performances to catch every hint of inspiration from nature or accident, to seize on the causes of each failure or success, and to utilize the experience for the future.

These same habits of punctuality and critical self-observation belonged to Mrs. Siddons, and were one of the secrets of her astonishing rise, just as they were of that of Forrest. The first time that Mrs. Siddons played the part of Lady Macbeth, she says, "So little did I know of my part when it came night that my shame and confusion cured me, for the remainder of my life, of procrastinating my business." After this first performance of Lady Macbeth, Mrs. Siddons recalled in her dressing-room what she had done, and practised various improvements. Trying to get the right look and tone for the words, "Here's the smell of the blood still," she did it so naturally that her maid exclaimed, "Dear me, ma'am, how hysterical you are! I vow, ma'am, it's not blood, but rose-paint and water!"

Perhaps the just sense which Forrest had of the dignity of his profession, and likewise his sense of manly behavior, will be shown most forcibly by an anecdote. An old schoolmate of his, who had become a clergyman, met him one day and asked the favor of a ticket to his performance of Lear that evening, but added that he wished his seat to be in a private box where he could see without being seen. "No, sir," was the reply with which the player rebuked the preacher; "when I look at my audience I should feel ashamed to see there one who is ashamed to be seen. Permit me to say, sir, that our acquaintance ends here." Had he remembered the lines of Richard Perkins to the old dramatic author Thomas Heywood, their quotation would have been apt and pungent:

"Still when I come to plays, I love to sit,
That all may see me, in a public place,
Even in the stage's front, and not to get
Into a nook and hoodwink there my face.
This is the difference: Some would have me deem
Them what they are not: I am what I seem!"

In no element or domain of his life was Forrest more misunderstood and belied than in regard to his general and particular relations with the other members of his profession. Justice to his memory requires that the truth be shown; and, besides, the subject has a strong interest.

The exercise of the dramatic faculty by itself is productive of tenderness, largeness, flexibility, and generosity of mind and heart. It is based on a rich, free intelligence and sensibility, and serves directly to quicken and invigorate the imagination and the sympathies. In fact, so far as its offices are fulfilled it delivers one from the hard, narrow limits of his own selfhood, familiarizes him with the conception and feeling of other grades and styles of character, conduct, and experience, through his passing assumptions of their parts and identification with their varieties develops the whole range of his nature, and makes him, while sensitive to differences, tolerant of them and full of charity. The true moral genius of the drama, supremely exemplified in Shakspeare, is the same genial gentleness and forbearing magnanimity towards every form of humanity as is shown by the God whose earth sustains and sky overarches and rain and sun and harvest visit and bless alike the coward and the hero, the saint and the scoundrel. For the moral essence of the drama consists in the recognition and appreciation of character and manners, not in asserting the will of self nor in assailing the wills of others. But there is a sharp contradiction between this natural tendency of the dramatic art by itself and the ordinary influence exerted by the professional practice of the art as a means of gaining celebrity and a livelihood. If the former would develop a generous emulation to see who can best reproduce in sympathetic imagination every height and depth of human nature and life, the latter instinctively stimulates a hostile rivalry to see who can secure the best parts and win the most pay and praise. Thus the members of the histrionic profession are drawn to one another in kindly sentiment by the intrinsic qualities of their art, but thrown into a hostile relation by those accidental conditions of their trade which make them selfish competitors for precedence. The breadth of the intrinsic tendency of the art is seen in the unparalleled mutual interest and kindness of actors and actresses, as a class standing by one another in all times of adversity with a generosity no other class exhibits; the aggravating power of the accidental influence of the profession is exposed in the notorious jealousy and irritability of these hunters after popularity. Accordingly, among the votaries of the stage a great many friendships are fostered and a great many rankling animosities are bred.

Forrest had all his life too profound an interest in his art, too exalted an estimate of the mission of the stage, too dignified and just a mind, too deep and ready a sympathy, to be capable of the contempt and dislike for his theatrical compeers and associates of which he was often accused. He was an irascible and imperious man. He was not a suspicious, an envious, or an unkind man. And the high spirit of affection and munificence breathing in his beautiful bequest of all his fortune to soothe the declining years of aged or disabled actors and to elevate their favorite art, will awaken a late remorse for the great wrong done his heart.

Others have suffered the same wrongs. Mrs. Siddons was accused of "pride, insolence, and savage insensibility to the distresses of her theatrical associates." She was satirized in the daily papers for her parsimony and avaricious inhospitality. The charges were cruelly unjust. The truth simply was that she was engrossed in labor, study, and the fulfilment of her duties to her family, while the meaner part of the profession and of the public wished her to give herself to their convivialities. Lawyers are not expected to plead cases for one another gratuitously, nor doctors to transfer a fee to a rival. Why should an actor alone be held bound to give his time and earnings to his associates whenever they ask? The practice of calling up and representing together the noblest sentiments of human nature is expected to create in them more friendship, more genial feeling, than is cultivated in others. This is a compliment to the profession. But any actor of high rank who protects his individuality and asks no favor beyond justice and good will, dignifies his profession and serves the true interests of its members.

Forrest had too profound and assured a sense of his own place and rank and worth to be restlessly inquisitive and sensitive as to what his associates thought or felt about him, or to feel any mean twinge of jealousy at any attention they could draw. He did not, as Macready and so many other renowned players did, desire to monopolize everything to himself when before an audience. On the contrary, nothing so much pleased him as to see another actor or actress studious, aspiring, and successful. Then the more applause they secured the better he liked it. But one point there was in his conduct which gave much offence to many and was not forgiven by them. He shrank from all familiar association with those of his profession who were not gentlemen and ladies in their personal self-respect and professional conduct. He had a horror for carelessness, sloth, unpunctuality, untruthfulness, drunkenness, or other common neglect of duty and thrift, whether arising from a slipshod good nature or from depravity. And it is notorious that the dramatic profession, although the freest of all professions from the darker crimes, is much addicted to indulgence in the vices associated with conviviality and a relaxed sternness of social conscience. The temptations to these snares of soul and body Forrest had felt and resisted. The opposite traits he had made a second nature. He liked men and women who kept their word, did their duty, saved their money, and aspired to do more excellent work and win a better position. It was because so many of those with whom he came in contact on the stage were not studious, prompt, careful, self-respectful, but idle, loose, negligent, reckless, that he stood socially aloof from them, censured them, and drew their hostility. But the more faithful and honorable body of the profession always cherished a warm appreciation of his sterling qualities of character and stood in the most friendly personal relations with him. Repeatedly, in different periods of his career, in Great Britain and in America, the whole company of a theatre, at the close of one of his engagements, united in bestowing some gift, with an address, in testimony of their sense of his courtesy, their admiration for his genius, and their gratitude for his professional example. John McCullough, who for five years played second parts to him and was his intimate comrade on and off the stage, speaks of him thus: "He was exact to a moment in every appointment; and the tardiness of any one delaying a rehearsal stirred his mightiest anger. He would sternly say to the offender, ' You have stolen from these ladies and gentlemen ten minutes of their time,—ten minutes that even God cannot restore.' But to those whom he saw attentive and industrious he was the kindest of men. No matter how incapable they might be, he aided them to the full extent of his power, often at rehearsal playing the most unimportant parts to teach an actor, and encouraging him by kind words and treatment. He never recognized the existence of weaknesses so long as they did not interfere with business. An actor might be what he pleased in private life until he carried the effects into moments of duty, and then he knew no mercy. On the stage he was the best and easiest of men. It was a pleasure to act with him. He would in every way assist those around him, aid them in every possible fashion, and do all to strengthen their faith in him and in themselves. Particularly was this so in the case of subordinates; while to equals who showed the slightest carelessness or injustice he was unrelenting." And in this connection the following letter written by Forrest to Thomas Barry, manager of the old Tremont Theatre and of the later Boston Theatre, is very characteristic:

"Baltimore, December 17th, 1854.

"My Dear Mr. Barry,—From an expression which you used to me while I had the pleasure to be with you last in Boston, I inferred that you could not justify my conduct towards Mr. —in refusing him permission to act with me during my late engagement there. When I briefly replied to your expression, I supposed I had answered your objections. But, thinking over the matter since, I am not so certain that I had convinced you of my undeniable right to pursue the course I then adopted. So I will now more fully state my views of the question.

"It is an axiom that a man in a state of liberty may choose his own associates, and if he find one to be treacherous and unworthy he may discard him. Therefore I discard Mr. —. Again, I never believed in the hypocrisy which tells us to love our enemies. *My* religion is to love the good and to eschew the evil. Therefore I eschew Mr. —. Physical cowardice may be forgiven, but I never forgave a moral coward; and therefore I forgive not Mr. —. He who insists upon associating, professionally or otherwise, with another known to despise him, is a wretch unworthy of the name of man. Consequently Mr. — is unworthy of the name of man. But, sir, besides all this; I have an indisputable right to choose from the company such actors as I consider will render me the most agreeable as well as the most efficient support.

"In my rejection of Mr. — I took the earliest care not to jeopardize any of the interests of your theatre. For I advised you in ample time of my resolution, warning you of my intentions, and giving my reasons therefore, so that you might choose between the services of Mr. —and my own. For, while I claim the right in these matters to choose for myself, I unhesitatingly concede the same right to another.

"And now if, after this expression of my views relative to this thing, you still hold to the opinion that my conduct was unjustifiable, you cannot with the slightest propriety ask me to fulfil another engagement so long as Mr. —remains in your company. For I pledge you my word as a man that he shall never, under any circumstances, act with me again.

"Yours truly,

"Edwin Forrest.

"Thos. Barry, esq."

Two incidents of a different kind will illustrate other qualities in the character of Forrest. A boy of sixteen or seventeen had a few lines to recite. At rehearsal his delivery was incorrect and annoying. Forrest repeated the lines, and asked to have them read in that manner. Each attempt failed more badly than the preceding. At last, quite irritated and out of patience, Forrest said, "Not so, not so. Read the passage as I do." The boy looked up with an injured but not immodest air, and replied, "Mr. Forrest, if I could read the lines as you do, I should not be occupying the low position I do in this company." Forrest felt that his petulance had been unjust. His chin sank upon his breast as he paused a moment in reflection. Then he said, "I am properly rebuked, and I ask your pardon." At the close of the rehearsal he went to the manager and inquired, "How much do you give that boy a week?" "Eight dollars."

"Well, during my engagement pay him sixteen, and charge the extra amount to me."

At another rehearsal the company had been waiting some time for the arrival of a subordinate player who was usually very prompt and faithful. When the delinquent entered, Forrest broke out testily, "Well, sir, you see how long you have detained us all." The poor man, pale, and struggling with emotion, answered, humbly, "I am very sorry. I came as soon as I could. I have suffered a great misfortune. My boy died last night." A thrill of sympathy went through the company. Forrest stepped forward and took the man respectfully by the hand, and said, "Excuse me, my friend, and go back to your home at once. You ought not to be here to-day, and we will get along in some way without you." Then, giving him a fifty-dollar bill, he added, "And accept this with my sincere apology."

The tremendous strength of Forrest, and the downright earnestness with which he used it on those unhappy men whose business it was to be seized, shaken, and hurled about, gave rise to scores of apocryphal stones concerning his violence in acting and the terrible sufferings of his subordinates. In many of these stories, under their exaggeration, something characteristic can be discerned: On a certain occasion when he impersonated a Roman hero attacked by six minions of a tyrant, he complained that the aforesaid minions were too tame; they did not come upon him as if it were a real struggle. After his storming against their inefficiency, the supernumeraries sulked and consulted. Their captain said, "If you want this to be a bully fight, Mr. Forrest, you have only to say so."

"I do," he replied. When the scene came on, the hero was standing in the middle of the stage. The minions entered and deployed in rapid skirmishing. One struck energetically at his face, a second levelled a strenuous kick at his paunch, and the remainder made ready to rush for a decisive tussle. For one instant he stood astounded, his chest heaving, his eyes flashing, his legs planted like columns of rock. Then came two minutes of powerful acting, at the end of which one supernumerary was seen sticking head foremost in the bass-drum of the orchestra, four were having their wounds dressed in the greenroom, and one, finding himself in the flies, rushed on the roof of the theatre shouting "fire!" Forrest, called before the curtain, panted his thanks to the audience, who, taking it as a legitimate part of the performance, protested that they had never before seen him act so splendidly. The story is questionable, yet through its grotesque dilatation undoubtedly one lower and lesser phase of the actor and of his public may be seen.

During the earlier years of his own pecuniary prosperity, Forrest lent at various times sums of money ranging from one dollar to five hundred dollars to a large number of his more improvident theatrical associates. In very few instances were these sums repaid. In most cases the obligation was suffered to go by default and in many the favor of the loans, so far from being felt as a claim for gratitude, proved a source of uneasiness and alienation. To a man of his just, careful, straightforward character and habits this multiplied experience of dishonesty, often coupled with treachery and slander, was extremely trying. It nettled him, it embittered him, it tended strongly to close his originally over-free hand against applications to borrow, and made him sometimes suspicious that friendly attentions were designed, as they not unfrequently were, as means to get at his purse. The rich man is much exposed to this experience, with its hardening and souring influence on character, especially the rich man in a profession like the dramatic abounding with impecunious and unthrifty members. Under these circumstances it was certain that many unsuccessful applicants for pecuniary favors, persons whom he refused because he thought them unworthy, would slander him. But throughout his life his heart and hand were generously open to the appeals of all distressed actors or actresses on whom he believed assistance would not be thrown away. In many an instance of destitution and suffering among his unfortunate brethren and sisters sick, deserted, dying, did his bounty come to relieve and console. Among his papers a score or more of letters were found, with widely-separated dates, from well-known members of the profession, containing requests of this sort or thanks for his prompt responses. For example, there was one from the estimable gentleman and veteran actor George Holland gratefully acknowledging a gift of two hundred dollars. The kind deeds of Forrest were not blazoned, but carefully concealed. Yet the few friends who had his inmost confidence, who were themselves the frequent channels of his secret beneficence, knew how free and full his charities were, especially to worthy and unfortunate members of the dramatic profession. In the course of his career he gave over, fifty benefits for needy associates, dramatic authors, and public charities,—from Porter, Woodhull, Devese, and Stone, to John Howard Payne and J. W. Wallack and the Dramatic Fund Association,—the proceeds of which were upwards of twenty-five thousand dollars. And when, in consequence of the thickening requests for such favors and the invidiousness of a selection, he made a rule not to play for the benefit of any one, unless in some exceptional case, he would still often give towards the object his price for a single performance, two hundred dollars. Yet, such is the unreasonableness of censorious minds, he was severely blamed, for showing an avaricious and unsympathizing spirit towards his theatrical contemporaries. The accusation frequently appeared in print and stung him, though he could never brook to answer it.

Many a time on the last night of his engagement at a theatre he would send for the treasurer and make him his almoner for the distribution of sums varying from five to fifteen dollars to the humbler laborers, the scene-shifter's, gasman, watchman, and others whose incomes were hardly enough to keep the wolf from their doors. During one of his engagements at Niblo's Garden the actors and actresses for some reason did not receive their regular salary. Learning the fact, he refused to take his share of the proceeds until they had been paid; and, going still further, he advanced a sum from his own pocket to make up what was due them.

More interesting and important, however, than his pecuniary attitude towards his fellow-players is his moral relation. And this in one aspect was eminently sweet and noble. If he avoided unworthy actors with contempt, he yielded to no one in the admiration, gratitude, and love he cherished for the gifted and faithful, the lustre of whose genius gilded the theatre, and the merit of whose character lifted and adorned the profession.

The earliest strong and distinct feeling of love, in the usual sense of the word, ever awakened in him, he said, was by a young and fascinating actress in the part of Juliet, whom he saw in a Philadelphia theatre when he was in his thirteenth year. What her name was he knew not, nor what became of her, nor could he remember who played Romeo to her; but the emotions she awakened in him by her representation of the sweet girl of Verona, the picture of her face and form and moving, remained as fair and bright and delicious as ever to the end of his days. Recounting the story to his biographer one evening in the summer of 1869 as he sat in his library, the moonlight streaming through the trees in at the open window and across the floor, he said, "A thousand times have I wondered at the intensity of the impression she made on my boyish soul, and longed to know what her after-fate was. She was a vision of enchantment, and, shutting my eyes, I seem to see her now. Years ago I came across the following lines, which so well corresponded to my remembrance of her that I committed them to memory:

"'Twas the embodying of a lovely thought,
A living picture exquisitely wrought
With hues we think, but never hope to see
In all their beautiful reality,
With something more than fancy can create,
So full of life, so warm, so passionate.
Young beauty, sweetly didst thou paint the deep
Intense affection woman's heart will keep
More tenderly than life! I see thee now,
With thy white-wreathed arms, thy pensive brow,
Standing so lovely in thy sorrowing.
I've sometimes read, and closed the page divine,
Dreaming what that Italian girl might be,
Yet ne'er imagined look or tone more sweet than thine.'"

An actor named James Fennell, endowed with a superb figure and a noble elocution, and a great favorite with play-goers in the boyhood of Forrest, made an indelible impression on him. The finished actor, however, was an unhappy man, thriftless in his affairs, and an inveterate drunkard. When he had become an old man his intemperance grew so gross, and his indebtedness to his landlady was so great, that she would keep him no longer. Driven away, he roamed about for some time in despair. Finally, on a bitter winter's night, amidst a pelting snow-storm, he came back and knocked at the door. The landlady opened the window and looked out Fennell, a picture of woebegone wretchedness struck an attitude and recited the lines,—

"Pity the sorrows of a poor old man,
Whose trembling limbs have borne him to your door;
His days are dwindled to the shortest span:
Oh, give relief, and heaven will bless your store;—"

with such powerful pathos that the heart of the woman relented, and she took him in and cared for him till, a little later, he died. The piteous case of this actor, whose infirmity destroyed the fruits of his genius, taught the youthful Forrest a lesson which he never forgot.

Instead of looking to artificial stimulants to prop up forces flagging under the strain of the irregular exertions and late hours of a player, he learned to depend on a sufficient supply of plain, wholesome food, carefully and slowly taken, and a scrupulous observance of full hours of sleep. Had they followed this wise course, how many—like the brilliant and wayward Kean, whose conduct disgraced the profession his genius glorified, and poor Mrs. George Barrett, whose beauty of person and motion intoxicated the beholder—would have been kept from their untimely and unhonored graves!

The first actor of really strong original power and commanding art under whose influence Forrest came in his early youth was Thomas A. Cooper. From him the boyish aspirant caught much that was valuable. He always retained a grateful recollection of his debt, and spoke warmly of his benefactor. In the destitute age of the veteran, Forrest was one of the first movers in securing a benefit for him. Unable himself to act on the occasion in New York, he got up another benefit at New Orleans, in which he acted the chief part, and raised a handsome sum for his old instructor. Cooper warmly acknowledged the kindness of his young friend in a published card. On another occasion also the same spirit was shown. One of the daughters of Cooper was to make her debut in the character of Virginia, the performance to be for the benefit of Cooper. Forrest agreed to give his services and play the part of Virginius. As soon as he heard that Miss Cooper would feel more confidence if her father played that part, Forrest consented to undertake the part of Dentatus. One of the daily journals remarked, "This is another instance of that generous kindness on the part of Mr. Forrest which has bought him golden opinions from all sorts of people. The public will award him the meed which such an act merits."

Another actor of consummate merit, both as artist and as man, there was in Philadelphia, in whose public performances and personal intercourse the boy Forrest took the keenest delight,— Joseph Jefferson, the incomparable comedian, great-grandfather of the present Joseph Jefferson the exquisite perfection and unrivalled popularity of whose Rip Van Winkle have filled the English-speaking world with his fame. The elder Jefferson was a man universally beloved for his charming qualities of character and universally admired for his inimitable art. Forrest's memory of him was singularly clear and strong and sweet. Whenever touching on this theme his tongue was full of eloquent music and his heart seemed steeped in tender reverence and love. He said the Theatre had produced some saints as well as the Church, and Jefferson was one of the most benignant and faultless. For thirty-five years he was the soul and life of the Philadelphia stage, the pre-eminent favorite of all, delighting every one who saw him with the quiet felicities and irresistible strokes of an art that was as nature itself. He played the characters of fools,—Launcelot Gobbo, Dogberry, Malvolio, the fool in Lear,—Forrest said, in a manner that made them actually sublime, suggesting something supernatural, through their mirth and simpleness insinuating into the audience astounding and overpowering meanings. In his age Jefferson risked his little fortune, the modest earnings of an industrious life, in an enterprise of his friend Warren, the theatrical manager. It was all lost. Once more he appealed to the patrons who had always smiled on him. The summer birds had flown, and his benefit-night showed him an empty house. The blow actually killed him. He left the city and went to Harrisburg, where he soon afterwards died among strangers. Hearing of his poverty and loneliness at Harrisburg, Forrest, who was then in his high tide of success, wrote to him that he would get up a benefit for him at the Arch Street Theatre and play Othello for him. But the heart-broken player replied that he would never be a suppliant for patronage in that city again. While he lay in his room very sick, the doctor called and found him reading Lalla Rookh. "I can assure you of a cure," said the physician. Jefferson replied, in a sad but firm voice, "My children are all grown up. I am of no further use to them; and I am weary of life. I care not to get well. I think it is better to be elsewhere." And so he died. Chief-Justice Gibson placed a marble slab over his dust, with a happy inscription which some nameless but gifted friend of the actor has appended to his own tributary verses.

> For thee, poor Player, who hast seen the day
> When stern neglect has bent thee to her state,
> With fond remembrance let the poet pay
> One tribute to thy melancholy fate.
> Haply some aged man may yet exclaim,
> "Him I remember in his youthful pride,
> When sober age ran riot at his name,
> And roaring laughter held his bursting side."
> There at his home, the father, husband kind,
> Oft have I noted his calm noon of life;
> With humor chastened, and with wit refined,
> Enjoy the social board with comforts rife.
> Him have I seen when age crept on apace,
> Portraying to the life some earlier part,
> The soul of mirth reflected from his face,
> While bitter pangs disturbed his throbbing heart.
> One night we missed him from his ancient chair,
> Placed by our host beside the blazing hearth;
> Another passed, yet still he was not there,
> Gone was the spirit of our former mirth!
> The future came, and with it came the tale,
> How Time had cured the wounds the world had given;
> How Death had wrapt him in his sable veil
> And gently borne him to the gates of heaven.
> Beneath the shadow of a sacred dome
> The pride and honor of our stage reclines;
> There stranger hands conveyed him to his home,
> And graced his memory with these sculptured lines:

Beneath this marble
Are deposited the ashes of
Joseph Jefferson,
An actor whose unrivalled powers
Took in the whole extent of Comic Character,
From Pathos to heart-shaking Mirth.
His coloring was that of nature, warm, fresh,
And enriched with the finest conceptions of Genius.
He was a member of the Chestnut Street Theatre,
Philadelphia,
In its most high and palmy days,
and the compeer
of cooper, WOOD, warren, francis,
and a host of worthies
Who,
like himself,
Are remembered with admiration and praise.

The love and reverence which Forrest cherished for this exquisite actor and good man were in the eyes of the numerous friends who often heard him express them in fond lingering reminiscences, a touching proof of the goodness of his own heart despite all the scars it had suffered.

When Forrest was playing at Louisville in his youth, during a rehearsal of *Macbeth* he came to the lines,—

"Till that Bellona's bridegroom, lapped in proof,

Confronted him with self-comparisons,"

when Drake, the manager of the theatre, who happened to be on the stage, said to him, "Boy, who was Bellona? And who was her bridegroom?" The stripling tragedian was forced to answer, "I do not know."

"Then," exclaimed Drake, "get a classical dictionary and study the thing out. Never go on spouting words ignorant of their meaning."

"Thank you, sir, for so good a piece of advice," replied young Forrest, with a little mortification in his air. "I have had that lesson before, but see that I have failed to practise it as I ought to have done." A long time after, in another city, when Drake had become a venerable white-haired gentleman; Forrest was rehearsing Othello in his presence. These lines were spoken relating to the magic handkerchief:

"A sibyl, that had numbered in the world
The sun to course two hundred compasses,
In her prophetic fury sewed the work;
The worms were hallowed that did breed the silk;
And it was dyed in mummy, which the skilful
Conserved of maidens' hearts."

A citizen who was standing by Drake asked him if he could explain these strange words. He said he could not. Forrest immediately gave, with great rapidity of utterance, an elegant and lucid exposition of the classical superstitions on which the passage is based. He did it with such grace and force that the whole company broke into applause. He turned to Drake with a low bow and said, "My dear sir, I owe this to you. Do you remember the lesson you taught me at Louisville, fifteen years ago, about Bellona and her bridegroom? Allow me now to thank you." As he took him by the hand the tears were rolling down the cheeks both of the old man and of the young man.

Forrest ever remembered with gratitude the kindness shown him by Mr. Jones, one of the managers under whom he made his first journey to the West and served his practical apprenticeship on the stage. And when the player had become a mature man, crowned with prosperity, living in his great mansion on Broad Street, in Philadelphia, and the manager was destitute and forsaken, bowed by misfortune and old age, he gave his early benefactor a home, taking him into his own house, treating him with kind consideration, comforting his last days, and following his dust to the grave with affectionate respect.

The relations of Forrest with the ladies who acted principal parts with him were almost uniformly of the most satisfactory character, marked by the greatest courtesy, justice, and delicacy. There were two or three instances of strong dislike on both sides. But in all the other examples, from his first assistants, Mrs. Riddle and Miss Placide, to his latest protégées, Miss Kellogg and Miss Lillie, there was nothing but the highest esteem and the most cordial good-will between the parties, their kind sentiments towards him ever sincere, his grateful recollections of them unalloyed. To that estimable woman and gifted actress, Mrs. Riddle, he especially felt himself indebted. In a letter to his biographer he says of her, "To her most kind and unselfish friendship, her motherly care, her wise counsels, the valuable instructions her artistic genius and experience enabled her to give me during two of the most critical years of my young life, I owe more of acknowledgment and affection than I can easily express or ever forget."

But the most beautiful of all his relations with women of the dramatic profession was the long and sacred friendship subsisting between him and Mrs. Sarah Wheatley. This honored lady, distinguished even more for the rare strength and beauty of her character than for her extraordinary histrionic talent, was a great favorite with the theatrical public of New York. She was one of the few examples that charm and uplift all who feel their influence, of a perfectly balanced womanhood, commanding the whole range of feminine virtues, from modest gentleness and self-denial to august dignity and authority, fitted to sweeten, adorn, or aggrandize any station. She first went upon the stage, without any preparatory training, to relieve and support her family, and, as it were by instinctive fitness, was instantly at home and a mistress there. And after withdrawing from the public, she lived amidst the worship of her children and her children's children to an extreme old age, full of exalted worth and serenity, the admiration and delight of the widest circle of friends, who felt that the atmosphere of her presence and manner more than repaid every attention they could lavish on her. Mrs. Wheatley saw the Othello of Forrest on the memorable night he played for the benefit of poor Woodhull. She felt his power, foresaw what he might become, and, with a generous impulse, went to him from behind the scenes and spoke kindly to him words of warm appreciation. The poor, unfriended youth was deeply touched. This was the beginning of an acquaintance which was never interrupted or shadowed by the faintest cloud, but grew stronger and holier to the end. She never noticed his foibles, for he never had them in her presence; and he thought of her with a loving veneration second only to that he felt for his mother. Her son, Mr. William Wheatley,— widely known to the dramatic profession as actor and manager, and esteemed by all for his talent, integrity, and refinement,—speaking of the beauty of this friendship after the death of the great tragedian, whom he had known long and most intimately, said, "If there was one sentiment deeper and keener than any other in the soul of Forrest, it was his reverence for a pure and good woman: and I know that his esteem for my mother approached idolatry, and that she regarded him with maternal fondness."

On a certain occasion when his friend James Oakes was with Forrest in his room at a hotel in New York, something had occurred which had greatly enraged him. He was pacing up and down the floor in a fury, tearing and swearing with the greatest violence. A servant knocked at the door, and announced that Mrs. Wheatley was in waiting. "The change that came over my friend at the announcement of this name," said Oakes, "was like a work of magic. The wrinkles left his brow, a smile was on his mouth, and his angered voice grew calm and musical."

"Mrs. Wheatley?" he said. "Ask her if she will do me the honor to come to my parlor!" Then, turning to his silent friend, he exclaimed, "Oakes, if you want to see a woman fit to be worshipped by every good man, a model of grace and dignity, a living embodiment of wisdom and goodness, you shall now have that grand satisfaction." As she entered he lifted his head illuminated with joy, threw open his arms, and cried, "Why, Mother Wheatley, how long it is since I saw you last,—more than a year!""It *is* a long time," she answered, with a sweet and grave fervor; "it *is* a long time; and how has it been with you all the while, my boy?" Oakes adds, "It was a picture as charming to behold as anything I ever saw. It stands in my memory holy to this day." When such experiences are found in the life of one whose biography is to be written, they should be recorded, and not, as is usually done, be carefully omitted; for these sacred passages are just what is most wholesome and needful in a world gone insane with selfish struggles, hatred, and indifference.

Of the appreciation Forrest had of the genius of the great comedian William E. Burton, he gave a striking expression in the last year of his life. He had been confined to his bed for several weeks in great agony. Oakes was sitting by him. Their talk turned upon the unrivalled gifts and charm of old Joseph Jefferson. Forrest poured out his heart warmly, as he always did, on this favorite theme. He then spoke of the wonderful pathos and instructiveness which might be thrown into the humblest comic characters, and added in close, "I would give twenty thousand dollars to have Burton alive again for ten years to go over the country and play the fools of Shakspeare!"

All who knew Forrest with any intimacy were well aware of his enthusiastic appreciation of the genius and affection for the memory of Kean. He never tired of expatiating on this subject. And he always felt a sharp pleasure in the recollection that when his friend Hackett, the incomparable American Falstaff, called on Kean in London, only a few days before his death, the first words of the dying tragedian were a kind inquiry after the welfare of Edwin Forrest. In his library one day, showing a friend a superb steel engraving of Sir Thomas Lawrence's portrait of John Philip Kemble, he said earnestly and with a regretful tone, "I would give a thousand dollars in gold for a likeness of Kean as good as this is of Kemble." He was familiar with the principal histories of the stage and biographies of players, and felt the keenest interest in their characters, their styles of acting, their personal fortunes. He also felt a pride in the fame and triumphs of his best contemporaries. He was always on kind terms with the elder Booth, to whom he assigned dramatic powers of a very extraordinary degree, although he believed that considerable of their effectiveness was caught from the contagious and electrifying example of Edmund Kean. In the last year of his life, when he was badly broken down in health and fortune, Booth said to Forrest one day, "I want to play the Devil."

"It seems to me," said Forrest, "that you have done that pretty well all your life."

"Oh, I don't mean that," replied Booth; "I am referring to the drama of Lord Byron. I want to play Lucifer to your Cain. Would not that draw,—you cast in the character of Cain, I in that of Lucifer?"

"I think it would," remarked Forrest. "We *must* do it before we die," replied Booth,—and went away, soon to pass into the impenetrable shadow, leaving this too with many another broken and unfulfilled dream.

Forrest assigned an exalted artistic rank to the very varied dramatic impersonations of Mr. E. L. Davenport, every one of whose roles is marked by firm drawing, distinct light and shade, fine consistency and finish. His Sir Giles Overreach was hardly surpassed by Kean or Booth, and has not been approached by anybody else. His quick, alert, springy tread full of fire and rapidity, the whole man in every step, fixed the attention and made every one feel that there was a terrific concentration of energy, an insane possession of the nerve-centres, portending something frightful soon to come. An old play-goer on witnessing this impersonation wrote the following impromptu:

"While viewing each remembered scene, before my gaze appears
Each famed depictor of Sir Giles for almost fifty years;
The elder Kean and mighty Booth have held all hearts in thrall,
But, without overreaching truth, you overreach them all!"

It is a satisfaction to put on record this judgment of one artist concerning another whose merit transcends even his high reputation,—especially as a coolness separated the two men, Mr. Davenport having through a misapprehension of the fact of the publication of Jack Cade by Judge Conrad inferred that it had thus in some sense become the property of the public, and produced the play on the stage, while Forrest held it to be his own private property. He had been so annoyed by such proceedings on the part of other actors before, provoking him into angry suits at law, that his temper was sore. He wrote sharply to Mr. Davenport, who, even if he had made a mistake, had done no conscious wrong and meant no offence, and who replied in a calmer tone and with better taste. Here the matter closed, but left an alienation,—for Forrest when irritated was relentlessly tenacious of his point. Mr. Davenport is a man of gentle and generous character, respected and beloved by all his companions. He is also in all parts of his profession a highly accomplished artist and critic. Accordingly, when he expresses the conviction, as he repeatedly has both before and since the decease of his former friend and great compeer, that Forrest was beyond comparison the most original and the greatest actor America has produced, his words are weighty, and their spirit honors the speaker as much as it does the subject.

In a letter written to Forrest twenty-five years earlier, under date of October 10th, 1847, Mr. Davenport had said, "I have not words to express the gratification and pleasure I felt in witnessing your masterly performance. It was probably the last time I shall have an opportunity to see you for years; but I assure you, however long it may be, the remembrance will always live in my mind as vividly as now."

The treatment also which Mr. John McCullough received from Forrest during his five years of constant service under him, the impression he made on his young coadjutor, and the permanent esteem and gratitude he secured from him, are all pleasant to contemplate. At the close of their business arrangement, Forrest said to McCullough, "I believe I have kept my agreement with you to the letter; but before we part I want to thank you for your strict fidelity to your professional duties at all times. And allow me to say that I have been most of all pleased to see you uniformly so studious and zealous in your efforts to improve. Continue in this course, firm against every temptation, and you will command a proud and happy future. Now, as a token of my esteem, I put in your hands the sum of five hundred dollars, which I want you to invest for your little boy, to accumulate until he is twenty-one years old, and then to be given to him." McCullough says that with the exception of two or three unreasonable outbreaks, which he immediately forgave and forgot, Forrest was extremely kind and good to him, sparing no pains to encourage and further him. And in return the young man would at any time have gladly given his heart's blood for his dear old imperious master, whom, in his enthusiasm, he held to be the most truthful and powerful actor that ever lived. Such an estimate by one of his talent and rank, making every allowance for the personal equation, is an abundant offset for the squeamish purists who have stigmatized Forrest as "a coarse ranter," and the prejudiced critic who called him "a vast animal bewildered with a grain of genius." It may well be believed that in the history of his country's drama he will be seen by distant ages towering in statuesque originality above the pigmy herd of his imitators and detractors.

Gabriel Harrison was another actor on whom the personality and the playing of Forrest took the deepest effect. He was a long time on the stage, and, though he afterwards became an author, a teacher, and a painter, he never abated the intense fervor of his enthusiasm for the dramatic art. His "Life of John Howard Payne," and his "Hundred Years of the Dramatic and Lyric Stage in Brooklyn," show him to be a man of much more than common intelligence and culture. He knew Forrest well for many years, and cherished the warmest friendship for him as a man whose nature he found noble and whose intercourse charming. The last Thanksgiving Day that Forrest had on earth, Harrison, by invitation, spent with him alone in his Broad Street mansion, enjoying a day of frank and memorable reminiscences, delicious effusions of mind and heart and soul. Harrison, writing to the biographer of his friend in protest against the epithet melodramatic, records his estimate thus: "Are the wonderful figures of Michael Angelo melodramatic because they are so strongly outlined? Is Niagara unnatural and full of trick because it is mighty and thunders so in its fall? When I looked at it, its sublimity made me feel as if I were looking God in the face; and I have never thought that God was melodramatic. I have seen Forrest act more than four hundred times. I have sat at his feet as a pupil artist learning of a master artist. In all his chief roles I have studied him with the most earnest carefulness, from his *tout ensemble* to the minutest particulars of look, tone, posture, and motion. And I say that without doubt he was the most honest, finished, and powerful actor that ever lived. Whenever I saw him act I used to feel with exultation how perfectly grand God had made him. How grand a form! how grand a mind! how grand a heart! how grand a voice! how grand a flood of passion, sweeping all these to their mark in perfect unison! My memory of him is so worshipful and affectionate, and so full of regret that I can see him no more, that my tears are blotting the leaf on which I write."

One further incident in the life of Forrest will also serve to illustrate his feeling towards the *personnel* of his profession. It is not without an element of romantic interest. It will fitly close the treatment of this part of the subject. At the end of the war he received a letter from a granddaughter of that Joseph Jefferson whose memory he had always cherished so tenderly. Residing in the South, the fortunes of war had reduced her to poverty, and she asked him to lend her a hundred dollars to meet her immediate necessities. With joyous alacrity he forwarded the amount, and deemed the ministration a great privilege. The sequel of the good deed will please every one who reads it. It need only be said that at the date of the ensuing correspondence Forrest had just been bereaved of his last sister, Eleonora:

"Philadelphia, June 13th, 1871.

"My Dear Mr. Forrest,—I understand from my aunt, Mrs. Fisher, that during my absence from America, and when she had become destitute from the effects of the war, you were kind enough to let her have one hundred dollars.

"My being nearly related to the lady sufficiently explains why I enclose you the sum you so generously gave.

"Permit me to offer my condolence in your late sad loss, and to ask pardon for addressing you at such a time.

"Faithfully yours,
"J. Jefferson.

"Philadelphia, June 15th, 1871.
"To Edwin Forrest."

"Dear Mr. Jefferson,—I received your note of 13th inst., covering a check for one hundred dollars, in payment of a like sum loaned by me, some years since, to your relative, Mrs. Fisher.

"I have no claim whatever on you for the liquidation of this debt. Yet, as the motive is apparent which prompts you to the kindly act, I make no cavil in accepting its payment from you.

"With thanks for the touching sympathy you express in my late bereavement, I am sincerely yours,

"Edwin Forrest.
"J. Jefferson, esq."

When an actor vanquishes the jealous instinct of his tribe and really admires another, his professional training gives a distinct relish and certainty to his praise. When Garrick heard of the decease of Mrs. Theophilus Cibber, a sister of Arne the musician, he said, "Then Tragedy is dead on one side." Also when seeing Carlin Bertinazzi in a piece where, having been beaten by his master, he threatened him with one hand while rubbing his wounded loins with the other, Garrick was so delighted with the truthfulness of the pantomime that he cried, "See, the back of Carlin has its expression and physiognomy." Old Quin had a strong aversion to Mrs. Bellamy, and a conviction that she would fail. But at the close of the first act, as she came off the stage, he caught her in his arms, exclaiming, generously, "Thou art a divine creature, and the true spirit is in thee." Within a year of the expulsion of Mrs. Siddons from Drury Lane as an uninteresting performer, Henderson declared that "she was an actress who had never had an equal and would never have a superior." She remembered this with deep gratitude to her dying day; and when his death had left his family poor she played Belvidera in Covent Garden for their benefit.

Forrest was abundantly capable of this same liberal spirit. No admirer of Henry Placide in his best day could be more enthusiastic in his eulogy than Forrest was, declaring that in his line he had no living equal. He said the same also of the Jesse Rural and two or three other parts of William R. Blake. He had likewise a profound admiration for the romantic and electrifying Othello of Gustavus Vasa Brooke. And of the performance of Cassio in *Othello* and of Cabrero in the Broker of Bogota, by William Wheatley, he said, "They were two of the most perfect pieces of acting I ever saw. One night when he had performed the part of Cabrero better than he ever had done it before, producing a sensation intense enough in the applause it drew to gratify the pride of any player, he said to me, as he left the stage, 'Never again will I play that part.' And, surely enough, he never did. The reason why was a mystery I have not been able to this day to fathom."

Forrest once said, "An intelligent, sympathetic actor, who resists the social temptations of his profession and keeps dignity of character and high purpose, ought to be the most charming of companions. In a great many cases this is the fact. With their insight into character, their power of interpreting even the most unpurposed signals, the secrets of society are more open to them than to others, and they have more adventures. This naturally makes them interesting." He gave two examples in illustration. When he was playing in England, he and James Sheridan Knowles became warm friends. Knowles had often seen Mrs. Siddons act. Forrest asked him what was the mysterious effect she produced in her celebrated sleep-walking scene of Lady Macbeth. He said, "I have read all the high-flown descriptions of the critics, and they fall short. I want you to tell me in plain blunt phrase just what impression she produced on you." Knowles replied, with a sort of shudder, as if the mere remembrance terrified him still, "Well, sir, I smelt blood! I swear that I smelt blood!" Forrest added that the whole life of that amazing actress by Campbell was not worth so much to him as this one Hogarthean stroke by Knowles.

The other anecdote related to an incident which happened to John McCullough, who for several years had been playing second parts to Forrest. He was staying in Washington. Two or three nights before the assassination of President Lincoln he was awakened by tears falling on his face from the eyes of some one standing over him. Looking up, he saw Wilkes Booth, and exclaimed, "Why, what is the matter?"

"My God," replied the unhappy man, already burdened with his monstrous crime, and speaking in a tone of long-drawn, melancholy indescribably pathetic, "My God, how peacefully you were sleeping! *I* cannot sleep."

Another element of strong interest in actors, giving them an imaginative attraction, is the obvious but profound symbolism of their art, the analogies of scenic life and human life. Harley, while playing Bottom in Midsummer Night's Dream, was stricken with apoplexy. Carried home, the last words he ever spoke were the words in his part, "I feel an exposition to sleep coming over me." Immediately it was so, and he slept forever. The aged Macklin attended the funeral of Barry. Looking into the grave, he murmured, "Poor Spranger!" One would have led him away, but the old man said, mournfully, "Sir, I am at my rehearsal; do not disturb my reverie." The elements of the art of acting are the applied elements of the science of human nature. They are the same on the stage as in life, save that there they are systematized and pronounced, set in relief, and consequently excite a more vivid interest. How rich it would have been to share in the fellowship of Lekain and Garrick when in the Champs Élysées they practised the representation of drunkenness!" How is that?" said Lekain. "Very well," replied Garrick. "You are all drunk except your left leg."

Such works as Colley Cibber's Apology, the several lives of Garrick, Boaden's Life of Kemble, Macklin's Memoirs, Campbell's Life of Mrs. Siddons, Gait's Lives of the Players, Proctor's Life of Kean, Collier's Annals of the Stage, Doran's His Majesty's Servants, were familiar to Forrest. His memory was well stored with their contents. He had reflected carefully and much on the general topics of which they treat, and he conversed on them with eloquence and with wisdom. He cherished an eager interest in everything pertaining to his profession viewed in its most comprehensive aspect. His intelligent and profound enthusiasm for the theatre gave him an entire faith that the drama is destined to flourish as long as human nature shall be embodied in men. Its seeming eclipse by cheaper and coarser attractions he held to be but temporary. Its perversion and degradation in meaningless spectacles and prurient dances will pass by, and its restoration to its own high mission, the exhibition of the grandest elements of the soul in the noblest situations, the teaching of the most beautiful and sublime lessons by direct exemplification in breathing life, will give it, ere many generations pass, a glory and a popular charm it has never yet known. Then we may expect to see a great purification and enrichment of the subject-matter presented on the stage. The mere animal affections will cease to have an exaggerated and morbid attention paid to them. Justice will be done to the generic moral sentiments of man, and to his noblest historic and ideal types. The passions of love of truth and spiritual aspiration will dilate in treatment, those of individual jealousy and social ambition dwindle. Instructive and inspiring plays will be constructed out of the veracious materials furnished by characters and careers like those of Columbus and Galileo.

Certainly the realization of such a vision is a great desideratum; because the theatre is a sort of universal Church of Humanity, where good and evil are shown in their true colors without formalism or cant. Its influence—unlike that of sectarian enclosures—is to draw all its attendants together in common sympathies towards the good and fair, and in common antipathies for the foul and cruel. Men are more open and generous in their pleasures than in their pains. Places of public amusement are the first to vibrate to the notes of public joy or grief, defeat or triumph. Telegrams announcing victories or calamities are read from the stage. Theatres are sure to be decked on great festival or pageant days, the popular pulse beating strongest there.

The taste for dramatic representations is native and ineradicable in man. It is a fixed passion with man to love to see the passions of men exhibited in plot and action, and to watch the mutual workings of characters on one another through their different manners of behavior. Just now, it is true, the great, complex, terribly exciting and exacting drama of real life, revealed to us in the newspaper and the novel and the telegraph, so fastens and drains our sympathies that we lack the ideal freedom and restful leisure to enjoy the stage drama so eagerly as it was enjoyed at an earlier and simpler time. But this will not always be so;—

"The world will grow a less distracting scene,
And life, less busy, wear a gentler mien."

Forrest looked for a revival, at no remote date, in America and Europe, of the ancient Greek pride and joy in athletic exercises and the development of nude strength and beauty. The reflex influence from such a revival, he imagined, would flood the stage with a new lustre, making it a resplendent and exalted centre for the inspiring exposure to the public of the perfected models of every form of human excellence. Then the gymnasium, the circus, the race-course, dance, music, song, and the intellectual emulations of the academy may all be grouped around the theatre and find their dazzling climax in the scenic drama, made religious once more as it was in the palmiest day of Greece.

Chapter XVII.
Outer and Inner Life of the Man

The external life of Forrest from the close of his first engagement after the divorce trial to the year 1869—the period stretching from his forty-sixth to his sixty-third year—was largely but the continual repetition of his old triumphs, varied now and then with some fresh professional glory or new personal adventure. To recite the details of his travels and theatrical experiences would be to make a monotonous record of popular successes without any important significance or general interest. A brief sketch of the leading incidents of this period is all that the reader will care to have.

The immense publicity and circulation given to the sensational reports of the long-drawn legal warfare between Forrest and his wife in their suits against each other added to his great fame a still greater notoriety, which enhanced public curiosity and drew to the theatre greater crowds than ever whenever he played. From Portland and Boston to Cincinnati and St. Louis, from Buffalo and Detroit to Charleston and New Orleans, the announcement of his name invariably brought out an overwhelming throng. The first sight of his person on the stage was the signal for wild applause. At the close of the performance he was often called before the curtain and constrained to address the assembly, and then on retiring to his hotel was not unfrequently followed by band and orchestra and complimented with a serenade.

The ranks of his enemies, reinforced with the malevolent critics or Bohemians whom he would not propitiate by any favor, social or pecuniary, continued to fling at him and annoy him in every way they could. But while their pestiferous buzzing and stinging made him sore and angry, it did not make him unhappy. His enormous professional success and broad personal following prevented that. One example of his remarkable public triumphs may stand to represent scores. It was the last night of a long and most brilliant engagement in New York. The "Forrest Light Guard," in full uniform, occupied the front seats of the parquet. No sooner had the curtain fallen on the performance of Coriolanus than the air grew wild with the prolonged shouts of "Forrest! Forrest!" At last he came forth, and the auditory, rising en masse, greeted him with stormy plaudits. "Speech! speech!" they cried. He responded thus:

"I need not tell you, ladies and gentlemen, that I am gratified to see this large assemblage before me; and I have an additional gratification when I remember that among my troops of friends I have now a military troop who have done me the honor to grace my name by associating it with their soldier-like corps. This night, ladies and gentlemen, ends my labors *inside* of the theatre for the season. I call them labors, for no one who has not experienced the toil of acting such parts as I have been called upon nightly to present to you, can have any idea of the labor, both mental and physical, required in the performance of the task. They who suppose the actor's life to be one of comparative ease mistake the fact egregiously. My experience has shown me that it is one of unremitting toil. In no other profession in the world is high eminence so difficult to reach as in ours. This proposition becomes evident when you remember how many of rare talents and accomplishments essay to mount the histrionic ladder, and how very few approach its topmost round. My earliest ambition was distinction upon the stage; and while yet a mere child I shaped my course to reach the wished-for goal. I soon became aware that distinction in any vocation was only to be won by hard work and by an unfailing self-reliance. And I resolved

'With such jewels as the exploring mind
Brings from the caves of knowledge, to buy my ransom
From those twin jailers of the daring heart,

Low birth and iron fortune.'

I resolved to educate myself; not that education only which belongs to the schools, and which is often comprised in a knowledge of mere words, but that other education of the world which makes words things. I resolved to educate myself as Garrick, and Kemble, and Cooke, and, last and greatest of all, Edmund Kean, had done. As he had done before me, I educated myself. The self-same volume from which the Bard of Avon drew his power of mastery lay open before me also,—the infallible volume of Nature. And in the pages of that great book, as in the pages of its epitome, the works of Shakspeare, I have conned the lessons of my glorious art. The philosopher-poet had taught me that

'The proper study of mankind is man;'

and, in pursuit of this study, I sojourned in Europe, in Asia, in Africa, as well as in the length and in the breadth of our own proud Republic. To catch the living lineaments of passion, I mixed with the prince and with the potentate, with the peasant and with the proletary, with the serf and with the savage. All the glorious works of Art belonging to the world, in painting and in sculpture, in architecture and in letters, I endeavored to make subservient to the studies of my calling. How successful I have been I leave to the verdict of my fellow-countrymen,—my fellow-countrymen, who. for a quarter of a century, have never denied to me their suffrages. Ladies and gentlemen, I have spoken thus much not to indulge in any feeling of pride, nor to gratify any sentiment of egotism, but I have done so in the hope that the words which I have uttered here to-night may be the means, perhaps, of inspiring in the bosom of some young enthusiast who may hereafter aspire to the stage a feeling of confidence. Some poor and friendless boy, perchance, imbued with genius, and with those refined sensibilities which are inseparably connected with genius, may be encouraged not to falter in his path for the paltry obstacles flung across it by envy, hatred, malice, and all uncharitableness. Let him rather, with a vigorous heart, buckle on the armor of patient industry,

with his own discretion for his tutor,
and then, with an unfaltering step,
despising the malice of his foes, 'climb

The steep where Fame's proud temple shines afar.'"

A shower of bravos broke out, bouquets were thrown upon the stage, and the actor slowly withdrew, crowned with the applauses of the people like a victorious Roman in the Capitol.

As the years passed on, Forrest came to take an ever keener interest in accumulating wealth. A good deal of his time and thought was devoted to the nursing of his earnings. He showed great shrewdness in his investments, which, with scarcely a single exception, turned out profitably. He was prudent and thrifty in his ways, but not parsimonious or mean. He lived in a handsome, generous style, without ostentation or extravagance, keeping plenty of servants, horses, and carriages, and a table generous in wholesome fare but sparing of luxuries. This love of money, and pleasure in amassing it, though it became a passion, as, with his bitter early experience of poverty and constant lessons of the evils of improvidence, it was natural that it should, did not become a vice or a disease; for it never prevented his full and ready response to every claim on his conscience or on his sympathy. And within this limit the love of accumulation is more to be praised than blamed. In final refutation of the gross injustice which so often during his life charged upon him the vice of a grasping penuriousness, a few specimens of his deeds of public spirit and benevolence—not a list, but a few specimens—may fitly be recorded here. To the fund in aid of the Democratic campaign which resulted in the election of Buchanan as President he sent his check for one thousand dollars. He gave the like sum to the first great meeting in Philadelphia at the outbreak of the war for the defence of the Union. In 1867, when the South was in such distress from the effects of the war, he gave five hundred dollars to the treasurer of a fund in their behalf, saying, "God only knows the whole suffering of our Southern brethren. Let us do all we can to relieve them, not stopping to question what is *constitutional*; for charity itself fulfils the law." He subscribed five hundred dollars towards the relief of the sufferers by the great Chicago fire in 1871. The ship "Edwin Forrest" being in distress on the coast, the towboat "Ajax," from New York, went to her assistance, having on board three pilots. The "Ajax" was never heard of afterwards. To the widows of the three lost pilots Forrest, unsolicited, sent one thousand dollars each. On two separate occasions he is known to have sent contributions of five hundred dollars to the Masonic Charity Fund of the New York Grand Lodge. These acts, which were not exceptional, but in keeping with his nature and habit, are not the acts of an unclean slave of avarice. The jealousy too often felt towards the rich too often incites groundless fault-finding.

It is true that an absorbing passion for truth, for beauty, for humanity, for perfection, is more glorious and commanding than even the most honorable chase of riches. But it is likewise true that reckless idlers and spendthrifts are a greater curse to society, breed worse evils, than can be attributed to misers. Self-indulgence, dependence, distress, contempt, the worst temptations, and untimely death, follow the steps of thriftlessness. Self-denial, foresight, industry, manifold power of usefulness, wait on a well-regulated purpose to secure pecuniary independence. Money represents the means of life,—the command of the best outer conditions of life,—food, shelter, education, culture in every direction. In itself it is a good, and the fostering of the virtues adapted to win it is beneficial alike to the individual and the community, despite the enormous evils associated with the excessive or unprincipled pursuit of it. Sharp and exacting as he was, the absolute honesty and honor of Forrest in all pecuniary dealings were so high above suspicion that they were never questioned. Although often wrongfully accused of a miserly and sordid temper, he never was accused of falsehood or trickery. The large fortune he obtained was honorably earned, liberally used, and at last nobly bestowed. He had a good right to the deep, vivid satisfaction and sense of power which it yielded him. His fortune was to him a huge supplementary background of support, a wide border of the means of life surrounding and sustaining his immediate life.

An extract from a letter written by him to his biographer may fitly be cited to complete what has been said above. Under date of August 28th, 1870, he wrote. "The desire I had for wealth was first fostered only that I might be abler to contribute to the comforts of those whose veins bore blood like mine, and to smooth the pathway to the grave of the gentlest, the truest, the most unselfish friend I ever knew—my mother!—and so, from this holy source, to widen the boundaries of all good and charitable deeds,—to relieve the wants of friends less fortunate than myself, and to succor the distressed wherever found. In early life, from necessity, I learned to depend solely upon myself for my own sustenance. This self-reliance soon gave me power in a small way to relieve the wants of others, and this I never failed to do even to the extent of my ability. So far did I carry this feeling for the distress of others that I have frequently been forced to ask an advance of salary from the theatre to pay the current expenses of my own frugal living. And this I have done when in the receipt of eight thousand dollars a year. I have been very, very poor; but in my whole life I have never from need borrowed more than two hundred dollars in all. I have lent two thousand times that sum, only an infinitesimal part of which was ever returned."

In 1851 Forrest moved from New York to Philadelphia, and took his three sisters to live with him. But he paid frequent visits to his romantic castle on the Hudson. During one of these visits an incident occurred which presents him to the imagination in real life in a light as picturesque and sensational as many of those scenes of fiction on the stage in which he had so often thrilled the multitude who beheld him. The steamboat "Henry Clay," plying on the Hudson between New York and Albany, when opposite Fonthill was suddenly wrapt in flames by an explosion of its boiler, and sunk with a crowd of shrieking passengers. The New York "Mirror" of the next day said, "We are informed that while the unfortunate wretches were struggling; Edwin Forrest, who was then at his castle, seeing their condition, rushed down to the river, jumped in, and succeeded in rescuing many from a watery grave, as well as in recovering the bodies of several who were drowned."

In 1856 Forrest sold Fonthill to the Catholic Sisterhood of Mount Saint Vincent, for one hundred thousand dollars. For the devout and beneficent lives of the members of this order he had a profound reverence; and immediately on completing the sale he made to the Mother Superior a present of the sum of five thousand dollars. And so ended all the dreams of domestic peace and bliss his fancy had woven on that enchanted spot, still to be associated with memories of his career and echoes of his name as long as its gray towers shall peer above the trees and be descried from afar by the sailers on the lordly river below.

In 1857 Forrest received an unparalleled compliment from the State of California. The Governor, Lieutenant-Governor, Secretary, Treasurer, and Comptroller of the State, twenty-seven members of the Senate, with the Secretary and Sergeant-at-Arms, the Speaker and forty-eight members of the House of Representatives, sent him a letter of invitation to make a professional visit to the Golden Coast. It read as follows:

"State Capitol, Sacramento, April 20th, 1857.

"Respected Sir,—The undersigned, State officers and members of the Senate and Assembly, a small portion of your many admirers on the coast of the Pacific, avail themselves of this, the only mode under their control, of signifying to you the very high estimation, as a gentleman and an actor, in which you are generally and universally held by all who have a taste for the legitimate drama. Genuine taste and rigid criticism have united with the verdict of impartial history to pronounce you the head and leader of the noble profession to which you have consecrated abilities that would in any sphere of life render you eminent. We believe that so long as Shakspeare is remembered, and his words revered, your name, too, will be remembered with pride by all who glory in the triumphs of our Saxon literature.

"In conclusion, permit us to express the hope that your existing engagements will so far coincide with our wishes as to permit us, at an early day, to welcome you to the shores of the Pacific, assuring you of a warm and sincere reception, so far as our efforts can accomplish the same, and we feel that we but express the feelings of every good citizen of the State."

To this he replied:

"Philadelphia, July 10th, 1857.

"Gentlemen,—With a grateful pleasure I acknowledge your communication of April 20th, delivered to me a short time since by the hands of Mr. Maguire.

"Your flattering invitation, so generously bestowed and so gracefully expressed, to enter the Golden Gate and visit your beautiful land, is one of the highest compliments I have ever received. It is an honor, I venture to say, that was never before conferred on one of my profession.

"It comes not from the lovers of the drama or men of letters merely, but from the Executive, the Representatives, and other high officials of a great State of the American Confederacy; and I shall ever regard it as one of the proudest compliments in all my professional career.

"Believe me, I deeply feel this mark of your kindness, not as mere incense to professional or personal vanity but as a proud tribute to that art which I have loved so well and have followed so long:

"'The youngest of the Sister Arts,
Where all their beauty blends.'

"This art, permit me to add, from my youth I have sought personally to elevate, and professionally to improve, more from the truths in nature's infallible volume than from the pedantic words of the schools,—a volume open to all, and which needs neither Greek nor Latin lore to be understood.

"And now, gentlemen, although I greatly regret that it is not in my power to accept your invitation, I sincerely trust there will be a time for such a word, when we may yet meet together under the roof of one of those proud temples consecrated to the drama by the taste and the munificence of your fellow-citizens."

During the crisis of his domestic unhappiness—1849-1852—Forrest had withdrawn from the stage for about two years. In 1856, stricken down with a severe attack of gout and inflammatory rheumatism, wearied also of his long round of professional labors, he retired into private life for a period of nearly five years. He now devoted his time to the care of his rapidly increasing wealth, and to the cultivation of his mind by reading, studying works of art, and conversing with a few chosen friends, leading, on the whole, a still and secluded life. At this time an enthusiastic religious revival was going on in the city, and it was reported that the tragedian had been made a convert. An old and dear friend, the Rev. E. L. Magoon, wrote to him a very cordial letter expressing the hope that this report was well founded. Here is the reply of Forrest:

"Philadelphia, March 27, 1858.

"I have much pleasure in the receipt of yours of the 23d instant.

"While I thank you and Mrs. Magoon with all my heart for the kind hope you have expressed that the recent rumor with regard to my highest welfare may be true, I am constrained to say the rumor is in this, as in most matters which pertain to me, most pitifully in error: there is not one word of truth in it.

"But in answer to your questions, my good friend,—for I know you are animated only by a sincere regard for my spiritual as well as for my temporal welfare,—I am happy to assure you that the painful attack of inflammatory rheumatism with which for the last three months I have combated is now quite overcome, and I think I may safely say that with the return of more genial weather I shall be restored once more to a sound and pristine health.

"Then, for the state of my mind. I do not know the time, since when a boy I blew sportive bladders in the beamy sun, that it was ever so tranquil and serene as in the present hour. Having profited by the leisure given me by my lengthened illness seriously to review the past

and carefully to consider the future, both for time and for eternity, I
have with a chastened spirit beheld with many regrets that there was
much in the past that might have been improved; more, perhaps, in the
acts of omission than in acts of commission, for I feel sustained that
my whole conduct has been actuated solely by an honest desire to
adhere strictly to the rule of right; that the past has been characterized,
as I trust the future will be, to love my friends, to hate my enemies,—
for I cannot be a hypocrite,—and to live in accordance with the Divine
precept: 'As ye would that men should do to you, do ye also to them
likewise.'

"And now for that 'higher welfare' of which you speak, I can only say
that, believing, as I sincerely do, in the justice, the mercy, the wisdom,
and the love of Him who knoweth the secrets of our hearts, I hope I
may with

'An unfaltering trust approach my grave,
Like one who wraps the drapery of his couch
About him, and lies down to pleasant dreams.'

"Hoping you are in the enjoyment of good health, and that you still
prosper in the ' good work,' which to you I know is a labor of love,

"I am your friend,
"Edwin Forrest."

At length, rested in mind and body, chastened in taste, sobered and
polished in style, but with no abatement of fire or energy, sought by the
public, solicited by friends, urged by managers, and impelled by his
own feelings, he broke from his long repose, and reappeared in New
York under circumstances as flattering as any that had ever crowned
his ambition. Niblo's Garden was packed to its remotest corners with
an auditory whose upturned expanse of eager faces lighted with smiles
and burst into cheers as he slowly advanced and received a welcome
whose earnestness and unity might well have thrilled him with pride
and joy. The following lines, strong and eloquent as their theme,

written for the occasion by William Ross Wallace, contain perhaps the most truthful and characteristic tribute ever paid to his genius, drawing the real contour and breathing the express spirit of the man and the player.

EDWIN FORREST.

Welcome to his look of grandeur, welcome to his stately mien,
Always shedding native glory o'er the wondrous mimic scene,
Always like a mighty mirror glassing Vice or Virtue's star,
Giving Time his very pressure, showing Nations as they are!
Once again old Rome—the awful—rears her red imperial crest,
And *Virginius* speaks her downfall in a father's tortured breast;
Once again far Albion's genius from sweet Avon leans to view,
As he was, her thoughtful Hamlet, and the very Lear she drew.
Nor alone does Europe glory in the Actor's perfect art,—
From Columbia's leafy mountains see the native hero start!
Not in depths of mere romances can you *Nature's* Indian find;
See him there, as God hath made him, in the *Metamora* shrined.
Where hast thou, O noble Artist,—crowned by Fame's immortal flower,—
Grasped the lightnings of thy genius? caught the magic of thy power?
Not, I know, in foreign regions,—for thou art too true and bold:
'Tis the *New* alone gives daring thus to paint the shapes of *Old*:
From the deep full wind that sweepeth through thine own wild native woods,
From the organ-like grand cadence heard in autumn's solemn floods,
Thou hast tuned the voice that thrills us with its modulated roll,
Echoing through the deepest caverns of the hearer's startled soul:
From the tender blossoms blooming on our haughty torrents' side—
Like some angel sent by Pity, preaching gentleness to Pride—
Thou didst learn such tender bearing, hushing every listener's breath,
When in thee poor *Lear*, the crownless, totters gently down to death:
From the boundless lakes and rivers, from our broad continuous climes,
Over which the bell of Freedom sounds her everlasting chimes,

Thou didst catch that breadth of manner; and to wreath the glorious
whole,

Sacred flames are ever leaping from thy democratic soul.

Welcome then that look of grandeur, welcome then that stately mien,

Always shedding native glory o'er the wondrous mimic scene,

Always like a mighty mirror glassing Vice or Virtue's star,

Giving Time his very pressure, showing Nations as they are!

After a long absence from Albany, Forrest fulfilled an engagement
there in 1864. It carried his mind back to his early struggles in the
same place, though few of the kind friends who had then cheered him
now remained. There was no vacant spot, however, any more than
there was any loss of fervor. On the last night the audience—so
crowded that "they seemed actually piled on one another in the
lobbies"—called him before the curtain and asked for a speech. He
said,—

"I am very glad, ladies and gentlemen, that an opportunity is thus
afforded me to say a few words, to thank you for your generous
welcome here, and also for the kind applause you have lavished on my
performances. In Albany I seem to live a twofold existence,—I live one
in the past, and I live one in the present, —and both alike are filled
with the most agreeable memories. Here, within these very walls, even
in my boyish days, I was cheered on to those inspiring toils

'Which make man master men.'

Here, within these walls, while yet in my boyish days, one of the
proudest honors of my professional life was achieved; for I here
essayed the part of Iago to the Othello of the greatest actor that 'ever
lived in the tide of times,'—Edmund Kean. To me there is music in the
very name,—Edmund Kean, a name blended indissolubly with the
genius of Shakspeare; Edmund Kean, who did more by his acting to
illustrate the Bard of all time than all the commentators from Johnson,
Warburton, and Steevens down to the critics of the present day. It was
said of Edmund Kean by a distinguished English poet, that 'he read
Shakspeare by flashes of lightning.' It is true; but those flashes of

lightning were the coruscations of his own divine mind, which was in affinity with the mind of Shakspeare. Now I must beg leave to express my heartfelt thanks for this demonstration of your favor, hoping at no distant day to meet you again."

Thus it is clear that, whatever the sufferings of Forrest may have been, however many trials and pangs his growing experience of the world may have brought him, he had great enjoyments still. Besides the proud delight of his professional successes and the solid satisfaction of his swelling property, he had an even more keen and substantial complacency of pleasure in his own physical health and strength. His enormous vital and muscular power supported a superb personal consciousness of joy and contentment. He trod the earth like an indigenous monarch, afraid of nothing. The dynamic charge, or rather surcharge, of his frame was often so profuse that it would break out in wild feats of power to relieve the aching muscles. For instance, one night when acting in the old Tremont Theatre in Boston, under such an exhilarating impulse he struck his sword against a wooden column at the side of the stage as he was passing out, and cut into it to the depth of more than three inches. An Englishman who sat near jumped from his seat in terror, and tremblingly said, as he hastened out, "He is a damned brute. He is going to cut the theatre down!" This full vigor of the organic nature, this vivid relishing edge of unsatiated senses, yielded a constant feeling of actual or potential happiness, and clothed him with an air of native pride which was both attractive and authoritative. He had paid the price for this great prize of an indomitable physique in systematic exercises and temperance. He wore it most proudly and kept it intact until he was fifty-nine years old. The lesson of his experience and example in physical culture is well worth heeding.

The fashion of society in regard to the education and care of the body has passed through three phases. The most extraordinary phase, in the glorious results it secured, was the worship of bodily perfection among the Greeks, a reflex revival of which was shown by the nobles and knights at the period of the Renaissance. The Greek gymnastic of the age of Pericles, as described by Plato so often and with such enthusiasm,—a gymnastic in which music, instead of being an end in itself, a sensuous luxury of the soul, was made a guide and adjunct to bodily training, giving rhythm to every motion, or that grace and economy of force which so much enhances both beauty and power,— lifted men higher in unity of strength and charm of health and harmony of faculties than has anywhere else been known. The Grecian games were made an ennobling and joyous religious service and festival. The eager, emulous, patriotic, and artistic appreciation of the spectators,—the wondrous strength, beauty, swiftness, rhythmic motions, imposing attitudes of the athletes,—the legends of the presence and contentions of the gods themselves on that very spot in earlier times,—the setting up of the statues of the victors in the temples as a worship of the Givers of Strength, Joy, and Glory,—served to carry the interest to a pitch hardly to be understood by us. The sculptures by Phidias which immortalize the triumph of Greek physical culture show a harmony of the circulations, a compacted unity of the organism, a central poise of equilibrium, a profundity of consciousness and a fulness of self-control, a perfect blending of the automatic and the volitional sides of human nature, which must have exalted the Olympic victors at once to the extreme of sensibility and to the extreme of repose. It is a million pities that this ideal should ever have been lost. But in Rome, under the military drill and unbridled license of the emperors, it degenerated into a brutal tyranny and sensuality, the gigantic superiority of potency it generated being perverted to the two uses of indulging self and oppressing others.

The next swing of the historic pendulum flung men, by the reaction of spirituality, over to the fatal opposite,—the ecclesiastic contempt and neglect of the body. The Christian ideal, or at least the Church ideal, in its scornful revulsion from gladiators and voluptuaries, glorified the soul at the expense of the loathed and mortified flesh. At the base of this cultus was the ascetic superstition that matter is evil, that the capacity for pleasure is an infernal snare, and that the only way to heaven is through material maceration and renunciation. Sound philosophy and religion teach, on the contrary, that the body is the temple of God, to be developed, cleansed, and adorned to the highest degree possible for His habitation.

The third phase in the history of bodily training is that neutral condition, between the two foregoing extremes, which generally characterizes the present period,—a state of almost universal indifference, or a fitful alternation of unregulated attention to it and neglect of it. The pedagogue gives his pupils some crude exercises to keep them from utterly losing their health and breaking down on his hands under the barbaric pressure of mental forcing; the drill-sergeant disciplines his recruits to go through their technical evolutions; the dancing-master trains the aspirants for the mysteries of the ballet; and the various other classes of public performers who get their living by playing on the curiosity, taste, or passion of the public, have their specialities of bodily education for their particular work. But a perfected system of aesthetic gymnastics, based on all that is known of the laws of anatomy, physiology, and hygiene,—a system of exercises regulated by the exactest rhythm and fitted to liberate every articulation, to develop every muscle, and to harmonize and exalt every nerve,—such a system applied from childhood to maturity for the purpose not of making professional exhibitors of themselves, but of perfecting men and women for the completest fulfilment and fruition of life itself, does not yet exist. It is the great educational desideratum of the age. Co-ordinating all our bodily organs and spiritual faculties, unifying the outward organism and the inward consciousness, it would remove disease, crime, and untimely death, open to men and women the highest conditions of inspiration, and raise them towards the estate of gods and goddesses. Avoiding equally the classic deification of the body and the mediaeval excommunication of it, emerging from the general indifference and inattention to it which belong to the modern absorption in mental work and social ambition, the next phase in the progress of physical education should be the awakening on the part of the whole people of a thorough appreciation of its just importance, and the assigning to it of its proportionate place in their practical discipline. This is a work worthy to be done now in America. As democratic Athens gave the world the first splendid gymnastic training with its transcendent models of manhood, so let democratic America, improving on the old example with all the new treasures of science and sympathy, make application to its citizens of a system of motions for the simultaneous education of bodies and souls to the full possession of their personal sovereignty, making them all kings and queens of themselves, because strong and beautiful and free and happy in every limb and in every faculty!

There is a vulgar prejudice among many of the most refined and religious people against the training of the body to its highest condition, as if that necessitated an animality fatal to the richest action of mind, heart, and soul. The fop whose delicacy is so exquisite that the least shock of vigorous emotion makes him turn pale and sicken, fancies the superb athlete a vulgar creature whose tissues are as coarse as wire netting and the globules of his blood as big as peas. But in reality the presence of fidgeting nerves in place of reposeful muscles gives feebler reactions, not finer ones, a more irritable consciousness, not a richer one. Were this squeamish prejudice well founded it would make God seem a bungler in his work, essential discord inhering in its different parts. It is not so. The harmonious development of all portions of our being will raise the whole higher than any fragment can be lifted alone. The two finest and loftiest and richest flowers of Greek genius, Plato and Sophocles, were both crowned victors in the Olympic games. But this strong, lazy prejudice has widely fulfilled itself in fact by limiting the greatest triumphs of physical culture to the more debased and profane types,—to professional dancers and pugilists. And even here it is to be affirmed that, on this low range of brawn and pluck and skill, physical power and prowess are better than physical weakness and cowardice. It is better, if men are on that level, to surpass and be admired there than to fail and be despised there. But since one God is the Creator of flesh and spirit, both of which when obedient are recipients of his influx and held in tune by all his laws, the best material states are not hostile, but most favorable, to the best spiritual fulfilments. The life of the mind will lift out of, not mire in, the life of the body. And hitherto unknown revelations of inspired power, delight, and longevity wait on that future age when the vindication of a divineness for the body equally sacred with that of the soul shall cause the choicest persons to be as faithful in physical culture for the perfection of their experience as prize-fighters are for winning the victory in the ring. Give us the soul of Channing, purest lover and hero of God, in the body of Heenan, foremost bruiser and champion of the world; the soul of Elizabeth Barrett Browning, tender poetess of humanity, in the body of Fanny Elssler, incomparable queen of the stage;—and what marvels of intuitive perception, creative genius, irresistible authority, and redemptive conquest shall we not behold!

Such is one of the prophecies drawn from the supremest examples of combined mental and physical culture in the dramatic profession. Forrest fell short of any such mark. His gymnastic was coarse and heavy, based on bone and muscle rather than brain and nerve. The sense of musical rhythm was not quick and fine in him. His blood was too densely charged with amorous heat, and his tissues too much clogged with his weight of over two hundred pounds, for the most ethereal delicacies of spirituality and the inspired imagination. But within his limitations he was a marked type of immense original and cultivated power. And his sedulous fidelity in taking care of his bodily strength and health is worthy of general imitation. He practised athletics daily, posturing with dumb-bells or Indian clubs, taking walks and drives. He was extremely attentive to ventilation, saying, "The first condition of health is to breathe pure air plentifully." He ever sought the sunshine, worshipping the smile of the divine luminary with the ardor of a true Parsee. "The weather has been pernicious," he says in one of his letters. "Oh for a day of pure sunshine! What a true worshipper of the Sun I have always been! And how he has rewarded me, in the light of his omnipotent and kindly eye, with health and joy and sweet content! How reasonable and how sublime was the worship of Zoroaster! I had rather be a beggar in a sunny climate than a Crœsus in a cloudy one." He was temperate in food and drink, shunning for the most part rich luxuries, complex and highly-seasoned dishes, falling to with the greatest relish on the simplest and wholesomest things, especially oatmeal, cracked wheat, corn-meal mush, brown bread, Scotch bannocks, cream, buttermilk. When fatigued, he turned from artificial stimulants and sought recovery in rest and sleep. When hard-worked, he never omitted going regularly to bed in the daytime to supplement the insufficient repose of the night. He had great facility in catching a nap, and at such times his deep and full respiration was as regular as clock-work. But above all the rest he attributed the greatest importance to keeping his skin in a clean and vigorous condition. Night and morning he gave himself a thorough washing, followed by energetic scrubbing with coarse towels and a percussing of his back and spine with elastic balls fastened to the ends of two little clubs. His skin was always aglow with life, polished like marble, a soft and sensitive yet firm and flowing mantle of protection and avenue of influences between his interior world and the exterior world. This extreme health and vigor of the skin relieved the tasks put on the other excretory organs, and was most conducive to vital energy and longevity.

The one fault in the constitution of Forrest was the gouty diathesis he inherited from his grandfather on the maternal side. This rheumatic inflammability—a contracted and congested state of some part of the capillary circulation and the associated sensory nerves accumulating force to be discharged in hot explosions of twinging agony—might have been cured by an aesthetic gymnastic adapted to free and harmonize all the circulations,—the breath, the blood, the nerve-force. But, unfortunately, his heavy and violent gymnastic was fitted to produce rigidity rather than suppleness, and thus to cause breaks in the nervous flow instead of an equable uniformity. This was the secret of his painful attacks and of his otherwise unexpectedly early death. There are three natures in man, the vital nature, the mental nature, the moral nature. These natures express and reveal themselves in three kinds or directions of movement. The vital nature betrays or asserts itself in eccentric movement, movement from a centre; the mental, in accentric movement, movement towards a centre; the moral, in concentric movement, movement around a centre. Outward lines of motion express vital activity, inward lines express mental activity, curved lines, which are a blending of the two other, express moral or affectional activity. This physiological philosophy is the basis of all sound and safe gymnastic. The essential evil and danger of the heavy and violent gymnastic of the circus and the ring is that it consists so largely of the outward and inward lines which express the individual will or vital energy and mental purpose. Each of these tends exclusively to strengthen the nature which it exercises. Straight hitting, pushing, lifting, jumping, in their two directions of exertion, tend to expand and to contract. That is vital, and this is mental. Both are expensive in their drain on the volition, but one tends to enlarge the physical organism, the other to shrink it and to produce strictures at every weak point. The former gives a heavy, obese development; the latter an irritable, irregular, at once bulgy and constricted development The vice of the vital nature dominating unchecked is gluttony, and its end, idiocy. The vice of the mental nature is avarice, both corporal and spiritual, and its end, madness. The vice of the moral nature, when it becomes diseased, is fanaticism; and its subject becomes, if the vital element in it controls, an ecstatic devotee; if the mental element controls, a reckless proselyter. Now, a true system of gymnastic will perfect all the three natures of man by not allowing the vital or the mental to domineer or its special motions to preponderate, but blending them in those rotatory elliptical or spiral movements which combine the generous expansion of the vital organs and the selfish concentration of the mental faculties in just proportion and thereby constitute the language of the moral nature. Rigid outward movements enlarge the bulk and strengthen sensuality. Rigid inward movements cramp the organism and break the unity and liberty of its circulations, leading to every variety of disease. But flowing musical movements justly blent of the other two movements, in which rhythm is observed, and the extensor muscles are used in preponderence over the contractile so as to neutralize the modern instinctive tendency to use the contractile more than the extensor,—movements in which the motor nerves are, for the same reason, used more than the sensory,— will economize the expenditure of force, soothe the sensibilities, and secure a balanced and harmonious development of the whole man in

608 Life of Edwin Forrest Volume II

equal strength and grace. Such a system of exercise will remove every tendency to a monstrous force in one part and a dwarfed proportion in another. It will secure health and beauty in a rounded fulness equally removed from shrivelled meagreness and repulsive corpulence. It will make its practiser far more than a match for the huge athletes of the coarse school, as the man whose every limb is a whip is thrice more puissant and terrible than the man whose every limb is a club. The deepest secret of the final result of this æsthetic gymnastic is that it gives one the perfect possession of himself in the perfected unity of his organism, *the connective tissue being so developed by the practice of a slow and rhythmical extensor action that it serves as an unbroken bed of solidarity for the whole muscular coating of the man*. Nothing else can be so conducive as this to equilibrium, and consequently to longevity. When the unity of the connective tissue is broken by strictures at the articulations or elsewhere, the waves of motion or force ever beating through the webs of nerves are interrupted, stopped, or reflected by devitalized wrinkles which they cannot pass. Thence result the innumerable mischiefs of inflammation in the outer membrane and catarrh in the inner.

The æsthetic gymnastic, which will serve as a diacatholicon and panacea for a perverted and sick generation, is one whose measured and curvilinear movements will not be wasteful of force but conservative of it, by keeping the molecular vibrations circulating in the organism in perpetual translations of their power, instead of shaking them out and losing them through sharp angles and shocks. This will develop the brain and nerves, the genius and character, as the old system developed the muscles and the viscera. It will lead to harmony, virtue, inspiration, and long life, as the old system led to exaggeration, lust, excess, and early death. How greatly it is needed one fact shows, namely, the steady process which has long been going on of lessening beauty and increasing ugliness in the higher classes of, society, lessening roundness and increasing angularity of facial contour. The proof of this historic encroachment of anxious, nervous wear and tear displacing the full grace of curved lines with the sinister sharpness of straight lines is given in most collections of family portraits, and may be strikingly seen by glancing from the rosy and generous faces of Fox and Burke or of Washington and Hamilton to the pinched and wrinkled visages of Gladstone and Disraeli or of Lincoln and Seward.

There is probably only one man now living who is fully competent to construct this system of æsthetic gymnastic,—James Steele Mackaye, the heir of the traditions and the developer of the philosophy of François Delsarte. It was he of whom Forrest, two years before his own death, said, "He has thrown floods of light into my mind: in fifteen minutes he has given me a deeper insight into the philosophy of my own art than I had myself learned in fifty years of study." If he shall die without producing this work, it will be a calamity to the world greater than the loss of any battle ever fought or the defeat of any legislative measure ever advocated. For this style of gymnastic alone recognizes the infinitely solemn and beautiful truth that every attitude, every motion, tends to *produce* the quality of which it is the legitimate expression. Here is brought to light an education constantly going on in every one, and far more momentous and fatal than any other. Here is a principle which makes the body and the laws of mechanics as sacred revelations of the will of God as the soul and the laws of morality. Here is the basis of the new religious education destined to perfect the children of men, abolish deformity, sickness, and crime, and redeem the earth.

Had Forrest practised such a style of exercise, instead of weighing upwards of two hundred pounds and suffering from those irregularities of circulation which often disabled, at length paralyzed, and at last killed him at sixty-seven, he would have weighed a hundred and sixty, been as free and agile as he was powerful, and lived without an ache or a shock to ninety or a hundred.

His faithful exercises, defective as they were in the spirit of beauty and economy, gave him enormous vital potency and tenacity. He felt this keenly as a priceless luxury, and was justly proud of it. He used to be extremely fond of the Turkish bath, and once said, "No man who has not taken a Turkish bath has ever known the moral luxury of being personally clean." He was a great frequenter of the celebrated establishment of Dr. Angell, on Lexington Avenue, in New York. After the bath and the shampoo, and the inunction and the rest, on one occasion, as he was striding up and down the room, feeling like an Olympian god who had been freshly fed through all the pores of his skin with some diviner viands than ambrosia, he vented his slight grief and his massive satisfaction in these words: "What a pity it is that a man should have to suffer for the sins of his ancestors! Were it not for this damned gouty diathesis, I would not swap constitutions with any man on earth,—damned if I would!"

It was in 1865, while playing, on a terribly cold February night, in the Holliday Street Theatre, in Baltimore, that Forrest received the first dread intimation that his so proudly cherished prerogative of bodily strength was insecure. He was enacting the part of Damon. The theatre was so cold that, he said, he felt chilled from the extremities of his hands and feet to the centre of his heart, and the words he uttered seemed to freeze on his lips. Suddenly his right leg began twitching and jerking. He nearly lost control of it; but by a violent effort of will he succeeded in getting through the play. Reaching his lodgings and calling a physician, he found, to his great grief and horror, that his right sciatic nerve was partially paralyzed.

An obvious lameness, a slight hobble in his gait, was the permanent consequence of this attack. It was sometimes better, sometimes worse; but not all his earnest and patient attempts to cure it ever availed to find a remedy. It was a mortifying blow, from which he never fully recovered, though he grew used to it. His strength of build and movement had been so complete, such a glory to him, he had so exulted in it as it drew admiring attention, that to be thus maimed and halted in one of its most conspicuous centres was indeed a bitter trial to him. Still he kept up good heart, and fondly hoped yet to outgrow it and be all himself again. He was just as faithful as ever to his exercises, his diet, his bathing, his rest and sleep; and he retained, in spite of this shocking blow, an astonishing quantity of vital and muscular energy. Still a large and dark blot had been made on his personal splendor, and all those roles which required grace and speed of bodily movement sank from their previous height. Notwithstanding his strenuous endeavors to neutralize the effects of this paralysis, its stealthy encroachments spread by imperceptible degrees until his whole right side—shoulder and chest and leg—shrank to smaller dimensions than the left, and at last he was obliged when fencing to have the sword fastened to his hand. And yet he continued to act to the end; acting still with a remarkable physical power and with a mental vividness not one particle lowered from that of his palmiest day. But, after the year 1865, for any of his old friends who remembered the electrifying spontaneity of his terrible demonstrations of strength in former days, to see him in such casts as Metamora, Damon, Spartacus, and Cade, was painful.

In the month of January, 1866, Forrest had a most gratifying triumph in Chicago. The receipts were unprecedentedly large, averaging for the five nights of his engagement nearly twenty-five hundred dollars a night He wrote to his friend Oakes: "Eighteen years since, I acted here in a small theatre of which the present mayor of Chicago, J. B. Rice, Esq., was manager. The population, then about six thousand, is now one hundred and eighty thousand, with a theatre that would grace Naples, Florence, or Paris. The applause I have received here has been as enthusiastic as I have ever known, and the money-return greater. It beats the history of the stage in New York, Boston, Philadelphia, Baltimore, Charleston, and New Orleans. Give me joy, my dear and steadfast friend, that the veteran does *not* lag superfluous on the stage."

Early in the same year he accepted the munificent offer made by the manager of the San Francisco theatre to induce him to pay a professional visit to California. He remembered the flattering letter sent him by the government of the State nine years before. He felt a keen desire, as a patriotic American, to view the wondrous scenery and products of the golden coast of the Pacific, and he also was ambitious that the youngest part of the country should behold those dramatic portrayals which had so long been applauded by the oldest. Landing in San Francisco on the third of May, he was serenaded in the evening by the Philharmonic Society, and on the fourteenth made his début in the Opera House in the rôle of Richelieu. The prices of admission were doubled, and the seats for the opening night were sold at auction. The first ticket brought five hundred dollars. "At an early hour last night," said one of the morning papers, "the tide of people turned with steady current towards the Opera House. Throng after throng approached the portal and melted into the vast space. Inside, the scene was one of extraordinary magnificence. Hundreds of flaming jets poured a flood of shadowless light on the rich painting and gilding of the amphitheatre, the luxurious draperies of the boxes, and the galaxy of wealth and beauty smiling beneath its rays." He played for thirty-five nights to an aggregate of over sixty thousand persons, and was paid twenty thousand dollars in gold. His engagement was suddenly interrupted by a severe attack of his old enemy the gout. He fled away to the cedar groves, the mineral springs, and the mountains, to feast his eyes on the marvellous California landscapes and to nurse his health. His enjoyment of the whole trip, and in particular of his long tarry at the Mammoth Tree Grove, was profound. He delighted in recalling and describing to his friends one scene in this grove, a scene in which he was himself a striking figure. Visible in various directions were gigantic trees hundreds of feet in height, whose age could be reckoned by centuries, bearing the memorial names of celebrated Americans, — Bryant, Lincoln, Seward, Longfellow, Webster, Kane, Everett, and the darling of so many hearts, sweet Starr King,—whose top, three hundred and sixty-six feet high, over-peers all the rest. Here the Father of the Forest, long ago fallen, his trunk four hundred and fifty feet long and one hundred and twelve feet in circumference at the base, lies mouldering in gray and stupendous ruin. A hollow chamber, large enough for one to pass through on horseback, extends for two hundred feet through the colossal trunk of this prone and dead monarch of the grove, whose descendants tower around him in their fresh life, and seem mourning his requiem as the evening breeze sighs in their branches. Forrest mounted a horse, and, with all the pageant personalities he had so long made familiar to the American people clustering upon his own, rode slowly through this incredible hollow just as the level beams of the setting sun illuminated the columns of the grove and turned it into a golden cathedral.

In September he wrote to Oakes,—

"Here I am still enjoying the salubrious air of the mountains, on horseback and afoot, and bathing in waters from the hot and cold springs which pour their affluent streams on every hand.

"My health is greatly improved, and my lameness is now scarcely perceptible. In a few weeks more I shall return to San Francisco to finish my engagement, which was interrupted by my late indisposition. My present intention is not to return to the East until next spring; for it would be too great a risk to encounter the rigors of a winter there which might prove disastrous. You are aware that the winter in San Francisco is much more agreeable than the summer; and after my professional engagement there I shall visit Sacramento and some few other towns, and then go to Los Angelos, where I shall enjoy a climate quite equal to that of the tropics. I am determined to come back to you in perfect health. How I should like to take a tramp with you into the mountains this blessed day! I can give you no reasonable idea of the beauty of the weather here. The skies are cloudless, save with the rare and rosiest shadows, not a drop of rain, and yet no drought, no aridity; the trees are fresh and green, and the air as exhilarating as champagne."

The news of the serious illness of his sister Caroline caused him to abandon the purpose of resuming his interrupted engagement in San Francisco, and, enriched with a thousand agreeable memories, on the twentieth of October he set sail for home.

The sentiment of patriotism was a fervid element in the inner life of Forrest, a source of strength and pleasure. He had a deep faith in the democratic principles and institutions of his country, a large knowledge and enjoyment of her scenery, a strong interest in her honor, industries, and fortunes, and an unshaken confidence and pride in her sublime destiny. His sympathy in politics, which he studied and voted on with intelligent conviction, had always been Southern as well as democratic; but at the first sound of the war he sprang into the most resolute attitude in defence of the imperilled cause of freedom and humanity. He wrote the following letter to one of his old friends in the West in June, 1861:

"The political aspect of our country is ominous indeed, and yet I hope with you that in the Divine Providence there will be some great good brought out of this evil state of affairs which will prove at last a blessing to our country. Oftentimes from that we consider evil comes a reviving good. I trust it may prove so in this case. I do not, however, condemn the South for their feelings of just indignation towards the intermeddling abolitionist of the North,—the abolitionist who for years by his incendiary acts has made the homestead of the planter a place of anxiety and unrest instead of peace and tranquillity. But I do condemn the leaders of this unwarrantable rebellion, those scurvy politicians who, to serve their own selfish ends, flatter and fool, browbeat and threaten honest people into an attitude which seems to threaten the safety of our glorious Union. I still believe in man's capacity to govern himself, and I prophesy that by September next all our difficulties will be adjusted. The South will know that the North has no hostile, no subversive feelings to gratify, that it is the Union of the States—that Union cemented by the blood of patriot sires—which is to be preserved unbroken and inviolate, and that under its fraternal aegis all discord shall cease, all wounds be healed. To this end we must be ready for the field; we must gird up our loins and put on our armor; for a graceful and lasting peace is only won when men are equals in honor and in courage. And to this end it gives me pleasure to know that my.namesake, your son —, has decided to take arms in defence of the Union of the States and the Constitution of our fathers; and, more, that his good mother, as well as yourself, approves his resolution. Now is the time to test if our Government be really a shield and a protection against anarchy and rebellion, or merely a rope of sand, an illusion, a chimera; and it is this spontaneous uprising of every friend of freedom rallying around the flag of his country—that sacred symbol of our individual faith—which will proclaim to the world in tones more potent than heaven's thunder-peal that we have a Government stronger and more enduring than that of kings and potentates, because founded on equal and exact justice, the offspring of man's holiest and noblest nature, the attribute of God himself."

Two years later, he wrote in a letter to another friend,—

"Great God! in what a melancholy condition is our country now! *An ineradicable curse begin at the very root of his heart that harbors a single thought that favors disunion.* May God avert the overwhelming evil!"

He made himself familiar with the triumphs of American genius in every department of industry and art, and glowed with pride over the names of his illustrious countrymen. The following brief letter reveals his heart. He never had any personal acquaintance with the brilliant man whose departure he thus mourns.

"New York, July 15th, 1859.

"My Dear Oakes,—It is with the deepest emotions I have just heard of the death of Rufus Choate. His decease is an irreparable loss to the whole country. A noble citizen, a peerless advocate, a great patriot, has gone, and there is no one to supply his place. In the fall of this great man death has obtained a victory and humanity suffered a defeat.

"Edwin Forrest."

One other letter of his should be preserved in this connection, for its eloquent expression of blended friendship and patriotism:

"Philadelphia, July 28th, 1862.

"My Dear Friend,—Where are you, and what are you doing? Are you ill or well? I have telegraphed to you twice, and one answer is that you are ill, another that you are much better. I called on Mr. Chickering during my recent visit to New York, and he assured me you could not be seriously ill, or he would have been advised of it; and so I calmed my fears. That you have greatly suffered in mind I have reason to know. The death of Colonel Wyman assured me of that. You must have felt it intensely. But he fell nobly, in the discharge of a most sacred duty which consecrates his name forever among the defenders of the Union of his country. I too have lost friends in the same glorious cause,— peace and renown to their ashes! Among them one, the noblest of God's manly creatures, Colonel Samuel Black, of Pennsylvania. Enclosed you have a merited eulogy of him by our friend Forney, who knew him well. Let us prepare ourselves for more of the same sad bereavements. This unnatural war, which has already widow'd and unchilded many a one,' has not yet reached its fearfullest extent. The Union cemented by the blood of our fathers must and shall be preserved; this is the unalterable decree of the people of the Free States. Better that all the slaves should perish and the blood of all those who uphold the institution of slavery perish with them, than that this proud Temple, this glorious Union consecrated to human freedom, should tumble into ruins. Do you remember what Tom Paine, the great Apostle of Liberty, wrote to General Washington in 1796? 'A thousand years hence,' he writes, 'perhaps much less, America may be what Britain now is. The innocence of her character, that won the hearts of all nations in her favor, may sound like a romance, and her inimitable virtue be as if it had never been. The ruins of that Liberty thousands bled to obtain may just furnish materials for a village tale. When we contemplate the fall of empires and the extinction of the nations of the Old World we see but little more to excite our regret than mouldering ruins, pompous palaces, magnificent monuments, lofty pyramids. But when the Empire of America shall fall the subject for contemplative sorrow will be infinitely greater than crumbling brass or marble can inspire. It will not then be said, here stood a temple of vast antiquity, a Babel of invisible height, or there a palace of sumptuous extravagance,—but here, oh painful thought! the noblest work of human wisdom, the greatest scene of human glory, THE FAIR CAUSE OF FREEDOM ROSE AND FELL!'

"May God in his infinite wisdom avert from us such a moral desolation! Write to me soon, and tell me all about yourself. I have been ill of late and confined to my bed. I am now better.

"Edwin Forrest.
"James Oakes, esq."

The earnestness of the feeling of Forrest as an American exerted a profound influence in moulding his character and in coloring his theatrical representations. The satisfactions it yielded, the proud hopes it inspired, were a great comfort and inspiration to him. And he said that one of his greatest regrets in dying would be that he should not see the unparalleled growth, happiness, and glory of his country as they would be a hundred years hence.

Another source of unfailing consolation and pleasure to him was his love of nature. He took a real solid joy in the forms and processes of the material creation, the changing lights and shades of the world, the solemn and lovely phenomena of morning and evening and summer and winter, the gorgeous upholstery of the clouds, and the mysterious marshalling of the stars. His letters abound in expressions which only a sincere and fervent lover of nature could have used. Writing from Philadelphia in early October, when recovering from a severe illness, he says, "It is the true Indian summer. The sunbeams stream through the golden veil of autumn with a softened radiance. How gratefully I receive these benedictions from the Universal Cause!" And in a letter dated at Savannah, November, 1870, he writes to his biographer, "Ah, my friend, could the fine weather you boast of having in Boston make me feel fresh and happy, Heaven has sent enough of it here to fill a world with gladness. The skies are bright and roseate as in summer, the air is filled with fragrance drawn by the warm sun from the balsamic trees, while the autumnal wild-flowers waft their incense to the glorious day. All these things I have enjoyed, and, I trust, with a spirit grateful to the Giver of all good. Yet all these, though they may meliorate in a degree the sadness of one's life, cannot bind up the broken heart, heal the wounded spirit, nor even, as Falstaff has it, 'set a leg.'"

This taste for nature, with the inexhaustible enjoyment and the refining culture it yields, was his in a degree not common except with artists and poets. While acting in Cleveland once in mid-winter, he persuaded a friend to walk with him for a few miles early on a very cold morning. Striding off, exulting in his strength, after an hour and a half he paused on the edge of the lake, his blood glowing with the exercise, his eyes sparkling with delight, while his somewhat overfat companion was nearly frozen and panted with fatigue. Stretching his hand out towards the magnificent expanse of scenery spread before them, he exclaimed, "Bring your prating atheists out here, let them look on that, and then say there is no God-—if they can!"

An eminent New York lawyer, an intimate friend of Forrest, who had spent his whole life in the city absorbed in the social struggle, was utterly indifferent to the beauties of nature. He had never felt even the loveliness of a sunset,—something which one would think must fill the commonest mind with glory. Walking with him in the environs of the city on a certain occasion when approaching twilight had caused the blue chamber of the west to blaze with such splendors of architectural clouds and crimsoned squadrons of war as no scenic art could ever begin to mock, Forrest called the attention of his comrade to the marvellous spectacle. "I have no doubt," said the lawyer, "that I have seen a great many of these things; but I never cared anything about them." The disciple of Shakspeare proceeded to discourse to the disciple of Coke upon Littleton on the charm of natural scenery, its soothing and delight-giving ministrations to a man of taste and sensibility, in a strain that left a permanent impression on his hearer, who from that time began to watch the phenomena of the outward world with a new interest.

But even more than in his professional triumphs, his increasing store of wealth, his animal health and strength, his patriotism, or his love for the works of God in nature, Forrest found during the last twenty years of his life a never-failing resource for his mind and heart in the treasures of literature. He gathered a library of between ten and fifteen thousand volumes, well selected, carefully arranged and catalogued, for the accommodation of which he set apart the finest apartment in his house, a lofty and spacious room running the whole length of the edifice. In this bright and cheerful room all the conveniences of use and comfort were collected. Beside his desk, where from his chair he could lay his hand on it, superbly bound in purple velvet, on a stand made expressly for it, rested his rare copy of the original folio edition of Shakspeare, valued at two thousand dollars. Around him, invitingly disposed, were the standard works of the historians, the biographers, the poets, and especially the dramatists and their commentators. Here he added to his shelved treasures many of the best new works as they appeared, keeping himself somewhat abreast with the fresh literature of the times in books like Motley's Netherlands, Grimm's Life of Michael Angelo, and Hawkins's Life of Kean, which he read with a generous relish. Here, ensconced in an arm-chair by the window, or lolling on a lounge in the centre of the library, or seated at his study-table, he passed nearly all the leisure time of his lonely later years. Here he would occupy himself for many an hour of day and night,— hours that flew swiftly, laden with stingless enjoyment,—passing from volume to volume sipping the hived sweetnesses of the paradisal field of literature. Here, alone and quiet in the peopled solitude of books, he loved to read aloud by the hour together, listening to himself as if some one else were reading to him,—the perfection of his breathing and the ease of his articulation being such that the labor of utterance took nothing from the interest of the subject, while the rich music and accurate inflections of his voice added much. Here his not numerous intimates, with occasional callers from abroad,—Rees, Forney, and his particular favorite, Daniel Dougherty,—would often drop in, ever sure of an honest welcome and genial fellowship, and speed the time with wit and humor, reminiscence, anecdote, argument, joke, and repartee, vainly seeking to beguile him into that more general society which would have gladly welcomed what he could so richly give and take.

An extract from a letter of his written in June, 1870, is of interest in this connection:

"I will read Forster's Life of Walter Savage Landor, of which you speak, at my first leisure; though I consider Forster personally to be a snob. You will find among my papers in your possession exactly what I think of him. For Landor, even as a boy, I had a great admiration. I sate with wonder while I quaffed instruction at the shrine of his genius. There is a book just published in England which I shall devour with an insatiable mental appetite. It is called 'Benedict Spinoza, his Life, Correspondence, and Ethics.' It is the first time that his works have been collected and published in English. So that I shall have a rare treat. His Ethics I have read in a French translation which I found in Paris years ago; and its perusal divided my time between the pleasures of the town and the intellectual culture which the study of his sublime philosophy gave me. It was called 'Spinoza's Ethics; or, Man's Revelation to Man of the Dealings of God with the World.'"

Yes, his library was indeed his sure refuge from care and sorrow, a sweet solace for disappointment and vacancy and heartache. Here, in the glorious fellowship of the genius and worth of all ages, he fully gratified that love of reading without whose employment he would hardly have known how to bear some of the years of his checkered life. An anecdote will illustrate the strength of this habit in him and afford an interesting glimpse of the interior of the man. In his library one summer afternoon, the notes of birds in the trees and the hum of bees in his garden languidly stealing in at the open window, he sat, with the precious Shakspeare folio in his lap, conversing with his biographer. He said, "If I could describe how large a space Shakspeare has filled of my inward life, and how intense an interest I feel in his personality, no one would believe me. I would this moment give one hundred thousand dollars simply to read—even if the instant I had finished its perusal the manuscript were to be destroyed forever—a full account of the first eighteen years of the life of Shakspeare,—such an account as he could himself have written at forty had he been so minded, of his joys and sorrows, hopes and fears, his aspirations, his disappointments, his friendships, his enmities, his quarrels, his fights, his day-dreams, his loves; in short, the whole inward and outward drama of his boyhood." It was certainly one of the most striking tributes ever paid to the genius of the immortal dramatist. A thorough familiarity with the works of Shakspeare is of itself an education and a fortune for the inner man. There all the known grades of experience, all the kinds of characters and styles of life seen in the world, are shown in their most vivid expressions. There all the varieties of thought and sentiment are gathered in their most choice and energetic forms of utterance. There are stimulus and employment for every faculty. There is incitement for all ambition, solace for all sorrow, beguilement for all care, provocation and means for every sort and degree of self-culture. Shakspeare is one of the greatest teachers that ever lived, and those players who have character, docility, and aspiration are his favorite pupils. Betterton, who was born in 1635, only twelve years after the death of Shakspeare, made a journey from London to Warwickshire on purpose to gather up what traditions and anecdotes remained of him. Garrick was the author of the remarkable centennial celebration of his memory. And the voice of Kemble faltered and his tears were visible as in his farewell speech on the stage he alluded to the divine Shakspeare.

Anecdotes of the conduct and expressions of a man when he is off his guard and unstudiedly natural give a truer picture of his character than elaborate general statements. And three or four brief ones may be given to close this chapter with an impartial view of the inner life of Forrest in its contrasted aspects of refinement and even sublimity at one time, and of rude severity and coarseness at another.

One summer evening, when he was paying a visit to his friend Oakes, they were at Cohasset, sitting on a piazza overhanging the sea. Mr. John F. Mills, one of the best men that ever lived, whose beautiful spirit gave pain to his host of friends for the first time only when he died, was with them. There had been a long storm, and now that it had subsided the moaning roar of the sea was loud and dismal. Forrest addressed it with this extemporaneous apostrophe, as reported by Mr. Mills: "Howl on, cursed old ocean, howl in remorse for the crimes you have committed. Millions of skeletons lie bleaching on your bed; and if all our race were swallowed there to-night you would not care any more for them than for the bursting of a bubble on your breast. There is something dreadful in this inhumanity of nature. Therefore I love to hear you groan, you heartless monster! It makes you seem as unhappy as you make your victims when they empty their stomachs into you or are themselves engulfed. Gnash your rocky teeth and churn your rage white. Thank God, your cruel reign will one day end, and there will be no more sea."

The next evening they sat in the same place, but the moon was up, and his mood was different, more placid and pensive than before. The swell and plunge of the billows on the beach made solemn accompaniment to the guttural music of his voice. There was a mournfulness in the murmur of his tones as elemental and sad as the tremendous sighing of the sea itself. "This world," he said, "seems to me a penal abode. We have all lived elsewhere and gone astray, and now we expiate our bygone offences. There is no other explanation that I can think of for the tangled snarl of human fates. True, since we are ignorant of these sins, our punishment seems not just. But then we may some time recover memory of all and so understand everything clearly. It is all mystery now, but if there is any explanation I am convinced we are convicts working out our penances, and hell is not hereafter but here. Just hear those breakers boom, boom, boom. Do they not seem to you to be drumming the funereal Rogue's March for this Botany Bay of a world?"

A stranger to Forrest, merely to gratify his vanity by drawing the attention of a company to his speech, said he had seen the celebrated actor drunk in the gutter. The friend who reported this to Forrest would not reveal who the man was. But one day he pointed him out on the opposite sidewalk. The outraged and angry tragedian went quietly over and accosted the slanderer; "Do you know Edwin Forrest, and do you say you once saw him drunk in the gutter?" On receiving an affirmative reply he broke out in the strong vernacular of which he was a master, "Now, you sneaking scoundrel and lying calumniator, I am Edwin Forrest. I ache all over to give you the damnedest thrashing you ever tasted. But it is against my principles. I should be ashamed of myself if I stooped to take such advantage of your cowardly weakness. But, while I will not do it with my body, in my mind I kick and spit on you. Now pass on, and relish yourself, and be damned, you human skunk."

Although Forrest used much profane language, his real spirit was not an irreverential one. His profanity was but an expletive habit, a safety-valve for wrath. When expostulated with on the custom, he said, "I never knowingly swear before ladies or clergymen, lest it should shock or grieve them. But at other times, when it is necessary either for proper emphasis or as a vent for passion too hot and strong, why I let it rip as it will."

In connection with the Broad Street mansion which he occupied at the time of his death, Forrest built and fitted up a handsome private theatre. John Wiser, a scenic artist, arranged and painted it. At its completion Forrest seated himself in a large chair, and, after expressing his pleasure at the effect, said, "John, do you know what would be the most delightful sight in the world, eh? If I could only see this room filled with children, and a company of little boys and girls playing on that stage."

One day when Forrest was walking with a friend in Brooklyn a beggar accosted them. Tears were in his eyes, and he had a ragged exterior as well as a tottering form and a pale and sunken look. With a plaintive voice he said, "For the love of heaven, gentlemen, give me a trifle for the sake of my starving family. You will not feel it, and it will relieve a half a score of hungry ones. Will you not aid me?" Forrest looked at the man for a moment as if reading his very soul, and then said, while placing a golden eagle in his hand, "Yes, my friend, you are either a true subject for charity or else the best actor I ever saw."

Forrest always carried his professional humor and docility with him. He gave a ludicrous description of an amateur grave-digger who lived in Philadelphia. He was worth fifty thousand dollars, yet whenever a grave was to be made he liked to have a hand in it. His nose was so turned up that his brains might have been seen, had he possessed any. And his voice was a perfect model for the second grave-digger in *Hamlet*, saying, "The crowner hath set on her, and finds it Christian burial."

A strolling exhibitor of snakes came to Louisville when Forrest was playing there in his youth. Wishing to feel the strongest emotions of fear, that he might utilize the experience in his acting, Forrest asked the man to take care of the head of a boa-constrictor some twelve feet in length and let the hideous reptile crawl about his naked neck. He never forgot the cold, clammy slip of the coils on his flesh and the sickening horror it awakened.

Chapter XVIII.
Prizes and Penalties of Fame

The next important feature to be studied in order to appreciate the character and life of Forrest is his experience of the prizes and the penalties of fame. For he had a great fame; and fame, particularly in a democratic country, inflicts penalties as well as bestows prizes. Not one man in a thousand has enough force and tenacity of character to determine to gain the solid and lasting prizes of life. Average men willingly put up with cheap and transient substitutes for the real ends, or with deluding mockeries of them. They seek passing pleasures instead of the conditions of permanent happiness; applause instead of merit; a crowd of acquaintances instead of true friends; notoriety or stagnant indifference instead of fame. There is nothing more worthy of contempt, although it is so miserably common, than the mean and whining cant which puts negation and failure above affirmation and success, constantly asserting the emptiness and deceit of all earthly goods. In opposition to this morbid depreciation of every natural attractiveness without and desire within, nothing is more wholesome or grand than a positive grasp and fruition of all the native worths of the world. A great deal of the fashionable disparagement and scorn of the prizes of wealth, position, reputation, is but unconscious envy decrying what it lacks the strength and courage to seize. The fame which a gifted and faithful man secures is the reflex signal of the effects he has produced, and a broad, vivid, healthy enjoyment of it is an intrinsic social good to be desired. It is one of the greatest forces employed by Providence for the education of men and the advancement of society. To condemn or despise it is to fling in the face of God. The fancied pious who do this are dupes of an impious error.

Fame is a life in the souls of other men added to our own. It is a feeling of the effect we have taken on the admiration and love of those who regard us with honoring attention and sympathy. It is a social atmosphere of respect and praise and curiosity, enveloping its subject, fostering his self-esteem, keeping his soul in a moral climate of complacency. The famous man has a secret feeling that the contributors to his glory are his friends, loyal to him, ready to protect, further, and bless him. Thus he is fortified and enriched by them, their powers ideally appropriated to his ideal use. Thus fame is the multiplication of the life of its subject, reflected in the lives of its givers. This is the real cause of the powerful fascination of fame for its votaries; for there is no instinct deeper in man than the instinct which leads him to desire to intensify, enlarge, and prolong his existence; and fame makes a man feel that in some sense his existence is multiplied and continued in all those who think of him admiringly, and that it will last as long as their successive generations endure. As Conrad makes Jack Cade say,—

"Fame is the thirst
Of gods and godlike men to make a life
Which nature made not, stealing from heaven
Its imaged immortality."

And so in its ultimate essence and use fame represents a magnified and prolonged idealization of direct personal experience. It is ideal means of life, a deeper foundation and wider range of reflected sympathetic life embracing and sustaining immediate individual life. This great prize is evidently a good to be desired, the evils connected with it belonging not to itself but to unprincipled methods of pursuing it, vulgar errors in distributing it, and the selfish perversion of its true offices. It exists and is enjoyed in various degrees, on many different levels, from the plebeian enthusiasm for the champion boxer to the aristocratic recognition of a great thinker. As we ascend in rank we lose in fervor. Fame is seen in its ruddiest intensity at the funeral of Thomas Sayers celebrated by fifty thousand screaming admirers; in its palest expansion in the renown of Plato, whose works are read by scattered philosophers and whose name glitters inaccessibly in the eternal empyrean. The reason for this greater heat of glory on its lower ranges plainly is that men feel the sharpest interest in the lowest bases of life, because these are the most indispensable. Existence can be maintained without transcendent talents, but not without health, strength, and courage. Animal perfection goes before spiritual perfection, and its glory is more popular because more appreciable.

Forrest drank the intoxicating cup of fame on widely separated levels, from the idolatrous incense of the Bowery Boys who at the sight of his herculean proportions shied their caps into the air with a wild yell of delight, to the praise of the refined judges who applauded the intellectual and imaginative genius of his Lear. It was a genuine luxury to his soul for many years, and would have been a far deeper one had it not been for the alloys accompanying it. He enjoyed the prize because he had honorably won it, not sacrificing to it the more commanding aims of life; and fame is a mockery only when it shines on the absence of the goods greater than itself,—honor, health, peace, and love. He suffered much on account of it, in consequence of the detestable jealousies, plots, ranklings, and slanders always kindled by it among unhappy rivals and malignant observers. But one suffering he was always spared, namely, the bitter mortifications of the charlatan who has snatched the outward semblance of the prizes of desert without paying their price or possessing their substance. Striving always to deserve his reputation, he did not forfeit his own esteem. The satisfaction he received from applause was the joy of feeling his own power in the fibres of the audience thrilling under his touch. Fame was the magnifying and certified abstract of this,—a vast and constant assurance in his imagination of life and power and pleasure. Dry sticks, leather men, may sneer at the idea, but the rising moral ranks of souls are indicated by the intensity with which they can act and react on ideal considerations. Fame puts a favorable bias on all our relations with the approving public, and thus enriches our inner life by aiding our sympathies to appropriate their goods.

The actor lives in an atmosphere electrized with human publicity, and walks between walls lined with mirrors. Everything in his career is calculated to develop an acute self-consciousness. And then by what terrible trials his sensitiveness is beset in his exposure to the opposite extremes of derision and eulogy!

Dr. Johnson, alluding at one time to the sensibility of Garrick, said, contemptuously, "Punch has no feelings." At another time, praising his genius, he said, sublimely, "His death eclipsed the gayety of nations." The actor tastes the sweetness of fame more keenly than any other, because no other lives so directly on it or draws the expression of it so openly and directly. Bannister was invited by the royal family at Windsor one evening to read a new play, and was treated with the utmost regard. The very next night he was stopped by a footpad, who, dragging him to a lamp to plunder him, discovered who he was, and said, "I'll be damned if I can rob Jack Bannister." Having thus the esteem of both extremes of society, it is safe to conclude that he enjoyed the admiration of all between. And this boon of public honor and love will seem valuable to a performer in proportion to the quickness and depth of his emotional power. "The awful consciousness," said Mrs. Siddons, "that one is the sole object of attention to that immense space, lined as it were with human intellect all around from top to bottom, may perhaps be imagined, but can never be described." A vulgar performer would rush on as if those heads were so many turnips. The genius of imaginative sensibility is the raw material for greatness. Forrest had much of this, although his self-possession was so strong; and under his composed exterior, even after he had been thirty years on the stage, he often shrank with temporary trepidation from the ordeal of facing a fresh audience. His enjoyment of the tributes paid to him was commensurately deep.

And, stretching through the long fifty years of his professional course, how varied, how numerous, how interesting and precious, these crowded tributes were! There was no end to the compliments paid him, echoes of the impression he had made on the country. Now it was a peerless race-horse, carrying off prize on prize, that was named after him. Then it was some beautiful yacht, club-boat, or pilot-boat, of which there were a dozen or more to whose owners he presented sets of flags. At another time it was a noble steamer or merchantman, of which there were a good many named for him, each adorned with a statue of some one of his characters as a figure-head. Locomotives and fire-engines also were crowned with his name and his likeness. Military companies, too, took their titles from him and carried his face copied on their banners. The following letter indicates another of the results of his fame:

"Waltham, February 12th, 1871.
"Edwin Forrest, esq.:

"Dear Sir,—Being one of the small army of boys called after you, I should feel happy to receive some token from my illustrious namesake, if nothing more than his autograph. Hoping to see you before you leave the stage,

"I am respectfully yours,
"Edwin Forrest Moore."

Seven different dramatic associations, composed of amateurs and professionals, were formed in the cities of Portland, Boston, New York, and elsewhere, bearing his name. And the notices of him in the newspapers were to be reckoned by thousands, ranging all the way from majestic eulogium to gross vituperation.

Portraits of him, paintings, engravings, photographs, in his own individuality and in his chief impersonations, were multiplied in many quarters. Numerous plaster casts of him, four or five busts in marble, and one full-length statue of surpasing grandeur, were taken. Many celebrated artists studied him, from Gilbert Stuart, whose Washington stands supremely immortal in American portraiture, to William Page, whose lovingly elaborated Shakspeare may become so in creative portraiture. Page has depicted Forrest in the rôle of Spartacus. He shows him at that moment of the scene in the amphitheatre where he utters the words which he never spoke without moving the audience to repeated bursts of applause: "Let them come in: we are armed!" The last portrait ever painted by the dying Stuart was of Forrest, then in his youth and only just beginning to become famous. Forrest used often to speak of his sitting to Stuart, whose strong fiery soul was enclosed in a frame then tottering and tremulous with age. "He was an old white lion," said Forrest, "and so blind that I had to tell him the color of my eyes and of my hair. By sudden efforts of will he *threw* the lines and bits of color on the canvas, and every stroke was speech."

Of the likenesses of Forrest published in this volume, the frontispiece is engraved from a daguerreotype of him at the age of forty-six; the succeeding one is from a painting by Samuel Lawrence, and shows him as he was at twenty-eight; the last one is from a photograph taken when he was in his sixty-seventh year. The illustrations of him in dramatic characters are from photographs made after he had passed sixty and had suffered partial paralysis. They do no justice to him as he appeared in his perfect meridian.

Of all the expressions of admiration, affection, pleasure, called forth by a professional artist, of all the forms or signals of fame, perhaps none is more flattering or more delightful to the recipient than the tributary verses evoked from souls endowed with the poetic faculty. As such natures are finer and higher than others, their homage is proportionally more precious. During his life more than fifty poems addressed to Forrest were published, and gave him a great deal of pure pleasure. A few specimens of these offerings may properly find a place here.

The following lines felicitously copied were thrown upon the stage to him one evening in a bouquet:

TO EDWIN FORREST.
When Time hath often turned his glass,
And Memory scans the stage,
Foremost shall then thy image pass,
The Roscius of this age.
The succeeding piece was written in 1828:
TO EDWIN FORREST.

Young heir of glory, Nature's bold and favorite child,
Nurtured 'midst matchless scenes of wild sublimity,
Thou who wert reared with sternest truth in groves of song,
To thy bare arm the grasp is given to hurl the bolts
Of wrathful heaven. 'Tis thine, with thundering voice to shake
Creation to her centre, wakening love or rage,
And show thyself as angels or as demons are.
Yea, thou didst seem, as at the shrine I saw thee kneel,
With that bold brow of thine, like some creation bright
From higher spheres breathing thy inspiration there,
As if the Altar's flame itself had lit thine eye
With all the dazzling radiance of the Deity.
Go forth. Already round thy brow the wreath of fame
Amidst thy godlike locks with classic grace is curled.
Go forth, and shine, the Sun of the dramatic world!
R. M. Ward.

The next piece, in which he is associated with his friend Halleck, is
dated 1830:

TO EDWIN FORREST.
When genius, with creative fancy fraught,
Moulds some new being for the sphere of thought,
How the soul triumphs as, supremely blest,
She opes her temple to the welcome guest,
And her white pulses feel, with answering glow,
The kindred breath of the young presence flow!
Such moments, bright as hours in heaven that bring
To spirits life, a pure and deathless thing,
Cheer him who, warm with poesy's true flame,
Rears in his bower of song the birds of fame;
He whose wreathed locks the lyric laurels wear
Green with immortal dew and cloudless air;
Whose harp-chords wildly echoed back the swell
Of glory's clarion when bozzaris fell,—

Thus knew his human fancies grow divine,
And poured their spirit o'er the happy line.
Yet not alone the sons of song can feel
This joy along the grateful senses steal.
To him who, musing, waits at Nature's throne,
And feels, at last, her wealth become his own,
Then with the priceless gold, thought, passion, heart,
And feeling, tempers to the test of art,
Blends these with poesy's mysterious spell
Strange as the sigh of ocean's rosy shell,
No less belong the triumph-throb, the pride
To mind-ennobling sympathies allied,
The deep emotion, and the rapture free;
And these, O Forrest, we behold in thee!
Who e'er has marked thine eye, thy matchless mien,
While, all forgetful of the mimic scene,
Spurning the formal, manner-taught control,
Thou bar'st the fire that lightens in the soul,
Has deemed there moved the form that Shakspeare drew
From visions bright with passion's warmest hue,
As, wildly garbed in awful tragic guise,
Macbeth, Othello, Lear, he saw arise.
When the last outrage of oppression falls
On man enthralled by man, and Freedom calls
Some champion to flash her steel where'er,
Bloody and black, death, shrieking, hovers near,
Who can portray like thee the throe of hate
Which warns the tyrant of his dreadful fate?
Who image forth th' exalted agony
Of strife and maddening hope of victory?
There thrills an echo of the pulse, the tone,
That universal man exults to own,
A voice which teaches craven souls that War
For right than guilty Peace is holier far;

Nor suffers them to breathe and pass away
As dust that ne'er forsook its primal clay.

The lines that follow next were printed in 1852, after the divorce trial:

TO EDWIN FORREST.
In every soul where Poesy and Beauty find a place,
Thy image, Forrest, sits enshrined in majesty and grace.
Could but the high and mighty bard, whose votary thou art,
Have seen with what a matchless power thou swayest the human heart,
He too had bowed beneath the spell and owned thy wondrous sway,
And bound thy brow with laurel, and with flowers strewn thy way.
The clouds of grief that for a time obscured thy brilliant morn,
Like to the envious shadows that would dim the rising sun,
Meridian's fame has put to flight. Cast not thy glances back,
But in the light of fearless genius hold thine onward track.
Margaret Barnett.

This sonnet was written in the same year:

TO EDWIN FORREST.
King of the tragic art! without compeer!
Thy sway is sovereign in the scenic realm;
And where thy sceptre waves, or nods thy helm,
All crowd to be thy royal presence near.
Thou speakest,—we are stilled; the solemn Past,
Rich with grand thought, and filled with noble men
Over whose lives and deeds time's veil is cast,
Rises to view, and they do live again!
While thou dost tread life's stage, thy lofty fame,
Undimmed, shall grow, and be the drama's pride
Centuries hence, when all shall see thy name
Carved deep and high her noblest names beside;

And, with the noblest placed, will aye be found,
In Thespis' fane, thy statue, laurel-crowned!
R. H. Bacon.

Here is a tribute penned in 1862, in the midst of our civil war:

EDWIN FORREST AS "DAMON."
Great master of the tragic art,
Whose genius moves the passions' spring,
To melt the eye and warm the heart
With love of virtue, hate of sin,
Is it our nation's bleeding fate
That gives thee such heroic fire
Singly to brave the Senate's hate
And faith for country's good inspire?
Yes; 'tis not all the mimic scene
We view when now beholding thee;
The heart-strung voice and earnest mien
Of "Damon" breathe pure liberty.
The test of friendship true is there;
But hope for freedom more than life
Starts the usurping tyrant near—
Pleads for the boy—weeps for the wife.
O art divine! when Forrest brings
His matchless eloquence to bear,
Denouncing treason's poisonous stings,
While for his loved land falls the tear,
The temple of the Muses, filled
With beauty, fashion, youth, and age,
Proves admiration for the skilled
And perfect artist of the stage.
G. C. Howard.

And a year later the following eloquent verses were published by
their author in the Philadelphia "Press:"

FORREST.
Pride of the Grecian art,
King of the glorious act,
Whose sceptre-touch can start
From airiest fancy fact!
Sole monarch of the stage!
Thy crowning is the truth
That garners unto age
The laurel-wreaths of youth.
Were massive mien or mould
Of Thespian gods divine
E'er richer in the gold
Of Thespian grace than *thine?*
A voice that thrills the soul
Through all her trembling keys,
From deepening organ-roll
To flute-born symphonies;
An eye that gleams the light
Of Tragedy's quiet fire,
And soul that sweeps aright
Each grandest poet-lyre,—
These into living thought,
FORREST! in thee sublime
The Thespian gods have wrought,
A masterpiece for Time!
Not from the clods of earth
'Mid grovelling toil and strife
Thy genius hailed her birth
To all her peerless life;
Her viewless home hath been
Where Poesy hath flung
Its sweetest words to win
The music of thy tongue!
How Manhood's honor rose,
How perished Woman's shame,

When robed in worth and woes
Thine own virginius came!
How Freedom claims a peal
And Tyranny a knell
When BRUTUS waves the steel
Where Slave and Tarquin fell!
When SPARTACUS leads on
Each gladiator-blade,
Or feudal tyrants fawn
To lion-hearted cade,—
How every listening heart
Outbeats its narrow span,
And, in that glorious art,
Adores the peerless man!
But dearer than the rest
We own thy mystic spell
To lave the lingering breast
Where Avon's sweetness fell!
To marshal from the page
And summon from the pen
Of SHAKSPEARE, to *thy* stage,
His living, breathing men!
No longer Shakspeare's line,
But *studious* gaze controls;
It girds and gilds from *thine*
The multitude of souls!
While Genius claims a crown,
Or mimic woe a tear,
Paled be the envious frown
And dumb the cynic sneer
That barreth from thy heart
Or veileth from thy name
The loftiest, grandest part
Of histrionic FAME!
C. H. B.

A single sonnet more shall end these examples of the poetic tributes to the genius and worth of Forrest; tributes Which, adding lustre to his career and shedding comfort and joy into his heart, were and are one of the most attractive illustrations of the value and sweetness of the prize of fame:

ON ROOT'S DAGUERREOTYPE OF MR. FORREST.
Light-born, and limned by Heaven! It is no cheat,
No image; but himself, his living shade!
With hurried pulse, the heart leaps forth to greet
The man who merits more than Tully said
Of his own Roscius, that the histrion's power
Was but a leaf amid his garland wreath.
His swaying spirit ruled the magic hour,
But his vast virtues knew no day, no death.
He seems not now, but is. And I do know,
Or think I do, what meaning from those lips
Would break; and on that bold and manly brow
There hangs a light that knows not an eclipse,
The light of a true soul. If art can give
The bodied soul this life, who doubts the soul will live?
Robert T. Conrad.

Public and private banquets were given in honor of the actor by distinguished men in all parts of the country, occasions drawing together brilliant assemblages and yielding the highest enjoyment to every faculty of sense and soul. To meet around the social table, decked with everything that wealth and taste can command, the most eminent members of the learned professions, artists, authors, statesmen, the leaders of the business world, beautiful and accomplished women, and pass the hours in friendly converse seasoned with every charm of culture and wit, is one of the choicest privileges society can bestow in recognition and reward of worth and celebrity. Among the more notable of these honors may be mentioned as especially brilliant and locally conspicuous at the time a dinner given him at Detroit by

General Lewis Cass, one at Cincinnati by his old friend James Taylor, one at New Orleans by a committee of the leading citizens, including some of his early admirers, and, later, one at Washington by his intimate and esteemed friend Colonel Forney, then Clerk of the House of Representatives. During one of his engagements in Washington he dined with a distinguished company under the princely auspices of Henry Clay. The great Kentuckian, in allusion to Pierre Soule, a Louisiana Senator, who was a passionate orator but wanting, perhaps, in sobriety of judgment and steadiness of character, said to one of the guests, "A mere actor, sir, a mere actor!" At that instant chancing to catch the eye of Forrest, he promptly added, with the courteous grace of self-possession and winsome eloquence native to his thoroughbred soul, "I do not allude, Mr. Forrest, when I use the word actor thus demeaningly, to those men of genius who impersonate the great characters of Shakspeare and the other immortal dramatists, holding the very mirror of truth up to nature; I refer to the man who in real life affects convictions and plays parts foreign to his soul."

At a banquet given in honor of John Howard Payne, the first vice-president, Prosper M. Wetmore, an old and dear friend of Forrest, paid him a compliment which, received as it was by the brilliant company with three times three enthusiastic cheers, must have given him a proud pleasure. Mr. Wetmore said, "Before mentioning the name of the gentleman whose health I am about to ask you to drink, I take this opportunity to say a word in relation to the generosity of his heart and the richness of his mind. He was one of the very first who took an interest in the festival of Thursday last, and kindly offered his name and services to add to the attractions of the evening. He has always been the foremost to do his share in honoring our sons of genius; and his purse has never been shut against the meritorious who stood in need of his bounty. His talents as an actor you all know and appreciate. Allow me to give you—Edwin Forrest:

"'His health; and would on earth there stood
Some more of such a frame,
That life might be all poetry,
And weariness a name.'"

Such as above described were the satisfactions afforded to Forrest by his fame. They are what thousands have vainly wished to win, fondly believing that if they could gain them they should be happy indeed. But to these advantages there are drawbacks, corresponding to these prizes there are penalties, which were experienced by Forrest in all their varieties of bitterness. The evils which dog the goods of public life, as their shadows, went far to disenchant him, to sour him, to make him turn sadly and resentfully into himself away from the lures and shams of society.

To any man of honorable instincts, clear perceptions, and high principles, the incompetency, corruption, and selfish biases of many of those who assume to sit in judgment on the claims of the competitors for public favor and glory, the shallowness and fickleness of the average public itself, the contemptible means successfully used by ignoble aspirants for their own advancement and the defeat of their rivals, the frequent reaction of their own modesty and high-mindedness to obscure and keep down the most meritorious, have a strong influence to rob ambition of its power, destroy all the relish of its rewards, and make fame seem worthless or even odious. Critics write in utter ignorance of the laws of criticism or standards of judgment, and even without having seen the performance they presume to approve or to condemn. Claqueurs are hired to clap one and to hiss another irrespective of merit or demerit. Wreaths, bouquets, rings, jewelled snuff-boxes, are purchased by actors or actresses themselves, through confederates, to be then presented to them in the name of an admiring public. A vase or cup or watch has been known to go with a popular performer from city to city to be presented to him over and over with eulogistic addresses of his own composition. A brazen politician, successful in compassing a nomination and election by shameless wire-pulling, mendacity, and bribery, then receives the tribute of an ostentatious testimonial of which he is himself the secret originator and prime manager. No one who has not had long experience of the world and been admitted behind the scenes, with the keys for interpreting appearances, can suspect how common such things are. They are terribly disheartening and repulsive to a generous soul. They destroy the splendor and value of the outward prizes of existence, and thus paralyze the grandest motives of action. When fools, charlatans, and swindlers carry off honors, then wisdom, genius, and heroism are tempted to despise honors. When the owl is umpire in a contest of song between the donkey and the nightingale, and awards the prize to the brayer, the lark and the mocking-bird may well decline to enter the lists.

In the fashionable rage for Master Betty, Kemble and Siddons were quite neglected; as the levee of Tom Thumb drew a throng of the nobility and fashion of London while poor Haydon, across the street, watched them with a gnawing heart from the door of his deserted exhibition. Cowper says in his "Task,"—

"For Betty the boy
Did strut and storm and straddle, stamp and stare,
And show the world how Garrick did not act."

When, with pompous incompetency, Lord Abercorn told Mrs. Siddons that "that boy would yet eclipse everything which had been called acting in England," she quietly replied, with crushing knowledge, "My lord, he is a very clever, pretty boy, but nothing more." Garrick said it was the lot of actors to be alternately petted and pelted. And Kemble, when congratulated on the superb honors given him at his final adieu to the stage, responded, "It was very fine, but then I could not help remembering that without any cause they were once going to burn my house." Genius and nobility naturally love fame, worship the public, would pour out their very life-blood to gain popular sympathy and admiration; but after such experiences of baseness and wrong and error the fascination flies from the prizes they had adored as so sacred, and never more do their souls leap and burn with the old enthusiasm of their unsophisticated days. The injustice of the world drives from it the love and homage of its noblest children.

Parasites and egotists seek association with a famous man merely to gratify their vanity, though they call it friendship. They fawn on him to share a reflection of his glory, to reap advantage from his influence, or to beg loans of his money; and when circumstances unmask their characters and show how they were preying on his frankness, he is revolted and his confidence in human nature shaken. Many a man of a sweet and loving nature, like the noble Timon, has gone out to the world with throbbing heart and open arms, and, met with selfishness and treachery, reacted into despair and hate. One of the penalties of a great reputation with its personal following is to be annoyed by sycophants, toadies, the impertinent curiosity of a miscellaneous throng who have neither genuine appreciation for talent nor sincere love for excellence, but a pestiferous instinct for boring and preying. Mrs. Siddons, bereaved of her children amidst her great fame, was so annoyed by worrying interruptions, assailed by envy, slandered by enemies, and vexed by parasites, that she breathed the deepest wishes of her soul in these lines:

"Say, what's the brightest wreath of fame,
But cankered buds that opening close?
Ah, what the world's most pleasing dream,
But broken fragments of repose?
"Lead me where peace with steady hand
The mingled cup of life shall hold,
Where time shall smoothly pour his sand,
And wisdom turn that sand to gold.
"Then haply at religion's shrine
This weary heart its load shall lay,
Each wish my fatal love resign,
And passion melt in tears away."

The falsehood, the injustice, the plots, insincerity and triviality that gather about the surfaces and course of a showy popular career Forrest experienced in their full extent. He was not deceived by them, but saw through them. They repelled and disgusted him, angered and depressed him. They did not make him a misanthrope, but they chilled his demeanor, hardened his face, checked the trustfulness of his sympathy, and gave him an increasing distaste for convivial scenes and an increased liking for his library and the chosen few in whom he could fully confide. He was a man who esteemed justice and sincerity above all things else. Flattery or interested eulogy he detested as much as he did venal prejudice and blame. He loathed the unmeaning, conventional praises of the journals, the polite compliments of acquaintances or strangers, but was glad of all honest estimates. His dignity kept him from mingling with the audience as they conversed on their way out of the theatre, but he loved to hear what they said when it was repeated by one whom he could trust. Nothing more surely proves that deep elements of love and pride instead of shallow vanity and selfishness formed the basis of his character than the fact that he hated to mix in great companies, either public or private, where he was known and noticed, but loved to mingle with the population of the streets, with festive multitudes, where, unrecognized, he could look on and enter into their ways and pleasures. "It is a great feat," he used to say, "to resist the temptations of our friends." He did it when he withdrew from the obstreperous enthusiasm of those who adulated him while revelling at his expense and shouting, "By heaven, Forrest, you are an institution!"—forsaking them, and giving himself exclusively to nature, his art, his books, and his disinterested friends.

The practice of the arts of purchasing unearned praise, the tricks of the mean to circumvent the noble, the accredited verdicts of titled ignorance, and the fickle superficiality of popular favor, lessen the value of common fame in the eyes of all who understand these things. They foul its prizes and repel ingenuous spirits from its pursuit. The same influence is exerted in a yet stronger degree by the experience of the malignant envy awakened in plebeian natures by the sight of the success of others contrasted with their own failure. It was long ago remarked that

"With fame in just proportion envy grows;
The man that makes a character makes foes."

The selfishness—not to say the innate depravity—of human nature, as transmitted by historic inheritance, is such that every one who has not been regenerated by the reception or culture of a better spirit secretly craves a monopoly of the goods which command his desires. He dislikes his competitors, and would gladly defeat their designs and appropriate every waiting laurel to himself. In 1865 Forrest wrote, in a letter to Oakes, "Yes, my dear friend, there are many in this world who take pleasure in the misfortunes of their fellow-men and gloat over the miseries of their neighbors. And their envy, hatred, and malice are always manifested most towards men of positive natures."

Souls of a generous type leave this base temper behind, and rejoice in the glory of a rival as if it were their own. But mean souls, so far from taking a disinterested delight in the spectacle of triumphant genius or valor justly crowned with what it has justly won, are filled with pain at the sight, a pain obscenely mixed up with fear and hate. Wherever they see an illustrious head they would fain strike it down or spatter it with mud. Their perverse instincts regard every good of another as so much kept from them. There was a powerful passage in the play of Jack Cade which Forrest used to pronounce with tremendous effect, ingravidating every word with his own bitter experience of its truth:

"Life's story still! all would o'ertop their fellows;
And every rank, the lowest, hath its height,
To which hearts flutter with as large a hope
As princes feel for empire! but in each
Ambition struggles with a sea of hate.
He who sweats up the ridgy grades of life
Finds in each station icy scorn above;
Below him, hooting envy!"

The extent to which this dark and malign power operates in the breasts of men is fearful. The careless see it not, the innocent suspect it not; carefully disguising itself under all sorts of garbs, it dupes the superficial observer. But the wise and earnest student of human life who has had large experience knows that it is almost omnipresent. In every walk of society, every profession,—even in the Church and among the clergy,—are men who fear and hate their superiors simply because they are superior, and the inferiors feel themselves obscured and taunted by the superiority. A good free man loves to reverence a superior, feels himself blessed and helped in looking up. But the slave of egotism and envy feels elevated and enriched only in looking down on those he fancies less favored than himself. It is a frightful and disheartening phase of human nature; but it ought to be recognized, that we may be guarded against it in others and stimulated to outgrow it in ourselves.

No other profession is so beset by the temptations and trials of this odious spirit as the histrionic, which lives directly in the public gaze, feeding on popular favor. And among all the actors America has produced, no other had so varied, so intense and immense an experience of the results of it as Forrest. He wrote these sad and caustic words in his old age: "For more than forty years the usual weapons of abuse, ridicule, and calumny have been unceasingly levelled at me, personally and professionally, by envious associates, by ungrateful friends turned traitors, by the hirelings of the press, and by a crowd of causeless enemies made such by sheer malignity." In a speech made twenty-two years previously in the Walnut Street Theatre, in response to a call before the curtain, he had said, "I thank you with all my heart for this glorious and generous reception. In the midst of my trials it is gratifying to be thus sustained. I have been assailed, ladies and gentlemen, by a fiendish combination of enemies, who, not content with striking at my professional efforts, have let loose their calumnies upon my private character and invaded the sacred precincts of my home. Apart from the support of my ardent and cherished friends is the consciousness that I possess a reputation far dearer than all the professional honors that the world could bestow,—a reputation which is dearer to me than life itself. I will therefore pursue unawed the even tenor of my way. I will, with God's blessing, live down the calumnies that would destroy me with my countrymen; and, turning neither to the right hand nor to the left hand, will fearlessly toil to preserve to the last the reputation of an honest and independent American citizen."

To a man of his keen feeling and proud self-respect it must have been a torture to read the studiously belittling estimates, the satires, the insults, the slanderous caricatures continually published in the newspapers under the name of criticism. No wonder they stirred his rage and poisoned his repose, as they wounded his heart, offended his conscience, and made him sometimes shrink from social intercourse and sicken of the world. One critic says, "He is an injury to the stage. He has established a bad school for the young actors who are all imitating him. He has a contempt for genius and a disrelish for literature." Against this extract, pasted in one of his scrap-books, Forrest had written, "Oh! oh!" A second writes, "It is impossible for us to admit that a man of Mr. Forrest's intelligence can take pleasure in making of himself a silly spectacle for the amusement of the ignorant and the sorrow and pity of the educated. We prefer to believe that it is even a greater pain for him to play Metamora than it is for us to see him play it In that case, how great must be his anguish!" A third philosophizes thus on his playing: "The best performances of Mr. Forrest are those tame readings of ordinary authors which offer no opportunity for enormous blunders. In the flat, dreary regions of the commonplace he walks firmly. But he climbs painfully up Shakspeare as a blind man would climb a mountain, continually tumbling over precipices without seeming to know it. He shocks our sensibilities, astonishes our judgment, bewilders and offends us; and this is at least excitement, if not entertainment. But his Brutus is a remarkably stupid performance. The only way in which he can redeem its stupidity is to make it worse; and if he wants to do this he must inspire it with the spirit of his Hamlet or his Othello." A fourth makes malicious sport at his expense in this manner: "Mr. Forrest excels every tragedian we remember in one grand achievement He can snort better than any man on the stage. It is an accomplishment which must have cost him much labor, and of which he is doubtless proud, for he introduces it whenever he gets a chance. His snort in Hamlet is tremendous; but that dying, swan-like note, which closes the career of the Gladiator, is unparalleled in the whole history of his sonorous and tragic nose. It must be heard, not described. We can only say that when he staggers in, with twenty mortal murders on his crown, with a face hideous with gore, and falls dying on the stage, he sounds a long, trumpet-like wail of dissolution, which is the most supernaturally appalling sound we ever heard from any nose, either of man or brute." And a fifth caps the climax by calling him "A herculean murderer of Shakspeare!" So did a critic say of Garrick, on the eve of his retirement, "His voice is hoarse and hollow, his dimples are furrows, his neck hideous, his lips ugly, especially the upper one, which is raised all at once like a turgid piece of leather." "He is a grimace-maker, a haberdasher of wry faces, a hypocrite who laughs and cries for hire!" Well might Byron exclaim,—

"Hard is his fate on whom the public gaze
Is fixed forever to detract or praise."

A servile fawning on the press, a cowardly fear of its censures, a tremulous sensitiveness to its comments, is one of the chief weaknesses of American society. Its unprincipled meddlesomeness, tyranny, and cruelty are thus pampered. A quiet ignoring of its impertinence or its slander is undoubtedly the course most conducive to comfort on the part of one assailed. But the man who has the independence and the courage publicly to call his wanton assailant to account and prosecute him, even though shielded by all the formidable immunities of an editorial chair, sets a good example and does a real service to the whole community. Every American who values his personal freedom should crown with his applause the American who seizes an insolent newspaper by the throat and brings it to its knees; for unkind and unprincipled criticism is the bane of the American people. The antidote for this bane is personal independence supported by personal conscience and honor in calm defiance of all prying and censorious espionage. This would produce individual distinction, raciness, and variety, resulting in an endless series of personal ranks, with perfect freedom of circulation among them all; whereas the two chief exposures of a democracy are individual envy and social cowardice, yielding the double evil of universal rivalry and universal truckling, and threatening to end in a dead level of conceited mediocrity. The envy towards superiors which De Tocqueville showed to be the cardinal vice of democracy finds its worst vent in the newspaper press, which assails almost every official in the country with the foulest accusations. Are these writers destitute of patriotism and of faith in humanity? Are they ignorant of the fact that if they convince the public that their superiors are all corrupt the irresistible reflex influence of the conviction will itself corrupt the whole public?

That American citizen who has original manhood and lives a fresh, honest life of his own, regardless of the dictation of King Caucus or Queen Average,—the most heartless and vulgar despots that ever reigned,—sets the bravest of examples and teaches the most needed of lessons. Fenimore Cooper did this, criticising the errors and defects of his fellow-citizens as an enthusiastic and conscientious patriot should who sets humanity and truth above even country and fashion, and in consequence he was misunderstood, lampooned, and insulted by the baser newspapers, and finally, after one or two hundred libel suits, hounded into his grave. If they ever come to their senses, his repentant countrymen will one day build him a monument. Forrest was much this sort of man. He asserted himself, resented and defied dictation, and wanted others to do the same. He secured at different times a verdict with damages against the proprietors of four newspapers, and threatened libel suits against three others, which he withdrew on receiving ample public apology. The apology given in one instance, where he had been professionally abused and personally accused of drunkenness, is of so exemplary a character that it ought to be preserved. And here it is:

"It will perhaps be remembered by most of our readers that Mr. Edwin Forrest brought a libel suit against the proprietors of this paper for articles which appeared in our issues of 10th, 17th, and 24th of November, 1867. The solicitations and representations of mutual friends have induced Mr. Forrest generously to consent to the withdrawal of the case. Under these circumstances it becomes our duty as it is our pleasure, to express our regret at the publication of the articles in question.

"The articles complained of were, we frankly admit, beyond the limits of dramatic criticism; and the present proprietors, who saw them for the first time when printed, were at the time and still are sincerely sorry they appeared. Though not personally acquainted with Mr. Forrest, we do know, what the world knows, that he has always been prompt and faithful in his professional engagements; and his bitterest enemies, if he have any, must admit that he is not only eminent in his profession but especially free from the vice of intemperance."

The newspaper attack from which he suffered the most was so peculiar in some of its features as to demand mention. In 1855 a series of elaborate critiques on his chief roles appeared in a leading metropolitan journal. They were so scholarly, careful, and strong in their analysis of the plays, and so cutting in their strictures on the player, that they attracted wide attention and did him much damage. Now, two hands were concerned in these articles. The learning, thought, and eloquence were furnished by a German of uncommon scholarship and talent, who deeply felt the power and merit of Forrest as an actor and considered him a man of accomplished dramatic genius. The articles, as he wrote them, were then padded with demeaning epithets and scurrilous estimates of Forrest by one who was filled with prejudices theoretical and personal. Could Forrest have totally disregarded the articles, fortified in a magnanimous serenity, it had been well. He could not do it. He took them home with extreme pain and with extreme wrath, intensely resenting their injustice and their unkindness. This is a specimen of what is inflicted and suffered in the battle of public life. It tempts one to say, Blessed is the man who escapes all publicity, and lives and loves and dies happily in private! No doubt, however, it is best to say, with the grand old Faliero,—

"I will be what I should be, or be nothing."

His long, crowded experience of unfairness and unkindness deposited in Forrest a burning grudge against the world, a fierce animosity towards his injurers, an angry recoil of self-esteem, and a morbid exaggeration of the real vices of society. In one of his letters to a friend he writes, "This human life is a wretched failure, and the sooner annihilation comes to it the better." An old poet makes one of his characters who had been deeply wronged say,—

"I will instruct my sorrows to be proud,
For grief is proud and makes his owner stout."

Mrs. Montagu wrote to John Philip Kemble under similar circumstances, "If you retire, from an opinion that mankind are insincere, ungrateful, and malignant, you will grow proud by reflecting that you are not like these Pharisees." How such an opinion in Forrest marred his peace of mind and rankled in his general feelings— although much kindliness to men and much enjoyment of life still remained—was obvious enough in his later years, and is vividly expressed in many of his letters. "It would amaze and shock the honest, upright people of this country," he writes, "could they but know as I do how these sage judges, these benign law-peddlers, are manipulated by outsiders to give any decree that malice and money may demand." Again he writes, "I have all my life been cheated and preyed on by harpies, right and left. While they have enjoyed my money and maligned me I have toiled on for the next batch of swindlers. I have squandered more than a quarter of a million dollars on friends who, with a few noble exceptions, have returned my kindness not only with ingratitude but with obloquy." And at another time he says still more at length, "Whatever my enemies may say of me—be it good or bad— matters but little. I would not buy their mercy at the price of one fair word. I claim no exemption from the infirmities of my temper, which are doubtless many. But I would not exchange the honest vices of my blood for the nefarious hypocrisies and assumed virtues of my malignant detractors. I am no canting religionist, and I cordially hate those who have wronged and backbitten me. I have—yes, let me own that I have—a religion of hate; not of revenge, for while I detest I would not injure. I have a hatred of oppression in whatever shape it may appear,—a hatred of hypocrisy, falsehood, and injustice,—a hatred of bad and wicked men and women,—and a hatred of my enemies, for whom I have no forgiveness excepting through their own repentance of the injuries they have done me. I have never flattered the blown-up fool above me nor crushed the wretch beneath me.

"'I have not caused the widow's tear.

Nor dimmed the orphan's eye;

I have not stained the virgin years,

Nor mocked the mourner's cry.'"

"As for those who misjudge and mislike me, I hate and defy them, and appeal for justice to Nature and God, confident that they will one day grant it."

These expressions but too plainly reveal the sore places in his heart. Ah, could he but have attained a sweet and magnanimous self-sufficingness, frankly forgiven and forgotten his foes, and outgrown all those chronic contempts and resentments,—could he but have turned his thoughts away from brooding over the vices of men, and dwelt prevailingly on the other side of the picture of the world,—how much more peaceful and dignified and happy his age would have been! But this is hardly to be expected of one passionately struggling in the emulous arena, his veins swollen with hot blood in which still runs the barbaric tradition, An eye for an eye, and a tooth for a tooth. To expurgate that old animal tradition and introduce in its place the saintly principle of forgiveness needs patient suffering and leisurely culture grafted on a fine spirit. When this result is secured, man rises superior to wrong, to enmity, to disgrace, is content to do his duty and fulfil his destiny in the love of truth and humanity, sure that every one will at last be rewarded after his deserts, and letting the cruel or ridiculous caprices of fortune and fame pass by him as unregarded as the idle wind.

It would not be fair to the truth of the case if this chapter left the impression that Forrest found on the whole the penalties of his fame bitterer to bear than its prizes were sweet to enjoy. The opposite was the face. The annoyances attendant on his great reputation alloyed but destroyed not the comfort it yielded in its varied tributes and in its vast supporting sense of sympathetic life. Besides, the very vexations consequent on it were often accompanied by their own outweighing compensations. Sallying out of the Tremont House in Boston, one forenoon, arm in arm with his friend Oakes, and passing down Washington Street, his attention was caught by a hideous caricature of himself in a shop-window. A group of boys were gazing at it in great merriment. "Good heavens, Oakes," he cried, "just look at that infernal thing! It is enough to make one curse the day he was born." At that moment one of the boys recognized him, and exclaimed to the others,

"Here he is!" Forrest whispered to his friend, "Boys are impartial; they have not the prejudices men have. I am going to ask them their opinion. Look here, boys, do I look like that?" One of them, a little older than the rest, answered, promptly, "Well, we knew that it was you; but then you see there is this difference,—this makes us laugh, and you make us cry." "Thank you, my lad, thank you," responded Forrest, "Come on, Oakes; I have got better than I bargained for. My enemy when he produced that beastly monstrosity little dreamed what a pleasure he was going to give me." And, as they swung slowly along, he said, half musingly, "I wonder why they always degrade me by caricature and never exalt me by idealization." The solution, which he left unattempted, is this. Caricature is the exaggeration of bad points, idealization is the heightening of good points. It is much easier to make the bad appear worse than it is to make the good appear better. Man intuitively likes to attempt what he feels he can succeed in, and dislikes to attempt what he feels he shall fail in. Therefore, when commonplace natures represent their superiors they lower them by travesty rather than raise them by improvement. And so in critical art caricature abounds over idealization.

Chapter XIX.
Friendships—Their Essential Nature and Different Levels—Their Loss and Gain, Grief and Joy

In addition to the satisfaction yielded by his professional triumphs, the growth of his fortune, the enjoyment of his health and strength, his taste for literature, his delight in nature, his love of country, and the tributes of his fame, there was another element in the life of Forrest which was of eminent importance, the source of a great deal of comfort and not a little pain,—his friendships. Some sketch of this portion and aspect of his experience must be essayed, though it will perforce be a brief and poor one because these delicate concerns of the heart are shy and elusive, leaving few records of themselves as they glide secretly to oblivion enriching only the responsive places which they bless and hallow as they pass. There are many histories which no historian writes, and the inmost trials and joys of the soul are mostly of them.

Friendship, in our times, is more thought about and longed for than it is talked of, and more talked of than experienced. Yet the experience itself of men differs vastly according to their characters, situations, and companions. To some, in their relations with humanity, the world is made up of strangers; they have neither acquaintances, enemies, nor friends. To some it consists of enemies alone. To a few it holds only friends. But to most men it is divided into four groups,—a wilderness of strangers, a throng of acquaintances, a snarl of enemies, and a knot of friends. Among the members of this larger class the chief distinctions lie in the comparative number and fervor of their lovers and of their haters, and in the comparative space they themselves assign to their experience respectively of sympathy and of antipathy. Some men pursued by virulent foes have the gracious faculty and habit of ignoring their existence, giving predominant attention to congenial persons, and forgetting annoyances in the charm of diviner employment. Others art continually infested by persecutions and resentments as by a species of diabolical vermin which tarnish the brightness of every prize, destroy the worth of every boon, and foster a chronic irritation in consciousness. To hate enemies with barbaric pertinacity of unforgivingness tends to this latter result, while to love friends with frank and joyous surrender tends to the former. Both the sinister and the benign experience were well illustrated in the life of Forrest, who had sympathetic companionship richly and enjoyed it deeply, although he was pestered by a mob of parasites, censors, and assailants whom he religiously abhorred and loathed. Hostility filled a large, dark, sad, cold place in his history, friendship a prominent, bright, warm, and happy place. The two facts have their equal lesson,— one of warning, one of example. Blessed is the fortunate man who cherishes his friends with loving enthusiasm, but never has a single grudge or fear or sneer for a foe.

The universal interest felt in the subject of friendship—the strange fascination the story of any ardent and noble instance of it has for all readers,—the intense longing for such an experience which exists explicit or latent in the centre of every heart in spite of all the corrupting and hardening influences of the world—is a pathetic signal of the mystery of our nature and a profound prophecy of our destiny. It means that no man is sufficient unto himself, but must find a complement in another. It means that man was not made to be alone, but must supplement himself with his fellows. The final significance of friendship—whereof love itself is but a specialized and intensified variety—is an almost unfathomable deep, but it would appear to be this. Every man in the structure and forces of his physical organism is an epitome of all Nature, a living mirror of the material universe; and in the faculties and desires of his soul he is a revelation of the Creator, a conscious image of God. As the ancients said, man is a little universe in the great universe,—*microcosmos in macrocosmo*. But every one of these divine microcosms has a central indestructible originality differencing it from all the rest. This is the eternal essence or monad of its personality, which reflects in its own peculiar forms and colors the substances and lights and shades of the whole. Thence arises that inexhaustible charm of idiosyncrasy, that everlasting play and shimmer of individual qualities, which constitutes the lure for all pursuit, the zest wherewith all life antidotes the monotonous bane of sameness and death. Now the secret of friendship becomes clear in the light of these statements. First, it is the destiny of every man eternally to epitomize in his own being the universe of matter and mind,—in other words, to be an intelligent focal point in the surrounding infinitude of nature and the interior infinitude of God. Secondly, he is to recognize such an epitome embodied and endlessly varied in the endless variety of other men, all of whom are perfectly distinguishable from one another by unnumbered peculiarities, every shape and tinge of their experience determined by their personal moulds and tints. Thirdly, the entire life of every person consists, in the last analysis, of a mutual communication between his selfhood and that surrounding whole made up of everything which is not himself,—an interchange of action and reaction between his infinitely concentrated soul and his infinitely expanded environment. Fourthly, when two men, two of these intellectual and sentient microcosms, meet, so adjusted as mutually to reflect each other with all their contents and possibilities in sympathetic communion, their life is perfected, their destiny is fulfilled, since the infinite Unity of Being is revealed in each made piquant with the bewitching relish of foreign individuality, and nothing more is required, save immortality of career in boundless theatre of space, to round in the drama with sempiternal adventures and surprises, as, beneath the sleepless eye of the One, the Many hide and peep beneath their incarnate masks in life after life and world beyond world. Thus the highest idea of the experience of friendship is that it is God glimmering in and out of the souls of the friends in revelation of their destiny,—as Plato would say, the perpetually varied perception of the same under the provocative and delightful disguise of the other. And every lower idea of it which has any truth is in connection with this and points up to it,—from the revellers who entwine their cups and attune their glee, the soldiers who stand side by side in battle, and the politicians who vote the same ballot, to the thinkers who see the same truths and the martyrs who die in allegiance to the same sentiment. Everywhere, on all its ranges, friendship means communion of lives, sharing of thought and feeling, cooperative fellowship of personalities, the reflection of one consciousness in another. Those who meet only at the bottom of the scale in sensual mirth should be able sometimes, at least by the aid of a literary telescope, to see those who commingle at its top in immortal faith and aspiration.

Forrest possessed in a marked degree many of the qualities of a good friend; although, of course, it is not pretended that he had the mental disinterestedness, the refined spirituality, or the profound philosophic and religious insight which calls one to the most exalted style and height of friendship as it is celebrated for perpetual remembrance in the In Memoriam of Tennyson. He was affectionate, quick of perception, full of spontaneous sympathy and a deep and wide humanity, strictly truthful, in the highest degree just in his principles and purposes though often badly warped by prejudice, prompt in attention, retentive in memory, and inflexibly faithful to his pledge. If he was proud, it was not an arrogant and cruel pride, but a lofty self-assertion bottomed on a sense of worth. And even in regard to his irascible temper, the inflammability and explosiveness were on the surface of his mind, while tenderness, justice, and magnanimity were in its depths, excepting where some supposed meanness or wrong had caused hate to percolate there. The keenness and tenacity of his feelings took effect alike in his attractions and repulsions, so that he was as slow to forget a comrade as he was to forgive a foe. In London he saw two carriage-dogs, who had been mates for years running along together, when one of them was crushed by a wheel and killed. The other just glanced at him, and, without deigning so much as to stop and smell of him, trotted on. From the sight of this Forrest caught such a contempt for the whole breed of carriage-dogs that he could never afterwards look at one without disgust. It was hardly fair perhaps to spread over an entire race what was the fault of one, but the impulse was generous. So long as any man with whom he had once been friends behaved properly and treated him justly he remained as true as steel to his fellowship. But open dereliction from duty, or clear degradation of character, or, in particular, any instance of baseness, cowardice, or treachery, moved his scorn and anger and fatally alienated him. It will be remembered that while yet a mere youth he played very successfully at Albany with Edmund Kean, whose genius he idolized.

After the play a man whom he had always liked said to him, "Your Iago was better than Kean's Othello." Forrest says, "I never spoke to that man again!"

There was a strong feeling of kindness and admiration between him and Silas Wright, the celebrated Democratic Senator from New York. The day was once fixed for an important debate between Silas Wright and Daniel Webster. Early in the morning a man who had seen Wright drinking deeply and somewhat overcharged went to Webster and said, "You will have an easy task to-day in overthrowing your adversary; he already reels." Indignant at the meanness of the remark, the great man frowned darkly and answered in his sternest tones, "Sir, no man has an easy victory over Silas Wright, drunk or sober," and stalked away. Forrest used to tell this anecdote with characteristic relish of the rebuke pride gave impertinence. He could well appreciate traits of character and modes of conduct which he did not profess to practise but openly repudiated for himself. For instance, though he preferred truth to charity when they were opposed, he often quoted with the warmest admiration the sentiment uttered by some one on the death of Robert Burns: "Let his faults be like swans' feet, hid beneath the stream." And he also once said, "The finest eulogy I ever heard spoken of General Grant was, as uttered by an old acquaintance of his, 'He never forgot a friend nor remembered an enemy.' Ah, is not that beautiful? If it be justly said, as I am sorry to say I very much doubt, it sets a grace around his head which he himself could never set there." It is certainly a very curious—though not at all an extraordinary—illustration of human nature to set against the above utterance of Forrest the following quotation from a letter of his dated Syracuse, October 5, 1868: "I saw by the telegraphic news in the paper this morning that George. W. Jamieson was killed last night by a railroad train at Yonkers. God is great; and justice, though slow, is sure. Another scoundrel has gone to hell—I trust forever!"

Of the very large number of friends Forrest had, his intimacy continued to the end of life with but comparatively few. Fatal barriers and chill spaces of separation came between him and a great many of them, caused sometimes by mere lapse of time and pressure of occupation or removal of residence and change of personal tastes, sometimes by alienating disagreements and collisions of temper. These estrangements were so numerous that he acquired the reputation of being a quarrelsome man and hard to get along with, which was not altogether the fact.

One class of his earlier friends were in many cases converted into enemies on this wise. Boon companions are easy to have, but cheap, superficial, fickle. Genuine friendship, on the other hand, generous community of life and aspiration, co-operative pursuit and enjoyment of the worthiest ends, is a rare and costly prize, requiring virtues and imposing tasks. Multitudes therefore are tempted to put up with jovial fellowship in the pleasures of the table and let the desire for an ennobling intercourse of souls die out. The parasitic and treacherous nature of most pot-fellowship is proverbial. How well Shakspeare paints it in his version of Timon! When the eyes of the generous Athenian were opened to the selfishness of his pretended friends he became so rankling a misanthrope that the Greek Anthology gives us this as the epitaph sculptured on his sepulchre:

"Dost hate the earth or Hades worse! Speak clear!
Hades, O fool! There are more of us here."

Forrest was not many years in learning how shallow, how selfish, how untrustworthy such comrades were. He had too much ambition, too much earnestness and dignity to be satisfied with a worthless substitute for a sacred reality. He would not let an ungirt indulgence of the senses in conviviality take the place of a consentient action of congenial souls in the enjoyment of excellence and the pursuit of glory. More and more, therefore, he withdrew from these scenes of banqueting, story-telling, and singing, and found his contentment more and more in books, in the repose and reflection of solitude, and in the society of a select few. The most of those whom he thus left to themselves resented his defection from their ways, and repaid his former favor and bounty with personal dislike and invidious speech.

Another class of his quondam friends he broke with not on the ground of their general principles and social habits but in consequence of some particular individual offence in their individual character and conduct. His standard for a friend—his standard of honesty, sincerity, and manly fairness—was an exacting one, and he brooked no gross deviation from it. When he believed, either correctly or incorrectly, that any associate of his had wilfully violated that standard, he at once openly repudiated his friendship and walked with him no more. In this way dark gaps were made in the ranks of his temporary friends by the expulsion thence of the satellites who preyed on his money, the actors who pirated his plays, the debauchees who dishonored themselves, the companions who betrayed his confidence and slandered his name. And thus the crowd of his revengeful assailants was again swelled. A single example in illustration of his conduct under such circumstances is marked by such racy vigor that it must be here adduced. A man of great smartness and of considerable distinction, with whom he had been especially intimate, but whom, having discovered his unworthiness, he had discarded, sought to reingratiate himself. Forrest wrote him this remarkable specimen of terse English:

"New York, January 14, 1859.

"I hope the motives which led you to address me a note under date of 13th inst. will never induce you to do so again. Attempts upon either my credulity or my purse will be found alike in vain. No person however malicious, as you assume to believe, could change my opinion of you. Your intention to write a book is a matter which rests entirely with yourself. May I, however, take the liberty of suggesting that at this late day such a thing is not really needed, to illustrate your character, to alter public opinion, nor to prove to the world how great a dust can be raised by an ass out of place in either diplomacy or literature? There is already enough known of your career to prove that your task of becoming the apologist for a prostitution which has girdled the globe is one congenial to your tastes, fitted to your peculiar abilities, and coincident with your antecedents even from your birth to the present day.

"Edwin Forrest."

Furthermore, an important circle of his most honored friends fell away from Forrest under circumstances peculiarly trying to his feelings. All those who in the time of his domestic unhappiness and the consequent lawsuits sympathized with the lady and supported her cause against him he regarded as having committed an unpardonable offence. He would never again speak with one of them. It was a heavy defection. It inflicted much suffering on him and bred a bitter sense of hostility towards them, with a sad feeling of impoverishment. For the places they had occupied in his heart and memory were thenceforth as so many closed and sealed chambers of funereal gloom.

But, after all the foregoing failures have been allowed for, there remain in the life we are contemplating a goodly number of friendships full of hearty sincerity and wholesome human helpfulness and joy,—friendships unstained by vice, unbroken by quarrels, undestroyed by years. Several of these have already been alluded to; especially the supreme example in his opening manhood, his relations with the eloquent, heroic, and generous William Leggett. Some account also has been given of his endeared intimacy with James Lawson, who first greeted him on the night of his first appearance in New York, and whose faithful attachment to his person and interests grew closer and stronger to the day of his death, never for an instant having seen the prospect of a breach or known the shadow of a passing cloud. "My friend Lawson," said Forrest, when near his end, "is a gentleman on whom, as Duncan remarked of the thane of Cawdor, I have always built an absolute trust. He has, in our long communion of nigh fifty years, never failed me in a single point nor deceived me by so much as a look, but has been as good and kind to me as man can be to man." Here is one of his letters:

"Philadelphia, Dec. 1, 1869.

"Dear Lawson,—I am glad you like the notice of *Spartacus*. It was written by our friend Forney, in his hearty and friendly spirit.

"My dear friend Lawson, it is not money that I play for now, but the excitement of the stage keeps me from rusting physically and mentally. It drives away the canker care, and averts the progress of decay. It is wholesome to be employed in 'the labor we delight in.' What prolonged the life of Izaak Walton, but his useful employments, which gave vigor to his mind and body, until mildly drew on the slow necessity of death? I hope to take you by the hand when you are ninety, and tell some merry tales of times long past. Day after to-morrow I leave home for Cincinnati, and shall be absent in the West for several months, and return with the birds and the buds, to see you once more, I hope, in your usual enjoyment of health and happiness. God bless you.

"Your sincere friend,
"Edwin Forrest."

And now some examples of less conspicuous but true and valued friendships, selected from among many, claim brief place in this narrative. William D. Gallagher, a Quaker by persuasion, a man of literary tastes and a most quiet and blameless spirit, cherished from boyhood a fervid admiration and love for Forrest ever gratefully appreciated by him. He took extreme pains to collect materials for the biography of his friend, materials which have been often used in the earlier pages of this volume. Forrest desired his biographer, if he could find appropriate place in his work, to record an acknowledging and tributary word in memory of this affectionate and unobtrusive friend. The fittest words for that purpose will be the following citation from a letter of Forrest himself. "I deeply regret to inform you of the death of William D. Gallagher, who on his recent visit to Boston was so much pleased in forming your acquaintance and hearing your discourses. He was a man to be honored and loved for his genuine worth. He was quite free from every vice of the world. He carried the spirit of a child all through his life. He was as pure and gentle, I believe, as an angel. Though he cut no figure in society, I was proud to know that so good a man was my friend. I used to feel that I had rather at any time clasp his hand than that of the heir apparent to the throne of England."

In the chief cities which Forrest every year visited professionally he formed many delightful acquaintances, many of which, constantly renewed and heightened by every fresh communion of heart and life, ripened into precious friendships. Of these, John C. Breckinridge, of Lexington, Kentucky, and John G. Stockly, of Cleveland, Ohio, and Charles G. Greene, of Boston, Massachusetts, may be named. But more particular mention should be made of James V. Wagner, of Baltimore. A Baltimore correspondent of the "National Intelligencer," in one of his communications, says, "We learn that the distinguished American tragedian during his recent sojourn in this city has presented a splendid carriage and pair of horses to his long-tried and faithful friend, our fellow-citizen James V. Wagner. When the celebrated actor was but a stripling and at the beginning of his career, Mr. Wagner took him warmly by the hand, and has been his ardent admirer and friend from that time to the present. The gift is a magnificent one, and reflects credit on bestower and receiver. It is an establishment altogether fit for a duke or a prince." In 1874 a son of Mr. Wagner gives this pleasing reminiscence of the frequent and ever-charming visits of Forrest at his father's house: "Often in childhood have I sat upon his knee, and, as I then felt, listened to the words of Metamora, Jack Cade, and Lear in broadcloth. Often did he stroke my little black locks and ask me if I would become a carpenter, a lawyer, a minister, or a merchant. I can testify to his fondness for young children, consequently his goodness of heart."

Judge Conrad, the eloquent author of Jack Cade, the high-souled, brilliant man, was a very dear and close friend of Forrest. The impulsive and generous writer gave the appreciative and steadfast player much pleasure and inspiration by his intercourse, and received a cordial esteem and many important favors in return. On Forrest's arrival from Europe with his wife in 1846 he was greeted with this hearty letter by Conrad:

"My Dear Mr. and Mrs. Forrest,—A thousand warm and hearty welcomes home! I had hoped to greet you in person, but my engagements preclude me that pleasure. You doubtless find that the creaking and crazy world has been grating upon its axis after the rough old fashion since you left us; that there are fresh mounds in the grave-yard, and fresh troubles in the way to it; but I am sure that you find the hearts of old as true as ever. Your wandering way has had anxious eyes watching over it; and your return is, in this city, hailed with general rejoicing. Absence embalms friendships: friends seldom change when so separated that they cannot offend. And to one who has a circle such as you have, I should think it almost worth while to go abroad for the luxury of returning home. Thank God that you are back and in health!

"Mrs. Conrad and our girls unite with me in bidding you welcome. The news of your arrival made a jubilee with the children. We all look forward anxiously for the privilege of taking you by the hand.

"Very truly your friend,
"R. T. Conrad."

One brief interruption to this friendship there was. It originated in some misunderstanding which provoked anger and pain. Forrest wrote at once, not unkindly, and asked an explanation. He was rejoiced by the immediate receipt of the following letter, which he endorsed with the single word "Reconciliation," and they were again united:

"Philadelphia, June 25th, 1849.

"My Dear Forrest,—Your letter throws the duty of apology upon me, and, from my heart, I ask your pardon, and will tear to tatters all record of what has passed. But there is no madness Coleridge tells us, that so works upon the brain as unkindness in those we love.

"Forget what has passed,—but not until you have forgiven one whose pulses beat sometimes too hotly, but will always beat for you. This single cloud in our past—a past all bright to me— has been absorbed by the nobler and purer atmosphere of your nature. Surely it cannot now cast a shadow.

"Before the receipt of your note I had written a letter under my own signature, replying to a brutal attack upon you in the Boston 'Aurora Borealis,' in relation to your course towards dramatic authors. It will appear in McMakin's 'Courier,' and I have seized the occasion to make some editorial remarks upon the subject that will not dissatisfy you; and, as the circulation of the 'Courier' is nearly wide as that of the wind, I think it will do good.

"Let me sign this hasty note as most truly and heartily

"Your friend,
"R. T. Conrad.
"E. Forrest, esq."

The friendship with James Taylor, described in a previous chapter of this biography, which was so pleasant and valuable to Forrest at the time, never died, but was kept fresh and strong to the last. This will appear from the interesting letters that follow:

"Fire Island, N.Y., July 14th, 1870.
"Edwin Forrest, esq.:
"My Dear Friend,—When you were last at my house I promised you a copy of my portrait of George F. Cooke. I could not until now

procure such a copy as I thought worthy to be sent you. It was first photographed and then painted, and is an exact counterfeit of the original. It is not full size. Several attempts were made to get a good photograph copy, or *negative,* and in the present size it was the most perfect. The history of this picture (I mean the one in my possession) is as follows: A young gentleman by the name of Jouitt studied portrait-painting with Sully in 1816, and on his leaving for his native State, Kentucky, Sully presented him with this picture of Cooke, being a copy of *his original picture of the great tragedian.* Jouitt presented the picture to Captain John Fowler, of Lexington, Ky., in 1818, and he on his death-bed in 1840 gave it to me. He was an old pioneer, and came to Kentucky with my mother in 1783. Now, my old and much-admired friend, please accept this portrait as a testimony of my high regard for you as a gentleman and a man of genius. I often have a vivid recollection of the old times when we were together,—the night you slept with me at Kean's Hotel, and the New Year's dinner at Ayer's Hotel with Clay, Merceir, and others. We were young then, full of life, hope, and enthusiasm; and I do not feel old yet. These days, my friend, I look back on with pleasure. I was not then vexed or troubled with the cares of life. If we should never meet again, I wish you much happiness and length of days. I am here enjoying the breezes of ' Neptune's salt wash,' fishing, and sailing. I shall return to New York in a week or ten days. Please write to me at the St. Nicholas, as I desire to know whether the picture reached you uninjured.

"Yours very sincerely,
"James Taylor."

"Fire Island, August 1st, 1870.
"Edwin Forrest:

"My Dear Friend,—Yours of the 21st of July was forwarded to me from New York at the close of last week, and I regret that it was out of my power to comply with your request to meet you at your home in Philadelphia. I have been here now over three weeks,—a most delightful cool place,—and I only regret that I have to leave it in the midst of the hot season to return to Kentucky, where business calls me. I am gratified that you liked the portrait;. it is in fact a true copy of the original. Dear Ned, I often think of our young days in Lexington with our friends Lewis, Turpin, Clay, and others, and how happy we were amidst those scenes. But they are gone, and we are almost old men. I hope we shall gracefully go down to death, having courageously fought the battle of life. You will leave a name and a fame behind you as one of the great masters of the dramatic art. Should you again visit the West, you know where to find your friend,

"James Taylor."

Another letter, much longer and more important, was addressed by Mr. Taylor to S. S. Smith, a common friend to the two persons,—a friend of whom Forrest once wrote to Oakes, "If my old friend S. S. Smith does not go to heaven when he dies, the office of door-keeper there is a sinecure and the place might as well be shut up. He is one of the most honest, kind-hearted, trustworthy men I have ever known. I have always cherished the warmest esteem for him." This letter was written after the death of Forrest, and contains a most interesting and touching tribute to him. It belongs in the closing chapter rather than here.

Among the long and well-cherished friends of Forrest, of a later date than Taylor, were the two distinguished New York counsellors John Graham and James T. Brady. The sudden death of the latter at the zenith of his manhood called from him a strong expression of feeling in a letter to one of their common friends: "The death of Brady shocked me very much. He was a genial, noble man, and an eloquent and honest lawyer,—every way so unlike the pettifogging peddlers of iniquity and the corrupt and ermined ruffians of the bench whom we have known. I feel honored in saying that I was his friend and that he was mine. His place will not easily be supplied with any of those who knew him, and could not know him without loving him. What an interesting figure he was, and how he drew all eyes where he came, with his beating heart, his bright frank face, his large and warm presence! He was a contrast indeed to those commonplace creatures concerning whom nobody cares anything, and never asks who they are, or what they do, or whence they come, or where they go. I regret that he should have died and not have made friends with John Graham. How I should like to have been instrumental with you in bringing about a reconciliation between them!"

And now we come to the central, crowning, supreme friendship which most of all alleviated the life and blessed the heart of Forrest alike when he was young and when he was old,—the glowing bond of cordiality that knit his soul with the soul of James Oakes. One of the two partners in this happy league of unselfish love and faithful service has passed through nature to eternity, while one still lives. To do justice to the relation on the side of the former it is necessary to know something of the character of the man who sustained the other side of it And though it is a delicate office, and one somewhat offensive to fashion, to speak frankly of the traits of the living, except indeed in assault and censure, yet, since truth is truth, and moral lessons have the same import whether drawn from those who are alive or from those who are dead, one who is called to tell the story of a departed Damon may perhaps venture honestly and with modesty to depict his lingering Pythias.

Oakes is a man of positive nature, downright and forthright, as blunt and strong in act and word as Forrest himself, and, so far, fitted to meet and mate him. He has made a host of foes by his bluff truth of speech and deed, his sturdy standing to his opinion, his straight march to his purpose. These foes, no matter who they were, high or low, he has always scorned and defied with unfaltering and unrepentant vigor. He has likewise made a host of friends, by his sound judgment always at their service, his genially affectionate spirit, and his unwearied devotion to gentle works of humanity in befriending the unfortunate and ministering to the distressed, the sick, and the dying. To these friends, rich and poor alike, and whether basking in popular favor or crushed under obloquy, he has always been steadfastly true. No fickle misliker or mere sunshine friend he, but, like Forrest, tenacious both in antipathies and sympathies. His nature has ever been wax to receive, steel to retain, the memory of injuries and of benefits, hostility and love. His sensitive openness to the beauty of nature, to the charm of poetry, to the voice of eloquence, to the touch of fine sentiment, is extreme. Anything pathetic, noble, or grand makes his tears spring quicker than a woman's, and his blood burns with instant indignation and his heart beats fast and loud against injustice, cruelty, or meanness. And yet he is not what is called a society man, a careful observer of the sleek proprieties of the polite world of conventional appearances. On the contrary, in many things his aboriginal love of free sincerity has shocked these. And he has been a strong lover of horses, of dogs, of sporting life, and of the rough, warm, honest ways of fearless and spontaneous sporting men. A soft heart, a true tongue, a clear head, self-asserting character and life, pity for suffering, defiance to pretension, contempt for fashion when opposed to nature, have been his passports to men and theirs to him. From his boyhood he has taken delight in doing kind deeds to the needy, carrying wines, fruits, flowers, and other delicacies to the sick, being a champion for the weak and injured, whether man or woman or child or quadruped or bird. Hundreds of times has he been seen in drifting snow-storms, undeterred by the pelting elements, in his wide-rimmed hat, shaggy overcoat, and long boots up to his thighs, loaded with good things, on his way to the bedside of some disabled friend or some poor sufferer forgotten by others. His enemies no doubt may justly bring many accusations against him. His friends certainly will confess his defects and faults. He himself would blush at the thought of claiming immunity from a full share of the weaknesses and sins of men. But no one who knows him, whether friend or foe, can question his extreme tenderness, tenacity, and fidelity of nature, his rare sensibility of hate for detestable forms of character and action, his heroic adhesion and indefatigable attentiveness to all whom he admires and loves.

His moral portrait is limned by the hand of one who had known him most thoroughly on his favorable side as a friend for nearly all his lifetime, in this private epistle:

"New York, Sunday morning, May 24, 1874.

"My Dear Oakes,—Your letter of the 22d reached me yesterday morning, and was read and re-read with pleasure. When you tell me you foot up sixty-seven, I find it difficult to believe you, and if you refer me to the record I shall still exclaim with Beau Shatterly (do you remember how poor Finn used to play it?), 'D—n parish registers! They're all impudent impositions and no authority!'

"There are a few exceptional men in the world who project their youth far forward into their lives, and this not so much from force of constitution as from the size of their hearts. You are one of these few phenomenal men. That you may long continue to flourish in perennial spring is my sincerest prayer. You have been just and generous (except to yourself),—to what extent you forget. I think the recording angel must sometimes curse your good deeds, you have given him or her or it (there is no sex to angels) so many to record in that huge log-book which is kept up aloft for future reference. In the race for salvation, while the saints (professional) are plying steel and whipcord, jostling each other and riding foul, you will distance them and go into the gate at an easy canter under no pull at all. As for me, it is different. I stood near the pyramid of Caius Sextius at Rome, at the grave of Keats, and read his epitaph by himself, ' Here lies one whose name was writ in water,' and said, That ought to be mine. However, I went up the steps of the Santa Scala on my knees, invested fifty francs or so in indulgences, and left the Eternal City whiter than snow,—but perhaps only as a whited sepulchre is sometimes whiter than snow.

"Excuse my levity. You will read between the lines and find plenty of sad and serious thoughts there. If I did not valiantly fight against bitter memories, I should cave.

"Yours entirely,
"F. A. D."

Oakes had many friends besides Forrest, some of whom he had known earlier and most of whom were friends in common to them both. Among the chief of these may be named—and they were men of extraordinary talent, force, racy originality of character, and depth of human passion—George W. Kendall and A. M. Holbrook, editors of the New Orleans "Picayune," William T. Porter, editor of the "Spirit of the Times," Dr. Charles M. Windship, of Roxbury, the romantic and tragic William Henry Herbert,— better known as Frank Forrester, a sort of modern Bertrand du Guesclin, who, when the woman he loved deceived him, resolutely severed every tie joining him with humanity and the world, requested that no epitaph should be written on him save "The Most Unhappy," and quieted his convulsed brain with a bullet, —Sargent S. Prentiss, of Mississippi, Thomas F. Marshall, of Kentucky, George W. Prentice, Albert Pike, Colonel Powell T. Wyman, and Francis A. Durivage. The inner lives of such characters as these, and others whose names are not given, fully revealed, show in human experience gulfs of delight and woe, degrees of intensity and wonder, little dreamed of by the peaceful and feeble superficialists who fancy in their innocence that the life of the nineteenth century is tame and dull, wholly wanting in the extremities of spiritual adventure and social excitement that marked the times of old. The knowledge of the sincere life of society to day—the real unconventional life behind the scenes—as it was uncovered and made familiar to Forrest and Oakes, when it is suddenly appreciated by a thoughtful scholar, an inexperienced recluse, gives him a shock of amazement, a mingled sorrow and wonder which make him cry, "What a sad, bitter, strange, beautiful, terrible world it is! O God! who knows or can even faintly guess from afar the meaning of it all? These fathomless passions of men and women, giving a bliss and a pain which make every other heaven or hell utterly superfluous,—these temptations and crimes which horrify the soul and curdle the blood,—these betrayals and disappointments that break our hearts, unhinge our reason, and precipitate us into self-sought graves, mad to pluck the secret of eternity,—who shall ever read the infinite riddle and tell us what it all is for?"

As the heaping decades of years rolled by, Oakes had to part with many of his dearest friends at the edge of that shadow which no mortal, only immortals, can penetrate. But, unlike what happens with most men, his friendly offices ceased not with the breath of the departed. For one and another and another and another of his old comrades, whom he had assiduously nursed in their last hours, when all was ended, with his own hands he tenderly closed the eyes, washed the body, put on the burial-garments, and reverently laid the humanized clay in the earth with farewell tears. To so many of his closest comrades had he paid this last service that at length in his twilight meditations he began to feel a chilly solitude spreading around. It was in such a mood that he wrote a letter to one of the surviving and central figures of that group of strong, brave, fiery-passioned men, who knew the full height and depth of the romance and tragedy of human experience, and had nearly all gone, most of them untimely, and several by their own hands. It was to Albert Pike that he wrote. What he wrote moved Pike to compose an essay, "Of Leaves and their Falling," in which this touching, tributary passage occurs. Having alluded to the dead of their circle,—Porter, Elliot, Lewis and Willis Gaylord Clark, Herbert, Wyman, Forrest, and others,—he proceeds: "James Oakes, of the old Salt-Store, 49 Long Wharf, Boston,—'Acorn' of the old 'Spirit of the Times,'—lives yet, as generous and genial as ever. He loved Porter like a brother, and, in a letter received by me yesterday, says, 'This is my birthday! 67 is marked on the milestone of my life just passed. Among the few old friends of my early days who are left on this side the river, none is dearer to me than yourself. As I creep down the western slope towards the last sunset, my old heart turns with irresistible longings to those early friends, my love for whom grew with my growth and strengthened with my strength. Alas, how few are left! As I look back upon the long line of grave-stones by the wayside that remind me of my early associates, a feeling of inexpressible sadness possesses me, and my heart yearns towards the few old friends left, to whom I cling with hooks of steel.' And so he thanks me for a poem sent him, and tells me how he has worked for the estate of Forrest, and sincerely and affectionately wishes that God may bless me and keep me in health for many years to come.

"Ah, dear old friend! the cold November days of life have come for both of us, and the dull bars of cloud scowl on the barren stubble-fields, the wind blows inhospitably, and the hills in the distance are bleak and gray and bare, and the winter comes, when we must drop from the tree, and be remembered a little while, and then forgotten almost as soon as the dead leaves.

"Well, what does it matter to us if we are to be forgotten before the spring showers fall a second time on our graves, as Porter was, except by two or three friends? What is it to the leaf that falls, killed by an untimely frost, whether it is remembered or forgotten by its fellows that still cling to the tree, to fall a little later in the season? Men are seldom remembered after death for anything that you or I would care to be remembered for.

"Porter would not have cared to be remembered by many, nor by any one, unless with affection for his unbounded goodness of heart and generosity. Nor am I covetous of large remembrance among men. If I should die before him, I should wish, if I cared for anything here after death more than a dead leaf does, to have Oakes come to my grave, as I wish that he and I could go to that of Porter, and there repeat, in the language to which no translation can do justice, this exquisite threnody of Catullus:

INFERS AD FRATRIS TUMULUM.
Multas per gentes et multa per sequora vectus,
Advenio has miseras, frater, ad inferias,
Ut te postremo donarem munere mortis,
Et mutum nequicquam alloquerer cinerem,
Quandoquidem Fortuna mihi tete abstulit ipsum,
Heu miser indigne frater ademte mihi
Nunc tamen interea haec prisco quae more parentum
Tradita sunt tristes munera ad inferias,
Accipe fratemo multum manantia fletu,
Atque in perpetuum, frater, ave atque vale.
"Discontented with the translations whereof by Lamb, Elton, and Hodgson, I have endeavored this more literal one:

"Through many nations, over many seas,
Brother, to this sad sacrifice I come
To pay to thee Death's final offices,
And, though in vain, invoke thine ashes dumb,
Since Fate's fell swoop has torn thyself from me,—
Alas, poor brother, from me severed ruthlessly!
"Therefore, meanwhile, these offices of sorrow,
Which, by old custom of our fathers' years
To the last sacrifice assigned, I borrow.
Flowing with torrents of fraternal tears,
Accept, though only half my grief they tell,—
And so, forever, brother, bless thee, and farewell!"

Such as he has been above described was the man who for forty-three years best loved Edwin Forrest and whom in return Edwin Forrest best loved. How much this means, the narrative of their friendship that follows will show.

At the time of their first meeting, which took place at the close of the actor's debut in Boston in the play of Damon and Pythias, Forrest was within a few weeks of twenty-one and Oakes a little less than twenty. They had so many traits and tastes in common that their souls chimed at once. When absent they corresponded by letter, and, seizing every opportunity for renewed personal fellowship, their mutual interest quickly ripened into a fervent attachment. Oakes had a passion for the theatre and the drama. He earnestly studied the principal plays produced, and soon began scribbling criticisms. These paragraphs he often gave to the regular reporters and dramatic critics of the newspapers, and sometimes sent them directly in his own name to the editors. Afterwards, over the signature of "Acorn," he acquired good reputation as a stated contributor to several leading journals in the East and the South. Both he and Forrest were great sticklers for a vigorous daily bath and scrub, and very fond of athletic exercises, which they especially enjoyed together, an example which might be copied with immense advantage by many daintily cultured people who fancy themselves above it. They were about equally matched with the gloves and the foils, if anything Forrest being the better boxer, Oakes the better fencer, as his motions were the more nimble.

As time passed and their mutual knowledge and confidence increased, the sympathies of the friends were more closely interlocked and spread over all their business interests and affectional experiences, and their constantly crossing letters were transcripts of their inner states and their daily outer lives. They scarcely held any secret back from each other. Forrest almost invariably consulted Oakes and carefully weighed his advice before taking any important step. Oakes made it his study to do everything in his power to aid and further his honored friend alike in his personal status and in his professional glory. For this end he wrote and moved others to write hundreds and hundreds of newspaper notices, working up every conceivable kind of item calculated to keep the name and personality of the actor freshly before the eyes of the public. His letters, with the alert instinct of love, were varied to meet and minister to the trials and condition of him to whom they were addressed, congratulating him in his triumph, counselling him in his perplexity, soothing him in his anger, consoling him in his sorrow. In the innumerable letters, transmitted for nearly fifty years at the rate of from two to seven a week, Oakes used to enclose slips snipped from the newspapers, and extracts from magazines and books, containing everything he found which he thought would interest, amuse, or edify his correspondent. Thus was he ever what a friend should be,—a mirror glassing the soul and fortunes of the counterpart friend; but a mirror which at the same time that it reflects what exists also reveals the supply of what is needed.

One of the charms of the correspondence of Oakes and Forrest is the ingenuous freedom with which their feelings are expressed. A shamefaced or frigid reticence on all matters of sentiment or personal affection between men seems to be the conspicuous characteristic of the Anglo-Saxon race. The most that the average well-to-do Englishman or American can say on meeting his dearest friend is, Well, old fellow, how goes it? Glad to see you! It is painful for a really rich and tender heart to move about in this sterile wilderness of dumb and bashful sympathy or frozen and petrified love. But these friends were wont to speak their free hearts each to each without reserve or affectation. Early in their acquaintance Oakes writes thus:

"My Dear Forrest,—I cannot tell you how much delight I had in your visit to me. When you left, the sinking of my heart told me how dear you had become. The more I see of you the more I find to honor and to love. I set your image against the remembrance of all the scamps I have known, and think more highly of the human race. How I long for the day when you will visit Boston again or I shall come to you! Command my services to the fullest extent in anything and in everything. For I am, from top to bottom, inside and out, and all through, forever yours,

"James Oakes."

And Forrest, replies:

"My Dearest and Best of Friends,—Thanking you for your hearty letter, which has given me a real pleasure, I assure you you could not have enjoyed my visit more than I did. Your encouraging smiles and delicate attentions gave a daily beauty to my life while I was under the same roof with you. In my life I have had the fellowship of many goodly men, brave and manly fellows who knew not what it was to lie or to be afraid. I have never met one whose heart beat with a nobler humanity than yours. I am proud to be your friend and to have you for mine. God bless you, and keep us always worthy of one another.

"Edwin Forrest."

Every summer for the last thirty years of his life Forrest made it a rule to spend a week or a fortnight with Oakes, when they either loitered about lovely Boston or went into the country or to the seaside and gave themselves up to leisurely enjoyment, "fleeting the time carelessly as they did in the golden world." Then the days and nights flew as if they were enchanted with speed. These visits were regularly repaid at New York, at Fonthill, at Philadelphia. Whenever they met, after a long separation, as soon as they were alone together they threw their arms around each other in fond embrace with mutual kisses, after the manner of lovers in our land or of friends in more tropical and demonstrative climes.

A single forlorn tomato was the entire crop raised at Fonthill Castle in the season of 1851. As the friends stood looking at it, Oakes suddenly plucked, peeled, and swallowed it. The tragedian gazed for some time in open-eyed astonishment. At length with affected rage he broke out, "Well, if this is not the most outrageous piece of selfishness! an impudent and barbarous robbery! That was the tomato which I had cherished and depended on as the precious product of all the money and pains I have spent here. And now you come, whip out your jack-knife, and, at one fell swoop, gulp down my whole harvest. I swear, it is the meanest thing I ever knew done." They looked each other in the eyes a moment, burst into a hearty laugh, and, locking arms, strolled down to the bank of the river.

When Forrest engaged his friend S. S. Smith to oversee the laying out of his estate of Forrest Hill, at Covington, opposite Cincinnati, he named one of the principal streets Oakes Avenue. When he purchased and began occasionally to occupy the Springbrook place he named the room opposite his own Oakes's Chamber. In his Broad Street Mansion, in Philadelphia, there was a portrait of Oakes in the entry, a portrait of Oakes in the dining-room, a portrait of Oakes in the picture-gallery, a portrait of Oakes in the library, and a general seeming presence of Oakes all over the house. Early one summer day, while visiting there, Oakes might have been seen, wrapped in a silk morning-gown of George Frederick Cooke, with a wig of John Philip Kemble on his head and a sword of Edmund Kean by his side, tackled between the thills of a heavy stone roller, rolling the garden walks to earn his breakfast. Forrest was behind him, urging him forward. Henrietta and Eleanora Forrest gazed out of a window at the scene in amazement until its amusing significance broke upon them, when their frolicsome peals of laughter caused the busy pair of laborers below to pause in their task and look up.

Oakes was fond of being with Forrest during his professional engagements as well as in his vacations. And the hours they then spent together yielded them a keen and solid enjoyment. This experience was most characteristic of their friendship, and is worthy of description. Oakes would go to the play and watch with the most vigilant attention every point in the performance. Then he would go behind the scenes to the dressing-room. There the excited and perspiring actor, blowing off steam, stripped and put himself in the hands of his body-servant, who sponged him, vigorously rubbed him dry, and helped him to dress. Locking arms, and avoiding all hangers-on who might be in the way, the friends proceeded to their room at the hotel. Forrest would then throw off his coat and boots, and loosen his nether garments so as to be perfectly at ease, and call for his supper. It was his custom, as he ate nothing before playing, to refresh himself afterwards with some simple dish. His usual food was a generous bowl of cold corn-meal mush and milk. This he took with a wholesome relish, the abstinent Oakes sharing only in sympathy. Then was the tragedian to be seen in his highest social glory; for he threw every restraint to the wind and gave full course to the impulses of his nature. "Now here we are, my friend," he would say, "and let the world wag as it will, what do we care? Is it not a luxury to unbutton your heart once in a while and let it all out where you know there can be no misunderstanding? Come, go to, now, and let us have a good time!" And a good time they *did* have. They recalled past adventures. They planned future ones. They gave every faculty of wit, humor, and affection free play, without heed of any law beyond that of their own friendly souls. Then, if he happened to be in the vein, Forrest would tell anecdotes of other players, and give imitations of them. He would take off with remarkable felicity the peculiarities of Irishmen, Frenchmen, Germans, Englishmen, and, above all, of negroes. Very few comic actors at their best on the stage appear better in portraying ludicrous dialect characters or in telling funny stories than Forrest did on these occasions when giving himself full swing with his friend alone, thoroughly unbent from professional duty and social stiffness. No one who then saw him sitting on the floor mimicking a tailor at work, rolling on the bed in convulsions of laughter, or representing the double part of two negro woodsawyers who undertook to play Damon and Pythias, would dream that this was the man whom the world thought so grim and sour and gloomy. He used to say, "It is often the case that we solemn tragedians when off the stage are your jolliest dogs, while your clowns and comedians are dyspeptic and melancholy in private." There was a genuine vein of humor in him very strong and active. He was extremely fond of indulging it. He read "Darius Green and his Flying Machine" with great effect. He said he would like very much to recite it to the author, Mr. Trowbridge, and then recite to him the "Idiot Boy," that he might perceive the contrast of the humor in the one and the pathos in the other as illustrated by a tragedian.

Another feature in the friendship of Forrest and Oakes was their frequent co-operation in works of mercy to the suffering and of championship for the weak and wronged. In reading over their voluminous correspondence many cases have been brought to light in which they took up the cause of a poor man, an orphan, or an unfortunate widow, against cruel and rapacious oppressors. One instance of this was where a rich man was endeavoring by legal technicalities to defraud a widow and her children of all the little property they had. Forrest heard of it, and his just wrath was stirred. He wrote to Oakes to stand in the breach and defeat this iniquity, promising to furnish whatever money was needed to secure justice. It was a difficult case, and the poor woman was in despair. But Oakes stood by her with acute advice and sympathy and courage that never failed. After a hard and long fight, and a good deal of expense, the right was vindicated. Writing to Forrest an account of the result, and thanking him for his check, Oakes said, "This act is in such keeping with your magnificent soul, and joins so with a multitude, of kindred deeds in reflecting lustre on you, that if my heart did not feel at least as much satisfaction for your sake as for my own I would tear it out and fling it at your feet."

The following extract is from another letter:

"Your letter enclosing a hundred and fifty dollars reaches me this moment. In an hour it will be in the hands of the poor forlorn creature who indeed has no claim but the claim of a common humanity on either of us, but whose near death of disease ought not to be anticipated by a death of neglect, starvation, and cold. Your charity will now prevent that. Once this unhappy woman moved in a high circle, envied and admired by all. Now everybody deserts her death-garret. The Day of Judgment, if there ever is one, will uncover strange secrets. Among the shameful secrets dragged to light there will be glorious ones too,—like this your response to my appeal for a desolated, forgotten outcast."

In 1856 Forrest had a severe illness which, in connection with his domestic sorrow and vexatious litigation, greatly depressed his spirit. Oakes, ever watchful and thoughtful for him, held it to be essential that he should take a prolonged respite from public life and labor. On purpose to persuade him to this course, to which he was obstinately averse, Oakes made a journey to Philadelphia. After their greetings he said, bluntly, "Forrest, I have come to ask a great favor." Forrest broke in on his speech with these words: "Oakes, in all our long acquaintance never once have you asked anything of me in a selfish spirit; and often as I have followed your advice I have never yet made a mistake when I have allowed myself to be guided by you. Whatever the request is which you have to make, it is granted before you make it." Oakes was deeply moved, but, commanding himself, he said, "Your professional life has been one of hard work. Your health is not good, and you are no longer young. You have money enough. You are now at the top notch of your fame. To keep your rank there you will have to make great exertions. You ought to have a good long rest. Now I want you to promise me that you will not act again for three years." Forrest drew a long breath and dropped his head forward on his breast. In a minute he looked up and said, "Ah, my friend, you have tested me in my tenderest point. But it shall be so." Nearly four years passed before he again confronted an audience from his theatrical throne and welcomed their applause.

A group of the most ardent admirers of Forrest combined and subscribed a handsome sum of money to secure a full-length marble statue of him in one of his classic characters. But he shrank from the long and tedious sittings, and refused to comply with their request. Oakes, who was doubly desirous of securing this memorial, first as a tribute to his illustrious friend, second as an important piece of patronage to a gifted artist then just entering his career, now undertook the work of persuasion. To his solicitation Forrest replied, "What troubles me is the weary sittings I must undergo. But since you put this matter on personal grounds, and ask me to endure the load for the sake of an old unselfish friendship,—which cannot appeal in vain,—I yield with pleasure to your request. Whenever Mr. Ball shall come to Philadelphia I will submit myself with alacrity to the torture."

The name of Thomas Ball has acquired celebrity in art since that day, but this statue of Forrest in the character of Coriolanus will always stand as a proud landmark in his sculptured path of fame. It was a true work of love not less than of ambition. For in the long hours of their fellowship in the preparatory studying and sketching and casting the sitter and the artist grew friends. The sculptor took his model and sailed for Florence, there to produce the work he had conceived. And when a year and a half had gone by, the complete result, safely landed in Boston and set up for view in an art-gallery, greeted the eyes of Oakes and gladdened his heart. For it more than met his expectations, it perfectly contented him. He wrote to Mr. Ball, "I am glad the statue came unheralded to our shores, and am content to let the verdict of the public rest on the merits of the work. I congratulate you on an unequivocal and grand success. As a personal likeness of Forrest it is most truthful, and as an illustration of the Shakspearean conception of the Roman Consul it is sublime. For more than forty years I have known this man with an intimacy not common among men. Indeed, our friendship has been more like the devotion of a man to the woman he loves than the relations usually subsisting between men. In all my intercourse with the world I have never known a truer man or one with a nobler nature than Edwin Forrest, whose real worth and greatness will not be acknowledged by the world until he is dead. I rejoice that one of his own countrymen has given to posterity this true and magnificent portrait of him in immortal marble. The eloquence of this marble will outlive the malevolence of all the enemies and of all the critics who have assailed him."

Forrest was indeed fortunate in the peaceful and time-enduring victory achieved for him by the artist in this sculptured Coriolanus, whose haughty beauty, and right foot insupportably advanced with the planted weight of all imperious Rome, will speak his quality to generations yet unborn. What a melancholy contrast is suggested by the words of Mrs. Siddons after seeing the marble counterfeit of John Philip Kemble: "I cannot help thinking of the statue of my poor brother. It is an absolute libel on his noble person and air. I should like to pound it into dust and scatter it to the winds."

The Coriolanus is colossal, eight feet and a half in height and weighing six tons. The forms and muscles of the neck, the right side of the chest, the right arm, left forearm, feet, and lower portion of the left leg, are delineated in perfection, the remaining parts being concealed by the folds of the mantle which is drawn around the left shoulder, while the head is slightly turned to the right. The face and head are superbly finished and seem pregnant with vitality. The whole expression is one of massive and imperious strength, adamantine self-sufficingness, reposeful, yet animated and resolute. It represents him at that point in the play where he repels the intercessions of his mother and wife, and says,—

"Let the Voices
Plough Rome and harrow Italy, I'll never
Be such a gosling to obey instinct, but stand
As if a man were author of himself
And knew no other kin."

So much pleased was Forrest with the statue, as his lingering gaze studied it and drank in its majestic significance reflected on him from the superb and classic pomp of marble, that he begged the privilege of purchasing it from the subscribers. And so it now stands in the Actors' Home founded by his will. The enthusiastic and efficient zeal of Oakes in securing this work drew his friend to him with an increased feeling of obligation and of attachment, which he frankly expressed in an eloquent letter of thanks.

Forrest and Oakes had from time to time many pleasing adventures together. A specimen or two may be related. Strolling in a quiet square in Baltimore, they came upon a company of boys who were playing marbles. "My little fellows," said the tragedian, with his deep voice of music, "will you lend me a marble and let me play with you?"

"Oh, yes," said a barefoot, smiling urchin, and held up a marble in his dirty paw. Forrest took it, sank on one knee, and began his game. In less than half an hour he had won every marble they had, and the discomfited and destitute gang were gazing at him in astonishment. "Don't you see," he then said, "how dangerous it is for you to play with a stranger, about whose skill or whose character you are wholly ignorant? Boys, as you grow up and mix in the fight of life it will always be useful to you to know in advance what kind of a fellow he is with whom you are going to deal." One of the boys, who had been sharply eying him, whispered to another, "I guess he is Mr. Forrest, the playactor, you know, at the theatre." The other replied, "Well, I should like to go there and see if he can playact as well as he plays marbles." "Yes," said Forrest, "come, all of you. I want you to come. I will do my best to please you." And he wrote an order of admission for them, gave them back their marbles, and bade them good-morning.

Once when he was filling an engagement in Boston, Oakes told him a story of a humble mechanic whose landlord had compelled him to pay a debt twice over, under circumstances of cruelty which had brought out proofs of a most heroic honesty and refined sensibility in the poor man. Forrest listened to the narrative with rapt attention. At its close he exclaimed, "That landlord is a stony-hearted brute, and this mechanic is a man of a royal soul! I must go and see him and his family before I leave Boston." Thanksgiving Day came that week. A friend of Oakes had sent him for his Thanksgiving dinner an enormous wild turkey, weighing with the feathers on twenty-seven and a half pounds. He showed this to Forrest on Wednesday and told him they were to feast on it the next day. "No, old chap," replied Forrest; "you and I will dine on a beefsteak, and take the wild turkey to the noble fellow who paid Shylock his money twice." Immediately after breakfast on Thanksgiving Day a barouche was ordered, the big black turkey, looking nearly as large as a Newfoundland dog, placed on the front seat, and Forrest and Oakes took the back seat. They drove to the theatre. Forrest accosted the box-keeper: "Mr. Fenno, I want for to-night's performance six of the best seats in the house, for an emperor and his family who are to honor me by their presence." Fenno gave him the tickets and declined to take pay for them. He insisted on paying for them, saying, "They are my guests, sir." They then rode over to East Boston to the house of the honest man, found him, announced their names, explained the cause and object of their visit, and were invited in by him and introduced to his wife and four children. Forrest kissed each one of the children. He brought in the huge turkey and laid it on the table. Then, turning to the wife, he said, "We have brought a turkey for your Thanksgiving dinner; and if you and your noble husband and children enjoy as much in eating it as my friend and myself do in offering it you will be very happy. And I am sure you deserve great happiness, and I have faith that God will give it to you all." He then presented the tickets for the play of Metamora, saying, "I shall look to see if you are all in the seats before I begin to act." Not one of them had ever been inside of a theatre. The sensations that were awaiting them may be imagined. When the curtain rose and Metamora appeared on the stage amidst that tumultuous applause which in those times never failed to greet his entrance, he walked deliberately to the front, fixed his eyes on the little family, bowed, and then proceeded. Throughout the play he acted for and at that group, who seemed far happier than any titular royalty could have been. Though this happened twenty years before his death, he never forgot when in Boston to inquire after the *American emperor*! The honest man is still living, and should this little story ever meet his eye he will vouch for its entire truth.

A few extracts taken almost at random from the letters of these friends will clearly indicate the substantial earnestness and warmth of their relation. Letters when honest and free reveal the likeness of the waiter, photographing the features of the soul, a feat which usually baffles artistic skill and always defies chemical action.

"You will doubtless receive this note to-morrow,—my birthday,— when, you say, you will *think* of me. Tell me the day, my dear friend, when you do *not* think of me! God bless you! Last night I acted at Washington in Damon and Pythias. The sound of weeping was actually audible all over the house as the noble Pythagorean rushed breathlessly back to save his friend and then to die. What a grand moral is told in that play! What sermon was ever half so impressive in its teaching! Had Shakspeare written on the subject he had 'drowned the stage with tears.'

"I cannot let this day pass without sending to you a renewed expression of the esteem and high regard with which through so many years my heart has unceasingly honored you. A merry Christmas to you, my glorious friend, and a happy New Year, early in which I hope again to take you by the hand."

"As the years go by us, my noble Spartacus, many things slip away never to return, and many things that stay lose their charm. But one thing seems to grow ever more fresh and precious,—the joy of an honest friendship and trust in manly worth. May this, dear Forrest, never fail for you or for me, however long we live."

"God bless you, Oakes, for your kindly greeting on the New Year's day! Though I was too busy to write, my soul went out to you on that day with renewed messages of love, and with thanks to Almighty God that he has quickened at least two hearts with an unselfish and unwavering devotion to each other, and that those two hearts are yours and mine."

"You are almost the only intimate friend I have had who never asked of me a pecuniary favor, and to whom I am indebted for as many personal kindnesses as I ever received from any. I will send you my portrait to hang in your parlor, with my autograph, and with such words as I have not written, and will never write, upon another."

"It gives me great pleasure, my much-loved friend, to know that in a few days more I shall see you again, and reach that haven of rest, the presence of a true friend, where the storms of trouble cease to prevail."

"And now, my friend, permit me to thank you for all the delicate attentions you so considerately showed me during my late visit, and for your noble manly sympathy for me in the wound I received from the legal assassins of the Court of Appeals, who by their recent decision have trampled upon law, precedent, justice, and the instinctive honor of the human heart."

On the eve of his professional trip to California, Forrest wrote to Oakes, "My dear friend, how much I should like, if your business matters would permit, to have you accompany me to California! I would right willingly pay all your expenses for the entire journey, and I am sure you would enjoy the trip beyond expression. Is it not *possible* for you to arrange your affairs and go with me? It would make me the happiest man in the world."

The scheme could not be realized, and after his own return he wrote, "Yes, in a few days I will come to you in Boston, my dear friend. We will talk of scenes long gone, and renew the pleasant things of the past in sweet reflections on their memory. We will hopefully trust in the future that our friendship may grow brighter with our years, and cease, if it must cease then, only with our lives."

In 1864 he had written, "I think we both of us have vitality enough to enjoy many happy years even in this vale of tears; but then we must occupy it together. For

"'When true hearts lie withered,
And fond ones are gone,
Oh, who would inhabit
This bleak world alone?'"

There was a partial change in his tone four years later, when he wrote, "I think with you that we ought not to live so much asunder. Our time is now dwindled to a span; and why should we not *together* see the sinking sun go brightly down on the evening of our day? What a blessed thing it would be to realize that dream of Cuba I named to you when we last met!"

In 1870 Oakes determined to retire from business, and Forrest wrote to him from Macon, Georgia,—

"I am glad to hear you are about to close your toils in the 'Old Salt House' and give your much-worn mind and body the quiet repose they need. In this way you will receive a new and happy lease of life, enlarge your sphere of usefulness to your friends, and be a joy to yourself in giving and taking kindnesses. I look forward with a loving impatience to the end of my professional engagements this season, that I may repair to Philadelphia, there to effect a settlement of such comforting means as shall make the residue of your life glide on in ceaseless ease. Do not, I beg you, let any pride or sensitiveness stand in the way of this my purpose. It is a debt which I owe to you for the innumerable kindnesses I have experienced at your hands, and for your unwearied fidelity to all my interests."

Oakes rejected the proposition, though keenly feeling how generous and beautiful it was. Argument and persuasion from friendly lips, however, at length overcame his repugnance, and the noble kindness—so uncommon and exemplary among friends in our hard grasping time—was finally as gratefully accepted as it was gladly bestowed. This gift was the most effective stroke of real acting that ever came from the genius of the player. Taken in connection with his traits of generous sweetness and his clouded passages of ferocious hate, it reveals a character like one of those barbaric kings who loom gigantic on the screen of the past, dusky and explosive with the ground passions of nature, but wearing a coronet of royal virtues and blazing all over with the jewelry of splendid deeds. It shows in him such a spirit in daily life as would enable him to utter on the stage with no knocking rebuke of memory the proud words of the noble Roman:—

"When Marcus Brutus grows so covetous
To lock his rascal counters from his friends,
Be ready, gods, with all your thunderbolts,
Dash him to pieces."

To anticipate here the sequel and earthly close of the friendship of Forrest and Oakes would be to detract too much from the proper interest of the last chapter of this biography. The story may well be left for the present as it stands at this point, where a half-century of unfaltering love and service was repaid not only by a heart full of gratitude but also with a munificent material Philadelphia, there to effect a settlement of such comforting means as shall make the residue of your life glide on in ceaseless ease."

When the hand that wrote these tender words had been nigh four years mouldering in the tomb the survivor was heard to say, "Every year, every month, every day, I more and more appreciate his noble qualities and miss more and more his precious companionship. And I would, were it in my power, bring him back from the grave to be with me as long as I am to stay."

In ending this chapter of the friendships of Forrest, the justice of history requires a few words more. For there are several names of friends, who were long very dear to him and to whom he was very dear, which should be added to those set down above. The reason why no account of their relationship has been embodied here, is simply that the writer had not knowledge of any incidents which he could so narrate as to make them of public interest. Yet the friendships were of the most endeared character, full of happiness, and never marred or clouded. The names of the Rev. Elias L. Magoon, Colonel John W. Forney, and Mr. James Rees should not be omitted in any list of the friends of Edwin Forrest. And still more emphatic and conspicuous mention is due to that intimate, affectionate; and sustained relation of trust and love with Daniel Dougherty, on which the grateful actor and man set his unquestionable seal in leaving him a bequest of five thousand dollars and making him one of the executors of his will and one of the trustees of his estate.

Chapter XX.

Place and Rank of Forrest as a Player— The Classic, Romantic, Natural, and Artistic Schools of Acting

Forrest being the most conspicuous and memorable actor America has produced, it is desirable to fix the place and rank which belong to him in the history of his profession. To do this with any clearness or with any authority we must first penetrate to the central characteristics of each of the great schools of acting, illustrate them by some examples, and explain his relation to them.

Omitting the consideration of comedy and confining our attention to tragedy, the most familiar distinction in the styles of dramatic representation is that which divides them into the two schools called Classic and Romantic or Ancient and Modern. But this enumeration is altogether insufficient. It needs to be supplemented by two other schools, namely, the Natural and the Artistic.

The antique theatres of Greece and Rome stood open in the air unroofed to the sky, and were so vast, holding from ten thousand to two hundred thousand spectators, that the players in order not to be belittled and inaudible were raised on the high cothurnus and wore a metallic mask whose huge and reverberating mouth augmented the voice. The word persona is derived from *personare*, to sound through. Dramatis personæ originally meant masks, and only later came to denote the persons of the play. The conditions suppressed all the finer inflections of tone and the play of the features. The actor had to depend for his effects on measured declamation, imposing forms and attitudes, slow and appropriate movements, simple pictures distinctly outlined and set in bold relief. The characters principally brought forward were kings, heroes, prophets, demi-gods, deities. It was the stately representation of superhuman or exalted personages, full of exaggerated solemnity and pomp both in bearing and in speech. All this naturally arose from the circumstances under which the serious drama was developed,—the audience a whole population, the player at a distance from them, in the scenery of surrounding sea and mountains and the overhanging heaven. The traditions of the Classic School came directly down to the subsequent ages and gave their mould and spirit to the modern theatre. They have been kept up by the long list of all the great conventional tragedians in their stilted pose and stride and grandiose delivery, until the very word theatrical has come to signify something overdone, unreal, turgid, hollow, bombastic.

But when, from the sixteenth to the eighteenth century, in Italy, Spain, Germany, France, and England, the drama revived and asserted itself in such an extended and deepened popular interest,—when the theatres were built on a smaller scale adapted for accurate seeing and hearing, and the actors and the stage were brought close to the limited and select audience,—when the plays, instead of dealing mainly with sublime themes of fate and the tragic pomp and grandeur of monarchs and gods, began to depict ordinary mortal characters and reflect the contents of real life,—the scene changed from an enormous amphitheatre where before a city of gazers giants stalked and trumpeted, to a parlor where a group of ladies and gentlemen exhibited to a company of critical observers the workings of human souls and the tangled plots of human life. The buskins were thrown off and the masks laid aside, the true form and moving displayed, living expression given to the features, and the changing tones of passion restored to the voice. Then the mechanical in acting gave way to the passionate; the Classic School, which was statuesque, receded, and the Romantic School, which was picturesque, advanced.

The Classic School modulates from the idea of dignity. Its attributes are unity, calmness, gravity, symmetry, power, harmonic severity. Its symbol is the Greek Parthenon, whose plain spaces marble images people with purity and silence. The Romantic School modulates from the idea of sensational effect. Its attributes are variety, change, excitement, sudden contrasts, alternations of accord and discord, vehement extremes. Its symbol is the Christian Cathedral, whose complicated cells and arches palpitate as the strains of the organ swell and die within them trembling with sensibility and mystery. The ancient tragedian represented man as a plaything of destiny, sublimely helpless in the grasp of his own doings and the will of the gods. The chief interest was in the evolution of the character, which had but one dominant chord raised with a cunning simplicity through ever-converging effects to a single overwhelming climax. The modern tragedian impersonates man as now the toy and now the master of his fate, a creature of a hundred contradictions, his history full of contrasts and explosive crises. The chief interest is in the complications of the character and the situations of the plot so combined as to keep the sympathies and antipathies in varying but constant excitement. The vices of the former school are proud rigidity and frigidity, pompous formality and mechanical bombast. The vices of the latter school, on the other hand, are incongruity, sensational extravagance, and affectation. The Classic virtue is unity set in relief, but a mathematical chill was its fault. The Romantic virtue is variety set in relief, but its bane was inconsistency. The true tone of the heart, however, and the breathing warmth of life which it brings to the stage more than atone for all its defects and excesses.

The Romantic School early began to branch in two directions. In one it degenerated into that Melodramatic Medley which, although it has a nameless herd of followers, does not deserve to be called a school, because it has no system and is but instinct and passion let loose and run wild. In the other direction, joining with the traditional stream of example from its Classic rival, the Romantic issued in what should be named the Natural School. So the Classic School, too, forked in a double tendency, one branch of which led to death in an icy formalism and slavish subserviency to empiric rules, while the other led to the perfecting of vital genius and skill in the rounded fulness of truth; not truth as refracted in crude individualities but as generalized into a scientific art. This higher result of the double issue of the Classic School, joined with the higher result of the double issue of the Romantic School, constitutes the Artistic School. The Natural School is to be defined as having merely an empiric foundation, in it the contents of human nature and their modes of manifestation being grasped by intuition, instinct, observation, and practice, with no commanded insight of ultimate principles. The Artistic School, on the contrary, has a scientific foundation, in it the materials and methods being mastered by a philosophical study which employs all the means of enlightenment and inspiration systematically co-ordinated and applied.

Betterton was a noble representative of the classic style with a large infusion of the romantic and the natural and with a strong determination towards the artistic. Garrick had less of the first two and more of the third and fourth. In the history of the British stage Garrick is an epochal mark in the progressive displacement of theatricality by nature. He ridiculed the noisy mechanical declamation of the stage and introduced a quiet conversational manner. He agreed with the suggestion of his friend Aaron Hill that Shakspeare, judging from his wise directions to the players in *Hamlet*, must himself have been a fine actor, but in advance of the taste of his time. Quin, Young, Kemble, Conway, and Vandenhoff were examples of the classic type of acting, while Barton Booth, Mossop, and Spranger Barry exemplified the more passionate and impulsive romantic type. Macklin was a bold and intelligent though somewhat coarse and hard representative of the Natural School. Cooper and Cooke, each of whom had a personality of great original power, veered between the three preceding schools, with a large and varying element of each one infused in their impersonations. But the fullest glory of the Romantic School was seen in Edmund Kean, the coruscations of whose meteoric genius blazed out equally in the sensational feats of the melodramatic and in the profound triumphs of the natural. In France, Lekain, Talma, and

Lemaître moved the stiff traditions of their art many degrees towards the simplicity and the free fire of truth, released the actor from his stilts, and did much to humanize the strutting and mouthing stage-ideal transmitted by tyrannic tradition.

The Classic and the Romantic School each had its separate reign. The Melodramatic offshoot of the latter also had and still has its prevalence, yielding its mushroom crops of empiric sensationalists. But in the historic evolution of the art of acting there must come a complete junction of two great historic schools in one person. The plebeian Lekain, a working goldsmith, was not bred in the laps of queens, as Baron said an actor ought to be; but, as Talma declared of him, Nature, a nobler instructress than any queen, undertook to reveal her secrets to him. And he broke the fetters of pedantry, repudiated the sing-song or monotonous chant so long in vogue, and brought the unaffected accents of the soul on the stage. Living, however, in the very focus of monarchical traditions and habits, subject to every royal and aristocratic influence, he could not establish in the eighteenth-century-theatres of France the true Democratic School of Nature. This was necessarily left for America and the nineteenth century. Edwin Forrest was the man. By his burning depth and quick exuberance of passion, his instinctive and cultivated democracy of conviction and sentiment, his resolute defiance of old rules and customs, and his constant recurrence to original observation of nature, it was easy for him to master the Romantic School, while the spirit and mode of the Classic School could not be difficult for one of his proud mind, imposing physique, and severe self-possession. The intense bias he caught from Kean in the melodramatic direction and the lofty bias imparted to him by Cooper in the stately antique way were supplemented, first, by his wild strolling experiences and training in the West and South, secondly, by his patient self-culture and studies at the prime fountain-heads of nature itself. In addition to this, he rose and flourished in the midst of the latest and ripest development of all the unconventional institutions and influences of the most democratic land and people the world has yet known. And so he came to represent, in the history of the drama, the moment of the fusion of the

Classic and Romantic Schools and their passage into the Natural School. As the founder of this school in the United States he has been followed by a whole brood of disciples,—such as Kirby, Neafie, Buchanan, and Proctor,—who have reflected discredit on him by imitating his faultiness instead of reproducing his excellence.

Substantially intellectual, impassioned, profoundly ambitious, with flaming physical energies, with a very imperfect education, and few social advantages, Forrest was early thrown into the company of men who had great natural force of mind, and were frank and generous, but comparatively unpolished in taste and reckless in habits, leading a life of free amusement, conviviality, and passion often exploding in frenzied jealousies, rages, duels, deaths. He resisted the temptations that would have proved fatal to him, as they did to so many of his fellows, kept his self-respect, and faithfully studied and aspired to something better. He was exposed to the widest extremes of praise and abuse,—petted without bounds and assailed without measure. He kept his head unturned by either extravagance, though not uninjured, and swiftly sprang into a vast and intense popularity. But under the circumstances of the case—his burning impulsiveness and exuberant energy and lack of early culture, his tempestuous associates, and the general rawness or sensational eagerness of our population at that time—he would have been a miracle if his acting had not been marred with faults, if he had not been extravagant in displays of muscle and voice, if he had not been in some degree what his hostile critics called a melodramatic actor. Yet even then there were excellences in his playing, virtues of sincerity, truthfulness, intelligence, electric strokes of fine feeling, exquisite touches of beauty, confluences of light and shade, sustained unity of design, which justified the admiration and gave ground for the excessive eulogies he received. In melodrama the action is more physical than mental, the exertions of the actor blows of artifice to produce an effect rather than strokes of art to reveal truth. But in this sense Forrest always, even in his crudest day, was more tragic than melodramatic, his efforts explosions of the soul through the senses rather than convulsions of the muscles,—vents of the mind and glimpses of the spirit rather than contortions of the person, limbs, voice, and face. And he went steadily on, reading the best books, studying himself and other men, scrutinizing the unconscious acting of all kinds of persons in every diversity of situation, sedulously trying to correct errors, outgrow faults, gain deeper insight, and secure a fuller and finer mastery of the resources of his art.

Consequently his career was a progressive one, and in his latest and mentally best days he gave impersonations of the loftiest and most difficult characters known in the drama which have hardly been surpassed. The prejudices against him as a strutting and robustious ranter who shivered the timbers of his hearers and tore everything to tatters were largely unwarranted at the outset, and for every year afterwards were a gross wrong. In the time of his herculean glory with the Bowery Boys it may be true that his fame was bottomed on the great lower classes of society, and made its strongest appeals through the signs he gave of muscle, blood, and fire; yet there must have been wonderful intelligence, pathos, and beauty, as well as naked power, to have commanded, as his playing did at that early day, the glowing tributes paid to him by Irving, Leggett, Bryant, Chandler, Clay, Conrad, Wetmore, Halleck, Ingraham, Lawson, and Oakes. He always had sincerity and earnestness. His audiences always felt his entrance as the appearance of a genuine man among the hollow fictions of the stage. His soul filled with power and passion by nature, without anything else was greater than everything else could be without this. A celebrated English actress generously undertook to train a young beginner, who was yet unknown, to assume higher parts. Tutoring her in the rôle of a princess neglected by the man she loved, the patroness could not get the pupil to make her concern appear natural. "Heaven and earth!" she exclaimed. "Suppose it real. Suppose yourself slighted by the man you devotedly loved. How would you act then in real life?" The hopeless reply was, "I? I should get another lover as quickly as I could." The instructress saw the fatal, fatal defect of nature. She shut the book and gave no more lessons. Nature must supply the diamond which art polishes.

The youthful Forrest not only had nature in himself, but he was a careful student of nature in others. He used to walk behind old men, watching every movement, to attain the gait and peculiarities of age. He visited hospitals and asylums, and patiently observed the phases of weakness and death, the features and actions of maniacs. His reading was a model of precision and lucidity in the extrication of the sense of the words. One of his earlier critics said, "He grasps the meaning of a passage more firmly than any actor we know. He discloses the idea with exactness, energy, and fulness, leaving in this respect nothing to be desired. His recitation is as clear as a mathematical demonstration." He had also an exquisite tenderness of feeling and utterance which penetrated the heart, and a power of intense mournfulness or delicious sadness which could always unseal the eyes of the sensitive. He studied the different forms of actual death with such minute attention that his stage deaths were so painfully true as to excite repugnance while they compelled admiration. The physical accompaniments were too literally exact. He had not yet learned that the highest artistic power lowers and absorbs the minor details in its broad grasp and conspicuous portrayal of the whole. The Natural School, as a rule, does not enough discriminate between the terror that paralyzes the brain and the horror that turns the stomach. In the part of Virginius, Forrest for some years had the hollow blade of the knife filled with a red fluid which, on the pressure of a spring as he struck his daughter, spurted out like blood following a stab. A lady fainted away as he played this scene in Providence, and, feeling that the act was artifice, and not art, he never afterwards repeated it. So it was nature, and not art, when Polus, the Roman tragedian, having to act a part of great pathos secretly brought in the urn the ashes of his own son. In distinction equally from artifice and from nature, art grasps the essential with a noble disregard of the accidental, and finely subordinates what is particular to what is general.

The Classic School modulates from the idea of grandeur or dignity; its aim is to set unity in relief, and its attribute is power in repose. The Romantic School modulates from the idea of effectiveness; its aim is to set the contrasts of variety in relief, and its attribute is power in excitement. The Natural School modulates from the idea of sincerity; its aim is to set reality in relief, exhibiting both unity in variety and variety in unity, and its attribute is alternation of power in repose and power in excitement, according to the exigencies of character and circumstance. The Artistic School modulates from the idea of truth; its attributes are freedom from personal crudity and prejudice, liberation of the faculties of the soul and the functions of the body, and an exact discrimination of the accidental and the individual from the essential and the universal; and its aim is to set in relief in due order and degree every variety of character and experience, every style and grade of spiritual manifestation, not as the workings of nature are made known in any given person however sincere, but as they are generalized into laws by a mastery of all the standards of comparison and classification. Sincerity is individual truth, but truth is universal sincerity. "Why do you enact that part in *Macbeth* as you do?" asked a friend of Forrest. "Because," he replied, "that is the way I should have done it had I been Macbeth." Ah, but the question is not how would a Forrestian Macbeth have done it, but how would a Macbethian Macbeth do it? The sincere Natural School of acting is hampered by the limiting of its vision to the reflections of nature in the refracting individuality of the actor. The true Artistic School purifies, corrects, supplements, and harmonizes individual perceptions by that consensus of averages, or elimination of the personal equation, which dispels illusions and reveals permanent principles.

Forrest stands at the head, of the Natural School as its greatest representative, with earnest aspirations and efforts towards that final and perfect School whose threshold he thoroughly crossed but whose central shrine and crown he could not attain. He attained a solitary supremacy in the Natural School, but could not attain it in the Artistic School, because he had not in his mind grasped the philosophically perfected ideal of that School, and did not in his preliminary practices apply to himself its scientifically systematized drill. His ideal and drill were the old traditional ones, based on observation, instinct, and empirical study, modified only by his originality and direct recurrence to nature. But Nature gives her empirical student merely genuine facts without and sincere impulses within. She yields essential universal truths and principles only to the student who is equipped with rectifying tests and a generalizing method. Destitute of this, both theoretically and practically, Forrest wanted that clearness and detachment of the spiritual faculties and the physical articulations, that consummated liberty and swiftness of thought and feeling and muscular play, which are absolutely necessary to the perfect actor. He was so great an artist that he gave his pictures background, foreground, proportion, perspective, light and shade, gradations of tone, and unity; but he fell short of perfection, because carrying into every character too much of his own individuality, and not sufficiently seizing their various individualities and giving their distinctive attributes an adequate setting in the refinements of an intellectualized representation of universal human nature.

The perfect artist—such an one as Delsarte was—will build a form of character in the cold marble of pure intellect and then transfuse it with passion till it blushes and burns. He will also reverse the process, seize the spiritual shape born flaming from intuitive passion, change it into critical perception, and deposit it in memory for subsequent evocation at will. This is more than nature: it is art superimposed on nature. Garrick, Siddons, Talma, Rachel, Salvini, Forrest, were natural actors, and, more, they were artists. But the only supreme master of the Artistic School known as yet, whose theoretic ideal and actual training were perfect, was the great dramatic teacher François Delsarte.

Nature is truth in itself. But it is the ideal operation of truth that constitutes art. Acting, like all art, is truth seen not in itself, but reflected in man. It should not exhibit unmodified nature directly. It should hold up the mirror of the human soul and reveal nature as reflected there. It is a Claude Lorraine mirror of intellectual sympathy, softening, shading, toning,— just as Shakspeare says, begetting a temperance which gives smoothness to everything seen. The fights of the gladiators and the butcheries of the victims in the Roman amphitheatre were not acting, but reality. The splendor of art was trodden into the mire of fact. The error, the defect, the exaggeration in the acting of Forrest, so far as such existed, was that sometimes excess of nature prevented perfection of art. If certainly a glorious fault, it was no less clearly a fault.

But as he advanced in years this fault diminished, and the polish of art removed the crudeness of nature. Step by step the tricks into which he had been betrayed revealed themselves to him as distasteful tricks, and the sturdy impetuous honesty of his character made him repudiate them. Too often in his earlier *Lear* he gave the impression that he was buffeting fate and fortune instead of being buffeted by them; but slowly the spiritual element predominated over the physical one, until the embodiment stood alone in its balanced and massive combination of sublimated truth, epic simplicity, exquisite tenderness, and tragic strength. So his young Damon was greatly a performance of captivating points and electrical transitions, stirring the audience to fever-heats of fear and transport. No one who saw his wonderful burst of passion when he learned that his slave had slain the horse that was to carry him to the rescue of his friend and hostage—no one who saw his reappearance before the block, stained and smeared with sweat and dust, crazed and worn, yet sustained by a terrible nervous energy— could say that in any class of passion he ever witnessed a truer or a grander thing. But the conception was rather of a hot-blooded knight of the age of chivalry than of a contemplative, resolute, symmetrical Greek senator. Gradually, however, the maturing mind of the actor lessened the mere tumult of sensational excitement, and increased and coordinated the mental and moral qualities into a classical and climacteric harmony. One of the most striking evidences of the progressive artistic improvement of Forrest was the change in his delivery of the celebrated lament of Othello, 'Farewell the tranquil mind.' He used, speaking it in a kind of musical recitative, to utter the words "neighing steed" in equine tones, imitate the shrillness of "the shrill trump," give a deep boom to the phrase "spirit-stirring drum," and swell and rattle his voice to portray "the engines whose rude throats the immortal Jove's dread clamors counterfeit." He learned to see that however effective this might be as elocution it was neither nature nor art, but an artificiality; and then he read the passage with consummate feeling and force, his voice broken with passionate emotion but not moulded to any pedantic cadences or flourishes. And yet it must be owned that after all his sedulous study and great growth in taste, his too strong individuality would still crop out sometimes to mar what else had been very nigh perfect. For instance, there was, even to the last, an occasional touch of vanity that was repulsive in those displays of voice which he would make on a favorite sonorous word. In the line of the Gladiator, "We will make Rome howl for this," the boys would repeat as they went homeward along the streets his vociferous and exaggerated downward slide and prolongation of the unhappy word *howl*. And the same fault was conspicuous and painful in the word *royal*, where Othello says,—

"'Tis yet to know,
(Which, when I know that boasting is an honour,
I shall promulgate,) I fetch my life and being
From men of royal siege."

Despite this and other similar flaws, however, he had an intense sincerity and force of nature, a varied truth blent in one consistent whole of grand moral effectiveness, that place him high among the most extraordinary players. His youthful Gladiator and Othello were as impetuous, volcanic, and terrible as any of the delineations of Frederick Lemaître. His mature Coriolanus had as imperial a stateliness, as grand a hauteur, as massive a dynamic pomp, as were ever seen in John Philip Kemble. His aged Lear was as boldly drawn and carefully finished, as fearfully powerful in its general truth, and as wonderfully tinted, toned, shaded, and balanced in its details, as any character-portrait ever pictured by David Garrick. In the various parts he played in the successive periods of his career he traversed the several schools of his art,—except the last one, and fairly entered that,—and displayed the leading traits of them all, the lava passion of Kean, the superb pomposity of Vandenhoff, the statuesque kingliness of Talma, the mechanically studied effects of Macready. His great glory was "magnanimous breadth and generosity of manly temperament." His faults were an occasional slip in delicacy of taste, inability always to free himself from himself, and the grave want of a swift grace and lightness in the one direction equal to his ponderous weight and slowness in the other. Thus, while in some respects he may be called the king of the Natural School, he must be considered only a striking member, and not a model, of the Artistic School. After his death his former wife, Mrs. Sinclair, who was in every way an excellent judge of acting, and could not be thought biased in his favor, was asked her opinion of him professionally. She replied, "He was a very great artist. In some things I do not think he ever had an equal; certainly not in my day. I do not believe his Othello and his Lear were ever surpassed. His great characteristics as an actor were power and naturalness." In illustration of this judgment the following anecdote, told by James Oakes, may be adduced:

"I was visiting my friend in Philadelphia, and went to the theatre to see his Virginius. He had said to me at sunset, 'I feel like acting this part to-night better than I ever did it before;' and accordingly I was full of expectation. Surely enough, never before in his life had I seen him so intensely grand. His touching and sublime pathos made not only women but sturdy men weep audibly. As for myself, I cried like a baby. I observed, sitting in the pit near the stage, a fine-looking old gentleman with hair as white as snow, who seemed entirely absorbed in the play, so much so that the attention of Forrest was drawn to him, and in some of the most moving scenes he appeared acting directly towards him. In the part where the desperate father kills his daughter the acting was so vivid and real that many ladies, sobbing aloud, buried their faces in their handkerchiefs and groaned. The old gentleman above alluded to said, in quite a distinct tone, 'My God, he has killed her!' Afterwards, when Virginius, having lost his reason, comes upon the stage and says, with a distraught air, 'Where is my daughter?' utterly absorbed and lost in the action, the old man rose from his seat, and, looking the player earnestly in the face, while the tears were streaming from his eyes, said, 'Good God, sir, don't you know that you killed her?' After the play Forrest told me that when he saw how deeply affected the old gentleman was he came very near breaking down himself. He esteemed it one of the greatest tributes ever paid him, one that he valued more than the most boisterous applause of a whole audience."

The following critical notice of the histrionic type and style of Forrest is from the gifted pen of William Winter, whose dramatic criticisms in the New York "Tribune" for the past ten years have been marked by a knowledge, an eloquence, an assured grasp and a conscientiousness which make them stand out in refreshing contrast to the average theatrical commenting of the newspaper press. Making a little allowance for the obvious antipathy and sympathy of the writer, the article is both just and generous:

"Mr. Forrest has always been remarkable for his iron repose, his perfect precision of method, his immense physical force, his capacity for leonine banter, his fiery ferocity, and his occasional felicity of elocution in passages of monotone and colloquy. These features are still conspicuous in his acting. The spell of physical magnetism that he has wielded so long is yet unbroken. The certainty of purpose that has always distinguished him remains the same. Hence his popular success is as great as ever. Strength and definiteness are always comprehensible, and generally admirable. Mr. Forrest is the union of both. We may liken him to a rugged old castle, conspicuous in a landscape.

"The architecture may not be admired; but the building is distinctly seen and known. You may not like the actor, but you cannot help seeing that he is the graphic representative of a certain set of ideas in art. That is something. Nay, in a world of loose and wavering motives and conduct, it is much. We have little sympathy with the school of acting which Mr. Forrest heads; but we know that it also serves in the great educational system of the age, and we are glad to see it so thoroughly represented. But, while Mr. Forrest illustrates the value of earnestness and of assured skill, he also illustrates the law of classification in art as well as in humanity. All mankind—artists among the rest—are distinctly classified. We are what we are. Each man develops along his own grade, but never rises into a higher one. Hence the world's continual wrangling over representative men,—wrangling between persons of different classes, who can never possibly become of one mind. Mr. Forrest has from the first been the theme of this sort of controversy. He represents the physical element in art. He is a landmark on the border-line between physical and spiritual power. Natures kindred with his own admire him, follow him, reverence him as the finest type of artist. That is natural and inevitable. But there is another sort of nature,—with which neither Mr. Forrest nor his admirers can possibly sympathize,—that demands an artist of a very different stamp; that asks continually for some great spiritual hero and leader; that has crowned and uncrowned many false monarchs; and that must for ever and ever hopelessly pursue its ideal. This nature feels what Shelley felt when he wrote of 'the desire of the moth for the star, of the night for the morrow.' To persons of this order—and they are sufficiently numerous to constitute a large minority—Mr. Forrest's peculiar interpretations of character and passion are unsatisfactory. They see and admire his certainty of touch, his profound assurance, his solid symmetry. But they feel that something is wanting to complete the artist. But enough of this. It is pleasanter now to dwell upon whatever is most agreeable in the veteran's professional attitude. Mr. Forrest is one of the few thorough and indefatigable students remaining to the stage. He has collected the best Shaksperean library in America. He studies acting with an earnest and single-hearted devotion worthy of all honor, worthy also of professional emulation. Every one of his personations bears the marks of elaborate thought. According to the measure of his abilities, Mr. Forrest is a true and faithful artist; and if, as seems to us, the divine spark be wanting to animate and glorify his creations, that lack, unhappily, is one that nearly all artists endure, and one that not all the world can supply."

And now it is left to show more clearly and fully, while doing justice to what Forrest was in his own noble School of Nature, how he fell short in that other School of Art which is the finest and greatest of all.

The voice of Forrest, naturally deep, rich, and strong, and developed by constant exercise until it became astonishingly full and powerful, ministered largely to the delight of his audiences and was a theme of unfailing wonder and eulogy to his admirers. It may not be said which is the most important weapon of the actor, the chest and neck, the arm and hand, the face and head, or the voice; because they depend on and contribute to one another, and each in its turn may be made the most potent of the agents of expression. But if the primacy be assigned to any organ it must be to the central and royal faculty of voice, since this is the most varied and complex and intellectual of all the channels of thought and emotion. A perfected voice can reveal almost everything which human nature is capable of thinking or feeling or being, and not only reveal it, but also wield it as an instrument of influence to awaken in the auditor correspondent experiences. But for this result not only an uncommon endowment by nature is necessary, but likewise an exquisite artistic training, prolonged with a skill and a patience which finally work a revolution in the vocal apparatus. Only one or two examples of this are seen in a generation. The Italian school of vocalization occasionally gives an instance in a Braham or a Lablache. But such perfection in the speaking voice is even rarer than in the singing. Henry Russell, whose reading and recitative were as consummate as his song, and played as irresistibly on the feelings, had a voice of perhaps the most nearly perfect expressive power known in our times. He could infuse into it every quality of experience, color it with every hue and tint of feeling, every light and shade of sentiment. To speak in illustrative metaphor, he could issue it at will in such a varying texture and quality of sound, such modified degrees of softness or hardness, energy or gentleness, as would suggest bolts of steel, of gold, of silver, or of opal; waves of velvet or of fire; ribbons of satin or of crystal. His organism seemed a mass of electric sensibility, all alive, and, in response to the touches of ideas within, giving out fitted tones and articulations through the whole diapason of humanity, from the very *vox angelica* down to the gruff basses where lions roar and serpents hiss. This is a result of the complete combination of instinctive sensibility in the mind and developed elocutionary apparatus in the body. The muscular connections of the thoracic and abdominal structures are brought into unity, every part playing into all the parts and propagating every vibration or undulatory impulse. At the slightest volition the entire space sounding becomes a vital whole, all its walls, from the roof of the mouth to the base of the inside, compressing and relaxing with elastic exactitude, or yielding in supple undulation so as to reveal in the sounds emitted precisely the tinge and energy of the dominant thought and emotion. Then the voice appears a pure mental agent, not a physical one. It seems to reside in the centre of the breath, using air alone to articulate its syllables. Commanding, without any bony or meaty quality, both extremes,—the thread-like diminuendo of the nightingale and the stunning crash of the thunderbolt,—it gives forth the whole contents of the man in explicit revelation.

This perfection of the Italian School has been confined to the lyric stage. Perhaps the nearest examples to it on the dramatic stage were Edmund Kean for a short time in his best period, and Forrest and Salvini in our own day. Forrest had it not in its complete finish. He grew up wild, as it were, on a wild continent, where no such consummate training had ever been known. Left to himself and to nature, he did everything and more than everything that could have been expected. But *perfection* of voice, a detached vocal mentality which uses the column of respiratory air alone as its instrument, sending its vibrations freely into the sonorous surfaces around it, he did not wholly attain. His voice seemed rather by direct will to employ the muscles to seize the breath and shape and throw the words. He could crash it in sheeted thunder better than he could hurl it in fagoted bolts, and he loved too much to do it. In a word, his voice lacked, just as his character did, the qualities of intellectualized spirituality, ethereal brilliancy, aerial abstraction and liberty from its muscular settings and environment. Had these qualities been fully his in body and soul, in addition to what he was, he would have been the unrivalled paragon of the stage. The fibres of the backbone and of the solar plexus were too much intertangled with the fibres of the brain, the individual traits in him were too closely mixed with the universal, for this. But nevertheless, as it was, his voice was an organ of magnificent richness and force for the expression of the elemental experiences of humanity in all their wide ranges of intelligence, instinct, and passion. It could do full justice to love and hate, scorn and admiration, desire, entreaty, expostulation, remorse, wonder, and awe, and was most especially effective in pity, in command, and in irony and sarcasm. His profound visceral vitality and vigor were truly extraordinary. This grew out of an athletic development exceptionally complete and a respiration exceptionally deep and perfect. When Forrest under great passion or mental energy spoke mighty words, his vocal blows, muffled thunder-strokes on the diaphragmatic drum, used to send convulsive shocks of emotion through the audience. The writer well remembers hearing him imitate the peculiar utterance of Edmund Kean in his most concentrated excitement. The sweet, gurgling, half-smothered and half-resonant staccato spasms of articulation betokened the most intense state of organic power, a girded and impassioned condition as terrible and fascinating as the muscular splendor of an infuriated tiger. The voice and elocution of Forrest were all that could be expected of nature and a culture instinctive, observational, and intelligent, but irregular and without fundamental principles. What was wanting was a systematic drill based on ultimate laws and presided over by a consummate ideal, an ideal which is the result of all the traditions of vocal training and triumphs perfected with the latest physiological knowledge. Then he could have done in tragedy what Braham did in song. Braham sang, "But the children of Israel went on dry land." He paused, and a painful hush filled the vast space. Then, as if carved out of the solid stillness, came the three little words, "through the sea." The breath of the audience failed, their pulses ceased to beat, as all the wonder of the miracle seemed to pass over them with those accents, awful, radiant, resonant, triumphant. He sat down amid the thunder of the whole house, while people turned to one another wiping their eyes, and said, Braham!

If the voice is the soul of the drama, facial expression is its life. In the latter as in the former Forrest had remarkable power and skill, yet fell short of the perfection of the few supreme masters. He stood at the head of the Natural School whose representatives achieve everything that can be done by a genuine inspiration and laborious study, but not everything that can be done by these conjoined with that learned and disciplined art which is the highest fruit of science applied in a systematic drill. Imitatively and impulsively, with careful study of nature in others, and with sincere excitement of his own faculties of thought and feeling, he practised faithfully to acquire mobility of feature and a facile command of every sort of passional expression. He succeeded in a very uncommon yet clearly limited degree. The familiar states of vernacular humanity when existing in their extremest degrees of intensity and breadth he could express with a fidelity and vigor possible to but few. His organic portraitures of the staple passions of man were exact in detail and stereoscopic in outline,—breathing sculptures, speaking pictures. Pre-eminently was this true in regard to the basic attributes and ground passions of our nature. His Gladiator in his palmiest day of vital strength was something never surpassed in its kind. Every stroke touched the raw of the truth, and it was sublime in its terribleness. At one moment he stood among his enemies like a column of rock among dashing waves; at another moment the storm of passion shook him as an oak is shaken by the hurricane. And when brought to bay his action was a living revelation, never to be forgotten, of a dread historic type of man,—the tense muscles, the distended neck, the obstructed breath, the swollen arteries and veins, the rigid jaws, the orbs now rolling like the dilated and blazing eyes of a leopard, now white and set like the ferocious deathly eyes of a bull, while smothered passion seemed to threaten an actual explosion of the whole frame. It was fearful, but it was great. It was nature at first hand. And he could paint with the same clear accuracy the sweeter and nobler phases of human nature and the higher and grander elements of experience. His expressions of domestic affection, friendship, honesty, honor, patriotism, compassion, valor, fortitude, meditation, wonder, sorrow, resignation, were marked by a delicate finish and a pronounced distinctness of truth seldom equalled. For example, when in Virginius he said to his motherless daughter, "I never saw you look so like your mother in all my life," the pensive and effusive tenderness of his look and speech irresistibly drew tears. When he said to her, "So, thou art Claudius's slave!" the combination in his utterance of love for her and ironic scorn for the tyrant was a stroke of art subtile and effective beyond description. And when, in his subsequent madness, he exhibited the phases of insanity from inane listlessness to raving frenzy, when his sinews visibly set as he seized Appius and strangled him to death, when he sat down beside the corpse and his face paled and his eyes glazed and his limbs slowly stiffened and his head dropped in death,—his attitudes and movements were a series of vital sculptures fit to be photographed for immortality.

Still, after every eulogy which can justly be paid him, it must be said that he remained far from the complete mastership of his art in its whole compass. Neither in conception nor execution did he ever grasp the entire range of the possibilities of histrionic expression. Had he done this he would not have stood at the head of the spontaneous and cultivated Natural School, but would have represented that Artistic School which practically still lies in the future, although its boundaries have been mapped and its contents sketched by François Delsarte. For instance, the feat performed by Lablache after a dinner at Gore House, the representation of a thunder-storm simply by facial expression, was something that Forrest would never have dreamed of undertaking. Lablache said he once witnessed, when walking in the Champs Élysées with Signor de Begnis, a distant thunder-storm above the Arc de Triomphe, and the idea occurred to him of picturing it with the play of his own features. He proceeded to do it without a single word. A gloom overspread his countenance appearing to deepen into actual darkness, and a terrific frown indicated the angry lowering of the tempest. The lightnings began by winks of the eyes and twitchings of the muscles of the face, succeeded by rapid sidelong movements of the mouth which wonderfully recalled the forked flashes that seem to rend the sky, while he conveyed the notion of thunder in the shaking of his head. By degrees the lightnings became less vivid, the frown relaxed, the gloom departed, and a broad smile illuminating his expressive face gave assurance that the sun had broken through the clouds and the storm was over.

By a Scientifically Artistic School of acting is not meant, as some perversely understand, a cold-blooded procedure on mechanical calculations, but a systematic application of the exact methods of science to the materials and practice of the dramatic art. It means an art of acting not left to chance, to caprice, to imitation, to individual inspiration, or to a desultory and indigested observation of others and study of self, but based on a comprehensive accurately formulated knowledge of the truths of human nature and experience, and a perfected mastery of the instruments for their expression. To be a worthy representative of this school one must have spontaneous genius, passion, inspiration, and mimetic instinct, and a patient training in the actual exercise of his profession, no less than if he belonged to the Classic, the Romantic, or the Natural School; while in addition he seizes the laws of dramatic revelation by analysis and generalization, and gains a complete possession of the organic apparatus for their display in his own person by a physical and mental drill minute and systematic to the last degree. The Artistic School of acting is the Classic, Romantic, and Natural Schools combined, purified, supplemented and perfected by adequate knowledge and drill methodically applied.

Human nature has its laws of manifestation as well as every other department of being. These laws are incomparably more elusive, obscure, and complicated than those of natural philosophy, and therefore later to gain formulation; but they are not a whit less real and unerring. The business of the dramatic performer is to reveal the secrets of the characters he represents by giving them open manifestation. Acting is the art of commanding the discriminated manifestations of human nature. If not based on the science of the structure and workings of human nature it is not an art, but mere empiricism, as most acting always has been.

Delsarte toiled forty years with unswerving zeal to transform the fumbling empiricism of the stage into a perfect art growing out of a perfect science. He was himself beyond all comparison the most accomplished actor that ever lived, and might, had he pleased, have raised whirlwinds of applause and reaped fortunes. But, with a heroic abnegation of fame and a proud consecration to the lonely pursuit of truth, he refused to cater to a public who craved only amusement and would not accept instruction; and he died comparatively obscure, in poverty and martyrdom. He mastered the whole circle of the sciences and the whole circle of the arts, and synthetized and crowned them all with an art of acting based on a science of man as comprehensive as the world and as minute as experience. It is to be hoped that he has left works which will yet be published in justification of his claim, to glorify his valiant, neglected, and saintly life, and to enrich mankind with an invaluable bequest.

Every form has its meaning. Every attitude has its meaning. Every motion has its meaning. Every sound has its meaning. Every combination of forms, attitudes, motions, or sounds, has its meaning. These meanings are intrinsic or conventional or both. Their purport, value, rank, beauty, merit, may be exactly determined, fixed, defined, portrayed. The knowledge of all this with reference to human nature, methodically arranged, constitutes the scientific foundation for dramatic representation. Then the art consists in setting it all in free living play. The first thing is a complete analysis and synthesis of the actions and reactions of our nature in its three divisions of intelligence, instinct, and passion; mind, heart, and conscience; mentality, vitality, and morality. The second thing is a complete command of the whole apparatus of expression, so that when it is known exactly what the action of each muscle or of each combination of muscles signifies, the actor may have the power to effect the requisite muscular adjustment and excitation. The first requisite, then, is a competent psychological knowledge of the spiritual functions of men, with a sympathetic quickness to summon them into life; and the second, a correspondent knowledge of anatomy and physiology applied in a gymnastic drill to liberate all parts of the organism from stiffness and stricture and unify it into a flexible and elastic whole.

The aesthetic gymnastic which Delsarte devised, to perfect the dramatic aspirant for the most exalted walks of his profession, was a series of exercises aiming to invigorate the tissues and free the articulations of the body, so as to give every joint and muscle its greatest possible ease and breadth of movement and secure at once the fullest liberty of each part and the exactest co-operation of all the parts. When the pupil had finished this training he was competent to exemplify every physical feat and capacity of man. Furthermore, this teacher arranged certain gamuts of expression for the face, the practice of which would give the brows, eyes, nose, and mouth their utmost vital mobility. He required his pupil to sit before a mirror and cause to pass over his face, from the appropriate ideas and emotions within, a series of revelatory pictures. Beginning, for instance, with death, he ascended through idiocy, drunkenness, despair, interest, curiosity, surprise, wonder, astonishment, fear, and terror, to horror; or from grief, through pity, love, joy, and delight, to ecstasy. Then he would reverse the passional panorama, and descend phase by phase back again all the way from ecstasy to despair and death. When he was able at will instantly to summon the distinct and vivid picture on his face of whatever state of feeling calls for expression, he was so far forth ready for entrance on his professional career.

Such is the training demanded of the consummate actor in that Artistic School which combines the excellences of the three preceding schools, cleansing them of their excesses and supplying all that they lack. The prejudice against this sort of discipline, that it must be fatal to all charm of impulse and fire of genius and reduce everything to a frigid construction by rule, is either a fruit of ignorance or an excuse of sloth. It is absurd to suppose that the perfecting of his mechanism makes a man mechanical. On the contrary it spiritualizes him. It is stiff obstructions or dead contractions in the organism that approximate a man to a marionette. It is a ridiculous prejudice which fancies that the strengthening, purification, and release of the organism from all strictures destroys natural life and replaces it with artifice, or banishes the fresh play of ideas and the surprising loveliness of impulse by reducing the divine spontaneity of passion to a cold set of formulas. The Delsartean drill so far from preventing inspiration invites and enhances it by preparing a fit vehicle and providing the needful conditions. The circulating curves of this aesthetic gymnastic, whose soft elliptical lines supersede the hard and violent angles of the vulgar style of exercise, redeem discordant man from his fragmentary condition to a harmonious unity. He is raised from the likeness of a puppet towards the likeness of a god. Then, as the influence of thought and feeling breathes through him, the changes of the features and the movement of the limbs and of the different zones of the body are so fused and interfluent that they modulate the flesh as if it were materialized music.

"Unmarked he stands amid the throng,
In rumination deep and long,
Till you may see, with sudden grace,
The very thought come o'er his face,
And by the motion of his form
Anticipate the bursting of the storm,
And by the uplifting of his brow
Tell where the bolt will strike, and how."

Delsarte could shrink and diminish his stature under the shrivelling contraction of meanness and cowardice or suspicion and crime until it seemed dwarfed, or lift and dilate it under the inspiration of grand ideas and magnanimous passions until it seemed gigantic. Every great emotional impulse that took possession of him seemed to melt all the parts of his organism together into a flexible whole with flowing joints, and then his fused movements awed the spectator like something supernatural. His face was a living canvas on which his soul painted the very proportions and hues of every feeling. His voice in tone and inflection took every color and shadow of thought and emotion, from the sombre cloudiness of breathing awe to the crystalline lucidity of articulating intellect. His inward furnishing even richer than the outward, he would sit down at the piano, in a coarse overcoat, in a room with bare walls, and, as he acted and sang, Œdipus, Agamemnon, Orestes, Augustus, Cinna, Pompey, Robert le Diable, Tartuffe, rose before you and revealed themselves in a truth that appeared almost miraculous and with a power that was actually irresistible. It was no reproduction by painful mimicry of externals, no portrayal by elaborate delineation of details. It was positive identification and resurrection. It was a real recreation of characters in their ensemble of being, and an exhibited reanimation of them by imaginative insight and sympathetic assimilation. Most wonderful of all, and greatest proof of the value of his system of drill, he could catch a part by inspiration and go through it under the automatic direction of nature, and then deliberately repeat the same thing by critical perception and conscious free will; and he could also reverse the process with equal ease, critically elaborate a rôle by analysis and then fix it in the nerves and perform it with inspired spontaneity. This was the highest possible exemplification of the dramatic art by the founder of its only perfect school. It was Classic, because it had the greatest dignity, repose, power, symmetry, unity. It was Romantic, because it was full of the most startling effects, beautiful combinations, sudden changes, surprising contrasts, and extremes. It was Natural, because exactly conformed to the facts of experience and the laws of truth as disclosed by the profoundest study of nature. And above all it was supremely Artistic, because in it intuition, instinct, inspiration, intelligence, will, and educated discipline were reconciled with one another in co-operative harmony, and everything was freely commanded by conscious knowledge and not left to accident.

True art is never merely an imitation of nature, nor is it ever purely creative; but it is partly both. It arises from the desire to convert conceptions into perceptions, to objectify the subjective in order to enhance and prolong it in order to revive it at will and impart it to others. Art, Delsarte said, with his matchless precision of phrase, is feeling passed through thought and fixed in form. Grace without force is the product of weakness or decay, and can please none save those whose sensibilities are drained. Force without grace is like presenting a figure skinned or flayed, and must shock every one who has taste. But grace in force and force in grace, combined impetuosity and moderation, power revealed hinting a far mightier power reserved,— this is what irresistibly charms all. This is what only the very fewest ever attain to in a superlative degree; for it requires not only richness of soul and spontaneous instinct, and not only analytic study and systematic drill, but all these added to patience and delicacy and energy. The elements of the art of acting are the applied elements of the science of human nature; yet on the stage those elements are different from what they are in life in this respect, that there they are set in relief,—that is, so systematized and pronounced as to give them distinct prominence. That is precisely the difference of art from nature. It heightens effect by the convergence of co-operative agencies. For instance, when the variations of the speech exactly correspond with the changes of the face, how the effect of each is heightened! Aaron Hill said of Barton Booth that the blind might have seen him in his voice and the deaf nave heard him in his visage. Of those in whom nature is equal he who has the greater art will carry the day, as of those in whom art is equal he who has more nature must win. A lady said, "Had I been Juliet to Garrick's Romeo, so ardent and impassioned was he, I should have expected that he would come up to me in the balcony; but had I been Juliet to Barry's Romeo, so tender, so eloquent and seductive was he, that I should certainly have gone down to him." In these two great actors nature and art contended which was stronger. Very different was it with Macready and Kean, of whom it used to be said respectively, "We go to see Macready in *Othello*, but we go to see Othello in Kean." The latter himself enjoyed, and delighted others by showing, a transcript of the great world of mankind in the little world of his heart. The former,—

"Whate'er the part in which his cast was laid,
Self still, like oil, upon the surface played."

Talma said, "In whatever sphere fate may have placed a man, the grand movements of the soul lift him into an ideal nature." The greatness of every truly great actor shows itself in the general ideal which characterizes his embodiments. If he has any originality it will publish itself in his ideal. Now, while most actors are not only second-rate but also second-hand, Forrest certainly was original alike as man and as player. He was distinctively original in his personality, original and independent in the very make of his mind and heart. This subtle and striking originality of personal mind and genius was thoroughly leavened and animated by a distinctively American spirit, the spirit generated by the historic and material conditions of American society and the social and moral conditions of American life. He was original by inherited idiosyncrasy, original by his natural education, original by his self-moulding culture which resented and shed every authoritative interference with his freedom and every merely traditional dictation. He was original in going directly to the instructions of nature and in drawing directly from the revelations of his own soul. He was original in a homely intensity of feeling and in a broad and unsophisticated intelligence whose honest edges were never blunted by hypocritical conformity and falsehood. And above all, as an actor he exhibited his originality in a bearing or style of manners thoroughly democratic in its prevailing scornful repudiation of tricks or squeamish nicety, and a frank reliance on the simplicity of truth and nature in their naked power.

Now, precisely the crowning originality of Forrest as an actor, that which secures him a distinctive place in the historic evolution of the drama, is that while the ideals which the great actors before him impersonated were monarchical, aristocratic, or purely individual, he embodied the democratic ideal of the intrinsic independence and royalty of man. Give Kemble only the man to play, he was nothing; give him the paraphernalia of rank and station, he was imposing. But Forrest, a born democrat, his bare feet on the earth, his bare breast to his foes, his bare forehead to the sky, asked no foreign aid, no gilded toggery, no superstitious titles, to fill the theatre with his presence and thrill the crowd with his spell. There is an egotism of pride, an egotism of vanity, an egotism of conceit, all of which, based in want of sympathy, are contemptible and detestable. Forrest was remarkable for a tremendous and obstinate pride, but not for vanity or conceit; and his sympathy was as deep and quick as his pride, so that he was not an odious egotist, although he was imperious and resentful. Many distinguished players have trodden the stage as gentlemen, Forrest trod it as man. The ideal of detachment, authority throned in cold-blooded self-regard, has been often set forth. He exhibited the ideal of identification, burning honesty of passion and open fellowship. The former is the ideal of polite society. The latter is the ideal of unsophisticated humanity. Macready asserted himself in his characters; Forrest asserted his characters in himself. Both were self-attached, though in an opposite way, and thus missed the perfect triumph which Delsarte achieved by abolishing self and always resuscitating alive in its pure integrity the very truth of the characters he essayed. Macready as an elaborate and frigid representative of titular kings was a sovereign on the boards, a subject elsewhere. Forrest as an inborn representative of natural kings was a true sovereign in himself everywhere and always. The former by his petulant pride and pomp and his drilled exemption from the sway of the sympathies secured the approval of a sensitive and irritable nil *admirari* class. The latter by the fulness of his sympathies and his impassioned eloquence as the impersonator of oppressed races awakened the enthusiastic admiration of the people. A line, said an accomplished critic, drawn across the tops of the points of Macready would leave Forrest below in matters of mechanical detail, but would only cut the bases of his pyramids of power and passion. His chief roles were all embodiments of the elemental vernacular of man in his natural virtue and glory rather than in the refinements of his choicest dialects. Always asserting the superiority of man to his accidents, he will be remembered in the history of the theatre as the greatest democrat that up to his time had ever stepped before the footlights. He had sincerity, eloquence, power, nobleness, sublimity. His want was beauty, charm. The epithets strong, fearless, heroic, grand, terrible, magnificent, were fully applicable to him; but the epithets bright, bold, brisk, romantic, winsome, graceful, poetic, were inapplicable. In a word, though abounding in the broad substance of sensibility and the warm breath of kindness, he lacked the artificial polish and finesse of etiquette; and consequently the under-current of dissent from his fame, the murmur of detraction, that followed him, was the resentment of the conventional society whose superfine code he neglected and scorned.

For this penalty, however, his sincerity and direct reliance on nature gave ample compensation in making him capable of inspiration. Adherence to mere authority, tradition, usage, or dry technicality, is fatal to inspiration. This carried to an extreme makes the most cultivated player a mere professor of postures and stage mechanics,— what the French called Macready, "*L'artiste de poses*." There is an infinite distance from such external elaboration to the surprises of feeling which open the soul directly upon the mysteries of experience, send cold waves of awe through the nerves, and convert the man into a sublime automaton of elemental nature, or a hand with which God himself gesticulates. Then the performing of the actor originates not on the volitional surfaces of the brain, but in the dynamic deeps of the spine and ganglia, and he seems an incarnate fagot of thunderbolts. Then the gesticulating arms, modulated by the profound spinal rhythms, become the instruments of a visible music of passion mysteriously powerful. For all action from the distal extremities of the nerves is feverish, twitching, anxious, with a fidgety and wasteful expensiveness of force, while action from their central extremities is steady, harmonious, commanding, economical of force. The nearer to the central insertions of the muscles the initial impulses take effect, so much the longer the lines they fling, the acuter the angles they subtend, the vaster the segments they cut and the areas they sweep. This suggests to the imagination of the spectator, without his knowing the meaning or ground of it, a godlike dignity and greatness. Forrest was full of this hinted and hinting power. It was the secret of his loaded personality and magnetizing port.

Art, while it is not pure and simple nature, is not anything substituted for nature nor anything opposed to nature. It is something superadded to nature, which gives the artist supreme possession of his theme, supreme possession of himself, and supreme command of his treatment of his theme. It is a grasped generalization of the truths of nature freed from all coarse, crude, and degrading accidents and details. The consummate artist, observing the principle or law, does everything easily; but the empiric, striving at the facts, does everything laboriously. Feeling transmuted into art by being passed through thought and fixed in form is transferred for its exemplification from the volition of the cerebral nerves to the automatic execution of the spinal nerves. This does not exhaust the strength, but leaves one fresh after apparently the most tremendous exertions. Talma, Rachel, Salvini, did not sweat or fatigue themselves, however violent their action seemed. But when feeling, instead of having been passed through thought and fixed in form for automatic exhibition, is livingly radiated into form by the will freshly exerted each time, the exaction on the forces of the organism is great. It is then nature in her expensiveness that is seen, rather than the art which secures the maximum of result at the minimum of cost. It was said of Barry that excessive sensibility conquered his powers. His heart overcame his head; while Garrick never lost possession of himself and of his acting. The one felt everything himself before he made his audience feel it; the other remained cool, and yet by his kingly self-control forced his audience to feel so much the more. In his direct honest feeling and exertion Forrest paid the expensive penalty of the Natural School. After playing one of his great parts he was drenched with perspiration and blew off steam like a locomotive brought to rest. The nerves of his brain and the nerves of his spinal cord were insufficiently detached in their activities, too much mixed. Like Edmund Kean, he was as a fusee, and the points of the play were as matches; at each electric touch his nerve-centres exploded and his muscles struck lightning. But in the Artistic School the actor is like a lens made of ice, through which the sunbeams passing set on fire whatever is placed in their focus. The player who can pour the full fire of passion through his soul while his nerves remain firm and calm has command of every power of nature, and reaches the greatest effects without waste. But, as Garrick said,—

"In vain will Art from Nature help implore
When Nature for herself exhausts her store."

The essence of the dramatic art or the mission of the theatre is the revelation of the different grades of character and culture as exhibited in the different styles of manners, so that the spectator may assign them their respective ranks. The skill or bungling of the actor is shown by the degrees of accuracy and completeness which mark his portraitures. And the predominant ideal illustrated in his impersonations betrays the personal quality and level of the actor himself.

Manners are the index of the soul, silently pointing out its rank. All grades of souls, from the bottom of the moral scale to its top, have their correspondent modes of behavior which are the direct expression of their immediate states and the reflex revelation of their permanent characters. The principle of politeness or good manners is the law of the ideal appropriation of states of feeling on recognition of their signs. Sympathy implies that when we see the sign of any state in another we at once enter into that state ourselves. Interpreting the sign we assimilate the substance signified and thus reflect the experience. Everything injurious, repulsive, or petty, pains, lessens, and lowers us. The signs of such states therefore are to be withheld. But the signs of beautiful, powerful, sublime, and blessed states enrich and exalt those who recognize them and reproduce their meaning. The refinement and benignity of any style of manners are measured by the largeness and purity of the sphere of sympathetic life it implies, the generosity of its motives, and the universality of its objects. The vulgarity and odiousness of mariners are measured by the coarseness of sensibility, the narrow egotism, the contracted sphere of consciousness implied by them. Thus the person who fixes our attention on anything spiritual, calming, authoritative, charming, or godlike, confers a favor, ideally exalting us above our average level. But all such acts as biting the nails or lips, taking snuff, smoking a cigar, talking of things destitute of interest save to the vanity of the talker, are bad manners, because they draw attention from dignified and pleasing themes and fasten it to petty details, or inflict a severe nervous waste on the sensibility that refuses to be degraded by obeying their signals.

Now, there are four generic codes of manners in society, each of which has its specific varieties, and all of which are exemplified in the theatre,—that great explicit "mirror of fashion and mould of form." First there is the code of royal manners, the proper behavior of kings. Kings are all of one family. They are all free, neither commanding one another nor obeying one another, each one complete sovereign in himself and of himself. The sphere of his personality is hedged about by a divinity through which no one ventures to peep for dictation or interference. In his relations with other persons the king is not an individual, but is the focal consensus of the whole people over whom he is placed, the apex of the collective unity of the nation. He therefore represents public universality and no private egotism. He is the symbol of perfect fulfilment, wealth, radiance, joy, peace. By personal will he imposes nothing, exacts nothing, but like the sun sheds impartially on all who approach him the golden largess of his own complete satisfaction. That is the genuine ideal of royal manners. But the actual exemplification is often the exact opposite,—an egotistic selfishness pampered and maddened to its very acme. Then the formula of kingly behavior is the essence of spiritual vulgarity and monopolizing arrogance, namely, I am the highest of all: therefore every one must bow to me and take the cue from me! Then, instead of representing the universal, to enrich all, he degrades the universal into the individual, to impoverish all. Then his insolent selfishness at the upper extreme produces deceit and fawning at the lower extreme. The true king imposes nothing, asks nothing, takes nothing, though all is freely offered him, because he radiates upon all the overflow of his own absolute contentment. Every one who sees him draws a reflected sympathetic happiness from the spectacle of his perfect happiness.

The formula expressed in truly royal manners is, I am so contented with the sense of fulfilment and of universal support that my only want is to see every one enjoying the same happiness! In a perfected state the formula of democratic manners will be identical with this. For then the whole community with its solidarity of wealth and power will be the sustaining environment whereof each individual is a centre. But as yet the private fortune of each man is his selfishly isolated environment; and the totality of individual environments bristles with hostility, while every one tries to break into and absorb the neighboring ones.

The code of aristocratic manners, too, has its sinister or false development as well as its true and benign development. The formula which, in its ungenial phase, it is forever insinuating through all its details of demeanor, when translated into plain words is this: I am superior to you and therefore command you! But the real aristocratic behavior does not say the inferior must obey the superior. On the contrary, it withholds and suppresses the sense of superiority, seems unconscious of it, and only indirectly implies it by the implicit affirmation, I am glad to be able to bless and aid you, to comfort, strengthen, and uplift you! The false aristocrat asserts himself and would force others to follow his lead. The true aristocrat joyously stoops to serve. His motto is not, I command, but Privilege imposes obligation.

The twofold aspect of plebeian manners affords a repetition of the same contrast The plebeian manner, discontented and insurrectionary, says, You are superior to me, and therefore I distrust, fear, and hate you! The plebeian manner, submissive and humble or cringing, says, I am inferior to you, and therefore beseech your favor, deprecating your scorn! But the plebeian manner, honest, manly, and good, says, You are superior to me, and I am glad of it, because, looking up to you with admiration and love, I shall appropriate your excellence and grow like you myself!

Finally, we come to the democratic code of manners. The spurious formula for democratic behavior is, I am as good as you! This is the interpretation too common in American practice thus far. It is the insolent casting off of despotic usages and authorities, and the replacing them with the defiant protest of a reckless independence. I am as good as you, and therefore neither of us will have any regard or deference for the other! But in wide distinction from this impolite and harsh extreme, the formula implied in the genuine code of democratic manners is, We are all amenable to the same open and universal standard of right and good, and therefore we do not raise the question at all of precedency or privilege, of conscious superiority or inferiority, but we leave all such points to the decision of the facts themselves, and are ready indifferently to lead or to follow according to the fitness of intrinsic ranks!

Spurious democracy would inaugurate a stagnant level of mediocrities, a universal wilderness of social carelessness and self-assertion. Genuine democracy recognizes every man as a monarch, independent and supreme in his interior personal sphere of life, but in his social and public life affiliated with endless grades of superiors, equals, and inferiors, all called on to obey not the self-will of one another, or of any majority, but to follow gladly the dictates of those inherent fitnesses of inspiration from above and aspiration from below which will remain eternally authoritative when every unjust immunity and merely conventional or titular rank has been superseded. This was the style of manners, this was the implied formula of behavior, embodied by Forrest in all his great roles. Affirming the indefeasible sovereignty of the individual, he neither wished to command nor brooked to obey other men except so far as the intrinsic credentials of God were displayed in them. Thus, under every accidental or local diversity of garb and bearing, he stood on the American stage, and stands and will stand in front there, as the first sincere, vigorous, and grand theatrical representative of the democratic royalty of man.

Chapter XXI.

Historic Evolution and Social Uses of the Dramatic Art—Genius and Relationship of the Liberal Professions—Hostility of the Church and the Theatre

In an early chapter of this biography an analysis was given of the dramatic art considered in its psychological origin and in its personal uses for those who practise it. This was done that, the reader might have in his mind the data requisite for forming an intelligent judgment on the life which was to be recorded and criticised in the succeeding chapters. But in order to appreciate the just moral rank and worth or the legitimate influences of such a life in its public sphere and aspects, it is necessary to understand something of the historic development and the social uses of the dramatic art,—its distinctive genius in contrast with the other liberal professions, and the natural effects on those who witness its exhibitions. The subject teems with matters of unsuspected importance, and its discussion will yield surprising revelations.

Before attempting to trace the rise of the Theatre and its struggle with its rivals, we must get an adequate idea of the essential substance of the art practised in the Theatre. For this purpose it will be necessary to approach the subject from a point of view different from those generally taken hitherto.

The practice of the dramatic art rests on the differences of men amidst their similarities. The whole intercourse of life really consists at bottom in a complex and subtle game of superiorities and inferiorities, full of tests and tricks, surprises, pains, and pleasures. Every one who has not been regenerated from the selfish heritage of history into a saintly disinterestedness is constantly impelled by a desire far deeper than his consciousness to wish to see others inferior to himself, to feel himself superior to others, and to get this relative estimate accepted in the imaginations of the bystanders. Human experience in society is a half-open and half-disguised battle for advantage and precedence, inward and outward, private and public, filled with attacks and defences, feints and traps, overtures and defiances, every conceivable sort of coarse or exquisite artifices for winning victories and inflicting defeats in the occult and endless game of personal comparisons.

All comparisons imply standards of judgment. There are eight of these standards,—four primary, and four secondary. The first of the primary standards of excellence by which we try ourselves and one another is bodily health, strength, grace, and beauty. The second is moral character, goodness of disposition, purity and nobility of motives. The third is genius and talent, brilliant powers of creative or beneficent action. The fourth is technical acquisitions, artificial learning and accomplishments, charm of manners, skill in doing attractive or important things. The first of the secondary standards by which men are estimated in society is hereditary rank or caste, birth, blood, and title. The second is official place and power, social position and influence. The third is reputation and fame. The fourth is wealth. All these standards, it will be observed, find their ultimate meaning and justification in the idea of adaptedness for the fulfilment of the ends of life. Good is the fruition of function. The highest personal beauty and genius imply the greatest fitness for the fulfilment of function. Wealth is a material means, fame an ideal means, for the fruition of life.

But obviously there are distinctions of grade and of authority among these standards, and he who ranks high when judged by one of them may rank low according to another. It is the continual subterfuge of self-love at the inner tribunal to evade the tests of the standards that are unfavorable to it, and to court comparison by those whose verdicts are surest to be flattering. On the contrary, in testing other people, the egotistic and ungenerous person instinctively applies the tests most likely to insure condemnation. This is the first vice of introspection and of mutual criticism.

The second evil is setting lower standards above higher ones, attributing more importance to apparent or conventional claims than to real and intrinsic merits. In all ignoble circles, among all men and women of low sensibility or of shallow routine, there is a steady tendency to estimate self and associates by factitious and hollow standards of good instead of the inherent and substantial standards. More deference is paid to dress and title than to form and bearing. Privileged descent and station are put before genius and worth. Deeds and deserts go to the wall in favor of shows and professions. Riches are esteemed above character. What others think of us is deemed of greater account than what God knows of us. This turning topsy-turvy of the standards for the judging of men is what fills the world with the confusion, wickedness, and misery of a rivalry that is as detestable as it is pernicious and sad.

No two men can be exactly alike. Inequality is the universal law of existence. Without it there would be an unbroken monotony and stagnation equivalent to death. It is the play of greater and lesser, fairer and homelier, wiser and foolisher, higher and lower, better and worse, richer and poorer, older and younger, that intersperses the spectacle of being and the drama of experience with the glimpsing bewitchments of surprise, the ravishing zest of pursuit and success, the everlasting freshness and variety of desire, change, suspense, risk, and adventure. The essential moral struggle for superiority, in which all men are forever engaged whether they know it or not, is the divine method of enchanting them with life and luring them forward. It would be an unmixed good, covering all intercourse with the charm of a theatrical beauty and spicing every day with the relish of a religious game, were it not for the predominant vices of fraud, envy, and tyranny surreptitiously introduced into the contest. Did all men regard their superiors with joyous reverence and aspiration, their equals with co-operative friendship, and their inferiors with respectful kindness and help, never of their own will raising the question as to who shall command or lead and who obey or follow, but leaving these points to be decided by the laws in the manifest fitness of things, the unlikenesses and inequalities which now set them at wretched odds would be the very conditions of their orchestral harmony and the chief elements of their converging delight. The general genius of the dramatic art, purified and perfected, tends directly to bring this about, while the special genius of each of the other liberal professions stands obstructively in the way. For the spirit of each of the other professional classes segregates it from general humanity into a privileged order whose members maintain its prerogatives by means of a necessary peculium for which their special interest makes them desire that the rest of the world shall depend exclusively on them. But the dramatic spirit freely enters the soul and lot of every condition of men for the sympathetic interpretation and intuitive feeling of their contents. The genuine temper of this art, separate from the depraved usages of society, would teach men to honor and copy those above, to love and blend with those around, and to example and help those beneath. Then the strong and cunning would no longer take selfish advantage of their power and hold the masses of mankind in subjection by the triple bond of interest, fraud, and fear. According to the principles of universal order, life would everywhere become a mutual partnership of teaching and blessing from above and learning and following from below, a spontaneous giving and taking of all good things in justice and love without violence and without money. Every one rendering his share of service in the co-operation of the whole, no portion would be victimized by the rest, but in the perfected equity and good will there would be abundant wealth for all and plenty of leisure for each.

There are certain select places or focal buildings in which all the secrets of human nature are revealed and the arts of power grasped. Each of these has become the centre of a profession which has employed the knowledge and skill given by its social position to secure certain advantages to its members and make the rest of mankind pay tribute to them in return for the benefits they claim to bestow or in acknowledgment of the authority they claim to possess. These are the ruling or leading classes of the world, in whose hands the keys of power are lodged. The advantages of their situation where all the secrets of experience are uncovered and all the arts of influence developed, their exemption from the hardships of physical drudgery, their varied training in mental accomplishments and cumulative inheritance of superiority, place the rest of mankind in subjection to them. Had they disinterestedly used their power to enlighten and free other men, to educate and enrich other men, the world would long since have been redeemed. They have used it to secure special advantages for themselves, making others their servants on whose uncompensated blood and sweat they live. Therefore the strife and crime and poverty and misery of the world continue.

All forms of experience are laid bare in the palace of the king. Every variety of character and of fortune is stripped of its disguises there; every mode of behavior, every rank of motives, exposed in its true signals. The lynx-eyed and selfish scrutiny which has its seat there utilizes this knowledge, and the rules and methods in which ages have generalized it, to endow the imperial profession with the peculiar attributes and treasures by which they govern. The true function of the king or other ruler is to represent the whole people with his superiority of position and endowment, to warn, guide, enlighten, and bless them, using all his privileges faithfully for their service. But the reverse of this has been his prevailing vice in all times. He has used his power for his own selfish luxury and the emoluments of his favorites, making government less a means of universal welfare and more a means of exalting the few at the cost of the many. The game of comparisons, instead of being made a divine play of variety and surprise in service and love, has been made a cruel engine for the oppression of the weak by the strong. The individual interest of the governing class has perverted its universal function into a personal privilege. The genius of the palace is selfish luxury in irresponsible power.

In the tent of the general the same revelation of the secrets of human nature is made as in the royal palace, and the skill in assuming authority and in controlling men thereby acquired is embodied in the military profession, which is always the right arm of the imperial profession. The genuine office of the martial profession is to raise the protecting and executive energy of a nation to its maximum by scientific precision of movement and unquestioning obedience to command. Its twofold vice has been the fostering of a love of war or reckless spirit of conquest, and the making of the officer a martinet and of the soldier a puppet utterly mindless of right or wrong in their blind obedience to orders. An army is a machine of destruction wielded by the most consummate art the world has yet known. When that absolute obedience and that perfect discipline and that matchless devotion become intelligent and free, and are directed to beneficent ends, they will redeem the world. But thus far the genius of the military headquarters is arbitrary power in automatic drill to avenge and to destroy.

By the sick-bed, in the hospital and the asylum, all the treasures of memory are yielded up, all the mysteries of passion exposed, all the operations of the soul unshrouded before the eyes of the physician. In this knowledge, and in the ability which the accumulated experience of so many centuries has gained to assuage pain, to heal disease, and to give alleviating guidance, an immense deposit of power is placed in the hands of the medical profession. The blessed function of the profession, in its universal aspect, is to instruct the people in the laws of health and to rescue them from suffering and danger. Its interest, in its class aspect, thrives on the ills of other men. The more sickness there is, the more completely dependent on them it is for remedy, the better for their interest. The great vices of the craft have been charlatanism and quackery, the owlish wisdom of the gold-headed cane and the spectacled nose, and a helpless addicted-ness to routine and prescription. All the defects of the profession, however, are fast vanishing, all its virtues fast increasing, as under the infiltrating inspirations of science it is shedding its bigotry and pride, subordinating pathology to hygiene, repudiating its besotted faith in drugging, and freely throwing open to the whole world the special discoveries and insights it used so carefully to keep to itself as sacred secrets. This is its disinterested phase. In its selfish phase its genius is a jealous guarding of its knowledge and repute as a means of power and gain.

The arts of rule are learned, the mechanism of human nature is unveiled in all the agencies of influence that work it, perhaps even more fully in the police-office, the court-house, and the prison, than in either of the places previously named. Brought before the bar of the judge, surrounded by the imposing and terrible array of the law with its dread apparatus of inquisition and punishment, every secret of the human heart is extorted. The culprit, the hero, the high and the low, the weak and the strong, all kinds and states of men, there betray their several characteristics in their demeanor, and uncover the springs of the world in its deepest interests, passions, and plots. Thus the legal profession, manipulating the laws, sitting as umpires for the decision of the complex conflicts of men in the endless collisions of their universal struggle of hostile interests, consummate masters of every method and artifice of power, have a place nearest to the seat of government. Their hands are on the very index and regulator of public authority. Their omnipresent instinct, ever since the rise of the black-gowned confraternity, has chiefly inspired and shaped as well as administered the judicial code of society. Now, their profound knowledge of the arts of sway, their matchless skill in victory and evasion, their vast professional prerogative, have been chiefly used not to bless mankind, but to win offices, honors, and fees from them. The universal function of the lawyer is justice, the prevention or reconciliation of disputes, the teaching of men to live in harmonious equity. But his private individual and class interest is litigation, the putting of the cause of a client above the public right, the retention of his light that other men in their darkness may be forced to look to him for guidance. The genius of the law is the nursing of its own authority by preserving occult technicalities, blind submission to precedents, and the pursuit of victory regardless of right or wrong.

But the priestly profession, in the temple of religion, has penetrated more profoundly into the soul than any of the other ruling castes to seize the secrets of character and elaborate the arts of sway. Through the lattice-work of the confessional breathes the dismal murmur of the sins and miseries of men and sighs the glorious music of their aspirations. The whole reach of experience in its degradations of vice and its heights of virtue, from apathy to ecstasy, is a familiar thing to the contemplation of the priest. Confided in or feared, set apart from other men that he may study them and manage their faiths, nothing is hidden from him. Suppressing or concealing his own passions, he learns to play on those of others and mould them to his will. So Jesuitism, entrenched in the superiority of its detaching and despotic drill, holds obedience by that cold eyeball which has read human nature so deeply and so long, plucking from it the tale of its weaknesses and thus the secrets of rule. Every mystery of man and his life is revealed to him who presides in the temple, at the altar, the confessional, and the grave, and who is called in to pronounce the will of God at every crisis of experience. His style and tenure of power are more ominous, pervasive, and fatal than any other, because claiming a sanction supernatural and absolute. It plants in heaven and hell the endless lever of its hopes and fears to pry up the primitive instincts of humanity and wrench apart the natural interests of the world. The sublime office of the priesthood, in its generous and universal aspect, is to teach men the truths of morality and religion and to administer their consolations to human sorrow and doom. But, perverting this benign office, it seeks to subdue all men to itself by claiming the exclusive deposit of a supernatural revelation. Then it seeks its class interest at the cost of the interests of the whole, puts authority in the place of demonstrated truth, and persecutes dissent as the unpardonable sin. The virtues of the clerical profession are studiousness, personal purity, philanthropic works, self-sacrifice, and conscientious piety. Its vices are the hideous brood of fanaticism, intolerance, cruelty, love of power, vanity, a remorseless greed for subjecting the real interests of the present world to the fancied interests of a future one. The historic animus of priesthoods has been dictatorial superstition and bigotry, setting their own favorite dogmas above the open truths of the universe, and either superciliously pitying or ferociously hating all outside of their own narrow folds.

The next place for the revelation of the contents of human nature in all the ranges of its experience is the studio of the artist. The open and impassioned sensibility of the great artist gives him free admission to the interiors of all whom he sees, and his genius enables him to translate what is there and record it in his works. All experiences are registered in the organism, and their signals, however invisible or mystic to ordinary observers, are obvious and full of meanings to the insight of genius. Sir Godfrey Kneller declared that the eyebrow of Addison seemed to say, "You are a much greater fool than you think yourself to be, but I would die sooner than tell you so!" The magic attraction of the greatest works of art resides really in their occult revelation of the inherent ranks of the persons depicted. Their clearness or foulness, their beauty or deformity, their grace or awkwardness, their radiant joy or their squalid and obscene wretchedness, are so many hints of the degrees of good and evil in men and women,—explicit symbols of their potencies of function, their harmony or discord of powers. In their forms, proportions, attitudes, gestures, lights and shades of expression, their respective capacities for woe or bliss are ranged along the scale of human possibility. Thus, in the paintings of Rubens the whole history of voluptuousness is made transparent from the first musical breath of desire to the last lurid madness of murder. In the sculptures of Phidias the most exquisite living development into unity of all the organs and faculties of man is petrified for posterity to behold and be stimulated to the same achievement. In the statues of Buddha is clearly seen by the initiated eye the intoxicating sense of godhead in the soul, the infinite dream and entrancement of nirvana,—the molecular equilibrium of the cells of the body and the dynamic equilibrium of the atoms of consciousness. This is the charm and mystery with which art fascinates even its unwitting beholders. But its great lessons of organic ranks and potencies, of higher and lower characters and experiences, are not distinctly taught. They are only suggested for those who have the keys to interpret them. Thus they often give an idle pleasure or provoke a piquant curiosity, but yield no moral fruit, no lasting benefit. The function of the artist is revelation by inspired genius, and through this revelation to exalt the ideals, purify and expand the sensibilities, and kindle the aspirations of men while giving them a refined pleasure. His vice is the luxurious enjoyment of his gifts as a subtile ministration to self-indulgence. His class interest is not to communicate his gifts, but to secure admiration and patronage for them. It is questionable whether as yet art has not on the whole done more to unnerve and mislead than to consecrate and uplift. Its genius is sympathetic insight catering to complacence and luxury rather than prompting to edification.

All other artists, however, must yield to the dramatic performer of genius and experience as to the completeness with which he pierces the secrecy of human nature and commands its manifestations. The actor gains his knowledge of men not indirectly by ruling and making use of them, but directly by intuitive perception and mimetic intelligence and sympathy entering into all their conditions and experiences, reproducing in himself their inner states of being and the outer signs of them. Then, on the stage, he gives systematic exhibitions of the varieties of character and life for the amusement and the instruction of the public. The ideal of his art is the exemplification in living action of the grades of personalities, the contrasts of conduct, the styles of manners, so set off with appropriate foils and true standards as to cause the spectators to discriminate the rank and worth of each, be warned from the unworthy with fear and loathing, and drawn to the excellent with admiration and love. This is contagious education disguised in beguiling entertainment. Thus the genius of the drama is earnest improvement concealed in free play, edification masked in recreation.

The vice that besets the player is not selfishness, despotism, avarice, indifference, or the subserving of a class interest opposed to the general interest. He is characteristically free from such faults. His great error is using his art for ostentation and vanity merely to win applause and profit. He is tempted to sacrifice the spirit of earnestness and teaching for the spirit of sport and pleasure, playing a part simply for people to enjoy, instead of adding to this lessons for them to learn. As the church, in order to escape from its barren routine of preceptive and ceremonial repetitions, needs the dramatic spirit of reflective sympathy and living action, so the theatre, in order to escape from its too frequent emptiness and tawdry frivolity, needs the academic spirit of earnest instruction. When the dramatic spirit whose home and throne are in the theatre shall add to what it already possesses moral and religious earnestness, making the scene of its art a school for training aspirants to perfection, it will be seen to be the purest and richest spirit in the world. It will teach all to enter into the soul and fortune of each, and each to feel himself bound up in one bundle of life and destiny with all,—even as he, the Christ, who was the divinest creature that ever wore this humanized and tearful mask of clay, played the rôle of no individual ego, but impersonated collective humanity, dramatically identifying himself to the end of time with all the broken and suffering members of our race, saying, "Inasmuch as ye have done it unto one of the least of these, ye have done it unto me." The universal prevalence of that same moralized and religious dramatic spirit in all men is all that is needed for the immediate and perfect redemption of the world. Dogmatic theology, ecclesiastical polity, and sectarian mechanism do more to delay than to expedite the time.

Thus it is plain that the professions that radiate from the palace, the tent, the hospital, the tribunal, the temple, the studio, and the theatre all have vices which largely neutralize their good offices and prevent the fulfilment of their true mission, namely, the spreading of the kingdom of heaven over the whole earth in the redemption of men from ignorance, oppression, strife, and want.

There is another building, the seat of another profession, quite exempt from the evils which alloy and burden the foregoing. The academy takes all knowledge, scientifically considered, for its province; and the teaching profession administer their possession as no *peculium* of their own, but as an open and free inheritance for all. They have no class interest to foster as against the welfare of the whole.

They have no dogma of authority to impose, aside from the inherent authority of truth and right They do not wish to rule, only to teach every one self-rule. The academic spirit would break open the enclosures bristling with technical secrets, the strongholds of partial power, and dispense freedom to all instead of despotic sway to the ruler, justice to all instead of victory for the client, health to all instead of a fee to the doctor, the grace of God to all instead of a salary for the priest. The vice of the teaching class is the pedagogic dryness of routine and verbal iteration. Academic education needs to add to itself everywhere the dramatic spirit of life, that creative action of free sympathy which will supplement the preceptive word with the exemplifying deed and change the prosaic aridity for poetic freshness and bloom. It also needs the military principle of drill, or organic habits of rhythm, wherever applicable; but not to displace spontaneous intelligence and choice. It likewise needs to proclaim the religiousness of scientific truth, that every truth of morals or things is a demonstrable revelation of the will of God, and the same for all men of all lands and faiths. Then the academic profession will in itself reject the excesses and supply the defects of all the other professions, and be the one guiding class in a condition of mankind which has thrown off obsolete leading-strings. For, while the ideal state of mankind will have no despotic or selfish ruler, soldier, lawyer, doctor, or priest, it will always have a class of teaching artists and artistic teachers, men of original genius and inspiration, to refresh, enlighten, and guide their less gifted brethren. To such a class the final government of the world will be intrusted, not governing by the force of authority but by the persuasion of light. Then partisan politics, ruling by human will declared in a majority of votes, will be transmuted into social science, guiding by the will of God revealed in demonstration. Those who desire to lift themselves at the expense of others, and to live without labor by appropriating the toil of others, will dislike such a conception, and scout it as visionary. But their spirit is bad and must pass away; because Christ, or God incarnate in man, is surely one day to reign, putting every enemy under his feet and being All in all.

This millennial state might soon be ushered in if the ruling professions, instead of guarding their class privileges and keeping the rest of the world under them, sought disinterestedly to fulfil their universal functions, securing order, justice, freedom, health, virtue, piety, and education to all. But in reality the chief desire which actuates them and shapes their policy and efforts is the instinctive desire to avoid hardships and secure luxuries by governing other men and appropriating the fruits of their labor without any equitable return. This is seen now concentrated in the universal struggle for money, because the superstition of money enables its possessor to command the products of others without producing anything himself. How can this fatal spell be broken, and that condition of society be inaugurated wherein all things shall be exchanged for love alone, except labor and its products, and these be exchanged on the principle of equivalences of cost, abjuring the tyrannical fraud of profit? It can only be brought about through an increased spirit of sympathy animating an improved social science. And this is primarily the office of the dramatic principle of imaginative identification, which is to make every one feel for all others as if he were in their place.

Thus it is clear that the genuine moral work of the drama is essentially the same as that of the gospel,—to redeem men from self-love by sympathy for their kind. And yet the theatre and the church have stood askance, and the priests and the players generally been enemies. What is the origin, what the significance, what the remedy, of this quarrel between those who should be friends and co-workers? A brief historic sketch and a little human analysis will answer these questions, perhaps with some profit as well as light.

The dramatic instinct and faculty are native in man in all times and conditions. When David was afraid of his life in the house of Achish, king of Gath, "he played the madman, scrabbling on the posts of the gate and letting his spittle fall down on his beard." But a theatre is a fruit only of a high civilization, and it always reflects that civilization. In India it seems to have been at first an appanage of the palace, designed to give amusement to the king and his nobles and favorites. It presented poetic descriptions of nature, romantic pictures of life, songs, dances, and satires. In the Hindoo temples also were sometimes enacted mythological religious and mystical dramas by the priests and their assistants, less with theatrical machinery than in words and movements, representing avatars of the gods, notably the avatars of Vishnu as Rama and Krishna, supernatural adventures, transmigrations, and scenes in other worlds. In China and Japan the drama was in ancient times, as it still is, largely confined to the illustration of history, presenting in long-drawn performances minute pictures of legendary or historic personages, events, costumes, manners, and customs. But it was in Egypt, where the priesthood was so distinct a caste, so powerful an order, possessed of so much secret knowledge and mechanism, that the doctrines and ritual of religion itself were first wrought into a drama of the most sensational and appalling kind. In the depths of the temple, with pomp of numbers and dresses, with music, gorgeous and terrible scenery, artificial thunders and lightnings, heavens and hells were unveiled, the dead shown in their immortal state, celestial spirits and demons and deities were revealed, and such lessons were enforced as suited the purposes of the managers of the spectacle. It was a tool in the hands of the priests to play on the fears and hopes of the people, who were taught to regard what they saw not as anything artificial but as a vision of the supernatural. This was the drama of the cryptic church, the theatre of the priestly conclave.

In Greece, as in Egypt,—possibly derived thence,—the earliest theatre and drama were religious and secret. In the Bacchic and Eleusinian and other mysteries, the incarnation, penance, death, and resurrection of some god were represented, and in connection with the spectacle various religious and philosophical doctrines were taught in symbolic shows. Every art of influencing the imagination and the senses was here employed,—the imposing forms and gestures of the hierophant and his helpers impersonating the demiurgus and his train,—light and darkness, colors, strange noises, music, incantations, rhythmic processions, enchanting and maddening dances. But, as there was in Greece no distinct priesthood separate from the rulers and leaders of the state, the intense interest and power of this mode of impression could not remain sequestered from the people and confined to a few sacred legends. The great freedom and restless intelligence and critical personal emulation of the Greeks soon brought forth from its seclusion this fascinating and peerless method of teaching, planted it on an open stage, applied it to sacred and political subjects, to character and experience, and gave the world the first public theatre of the people. Still retaining in its best examples its original religious dignity and solemnity, it added many other qualities, developed comedy alongside of tragedy, and in its combination of ideal and satirical types and manners rendered the stage a mirror for the mimic reflection of the real scenes of human life. Thus it escaped from privacy and priestly management into publicity under the direction of a literary and political class. It was wielded for the threefold purpose of moral and religious impression, of social or party influence, and of displaying various styles of character and behavior for popular amusement and edification.

In Rome the drama was modified and varied in some particulars from its Greek model, but no new feature was added. It nearly lost its religious quality, became more exclusively social and sensational, extended its range only to profane and degrade it into the barbarity of the circus and the arena. The Greek poet dealing with the simulated woes of the soul was displaced by the Roman gladiator dealing in the real agonies of the body, and the supernal beauty of classic tragedy expired in the applauded horrors of butchery.

As the drama and the theatre in the Oriental and in the Classic world had a priestly and religious origin and character, so was it with their revival and first development in Christendom. The early Christian Church regarded the games, spectacles, and plays of the moribund civilization amidst which it arose in regenerating energy, with intense abomination, as intimately associated with and characteristic of the idolatrous pagan faith, the persecuting pagan power, and the corrupt pagan morals, against whose insidious influence and threatening array the new type of belief and life had to maintain itself. Tertullian and other distinguished Christian fathers fulminated against the actors and their associates excommunication in this world and damnation in the next. But after a while, as the young religion got established, spread among millions of adherents, and had itself a vast popular sway to uphold and extend, the love of power and the spirit of politic conformity entered into it. Seeing what a strong attraction for the public was inherent in the spectacular drama, with its costume, scenery, dialogue, and action, and what a power it possessed for insinuating persuasion and instruction, the church began to adopt its methods, modified to suit the new ideas and situation. First the bait of amusement, sport, and burlesque was thrown out to draw in and please the rabble by licensing to be held in the church the Feast of Asses, the Feast of Fools, and other like riotous and farcical mummeries borrowed with certain alterations from the pagan Saturnalia. Then, to add a serious element of edification, the priests dramatically constructed and enacted in Miracle-Plays, Mysteries, and Moralities the chief events in Scriptural history, the outlines of dogmatic theology, the lessons of practical duty, and the claims of ecclesiastical authority, seeking thus to draw the crowd and teach and drill them to obedience. The virtues and vices of men, temptation, death, judgment, were allegorized, personified, and brought on the stage to impress the rude audience. The Creation, the Flood, the Crucifixion, the Day of Judgment, were represented. God, Christ, the Virgin, angels, the devil and his imps, were shown. John Rastale, brother-in-law of Sir Thomas More, composed a Merry Interlude to serve as a vehicle of science and philosophy, explaining the four elements and describing various strange lands, especially the recently-discovered America. The characters were Nature, Humanity, Studious Desire, Sensual Appetite, a Taverner, Experience, Ignorance, and a Messenger who spoke the prologue. These plays, simple, crude, fantastic, grotesque, as they were, suited the tastes of the time, administered fun and terror to the spectators, who alternately laughed and shuddered while the meaning of the creed and the hold of its power sank deeper into their souls. There was a mixture in it of good and evil, recreation and fear, truth and superstition, fitted to the age and furnishing a transition to something better.

"When friars, monks, and priests of former days
Apocrypha and Scripture turned to plays,
The Festivals of Fools and Asses kept,
Obeyed boy-bishops and to crosses crept,
They made the mumming Church the people's rod,
And held the grinning bauble for a God."

But quite aside from all these dramatic excrescences of the church, these artifices for catering to and influencing the public, there has been always imbedded in the very substance of Christianity, ever since the great ecclesiastical system of dogmatic theology was evolved, a profound and awful tragedy, the incomparable Drama of Redemption, whose subject is the birth, life, teachings, sufferings, death, and resurrection of Christ, whose action sweeps from the creation of the world to the day of doom, whose characters are the whole human race, God and his angels, Satan and his demons, and whose explicating close opens the perfect bliss of heaven for the elect and seals the hopeless agony of hell for the damned. This is the unrivalled ecclesiastical drama whose meaning the Protestant Church makes implicit in its creed but the Catholic Church makes explicit not only in the colossal pathos and overpowering *miserere* of Passion Week, but also in every celebration of the mass, at whose infinite denouement of a dying God the whole universe might well stand aghast.

In the course of time the companies of actors who, in connection with the priests or under their permission and oversight, had played in the Mysteries and Moralities, gradually detached themselves from ecclesiastical localities and management, and, with licenses obtained from sacred and secular authority, set up on their own account, strolled from place to place, giving entertainments in public squares, at fairs, in the court-yards of inns, in the mansions of nobles, and in the palaces of royalty. Then kings and great dukes came to have their own select companies of players, who wore their livery, obeyed their orders, and ministered to their amusement and ostentation. Herein the drama was degraded from its proper dignity to be a vassal of vanity and luxury. In a masque performed at the marriage of an Italian duke in the sixteenth century, Jupiter, Juno, Apollo, Diana, Venus, and Mars appeared bringing in dishes of dainties and waiting on the guests. The immortal gods represented as servants to honor and ornament a human festival!

At length the dramatic profession, forsaking courts and inns, secured a separate home of its own, and became a guild by itself, independently established in the distinct theatre and appealing directly to the general public for support. In the secret theatre of the priests the substance of the drama, based on such legends as those of the Hindoo Krishna, the Egyptian Osiris, and the Greek Dionysus, was fiction exhibited as fact or poetry disguised as revelation. In the open theatre of the state the substance of the drama, in such examples as the Prometheus of Æschylus, was mythology, moral philosophy, or poetry represented as history. In the plays foisted on the mediaeval Christian church the dramatic substance was tradition, ceremonial, and dogma taught as religion. But now, with the rise of the educated histrionic profession, all this passed away, and in the freed theatre of the people the substance of the drama became coincident with the realities of human life, a living reflex of the experience of society. In Portugal and Spain, Lope de Vega and Calderon developed the highest flower and finish of the Mysteries and Miracle-Plays in their transition from the ecclesiastical to the social type of the drama, while in England, France, Italy, and Germany the stage became a rounded mirror of the world, reflecting human nature and conduct in their actual form, color, and motion. Then the theatrical art was rapidly developed in all its varieties,—the drama of character and fate, or tragedy; the drama of plot and intrigue, or romance; and the drama of manners, or comedy and farce. Then the theatre instinctively assumed for its whole business what its comprehensive function now is and must ever remain, yet what it has never grasped and wielded with distinct consciousness, but only blindly groped after and fumbled about,— namely, the exhibition of the entire range of the types of human character and behavior so set off with the contrasts of their foils and in the light of their standards as to make the spectators feel what is admirable and lovely and what is contemptible and odious, as the operation of the laws of destiny is made visible before them. But all who penetrate beneath mere appearances must perceive that just in the degree in which the theatre does this work it is trenching on the immediate province of the church, and the players fulfilling a function identical in moral substance with that of the priests.

The church aims directly to teach and to impress, to persuade and to command. The theatre aims directly to entertain, indirectly to teach, persuade, and impress. It often accomplishes the last three aims so much the better because of the surrendered, genial, and pleased condition of soul induced by the success of the first one. Another advantage the theatre has had over the church, in attempting to educate or exert influence, is that it does it without the perfunctory air or the dogmatic animus or repulsive severity of those who claim the tasks of moral guidance and authority as their supernatural professional office. The teachings of the theatre have also a freshness and attraction in their inexhaustible range of natural variety which are wanting to the monotonous verbal and ritualistic routine of the set themes and unchanging forms in the ecclesiastical scheme of Sunday drill. And then, finally, all natural competition of the dry, bleak pulpit with the stage becomes hopeless when the priest sees the intense sensational pleasure and impression secured for the lessons of the player by the convergent action of the fourteen-fold charm of the theatre,—namely, the charm of a happy and sympathetic crowd; the charm of ornate architectural spaciousness and brilliancy; the charm of artistic views of natural scenery; the charm of music; the charm of light and shade and color in costumes and jewelry and on figures and landscapes now illuminated and now darkened; the charm of rhythmic motion in marches and processions and dances; the charm of poetry; the charm of eloquence in word and tone and look and gesture; the charm of receiving beautiful lessons exquisitely taught; the charm of following an intricate and thickening plot to its satisfactory explication; the charm of beholding in varied exercise human forms which are trained models of strength, beauty, and grace; the charm of seeing the varieties of human characters act and react on one another; the charm of sympathy with the fortunes and feelings of others under exciting conditions rising to a climax; the charm of a temporary release from the grinding mill of business and habit to disport the faculties of the soul freely in an ideal world.

Is it not obvious that such a power as this should be utilized by the most cultivated minds in the community for the highest ends?

When in the independent theatre such a power as this arose, no longer asking favors or paying tribute, bidding with such a fearful preponderance of fascinations for that docile attention of the populace whereof the clergy had previously held a monopoly, it was no wonder that the church looked on its rival with deadly jealousy. And there was good ground for this jealousy separate from any personal interests or animosities. For *the respective ideals of life held up by the priest and the player* are diametrically opposed to each other. This is the real ultimate basis of the chronic hostility of the church and the theatre. The deepest genius of the one contradicts that of the other. The ecclesiastical ideal of life is abnegation, ascetic self-repression and denial; while the dramatic ideal of life is fulfilment, harmonic exaltation and completeness of being and function. Which of these ideals is the more just and adequate? If God made us, it would appear that the fulfilment of all the normal offices of our nature in their co-ordinated plenitude of power is his will. It is only on the theory that the Devil made us in opposition to the wisdom and wish of God, that intrinsic and sheer denial can be our duty. Lower abnegation as a means for higher fruition, partial denial for the sake of total fulfilment, are clear and rational obligations. But the idea that ascetic self-sacrifice as an end pure and simple in itself is a virtue or a means of salvation is a morbid superstition with which the church has always been diseased, but from which the theatre has always been free. Accordingly, the two institutions in their very genius, as interpreted from the narrow professional point of view, are hostile. The vices of the church have been sour asceticism, fanatical ferocity, sentimental melancholy, dismal gloom, narrow mechanical formalism and cant, and a deep hypocrisy resulting from the reaction of excessive public strictness into secret indulgence. The vices of the theatre, on the other hand, have been frivolity, reckless gayety, conviviality, and voluptuousness. But these vices have been envisaged with the virtues of quick sympathy, liberal sentiment, an ingenuous spirit of enjoyment, open docility, universal tolerance and kindliness.

Purified from its accidental corruptions and redeemed from its shallow carelessness, the theatre would have greater power to teach and mould than the church. Aside from historic authority and social prestige, its intrinsic impressiveness is greater. The deed must go for more than the word. The dogma must yield to the life. And while in the pulpit the dogmatic word is preached in its hortatory dryness, on the stage the living deed is shown in its contagious persuasion or its electric warning. Character is much more plastic to manners than to opinions. Manners descend from the top of society; opinions ascend from the bottom. This is because opinions indirectly govern the world while manners directly govern it. And the ruling class desire to maintain things as they are, that they may keep their prerogatives. Therefore they are opposed to new doctrines. But the ground masses of the people, who are ruled, desire to change the status quo for their own betterment. Now the church, representing the vested interests of traditional authority and the present condition of things, has become a school of opinions, not for the free testing and teaching of the True, but for the drill of the Established; while the theatre, in its genuine ideal, is what the church ought to be,—a school of manners, or manufactory of character.

Another superiority of the genius of the drama to the genius of theology is the freedom and largeness of the application of its method. The moral principle of the dramatic art is *disinterested sympathy animating plastic intelligence for the interpretation and free circulation of souls and lives.* It is the redemptive or enriching supplementation of the individual with society. For in order to put on a superior we must first put off self. And there is nothing nobler in the attributes of man than his ability to subdue the tyranny of old egotistic custom with new perception and impulse, and thus start on a fresh moral career endlessly varied and progressive. The theatre gives this principle a natural and universal application through the whole moral range of human life. The ecclesiastical dogmatist restricts it to a single supernatural application to the disciple of Christ, and would monopolize its influence to that one channel. Notoriously every bigot would drill the whole world in his own fixed mould, to his own set pattern, stiff, harsh, ascetic, exclusive. But the cosmopolite would see exemplified in mankind the same generous liberty and variety which prevail in nature. He would, instead of directing attention only to the sectarian type of saint, hold up all sorts of worthy ideals that each may be admired and copied according to its fitness and beauty.

The church paints the world as a sad and fearful place of probation, where redemption is to be fought for while the violent and speedy end of the entire scene is implored. The theatre regards it as a gift of beauty and joy to be graciously perfected and perpetuated. The ideal of the priest and the ideal of the actor contrast as Dominic and Pericles, or as Simeon Stylites and Haroun-al-Raschid. All the words denoting the church and its party—ecclesia, église, kirche, congregation—signify a portion selected or elected and called aside by themselves for special salvation, apart from the great whole who are to be left to the general doom. But the word theatre in its etymology implies that the world of life is something worthy of contemplation, beautiful to be gazed at and enjoyed.

The priest naturally disliked the player because he was more attractive to the public than himself. He also disliked him because disapproving his art. The very object of the drama is by its spectacle of action to rouse the faculties and excite the feelings of the assembly who regard it. But the priest would not have the passions vivified; he would have them mortified. The contemplation of the dread passion and sacrifice of Christ, the fear of sin and of death and judgment, should exclude or suppress all other passions. On the contrary, the dramatist holds to the great moral canon of all art, that perfected life is the continuous end of life, and that the setting of intelligence and emotion into ideal play, a spiritual gymnastic of the passions in mental space disentangled from their muscular connections, purifies and frees them.

The priest not only holds that the dramatic ideal of the natural fulfilment of the offices of being is opposed to the religious ideal of grace, is profane, and tends directly to ruin; he likewise, from all the prejudices of his own rigidity of mould and bigoted routine, believes that the facility and continual practice of the actor in passing from assumption to assumption and from mood to mood must be fatal to moral consistency, must loosen the fibre of character, and produce dissoluteness of soul not less than of life. This is mostly a false prejudice. Those of the greatest dramatic mobility of genius and versatile spiritual physiognomy, like Cervantes, Molière, Goethe, Schiller, Dickens, Voltaire, and the very greatest actors and actresses, like Talma, Garrick, Rachel, Siddons, had the most firm and coherent individuality of their own. Their penetrations and impersonations of others reacted not to weaken and scatter but to define and gird their own personal types of being and behavior. The dramatic type of character is richer and freer than the priestly, but not less distinctly maintained.

Another circumstance stirring a keen resentment in the church against the theatre is that it has often been attacked and satirized by it. When the divines, who had long enjoyed a monopoly of the luxurious privilege of being the censors of morals, the critics of other men, found themselves unceremoniously hauled over the coals by the actors, their vices exposed to the cautery of a merciless ridicule, their personal peculiarities caricatured, it was but human nature that they should be angry and try to put down the new censorship which with its secular vigor and universal principles confronted the ecclesiastical standard. The legal, medical, and clerical professions have often had to run the gauntlet of a scorching criticism on the stage. Herein the drama has been a power of wholesome purification; but it could not hope to escape the penalty of the wrath of those it exposed with its light and laughter. It has done much to make cant and hypocrisy odious and to vindicate true morality and devotion by unmasking false. Louis XIV said to Condé, "Why do the saints who are scandalized at Tartuffe make no complaint of Scaramouche?" Condé replied, "Because the author of Scaramouche ridicules religion, for which these gentry care nothing; but Molière ridicules themselves, and this they cannot endure." The censure and satire on the stage, concealed in the quips of fools or launched from the maxims of the noble, have often had marked effect. Jesters like Heywood and Tarleton, who were caressed by kings and statesmen, under their masks of simplicity and merriment have shot many a brave bolt at privileged pretences and wrongs and pompous imposition. The power of satire is often most piercing and most fruitful. The all-wise Shakspeare makes his melancholy Jaques say,—

"Invest me in my motley: give me leave
To speak my mind, and I will through and through
Cleanse the foul body of the infected world
If they will patiently receive my medicine."

Furthermore, the priest often has an antipathy for the player because in spite of his arrogated spiritual superiority feeling himself personally inferior to him. The preacher, rigid, hide-bound, of a dogmatic and formal cast, cannot take off the mobile, hundred-featured actor, who, on the contrary, can easily include and transcend him, caricature him, and make him appear in the most ridiculous or the most disagreeable light.

"If comprehension best can power express,
And that's still greater which includes the less,
No rank's high claim can make the player's small,
Since acting each he comprehends them all."

Molière can show up Tartuffe, Tartuffe cannot show up Molière. Therefore Tartuffe fears and hates Molière, excommunicates him, denies his body consecrated burial, and, with a sharp relish, consigns his soul to the brimstone gulf. The prevailing temper of the clerical guild towards the histrionic guild, from the first till now, has been uncharitable and unjust, intellectually unappreciative and morally repulsive. This is shown all the way from the frenzied De Spectaculis of Tertullian and the vituperative Histrio-Mastix of Prynne to the sweeping denunciation of the drama by Henry Ward Beecher, who, never having seen a play, condemns it from inherited prejudice, although himself every Sunday carrying a whole theatre into his pulpit in his own person. An English clergyman in 1792 uttered these words in a sermon on the drama: "No player or any of his children ought to be entitled to Christian burial or even to lie in a church-yard. Not one of them can be saved. And those who enter a play-house are equally certain with the players of eternal damnation. No player can be an honest man." Richard Robinson, who played Wittipol in "The Devil is an Ass" so as to win warm praise from Ben Jonson, was, at the siege of Bassinge-House, shot through the head after he had laid down his arms. A puritan named Harrison shot him, crying, "Cursed be he that doeth the work of the Lord deceitfully!" The body of the favorite Parisian actor Philippe in 1824 was refused religious rites by the priests, and his friends were so incensed that the military had to be called out to quell the riot. A kindred disturbance was narrowly escaped at the death of Talma. When the wife of Nokes, a dancing-master, had rescued Edmund Kean and his wife and children from actual starvation and lent them a room, the landlord, a Christian clergyman named Flower, said that "no theatrical people should have the room." And it is matter of fresh remembrance how the same spirit of bigotry was manifested by a Boston bishop in refusing confirmation to the universally respected and beloved Thomas Comer because he led the orchestra in a theatre, and by a New York pastor who declined to read the funeral-service over the estimable George Holland because he had been an actor.

It must be affirmed that the chief animus of the clerical profession has been the desire to be obeyed, and that this is less Christian and less amiable than the ruling spirit of the dramatic profession, which is the desire to be loved. But the real spirit which ought to reign supreme in every one is neither the desire to be obeyed nor the desire to be loved, but the desire to be harmonized with the principles of universal order, giving and taking accordingly without egotistic exactions of any kind whether dictatorial or sympathetic. And this result can only be attained by means of the dramatic art of mutual sympathetic interpretation universally applied under the guidance of moral and religious principles.

The church of Christ, in opposition to the example of its divine Founder, has been made an exclusive enclosure for a privileged class of believers. In it their prejudices are cherished and their ascetic ideal glorified and urged on all. The Saviour himself was a miracle of tolerance and inclusiveness, mingling freely with the common people, not spurning the publican, the sinner, or the harlot, but regarding all ranks in the great brotherhood of humanity with a sweet and inexhaustible kindness. There was one exception alone. Towards the bigot, the pharisee, the hypocrite, the tyrant, his scorn and indignation burned. But all other forms of man moved only his impartial love or his healing compassion. This was the divinely democratic genius of Christ, but has not been the genius of the priesthood who with arrogance and persecution have claimed to represent him. The theatre has been far more expansive in the range of its sympathies than the church. The highest dramatic genius that has ever appeared in the world, Shakspeare, shows in his works a serene charity, a boundless toleration, a genial appreciation of the widest extremes, kindred to that of God in nature and grace. His loving imagination, like the all-holding sky, embraces Trinculo, Bardolph, Poins, Falstaff, and Malvolio, as well as Bassanio, Prospero, Hamlet, Cæsar, and Lear; Audrey and Quickly, as well as Portia and Cordelia.

The first glory of the theatre is its freedom from sectarianism; and its first use is to radiate abroad this generous spirit of universality, not bigotedly limiting attention to any one province of life or any single ideal, but revealing the whole world of man in its heights and breadths and depths, exhibiting in turn every variety of ideal and doing justice to them all. "The drama," Macklin said, "should be a perfect reproduction of general nature as it passes through human life in every character, age, rank, and station." Taught this by genius, experience, and learning, it teaches the common observer how wondrously large and rich is the world of mankind. Emperors and clowns pass, saints and villains jostle, heroes and murderers meet, the divine lady and the foul virago appear and vanish,—and all the meanings and values of their traits and fortunes are laid bare to those who see and can understand. There is indeed no other revelation of the complex contents and destinies of humanity in this world so competent as that afforded in dramatic literature and the theatre. For here all is concentrated, heightened, set off, and revealed by aid of the most exquisite contrivances of art of every sort.

One of the most penetrative and wonderful but least generally appreciated of these contrivances is the explication of the good and evil or beauty and ugliness of souls and deeds, the moral worth and significance of dispositions and situations, by means of music. Rubinstein has depicted in his symphony of Ivan the Terrible the character of that frightful monster of the Russian throne. In this musical character-picture he has painted his hero in the blackest colors, revealing his hideous traits and moods by violent and spasmodic tones repulsively combined. But Mozart is the most dramatic of the composers,—the very Shakspeare of the musicians. The personages of his operas are distinctive creations, true to life. They appear to think, feel, and act in tones and combinations of tones. Each of the musical characters keeps his individuality, however the passions and scenes and events change. The features and outlines of the characters are defined or determined by the style, the phrases, the time, rhythm, range, inflections, and accompaniment. In place of this, Wagner marks his chief personages by the mannerism of repeating the same phrase with the same instruments whenever one of them reappears. In the Tannhäuser, as often as Venus enters the high chromatic violin tremolo and rhythmical whisper of the wind instruments are repeated. The artifice is profound, and its effect mysteriously impressive. The meaning of the mystery lies in the facts that the sounds of the music correspond with vibrations in our nerves, and that every quality of passion has its peculiar forms and rates of vibration. The ratios in the physical sound are parallel with other ratios in the spiritual consciousness. And so Giovanni and Leporello, Elvira and Anna, are distinguished. And so the Benediction of the Poignards and the Mass for the Dead are contrasted.

Characters are interpreted on the stage by means of their visible motions also. For the upper classes, the most dignified personages in the stately tragedy, there is a solemn pomp of bearing, and the employment of marches and processions. Everything partakes more of slowness and formality. The most heavenly human characters, or angelic visitants from another world, are indicated by floating contours and melodious lines of motion. Perfected equilibrium in the body is the sign of perfected harmony in the soul. Devils or demoniac men are suggested by dances full of excessive energy, hideous and sudden contortions, convulsive jumps and climaxes.

The central characteristic of the genuine melodrama, now nearly or quite obsolete, was its combination of musical tone and muscular movement as a method of dramatic revelation and impression. Its theme and scene lay in the middle or lower class and in a limited sphere. Thus, while the assassination of a monarch suggested a tragedy, a village murder would form the subject of a melodrama. But all the gestures and pantomime of the performers were regulated or accompanied by instrumental music played forte or fortissimo, piano or pianissimo, as the situation required. The villain was marked by an orchestral discord or crash, while lovers billed and cooed to the mellifluous breathings of the German flute. Villagers always came over a bridge at the rise of the curtain to lively music. The heroine entered to eight bars of plaintive melody. Four harsh and strongly accented bars heralded the approach of the villain. The characters struggled to hurried music, recognized one another and were surprised to chords, and crept about in caves and dark apartments to mysterious pizzicato strains. All this correspondence of sound, color, and motion works on the souls of the audience in the profoundest manner, obscurely suggestive of innumerable things beyond the reach of any clear memory and below the depths of any distinct apprehension. It stirs up that automatic region of our nature compacted of prehistoric experiences.

Few persons have any idea how closely the theatre even in its romantic extravaganzas and fairy spectacles reflects the truths of human life. It merely intensifies the effect and produces a magical impression by expanding and shrinking the measures of space and time. But all its seeming miracles are in the outer world slowly brought about in prosaic reality. The suddenness of the changes in the mimic scenes ought to open our eyes to the equal marvellousness of them in the gradual substance of history. Harlequin in his spangled vestment, with his sword of enchantment, pursuing the lovely Columbine, and always outwitting and baffling the clumsy attempts of the Clown and Pantaloon to circumvent him, is the type of how the aristocracy of genius has always snatched the sweet prizes of the world from blundering plebeianism amidst the astonishment, laughter, and rage of the bewildered bystanders, who so imperfectly comprehend the game. The relations of coexistence and sequence, the working of laws of cause and effect that preside over events in the actual world, are not altered in the theatre. It is only their measures or rates of action that are trifled with so to the amazement of the senses. Appreciating this, it is obvious that no transformation scenes on the stage can possibly equal the real ones in life itself. Mohammed, the poor factor of Kadijah, receives an inspiration, preaches a new faith, is hunted by his foes, conquers nation after nation, till a quarter of the earth exults under his crescent flag and hails him infallible prophet of Allah. Columbus conceives a thought, his frail pinnaces pierce their perilous way over the ocean, and a new world is discovered. Louis Napoleon is taken from teaching French for a livelihood in New York to be throned in the palace of the Tuileries and to inaugurate the *Exposition Universelle* surrounded by the leading monarchs of the earth. The young Rachel, haggard and ill clad, begged an influential person to obtain leave for her to appear on the stage of the Théâtre Français. He told her to get a basket and sell flowers. When she did appear, and heaps of bouquets were thrown at her feet, after the curtain fell she flung them all into a basket, slung it from her shoulders, and, kneeling to the man who had advised her to go and sell flowers, asked him, half in smiles and half in tears, if he would not buy a nosegay. Nothing that befalls the glittering Harlequin or Columbine amidst the swift enchantments of the theatre is fuller of astounding contrasts than these realities, if our thought but escapes the tyranny of space and time.

An artifice of vast power by which the theatre intensifies its revelations of character and experience, conduct and destiny, so as to make them more effective and apparently more significant than the original realities themselves are in actual life, is by increasing the range and vividness of the standards and foils by which they are judged, carrying them lower and raising them higher and making their contrasts sharper than they are seen elsewhere. The fool used to have the head of his stick or mock sceptre painted with human features, and talk and play with it as if it were an intelligent comrade. This was his bauble, in allusion to which Shakspeare says, "The fool holds his bauble for a god." Scoggan, the famous mummer, used to dress up his fists and make them act for the amusement of a dinner company. This is the secret of the vulgar delight in the clown, with his ridiculous dress made up of absurdities, his face whitened with chalk and flour and blotched with red patches and black and yellow streaks, his lips painted in elongations so that when he laughs his mouth seems to open from ear to ear. The mental disparity of his standard of intelligence and manners with that in the minds of the spectators elicits roars of coarse joy from them. It was said of Mazurier, the great Punchinello, that he was in deformities what Apollo was in perfections. Humped equally before and behind, perched on the legs of a heron, equipped with the arms of an ape, he moved with that stiffness without force, that suppleness devoid of reaction, characterizing the play of a body which has not in itself the principle of its movement, and whose members, set in action by a wire, are not attached to the trunk by articulations, but by rags. He imitated mechanism with as close a fidelity as in another rôle mechanism is made to imitate man. He seemed to be human and yet to have nothing human. His motions and falls were such that one believed him made not of flesh and bone but of cotton and thread. His face was wooden, and he carried illusion to such a pitch that the children took him for a gigantic puppet which had grown.

Even below this there is a lower dramatic depth still, and filled with yet keener sport for a large class. The reflection of human life in the marionette or puppet-show makes a revelation of a phase of human nature as profound and fearful as it is unexpected. The revelation is not consciously made, but springs from an intuitive perception of truth and sense of fitness as marvellous as anything in the history of the drama. It has long been known that there is an intimate likeness between the insane class and the criminal class. They both show the effect of removing the restraints exerted on the ego by its sympathetic connections with the general public. The restraint exercised on the indulgence of egotistic feelings and interests by a consideration of the feelings and interests of others being lifted off, these selfish instincts, which are the deepest organic heritage from ancestral history, break recklessly out. Now, the puppet has no sympathy. Moved not by his brain and heart but by wires attached to his limbs, his character shows the result. He is personified selfishness and whim. His individual will is absolutely reckless of other wills or of consequences. His ferocity is murderous, his jollity fiendish, his conduct a jumble of animal passions, cunning impulses, and chaotic impressions. This is unregenerate man released from social order and given over to himself. And there is a deep, sinister, raw pleasure for an uncultivated soul in the sight of a being freed from every law but that of self-indulgence. This is the secret of the fascination of the plebeian puppet-show.

Sometimes there has been in it a strange and terrible element of social satire. The lower class vent through it their hatred for their oppressors. One type of the Italian Polichincllc was a representative of the populace angered and made vindictive by their wrongs. He lays the stick lustily on the shoulders of his master and on the necks of the police, and takes summary vengeance for the iniquities of official justice. He is also a frightful cynic. He says, "I despise men so much that I care not what they think or say of me. I have suffered as much as others, but I have turned my back and my heart into leather. I am laughter personified, triumphant laughter, wicked laughter. Pshaw for the poor creatures knocked over by a breath! I am of iron and wood, old also as the world."

"In thus speaking," says his French historian, "he is truthful; for his heart is as dry as his baton, and he is a thorough egotist. Ferocious under his seeming good humor, he does evil for the love of it. Valuing the life of a man no more than that of a flea, he delights in quarrels and massacres." He has no sincere affection, no reverence, no fear either of God or devil, is always eager for coarse and low enjoyment, and laughs most loudly when he has done the cruellest deeds. He is the very type of the strong, vital, abandoned criminal; and he opens a huge vista into the most horrible experience of the human race.

And now it will be a relief to turn attention aloft in the opposite direction. The upward action of the dramatic art is its benign aspect. The egotist looks down to learn how great he is, and up to learn how little. The generous man looks up to feel how rich he is, and down to feel how poor. The former sees himself in contrast with others, the latter sees himself in unison with them. This may be exemplified in comedy as well as in tragedy. The portraiture of reality on the stage hitherto has perhaps chiefly aimed to amuse by exhibiting the follies and absurdities of people and making the spectators laugh at them in reaction from standards in their own minds. It will one day aim to correct the follies and absurdities of the spectators by setting before them models of superiority and ideals of perfection.

To enter into and appropriate the states and prerogatives of those happier, greater, and better than we, either for an admiring estimate of them, for the enrichment of ourselves, or for the free play of desirable spiritual qualities, is at once recreation, luxury, redemption, and education. This is the highest application of the dramatic principle, the mending of the characters of men with the characters of superior men. And it tends to the reconciliation and attuning of all the world. This is the principle which Paul illustrates in his doctrine that true circumcision is not of the flesh but of the soul, and that the genuine children of Abraham are the new race of spiritual characters which, reproducing his type of faith and conduct, will supersede his mere material descendants. He also says that those who measure themselves by themselves and compare themselves among themselves are not wise. The complement of this statement would be that we should compare ourselves with all sorts of people, that we may put off every imperfection of our own and put on every perfection of theirs. And the same apostle gives this principle its supremest application in his immortal text, "Put ye on the Lord Jesus Christ." The Pauline formula for the salvation of the world embodies the regenerating essence of the dramatic art, which is the assimilation by less divine characters of a more divine one, raising them into fellowship with the Divinest. It calls on all men to "behold with open face, as in a mirror, the glory of the Lord," and gaze on it until "they are changed into the same image, from glory to glory, by the Spirit of the Lord."

In distinction from this high use of the dramatic life and spirit, the fault of the ordinary range of coarse and careless men is the utter absence of all vital sympathetic insight. Fixed in the grooves of habit, shut up in their own hard and narrow type, they move stolidly among other men, insensible to the treasures they contain, giving and taking no more than so many sticks would.

And in some who have a fair share of the dramatic instinct it suffers a direct inversion of its purest office. For the weak and reckless allow themselves to be degraded to the level of the worst characters they behold, adopt their customs, assume their traits, copy their vices, and repeat their retributive ruin. The man of moral earnestness is warned and armed by a dramatic knowledge of the profligate and criminal. Only the impure or heedless idler will be led astray by it.

Yet there is another abuse of this art of dramatic penetration, which, if less fearful, is more frequent and almost as much to be reprehended, namely, a fruitless toying with it in a spirit of mere frivolity. A great many persons enter imaginatively into the states of other people, neither to honor and imitate nor to disapprove and avoid, but in empty sport and as an ostentatious luxury of vanity and pride. There is nothing which vulgar natures are so fond of as, in vulgar phrase, feeling their oats, pampering their fancied superiority to those they contemplate. They hate to be rebuked and commanded by excellences beyond their own attainment. They love to look down on something beneath their own arrogated estimate of self. And so they come to interpret almost everything they see as being inferior, and to draw from it a reflex complacency. Their noisy laughter is but an indirect self-applause consisting of what Emerson has called "contemptible squeals of joy." For whatever a man can laugh at he deems he is superior to. Nothing did the audiences at the old miracle-plays enjoy half so keenly as laughing at the devil when he was driven through a trap-door in a sulphurous shower of fire and squibs. The reason why a superficial exhibition of wit or humor is so popular is that it affords, at so low a price of effort, the luxury of the feeling of detachment and mastery. The insincere or unconsecrated nature always prefers a cheap seeming superiority to a costly real one. However much Harlequin and Punch and Judy may relieve and amuse, and thus find justification, they do not purify nor lift nor inspire nor educate the ordinary spectator. The genuine drama does all these in addition to bestowing the richest entertainment. Still, it must be remembered that the influence of a performance depends ultimately on the character and spirit of the spectator. Some persons seeing Washington would think nothing of his character, but be absorbed in admiration of his regimentals. One, at a given exhibition, will be simply entertained. Another will be debauched. A third will be lastingly impressed, stimulatingly edified. A fourth may enjoy the delusive luxury of a criticising superiority, persuading himself that he includes and transcends the characters whose enactments he so clearly understands and sees around. Those who laugh at those who weep fancy they are above them while really grovelling below in vulgar insensibility. One may easily lift armor he cannot wear.

The next use of the theatre, the most obvious of its serious uses, lies in the force with which it carries the great practical truths of morality home to the heart and the soul. The power of the stage in enforcing moral lessons, the rewards of virtue, the beauty of nobleness, the penalties of vice and crime, the horrors of remorse and disgrace, the peace and comfort of a self-approving conscience, is greater than that of any other mode of teaching. Its living exemplification of the workings of good and evil in the secret soul and in the social sphere has an effectiveness of incitement and of warning far beyond that of the mere didactic precept or exhortation of the pulpit. It is said that many a dissipated and felonious apprentice who saw Ross play George Barnwell was turned from his evil courses by the terrible force of the representation. One who was thus saved used every year anonymously to send Ross on his benefit-night the sum of ten guineas as a token of his gratitude. And Dr. Barrowby assured the player that he had done more good by his acting than many a parson had by his preaching. This educational function or moral edification in uncovering the secrets of experience and showing how every style of character and conduct entails its own compensatory consequences is even now a high and fruitful office of the theatre, frivolous and corrupt as it often is. And when the drama shall be made in all respects what it ought to be, fulfilling its own proper ideal, it will be beyond comparison the most effective agency in the world for imparting moral instruction and influence. The teaching of the stage is indeed all the more insinuating and powerful because it is indirect and not perfunctory or interested. The audience are not on their guard against it. It works with the force of nature and sincerity themselves.

"I have heard
That guilty creatures, sitting at a play,
Have by the very cunning of the scene
Been struck so to the soul that presently
They have proclaimed their malefactions."

No thoughtful and earnest person could possibly see the wickedness of Iago, the torture of Othello, the struggle and remorse of Macbeth, depicted by a great actor and not be profoundly instructed, moved, and morally fortified.

Not only does the drama array its teachings of morality in living forms so much more contagious and powerful than abstract precepts, but it also gives the highest examples of didactic eloquence. It abounds in the most beautiful expressions of poetry and philosophy, the wisest and most charming instances of insight and moralizing experience, verbal descriptions of character and of nature set off with every adjunct of oratoric art and heightening scenery. The preaching on the stage is often richer and sounder as well as more splendid than that heard from the pulpit. Besides, the pleasing excitement of the scene, the persuasive interest of the play, the surrendered and receptive spirits of the crowd blending in quickest sympathy and applause always over the most disinterested and exalted sentiments, predispose every hearer to the most favorable mood for being impressed by what is lovely, good, and great. The actor, inspired by his theme and his audience, makes thousands thrill and weep as he gives burning utterance to burning thoughts or infuses his own high spirit into beautiful and heroic examples of eloquence and virtue. When in Macbeth Forrest said,—

"I dare do all that may become a man, Who dares do more is none;"—

when in the Peruvian hero he replied to the accusation from Pizarro of haying spoken falsely, "Rolla utter falsehood! I would I had thee in a desert with thy troop around thee, and I but with my sword in this unshackled hand!" when in Damon he said, in rebuke of the corrupt and sycophantic office-seeker,—

"I told you, boy, I favored not this stealing
And winding into place: what he deserves,
An honest man dares challenge 'gainst the world,"—

it must have been a brutish breast in which his words did not start generous and ennobling, echoes. Tell says,—

"Ha! behold in air
Where a majestic eagle floats above
The northern turrets of the citadel,
And as the sun breaks through yon rifted cloud

is plumage shines, embathed in burning gold,
And sets off his regality in heaven!"

To have such a picture painted in speech and action so vividly that the hearers are transported out of themselves and tremble with pleasure is an educational influence of a pure and lofty order. The victorious Spartacus soliloquizes,—

"A cloud is on my path, but my ambition
Sees glory in it. As travellers, who stand
On mountains, view upon some neighboring peak
Among the mists a figure of themselves
Traced in sublimer characters; so I
Here see the vapory image of myself
Distant and dim, but giant-like."

All who take the impression of the actor and his imagery in this passage must receive some sense of the greatness of man and the mystery of his destiny, and feel themselves magnified beyond their wonted state. And when Forrest spoke these words of Virginius whole audiences were electrified by their power and inspirited with their sublime faith:

"Whoever says Justice will toe defeated—
He lies in the face of the gods. She is immutable,
Immaculate, and immortal. And though all
The guilty globe should blaze, she will spring up
Through the fire and soar above the crackling pile
With not a downy feather ruffled by
Its fierceness!"

The noble lines of the poet full of great thoughts, scarcely heeded and soon forgotten by the reader, are by the fiery or solemn elocution of the actor sculptured on the memories of his auditors for ineffaceable retention.

The theatre is always in some degree a school of manners, but it ought to be far more distinctly and systematically such. The different personages are foils and contrasts to set one another off. As they act and react in their various styles of being and of behavior, they advertise and illuminate what they are, and tacitly, but with the most penetrative effect, teach the spectator to estimate them by mutual comparisons and by reference to such standards as he knows. Grandeur and meanness, awkwardness and grace, brutal or fiendish cruelty and divine sensibility, selfish arrogance and sweet renunciation, grossness and delicacy, —in a word, every possible sort and grade of inward disposition and of outward bearing are exemplified on the stage. The instructive spectacle is too often gazed at with frivolity and mirth alone. But more profound, more vital, more important lessons are nowhere in the world taught. This art of manners precisely fitted to the character and rank of the person has been particularly studied in the Théâtre Français. The writer saw a play represented there in which there were three distinct sets of characters. The first belonged to the circle of royalty, the second to the gentry, and the third were of the laboring class. The second carefully aped the first, and the third painfully aped the second. The bearing of the first was composed, easy, dignified; that of the second was a lowered copy with curious differences made most instructively perceptible; while the third was a ludicrous travesty. The superior always, as by a secret magic, overswayed and gave the cue to the inferior. The king, disguised, sat down at table with a plebeian. The king ate and drank slowly, quietly, with a silent refinement in every motion; but the plebeian hurried, shuffled, fussed, choked, and sneezed. The actor who is really master of his whole business teaches in a thousand indescribably subtile ways a thousand indescribably valuable lessons for all who have eyes to see and intelligence behind the eyes to interpret what they see and apply its morals to their own edification.

Another service rendered by the theatre is in uncovering the arts of deceit and villany. In their unsophisticated openness the innocent are often the helpless victims of seductive adepts in dissipation and crime.

All the designing ways and tricks of the votaries of vice, the hypocritical wiles of brilliant scoundrels, their insinuating movements, the magnetizing spells they weave around the unsuspicious, are exposed on the stage in such a manner as fully to put every careful observer on guard. This unmasking of dangers, this warning and arming, is a species of moral instruction quite necessary in the present state of society, and nowhere so consummately exhibited as before the footlights. Nor is it to be fancied that the instruction is more demoralizing than guardian; for the instinctive sympathies of a public assembly move towards virtue, not towards vice. They who seem to be corrupted by public plays are inwardly corrupt beforehand.

A further and fairer utility of the stage is the exact opposite of that last mentioned. It is the delightful privilege of dramatic performers to exhibit pleasing and admirable types of character and display their worths and graces so as to kindle the love and worship of those who behold, and awaken in them emulous desires for the noble virtues and the exquisite charms which they see so divinely embodied. If the manifestation of heroism, piety, modesty, tenderness, self-sacrifice, glorious aspiration in the drama is not an educational and redemptive spectacle, it must be because the stolidity and shallowness of the audience neutralize its proper influence. Then it is they who are disgraced, not the play which is discredited.

It is also a signal function of dramatic acting to reveal to ordinary people the extraordinary attributes of their own nature by exemplifying before them the transcendent heights and depths of the human soul. Average persons and their average lives are prosaic and monotonous, often mean and tiresome or repulsive. They have no conception of the august or appalling extremes reached by those of the greatest endowments, the intensities of their experience, the grandeurs and the mysteries of their fate. In contrast with the tame level of vulgar life, the dull plod of the humdrum world, the theatre shows the romantic side of life, the supernal passions and adventures of genius, the entrancements of dreaming ideality, the glimpsing hints and marvels of destiny. An actor like Garrick or Salvini, an actress like Rachel or Ristori, carrying the graduated signals of love to the climax of beatific bliss, or the signals of jealousy to the explosive point of madness, makes common persons feel that they had not dreamed what these passions were. In beholding a great play greatly performed an audience gain a new measure for the richness of experience and the width of its extremes. Thus average people are brought to see the exceptional greatnesses of humanity and initiated into some appreciation of those astonishing passions, feats, and utterances of genius which must otherwise have remained sealed mysteries to them. Rachel used to stand, every nerve seeming an adder, and freeze and thrill the audience with terror, as her fusing gestures, perfectly automatic although guided by will, glided in slow continuity of curves or darted in electric starts. The commanding majesty, intelligence, and passion of Siddons seemed to bring her audience before her and not her before her audience.

A great actor enlarges the diapason of man. Our kind is aggrandized in him. He is copy to men of grosser faculty and teaches them how to feel. It was this sort of association in his mind that made Dryden say of the aged Betterton, with such magnifying pomp of phrase,—

"He, like the sun, still shoots a glimmering ray,
Like ancient Rome majestic in decay."

But the central and essential office of the drama is to serve as a means of spiritual purification, freedom, and enrichment. It is a most powerful alternative for those wearied, sickened, and soured with egotism. It takes them out of themselves, transfers their thoughts from their own affairs, and trains them in disinterested sympathy. They are made to hate the tyrants, loathe the sycophants, admire the heroes, pity the sufferers, love the lovers, grieve with the unhappy, and rejoice with the glad. Redeemed from the dismal treadmill of the ego, they enter into the fortunes of others and put on their feelings, and, exulting to be out of the purgatory of self-consciousness, they roam at large in the romantic paradise of sympathetic human kind. As we sit in the theatre and follow the course of the play, a torrent of ideal life is poured through the soul, free from the sticky attachments of personal prejudices, slavish likes and dislikes, viscous and disturbing morbidities. It therefore cleanses and emancipates. This is what Aristotle meant in saying that the soul should be purged by the passions of pity and terror. The impure mixture of broken interests and distracted feelings known in daily life is washed away by the overwhelming rush of the emotions and lessons of a great tragedy. One may recognize in another the signs of states—a glow of muscle, a vigor of thought, a height of sentiment—which he could not create in himself, but which he easily enters into by sympathy. An actor of splendid genius and tone, in the focus of a breathless audience, is for the hour a millionaire of soul. Two thousand spectators sitting before him divest themselves of themselves and put him on, and are for the hour millionaires of soul too. And so the stage illustrates a cheap way to wealth of consciousness, or every man his own spiritual Crœsus.

The histrionic art is likewise the best illustration of history. No narrative of events or biographic description can vie with a good play properly set on the stage in giving a vivid conception of an ancient period or a great personage. It steals the keys of time, enters the chambers of the past, and summons the sleeping dead to life again in their very forms, costumes, and motions.

"Time rushes o'er us: thick as evening clouds
Ages roll back. What calls them from their shrouds?
What in full vision brings their good and great,
The men whose virtues make a nation's fate,
The far forgotten stars of human kind?
The Stage, that mighty telescope of mind!"

What are the words of Tacitus or Livy in their impression on the common mind compared with the visible resurrection of the people and life of Rome in "Virginius,""Brutus,""Julius Cæsar," or "Antony and Cleopatra"? Colley Cibber said, with felicitous phrase, "The most a Vandyke can arrive at is to make his portraits of great persons seem to think. A Shakspeare goes further, and tells you what his pictures thought. A Betterton steps beyond both, and calls them from the grave

to breathe and be themselves again in feature, speech, and motion."
The theatrical art puts in our hands a telescope wherewith we pierce
distant ages and nations and see them as they were.

And as it revives the truths and wonders of antiquity, so it reflects the
present world, depicting in its successive scenes all forms of society
and experience, from the luxuries of the palace to the wretchedness of
the hovel. Moreover, in addition to thus lifting the curtain from the
past and the present, it gives prophetic glimpses of the future, in its
representations of ideal types of men and women and in its poetic
pictures of happier times yet to bless the world. While most buildings
are devoted to the mere interests and comforts of the private
individual or family, or to mechanical business and selfish scheming,
well is it that there should be one fair and open edifice dedicated to the
revelation of human nature in its whole extent, of human experience
in all its seriousness and mirth, of human love and hope in all their
beautiful glory.

But, after all the uses of the theatre enumerated above, there remains
to be stated what is perhaps its most constant, most valuable and
universal benefit; namely, its delightful ministry of recreation and
amusement. In its charmed enclosure there is a blessed escape from
the jading cares and toils and hates and griefs and fears that so harass
and corrode heart and mind in the emulous strifes of the world. Here
pictures of beauty and bravery are exhibited, adventures of romantic
interest set forth, the most sublime deeds and engaging traits of men
lifted into relief, a tide of pride and joy and love sent warm to the
hearts of the crowd, and all factitious distinctions swept away, as
thousands of eyes gaze on the same scenes and thousands of bosoms
beat together with one emotion. In the drama all the arts are
concentrated, and made accessible to those of the most moderate
means, with a splendor which elsewhere, if found at all, can be
commanded only by the favored few. There is the rich and imposing
architecture of the theatre itself, with its stately proportions and fair
ornaments. There is the audience with its brilliant toilets and its array
of celebrity, beauty, and fashion. There are colors in every direction,
and painting in the elaborate scenery heightened by the gorgeous

illumination poured over all. There is sculpture in the most exquisite forms and motions, the living statuary of the trained performers. There are poetry and oratory in the skilled elocution of the speakers. There are the interest of the story, the interplay of the characters, and the evolution and climax of the plot. There is the profound magnetic charm of the sympathetic assembly, all swayed and breathing as one. And then there is the penetrative incantation, the omnipotent spell of rhythm, in the music of the orchestra, the chant of the singers, the dancing of the ballet.

Here indeed is an art equally fitted to amuse the weary, to instruct the docile, and to express the inspired. The prejudiced deprecators of the drama have delighted to depict the kings and queens of the stage descending from their scenic pedestals, casting off their tinsel robes, and slinking away in slovenly attire into cellar and garret. How much worthier of note is the reverse aspect, the noble metamorphosis actors undergo when the prosaic belittlement of their daily life of poverty and care slips off and they enter the scene in the greatest characters of history to enact the grandest conceptions of passion and poetry! And there is an influence in great impersonations to purify and ennoble their performers. The law of congruity necessitates it. "If," said Clairon, "I am only an ordinary woman for twenty of the twenty-four hours of the day, no effort I can make will render me more than an ordinary woman when I appear as Agrippina or Semiramis." The actor, to make heroic, sublime, or tender manifestations of the mysterious power and pity and doom of human nature, must have these qualities in his soul. No petty or vulgar nature could be competent to such strokes of wonder and pathos as the "Prithee, undo this button!" of Garrick; the "Fool, fool, fool!" of Kean; the "Vous pleurez, Zaïre!" of Lekain; the "After life's fitful fever he sleeps well!" of Forrest.

The theatre offers us an unrivalled opportunity for the economical activity of all our faculties, especially of our finer sentiments, which there play freely, disconnected from the exacting action of the studious intellect. The whole concentrated mass of life shown in action on the stage is ideally radiated into the bosoms of the beholders without cost to them. They despise, they admire, they laugh, they weep, they feel complacent in their contempt or in their reverence. Many who are too poor and outcast, or too busy and worn, or too proud and irascible, or too grieved and unfortunately circumstanced, for the indulgence of these feelings in real life, find the luxuries copiously and cheaply supplied in the scene. This is one reason why so many play-goers retain such grateful recollections of their favorites. Steele said, "From the acting of Mr. Betterton I have received more strong impressions of what is great and noble in human nature than from the arguments of the most solid philosophers or the descriptions of the most charming poets." Robson declared, "I never came away from seeing Bannister without feeling ten years younger, and that if I had not, with Christian, got rid of my sins, I had got rid of what was pretty nearly as heavy to carry, my cares." A noble lady of Edinburgh who in her youth had seen Siddons, when blind and nearly speechless in the torpor of extreme age, on being reminded of the great actress, broke into enthusiastic expressions, while smiles lighted up the features pale and wrinkled with nearly a hundred years.

An old English writer asking how he shall seclude and refresh himself from fretting care and hardship puts aside every form of vicious dissipation, and says,—"My faculties truly to recreate

With modest mirth and myself to please,
Give me a PLAY that no distaste can breed.
Prove thou a spider and from flowers suck gall;
I will, bee-like, take honey from a weed,
For I was never puritanical."

Collective history looked at from the human point of view may sometimes appear a chaos, but seen from the divine auditorium above it is a perfect drama, the earth its stage, the generations its actors. Thus the argument of Thomas Heywood was sound, No Theatre, No World!
"If then the world a theatre present,

As by the roundnesse it appears most fit,
Built with starre-galleries of high ascent

In which Jehove doth as spectator sit
And chief determines to applaud the best,
But by their evil actions doome the rest,
He who denies that theatres should be
He may as well deny the world to me!"

For as the world is a stage, so the stage is a world. It is an artistic world in which not only the natural but also the supernatural world is revealed. This is shown with overwhelming abundance of power in William Winter's description of the Saul of Alfieri as rendered by Salvini:

"It depicts the condition of an imaginative mind, a stately and robust character, an arrogant, fiery spirit, an affectionate heart, and, altogether, a royal and regally-poised nature, that have first been undermined by sin and the consciousness of sin, and then crazed by contact with the spirit-world and by a nameless dread of the impending anger of an offended God. It would be difficult to conceive of a more distracting and piteous state. Awe and terror surround this august sufferer, and make him both holy and dreadful. In his person and his condition, as these are visible to the imaginative mind, he combines all the elements that impress and thrill. He is of vast physical stature, which time has not bent, and of great beauty of face, which griefs have ravaged but not destroyed. He is a valiant and bloody warrior, and danger seems to radiate from his presence. He is a magnanimous king and a loving father, and he softens by generosity and wins by gentleness. He is a maniac, haunted by spectres and scourged with a whip of scorpions, and his red-eyed fury makes all space a hell and shatters silence with the shrieks of the damned. He is a human soul, burdened with the frightful consciousness of the Almighty's wrath, and poised in torment on the precipice that overhangs the dark and storm-beaten ocean of eternity. His human weakness is affrighted by ghastly visions and by all manner of indefinite horrors, against which his vain struggles do but make more piteous his awful condition. The gleams of calm that fall upon his tortured heart only light up an abyss of misery,—a vault of darkness peopled by demons. He is already cut off from among the living by the doom of inevitable fate, and while we pity him we fear him. His coming seems attended with monstrous shapes; he diffuses dissonance; his voice is a cry of anguish or a wail of desolation; his existence is a tempest; there can be no relief for him save death, and the death that ends him comes like the blessing of tears to the scorched eyelids of consuming misery. That is the Saul of the Bible and of Alfieri's tragedy; and that is the Saul whom Salvini embodies. It is a golossal monument of human suffering that the actor presents, and no man can look upon it without being awed and chastened and lifted above the common level of this world."

But the culminating utility and glory and eulogy of the art of the theatre are not that it furnishes common people an opportunity for learning what are the exceptional greatness, beauty, and wonder of human nature by the sight of its most colossal faculties unveiled and its most marvellous terrors, splendors, sorrows, and ecstasies exposed for study, but that *its inherent genius tends to produce expansive sympathy, sincerity of soul, generous deeds, and an open catholicity of temper*. No other class is so true and liberal to its own members in distress or so prompt in response to public calamity as that of the actors. Their constant familiarity with the sentiments of nobleness and pity imbues them with the qualities. In trying exigencies, personal or national, their conduct has often illustrated the truth of the compliment paid them by the poet:

"These men will act the passions they inspire,
And wave the sabre as they sweep the lyre."

Macklin said, "I have always loved the conscious worth of a good action more than the profit that would arise from a bad one." A famous singer was passing through the market-place of Lyons one day, when a woman with a sick child asked alms of him. He had left his purse behind, but, wishing to aid the woman, he took off his hat, sang his best, and hastily gave her the money he collected.

"The singer, pleased, passed on, and softly thought,
Men will not know by whom this deed was wrought;

But when at night he came upon the stage,
Cheer after cheer went up from that wide throng,
And flowers rained on him. Nothing could assuage
The tumult of the welcome save the song
That for the beggars he had sung that day
While standing in the city's busy way."

So when in his old age the great tenor, Duprez, reappeared to sing some stanzas he had composed in behalf of the sufferers by an inundation, as he said he could no longer utter the sensational cry of Arnold in William Tell, *Suivez-moi*, but that he still had strength to sing *Secouronsle malheur*, the house rang with plaudits.

The flexibility of the actor, his sympathetic art, the affecting poetic situations in which he is seen set off by aggrandizing and romantic adjuncts, clothe him with fascinating associations, make him gazed after and courted. This is one secret of the keen interest felt in him. He who gives the most powerful signs of soul is naturally thought to have the greatest soul. The great have always been drawn to make favorites of actors. Demosthenes was the friend of Satyrus; Cicero, of Roscius; Louis the Fourteenth, of Molière; Bolingbroke, of Barton Booth; Napoleon, of Talma; Byron, of Kean. The Duke of Northumberland gave Kemble ten thousand pounds sterling. Lord Loughborough settled a handsome annuity on Macklin in his destitute age; and when the old actor in his one hundred and eighth year was about to die he besought the friend who had agreed to write his life to make grateful mention of this.

Players have given kings and nobles greater benefits than they have received from them, often teaching them character as well as manners. When the Earl of Essex told Edmund Kean that by continuing to associate with Incledon, the decayed singer, he would endanger his own further welcome in the upper class, the actor replied, "My lord, Incledon was my friend, in the strictest sense of the word, when I had scarcely another friend in the world; and if I should now desert him in the decline of his popularity and the fall of his fortunes I should little deserve the friendship of any man, and be quite unworthy of the favorable opinion your lordship has done me the honor to entertain for me." Thus speaking, he rose, and, with a profound bow to the earl, left the room.

The greatest social characters have not only always affected the society of gifted players, but have themselves had a profound passion for the personal practice of the art. This is because the art deals with all the most subtile secrets of human nature and experience, out of which grow those arts of power which they feel to be their peculiar province. It is also because in this practice they escape from the empty round of the merely conventional and titular which soon becomes so wearying to the soul and so nauseous to the heart, and come into the realm of reality. The effect produced by the king, the deference paid to him, may be hollow. The power of the actor depends on genuine gifts; on his own real being and skill and charm. And he sees through all cold forms and shallow pretences. His very art, in its bedizenments and factitious accessories, sickens him of all shams in private life. There he wants sincerity and the unaffected substantial goods of nature, a friendly fellowship springing straight from the heart. When the wife of Kean asked him what Lord Essex had said of his Shylock, the actor replied, "Damn Lord Essex. The pit rose at me!" A common soldier with whom Cooke had quarrelled refused to fight him because he was rich and the persons present would favor him. Cooke said, "Look here, sir. This is all I possess in the world," showing three hundred and fifty pounds in bank-notes, which he immediately thrust into the fire, holding the poker on them till they were consumed. Then he added, "Now I am a beggar, sir. Will you fight me now?"

This democratic spirit which spurns social affectations and tramples unreal claims, keenly recognizing distinctions but insisting that they shall be genuine and not merely supposititious, is the very genius of the drama as felt in its inmost essence.

Rulers have ever delighted to evade their imprisonment in etiquette, put on an incognito, and disport themselves in the original relishes of human intercourse on the basis of facts. Nothing in literature is more charming than the adventures in this kind of Haroun-al-Raschid and his Vizier in the Arabian Nights' Entertainments. Nero and

Commodus were proudest of all to strip off their imperial insignia and win plaudits by their performances in the amphitheatre. Julius Caesar acted in his own theatre the part of Hercules Furens. He was so carried away by the spirit of the rôle that he actually killed the youth who played Lycus and swung the body two or three times round his head. Louis the Fourteenth appeared in the Magnificent Lovers, by Molière, and pantomimed, danced, sang, and played on the flute and the guitar. He especially loved in gorgeous ballets to perform the rôle of the Sun; and in the ballet of the Seasons he repeatedly filled the rôle of the blonde Ceres surrounded by harvesters. Even Oliver Cromwell once acted the part of Tactus in the play of "Lingua, or the Combat of the Five Senses for Superiority."

But the life of the dramatic profession is not all a brilliant round of power, gayety, and indulgence. It too has sacrifices, toils, tears, strenuous duty and virtue, tragedy, mystery, and triumph. The strange picture of human life and death is nowhere more vividly reflected than in the theatrical career. The little prodigy James Speaight, whose performances on the violin had for three years been applauded by crowds, when he was not yet seven years old, was one evening slightly ill as he left the stage. About midnight his father heard him say, "Gracious God, make room for another little child in heaven." The father spoke, received no answer, and on going to him found him dead. In 1819, a Mlle. Charton made her début at the Odéon. Her enchanting loveliness and talent captivated all. Intoxicated Paris rang with her praises. Suddenly she ceased to act. A jealous lover had flung into that beautiful and happy face a cup of vitriol, destroying beauty, happiness, and eyesight forever. She refused to prosecute the ruffian, but sat at home, suffering and helpless, and was soon absorbed in the population and forgotten. What could be more dreadful than such a doom, or more pathetic than such submission! In fact, many of those who lived by acting on the stage have given as noble specimens of acting off of it as are to be found in history. Mrs. Porter, a famous actress of the generation preceding Garrick, riding home after the play, in a one-horse chaise, was accosted by a highwayman with a demand for her money. "She levelled a pistol at him, when he changed his tone to supplication, told her his name and the abode of his starving family, and appealed to her compassion so strongly that she gave him ten guineas. He left her, and, as she lashed her horse, the animal started aside, upset the chaise, and in the fall her hip-joint was dislocated. Notwithstanding all the pain and loss the man had thus occasioned her, she inquired into his circumstances, and, finding that he had told her the truth, raised sixty pounds among her acquaintances and sent it to his family." Her lameness forced her to leave the stage, and she had herself to subsist upon charity.

The dread shrinking and anxiety felt by Mrs. Siddons on the night of her first successful appearance in London, after her earlier failure, were such as common natures cannot imagine, and such as nothing but a holy love for her young dependent children could have nerved even her heroic nature to bear. The dying away of the frenzied shouts and plaudits left her half dead, as she wrote to a friend. "My joy and thankfulness were of too solemn and overpowering a nature to admit of words or even tears. My father, my husband, and myself sat down to a frugal supper in a silence uninterrupted except by exclamations of gladness from Mr. Siddons. My father enjoyed his refreshments, but occasionally stopped short, and, laying down his knife and fork, and lifting up his venerable face, and throwing back his silver hair, gave way to tears of happiness."

The essence of the ecclesiastical and theatrical quarrel lies in the relation of the natural passions to duty. It is especially concentrated and prominent in regard to the passion of love, concerning which the opposed views are seen on the one side in the prurient plays constantly produced on the boards, and on the other side in the repressive injunctions as constantly iterated from the pulpit. The latter loudly commands denial, the former silently insinuates indulgence. The one is inflamed with the love of power, the other is infected with the love of pleasure. The battle can never be ended by the victory of either party.

The strife is hopeless so long as the ascetic ideal is proclaimed alone, kindling the bigoted mental passions, and the voluptuous ideal is exhibited alone, inflaming the loose sensual passions. Each will have its party, and they will keep on fighting. The only solution lies in the appearance and triumph of that juster and broader ideal which shows that the genuine aim and end of life are not the gratification of any despotic separate passions, whether spiritual or physical, but the perfection of individual being in social unity. The two combatants, therefore, must be reconciled by a mediator diviner than either of them, armed with a truer authority than the one and animated by a purer mind than the other. That mediator is Science, unfolding the psychological and physiological laws of the subject, and bringing denial and indulgence into reconciliation by giving wholesomeness and normality to every passion, which shall then seek fulfilment only in accordance with the conditions of universal order, securing a pure harmony at once of all the functions of the individual and of all the interests of society. The incomplete and vain formula of the church is, Deny thyself. The equally defective and dangerous formula of the theatre is, Indulge thyself. But the perfect and bridging formula of science is, So deny or rule in the parts of thy being and life as to fulfil thyself in the whole.

Virtue is not confined to the votaries of the pulpit, but is often glorified in the votaries of the stage. Vice, if sometimes openly flaunted in the theatre, is sometimes secretly cherished in the church. Neither should scorn the other, but they should mutually teach and aid each other, and combine their methods as friends, to purify, enlighten, and free the world. Each has much to give the other, and as much to receive from it. For, while the mischief of the ascetic ecclesiastic ideal of repression and denial is the breeding of a spirit of sour and fanatical gloom, its glory is the earnest conscience, the trimmed lamp, and the girt loins. Add this sacred self-restraint, which allows no indulgence not in accordance with the conditions of universal order, to the genial dramatic ideal of man and life,—a perfect organism and perfect faculties in perfect conditions of fulfilment and liberty, or the greatest amount of harmonious experience rooted in the physical nature and flowering in the spiritual,— and it is the just ideal.

The true business of the church is to inculcate morality and religion. Its perversions are traditional routine, creed authority, and ceremony.

The true business of the theatre is to exhibit characters and manners in their contrasts so as to secure appropriating approval for the best, condemnation and avoidance for the worst. Its perversions are carelessness, frivolity, and license. When the church purifies itself for its two genuine functions,— truth and consolation,—and the theatre cleanly administers its two genuine functions,—wholesome recreation and earnest teaching,—their offices will coincide and the strife of priest and player cease.

Chapter XXII.

Forrest in Seven of His Chief Roles— Characters of Imaginative Portraiture— Richelieu—Macbeth—Richard— Hamlet—Coriolanus—Othellow—Lear

At the date of this writing, although there are many good actors in America, there are none who are generally recognized as great. There also appears for the time to be a decline in the popular taste for the serious and lofty drama, and a general preference for sensational, comic, and spectacular plays. In vain does the call-boy summon the sublime characters and parts that entranced the audiences of a bygone generation. They seem to have died with the strong and stately actors who gave them such noble life and motion. The sceptred pall of gorgeous tragedy has vanished from the stage, it may almost be said, and for the poet and the thinker have been substituted the carpenter, the scene-painter, the upholsterer, and the milliner. Nudity, prurience, broad appeals to sensual passion, extravagant glare and movement and noise, have largely thrust aside tragic action, romantic sentiment, and moral grandeur. Even though the depravation be but temporary, marking a transitional crisis, it is a feature unpleasant to contemplate. And it may be of some service, not only in completing the picture of the life of Forrest, but likewise in revealing the higher social uses and lessons of his art, to give a description of the chief of those massive and heroic roles he loved best to fill in the ripest period of his professional career. The accounts must be brief and fragmentary, and very inadequate at the best. To preserve or re-create the full impression of a great actor in a great part, he should be sculptured in every attitude and movement, with every gesture and look, and painted in every tone, emphasis, and inflection of his voice. Yet, without attempting this impossible feat in the case of Forrest, enough may be rapidly indicated in general sketches to enable intelligent readers to form some approximate conception of his leading impersonations and of the influences they were calculated to exert.

The pictures of the acting of Forrest now to be essayed must be tantalizingly faint and imperfect, in the absence of an art to translate and reproduce all the other eight dramatic languages of human nature in the one language of words. But to appreciate even these poor attempts at their worth one preliminary condition on the part of those who read is pre-eminently necessary. They must remember that Forrest was one of those rare men profusely endowed with that mysterious power to interest and impress which is popularly called personal magnetism. He was signally charged with that secret spell, that loaded and swaying fascination, which all feel though no one understands, which contagiously works on those who come within its reach, seizing curiosity, enlisting sympathy, or evoking repulsion. The distinguishing differences of men in this respect are indescribable and fatal. No art can efface them or neutralize them. For an artist who makes direct personal appeal to an audience the having or the not having this magnetic gift is as the hidden core of destiny. With it obstacles are removed as by magic, friends won, enemies overthrown, and wherever the possessor sails through the community he leaves a wide phosphorescent wake of social interest and gossip. Without it, though flags are waved and trumpets are blown and all pains taken to make an impression and secure a victorious career, yet the efforts prove futile and public attention wanders listlessly away. One seems created to be the victim of perpetual slights, dry; trivial, destitute of charm, nobody caring anything about him; while another, freighted with occult talismans, strangely interests everybody. The recognition of such contrasts is one of the most familiar facts of experience. These phenomena are suggested by the word sphere as applied to the characteristic influence of personality. The spiritual sphere or signalling power of an individual is described as attractive or repulsive, strong or weak, vast or little, harmonious or discordant. The mystery is not so blankly baffling as it has been supposed, but is in a large degree susceptible of rational explication.

Out of a hundred accomplished singers, beautiful in person and marvellous in voice, one prima donna shall surpass all the rest in fascinating the public. There is a nameless distinction in her bearing, there is an indescribable charm in her song, which bewitch and enthrall, are her irresistible passports to public enthusiasm, and make her sure of a long and dazzling career; while one after another of the rest with desperate exertions and fitful plaudits disappear. Here is a tragedian who exercises the same spell and quickly obscures his distanced rivals. He advances on the stage with a quiet step, his mantle negligently crossing his breast, his countenance calm. Without a start, without a gesture, without a word, he simply is. and looks. Yet, as he approaches, awe spreads around him. Why this breathless silence all over the theatre, this rooted attention from every one? He seats himself, he leans on the arm of the chair; his voice, quick and deep, seems not to utter common words, but to pronounce supernatural oracles. By what transcendent faculty does he render hate so terrible, irony so frightful, disdain so superhuman, devotion so entrancing, love so inexpressibly sweet, that the whole assembly rivet their eyes and hold their breath while their hearts throb under the mystic influence of his action? The secret is purely a matter of law without anything of chance or whim or caprice in it. It is the profound and universal law which regulates the exercise of sympathetic influence by one person on another. It has two elements, namely, beauty and power. Beauty and power both can be expressed in shapes, features, motions, and tones. Shapes, features, and tones are results and revelations of modes of motion. The face is shaped and modulated by the ideal forces within, the rhythmical vibrations which preside over the processes of nutrition. All those shapes or movements in a person which in their completeness constitute, or in their segments imply, returning curves or undulations, such as circles, ellipses, and spirals, are beautiful. They suggest economy of force, ease of function, sustained vitality, and potency. But abrupt changes of direction, sudden snatches and breaks of movement, sharp angles, are ugly and repellent, because they suggest waste of force, difficulty of function, discord of the individual with the universal, and therefore hint evil and death. The serpent was anciently considered a symbol of immortality on account, no doubt, of all its motions being endless lines or undulations circling in themselves. This is the law of beauty which just in proportion to its pervasive prevalence and exhibition in any one gives its possessor charm. The subtile indication of this in the incessant and innumerable play of the person fascinates and delights all who see it; and those who do not consciously perceive it are still influenced by it in the unconscious depths of their nature.

The element of power is closely allied in its mode of revelation and influence with that of beauty. Every attitude, gesture; or facial expression is composed of contours and lines, static and dynamic, latent and explicit, fragmentary and complete, straight, curved, or angularly crooked. Now, the nature of these lines, the degree in which their curves return or do not return into themselves, the nature and sizes of the figures they describe, or would describe if completed according to their indicative commencements, determine their beauty or ugliness and decide what effect they shall produce on the spectator. The beauty and the pleasure it yields are proportioned to the preponderance of endless lines suggestive of circulation of force without waste, and therefore of perfect grace and. immortal life. But that sense of power which breeds awe in the beholder is measured by the proportion of exertion made to effect produced. All force expended passes off on angular lines. The angles of movement may be obtuse or sharp in varying degrees, and consequently subtend lines of different lengths. All attitudes and gestures compose curves and figures, or cast lines and form angles, which constitute their æsthetic and dynamic values, those measuring beauty, these measuring power. For, on the principle of the lever and momentum, the power expended at the end of a line is equal to that exerted at the beginning of the line multiplied by its length. The amounts of exertion and the lengths of lines are unconsciously estimated by the intuitions of the observer, and the unconscious interpretations to which he is led are what yield the impressions he experiences on seeing any given actor. The greatest sense of power is received when the minimum of initial effort is seen with the maximum of terminal result; when the smallest weight at the central extremity balances the largest one at the distal extremity. The law of combined beauty and power of action, then, is contained in the relations of returning lines and lengths of straight lines. The measure of dramatic expression is this: impression of grace is according to the preponderance of perpetuating curves, and impression of strength according to the degrees of the angles formed by the straight lines. That actress or actor in whose organism there is the greatest freedom of the parts and the greatest unity of the whole, the most perfect cooperation of all the nerve-centres in a free dynamic solidarity and the most complete surrender of the individual will to universal principles, will make the deepest sensation,—in other words, will have the largest amount of what has been vaguely called personal magnetism. The divinest character expresses itself in softly-flowing forms and inexpensive movements. The most royal and august majesty of function indicates its rank of power by the slightest exertions implying the vastest effects. Frivolous, false, and vulgar characters are ever full of short lines, incongruous, fussy, and broken motions, curves everywhere subordinated and angles obtrusive. Such persons are, as it is said, destitute of magnetism. They do not interest. They cannot possibly charm or awe. It is a law of inexpressible importance that *the quality, grade, and measure of a personality are revealed primarily in the proportions, secondarily in the movements, of the physical organism.* These proportions and movements betray alike the permanent features of the indwelling character and all its passing thoughts and emotions. The truth is all there, though the spectator may be incompetent to interpret its signals. The most harmonious and perfect character will show the most exquisite symmetry and grace of repose and action. The irregulated, raw, and reckless type of character expresses itself in awkward, violent, or incongruous movements, wasteful of energy yet not impressive in result. Beauty of motion, the implication of endless lines, is the normal sign of loveliness of soul. Grandeur of soul or dynamic greatness of mind is indicated by implicit extent and ponderous slowness of motion. When the smallest displays of motion at the centres suggest the most sustained and extended lines, the impression given of power is the most mysterious and overwhelming. The most tremendous exertions, in lines and angles whose invisible complements are small, produce a weak impression, because they make no appeal to the imagination. The beauty of the figures implied in the forms of the movements of a man is the analogue of his goodness; the dimensions of the figures, the analogue of his strength. And in the case of every one the spectators are constantly apprehending the forms of these figures and how far they reach, and emotionally reacting in accordance with the results thus attained. It is not a conscious and critical process of the understanding or the senses, but a swift procedure of the intuitions or organic habits, including the sum of ancestral experiences deposited in instinctive faculty. Many who are ignorant of this law of the revelation of human nature, and of the sympathetic influence of man on man involved in it. may feel that the whole conception is merely a fine-spun fancy, with no solid basis in fact. But a perfect parallel to the process here described as taking place through the eye has been both mathematically and visibly demonstrated in the case of the ear. The beauty of form as perceived by the eye depends on implicit perception of geometric law, and is proportioned to the simplicity of the law and the variety of the outline embodying it, just as the harmony of colors or the harmony of sounds depends on the implicit perception of arithmetical ratios, and is proportioned to the harmony of times in which the vibrations of the visible or audible medium occur. We distinguish the beauty and the quality of a tone of the same pitch produced by different instruments or voices, and our feelings are differently affected with pleasure or pain as we listen to them. But the beauty of a tone consists in the equidistance of the pulsations of air composing it, and the quality of a tone consists in the forms of the pulsations. The auditory apparatus reports the symmetry or asymmetry of the pulsations in form and rate, and the soul, intuitively grasping the secret significance, is delighted or disturbed accordingly. The charm of a delicious, musical, powerful voice has these four elements, beautiful forms in its vibrations, perfect rhythm or equidistance in its vibrations, varying breadth in its vibrations, and varying extent of vibratory surface in the sounding mechanism. Without knowing anything about any of these conditions, the sensitive hearer, played on by them through his ear, accurately responds in feeling. It is exactly the same, in the case of the eye, with the geometrical lines and figures involved in the bearing of a person. If these are beautiful in forms, graceful in motions, sublime in implicit dimensions, the impression is delightful and profound; while if they are petty and incoherent, or clumsy and unbalanced, their appeal is superficial and disagreeable. This is the law of personal magnetism, which always exerts the vastest swing of power from the most exactly centred equilibrium. The mysteries of God are revealed in space and time through form and motion. They are concentrated in rhythm, which, as defined by Delsarte, is the simultaneous vibration of number, weight, and measure. We are creatures of space and time; all our experience has been written and is organized in that language. Our whole nature therefore in its inmost depths corresponds and thrills to the mystic symbols of harmony or discord with love and pleasure or with fear and pain. The secret of the delight that waits on the perception or feeling of beauty and power is the recognition of sequent ratios which express symmetry in time or algebraic law, and coexistent ratios which express symmetry in space or geometric law. Spatial symmetry is the law of equilibrium, the adjustment of the individual with the universal, and measures power. Temporal symmetry is the law of health, the pulsating adjustment of function with its norm, and measures the melodious flow of life. Rhythm is the constant dynamic reproduction of symmetry in space and time combined. It is the secret of personal magnetism. Its charm and its power are at their height when the symmetries are most varied in detail and most perfect in unity.

Now, Forrest ever possessed this magnetic temperament, this firmly poised and ingravidated personality, and ever wielded its signals with startling effect. The tones and inflections of his sweet and majestic voice in its wide diapason were felt by his hearers palpitating among the pulses of their hearts. His attitude, look, and gesture in great situations often produced on a whole assembly the electric creep of the flesh and the cold shudder of the marrow. His fearlessness and deliberation were conspicuous and proverbial. A censorious critic said, "Mr. Forrest is the most painfully elaborate actor on the stage. He swings in a great slow orbit, and, though he revolves with dignity and sublimity, the sublimity is often stupid and the dignity a little pompous. He dwells so long on unimportant passages that one might imagine he intended to take up an everlasting rest on a period, to go to sleep over a semicolon, or spend the evening with a comma. His pauses are like the distances from star to star, and if he continues in his course people will have time to stroll in the lobbies between his sentences. His performances might be defined by his enemies as infinite extensions of silence with incidental intervals of speech." Through this enveloping burlesque one discerns the poise, sang-froid, and grandeur of the man.

Senator Stockton, passing the Broadway Theatre one evening, met a friend coming out, and asked him, "What is going on in there?" The reply was, "Oh, nothing: Forrest is in one of his pauses!" An admiring critic said of him, and if the diction be exaggerated it yet invests the truth, "There is no actor living who takes a stronger hold of the feelings of his audience or grasps the passions of the human heart with such a giant-like clutch. He is as imposing and daring in his action as the mountain condor when he darts on the flock, or the bird of Jove when he wheels from the peaks and burnishes his plumage in the blaze of the sun. It is not one here and there that submits to his sovereignty. The entire audience are swayed and fashioned after the workings of his soul. He permits none to escape the potency of his sceptre, but makes all bow to his terrible and overwhelming mastery." Of course different persons had different degrees of susceptibility to this elemental power and earnestness of nature and to this trained and skilled display of art, though all must feel it more or less either as attraction or as repulsion. The varying effects of the playing of character through its signs is the genuine drama of life itself. The idiot holds his bauble for a god, as Shakspeare says. The ruffian is hardened against all delicate and noble manifestations of mind. The dilettante, in his dryness, veneer, and varnish, is incapable of any enthusiasm for persons. And there are multitudes so harassed and exhausted in the selfish contests of the day, their hearts and imaginations so perverted or shrivelled, that the brightest signals of heroism, genius, and saintliness shine before them in vain. The play of personal qualities, the study and appreciation of them, are more neglected now than they ever were before. It is one of the greatest of social calamities; for it takes the social stimulus away from spiritual ambition or the passion for excellence. And it is one of the supreme benefactions conferred on society by a great actor that he intensifies and illuminates the revelatory language of character and fixes attention on its import by lifting all its modes of expression to their highest pitch.

RICHELIEU.

In a previous chapter an attempt was made to describe Forrest in those characters of physical and mental realism with which his fame was chiefly identified during the earlier and middle portions of his popular career. It remains now to essay a similar sketch of those characters of imaginative portraiture which he best loved to impersonate in the culminating glory and at the close of his artistic career. In the Rolla, Damon, Spartacus, Metamora of his young manhood he was, rather than played, the men whose parts he assumed, so intensely did he feel them and so completely did he reproduce nature. He wrestled with the genius of his art as Hercules with Antæus, throwing it to the ground continually, but making its vitality more vigorous with every fall. As years passed, and brought the philosophic mind, they tempered and refined the animal fierceness, strained out the crudity and excess, and secured a result marked by greater symmetry in details, fuller harmony of accessories, a purer unity in the whole, and a loftier climax of interest and impression.

Then studious intellect and impassioned sentiment, guided by truth
and taste, preponderated over mere instinct and observation, and
imaginative portraiture took the place which had been held by
sensational realism. This is what in dramatic art gives the violence of
passion moderating restraint, puts the calm girdle of beauty about the
throbbing loins of power. Imagination, it is true, cannot create, but it
can idealize, order, and unify, unravel the tangled snarl of details, and
wind the intricacies in one unbroken thread, making nature more
natural by abstraction of the accidental and arrangement of the
essential. This was what the acting of Forrest, always sincere and
natural, for a long time needed, but at last, in a great degree, attained,
and, in attaining, became genuinely artistic.

The Richelieu of Forrest was a grand conception consummately
elaborated and grandly represented. It was a part suited to his nature,
and which he always loved to portray. The glorious patriotism which
knit his soul to France, the tender affection which bound his heart to
his niece, the leonine banter with which he mocked his rivals, the
indomitable courage with which he defied his foes, the sublime self-
sufficingness with which he trusted in fate and in the deepest
emergencies prophesied the dawn while his followers were trembling
in the gloom, his immense personal superiority of mind and force
swaying all others, as the sun sways its orbs,—these were traits to
which Forrest brought congenial qualities and moods, making their
representation a delight to his soul.

He dressed for the part in long robes, an iron-gray wig, and the
scarlet cap of a cardinal. He stooped a little, coughed, but gave no signs
of superannuation. As the conspiracies thickened about him and the
end drew on, he seemed visibly to grow older and more excitable. His
age and feebleness, though simulated with an exquisite skill, were not
obtruded. Though the picture of an old man, it was the picture of a
very grand old man, like the ruin of a mighty castle, worn by time and
broken by storms, yet towering proudly in its strength, with
foundations the earthquake could not uproot and battlements over
which the thunder crashed in vain. Forrest made the character not
only intensely interesting and exciting by the great variety of sharp

contrasts he brought into reconciliation in it, but also admirable and lovable from the honest virtues and august traits it embodied. He represented Richelieu as a patriotic statesman of the loftiest order, and also as a sage deeply read in the lore of the human heart, tenaciously just, a careful weigher of motives, his sometimes rough and repellent manner always covering a deep well of love and a rich vein of satire.

In the opening scene, the cunning slyness of the veteran plotter and detective, the dignity of the great statesman, and the magnetic command of the powerful minister were revealed in rapid alternation in a manner which was a masterpiece of art.

"And so you think this new conspiracy
The craftiest trap yet laid for the old fox?
Fox? Well, I like the nickname. What did Plutarch
Say of the Greek Lysander?
That where the lion's skin fell short, he eked it
Out with the fox's! A great statesman, Joseph,
That same Lysander!"

There was in the delivery of these words a mixture of sportiveness and sobriety, complacency and irony, which spoke volumes. Then, speaking of Baradas, the conceited upstart who expected to outwit and overthrow him, the expression of self-conscious greatness in his manner, combined with contempt for the mushroom success of littleness, made the verbal passage and the picture he painted in uttering it equally memorable as he said,—

"It cost me six long winters
To mount as high as in six little moons
This painted lizard. But I hold the ladder,
And when I shake—he falls!"

As his hand imaginatively shook the ladder, his eye blazed, his voice grew solid, and the audience saw everything indicated by the words as distinctly as if it had been presented in material reality. Nothing could be more finely drawn and colored than the variety of moods, the changing qualities of character and temper, called out in Richelieu by the reactions of his soul on the contrasted persons of the play and exigencies of the plot as he came in contact with them. When, alluding to the attachment of the king for his ward as an ivy, he said—

"Insidious ivy,
And shall it creep around my blossoming tree,
Where innocent thoughts, like happy birds, make music
That spirits in heaven might hear?"—

there was a fond caressing sweetness in his tones that fell on the heart like a celestial dew. Into what a wholly different world of human nature we were taken in the absolute transformation of his demeanor with Joseph, the Capuchin monk, his confidant! Here there was a grim humor, an amusing yet sinister banter:

"In my closet
You'll find a rosary, Joseph: ere you tell
Three hundred beads I'll summon you. Stay, Joseph.
I did omit an Ave in my matins,—
A grievous fault. Atone it for me, Joseph.
There is a scourge within; I am weak, you strong.
It were but charity to take my sin
On such broad shoulders. Exercise is healthful."

His interview with De Mauprat reminded one of a cat playing with a mouse, or of a royal tiger which had laid its paw on one of the sacred cattle and was watching its quiverings under the velvet-sheathed claws. When De Mauprat expects to be ordered to the block, Richelieu sends him to his darling Julie:

"To the tapestry chamber. You will there behold
The executioner: your doom be private,
And heaven have mercy on you!"

The delightful humor here follows the desperate terror like sunlight streaming on a thunder-cloud. What a contrast was furnished in the allusion to the detested Baradas and his confederates when the aroused cardinal, after the failure of every method to conciliate, towers into his kingliest port, and exclaims, with concentrated and vindictive resolution,—

"All means to crush. As with the opening and
The clenching of this little hand, I will
Crush the small vermin of the stinging courtiers!"

The central and all-conspicuous merit of Forrest's rendering of Richelieu was the unfailing felicity of skill with which he kept the unity of the character clear through all the variety of its manifestations. It was a character fixed in its centre but mobile in its exterior, dominated by a magnificent patriotic ambition, open to everything great, tinged with cynicism by bitter experience, if irascible and revengeful yet full of honest human sympathy. He enjoyed circumventing traitors with a finesse keener than their own, and defying enemies with a haughtiness that blasted, while ever and anon gleams of gentle and generous affection lighted up and softened the sombre prominences of a nature formed to mould rugged wills and to rule stormy times.

It is only great actors who are able to make the individuality of a character imperially prominent and absorbing yet at the same time to do equal justice to every universal thought or sentiment occurring in the part. Forrest was remarkable for this supreme excellence. Whenever the author had introduced any idea or passion of especial dignity from the depth of its meaning or the largeness of its scope, he was sure to express it with corresponding emphasis and finish. This makes a dramatic entertainment educational and ennobling no less than pleasurable. When François, starting on an important errand, says, "If I fail?" Richelieu gazes on the boy, while recollections of the marvellous triumphs of his own career flit over his face, and exclaims, with an electric accentuation of surprise and unconquerable assurance,—

"Fail?
In the lexicon of youth, which fate reserves
For a bright manhood, there is no such word
As fail!"

When the huge sword of his martial period at Rochelle drops from his grasp, and he is reminded that he has other weapons now, he goes slowly to his desk, the old hand from which the heavy falchion had dropped takes up the light feather, his eyes look into vacancy, the soldier passes into the seer, an indefinable presence of prophecy broods over him, and the meditative exultation of his air and the solemn warmth of his voice make the whole audience thrill as his sculptured syllables fall on their ears:

"True,—*this*!
Beneath the rule of men entirely great
The pen is mightier than the sword. Behold
The arch-enchanted wand! Itself a nothing,
But taking sorcery from the master hand
To paralyze the Cæsars and to strike
The loud earth breathless. Take away the sword:
States can be saved without it."

When Julie, appealing to him for aid which he cannot promise, expostulatingly asks,—

"Art thou not Richelieu?"—

he answers in a manner whose attitude, look, and tone instantly carry the imagination and sympathy of the soul-stricken auditors from the individual instance before them to the solemn pathos and mystery of the destiny of all mankind in this world:

"Yesterday I was:
To-day, a very weak old man: to-morrow,

I know not what!"

So, when, amidst unveiled treason, hate and fear and sickening ingratitude, left alone in his desolation, his spirit for a moment wavered under the load of suspicion and melancholy, but quickly rallied into its own invincible heroism, he so painted and voiced the successive moods that every bosom palpitated in living response:

"My leeches bribed to poisoners; pages
To strangle me in sleep; my very king—
This brain the unresting loom from which was woven
The purple of his greatness—leagued against me!
Old, childless, friendless, broken—all forsake,
All, all, but the indomitable heart
Of Armand Richelieu!"

Never was transition more powerful than from the minor wail of lamentation with which Forrest here began to the glorious eloquence of the climax, where his vocal thunderbolts drove home to every heart the lesson of conscious greatness and courage. The treachery was depicted with a look and voice expressive of a weary and mournful indignation and scorn touched with loathing; the desertion, with bowed head and drooping arms, in low, lingering, tearful tones; the self-assertion was launched from a mien that swelled with sudden access of inspiration, as if heaving off its weakness and stiffened in its utmost erection.

Another imposing instance in which Forrest so rendered a towering sense of genius and personal superiority as to change it from egotism to revelation, merging the individual peculiarity in a universal attribute, was where the armed De Mauprat comes upon the solitary cardinal and tells him the next step will be his grave. The defiant retort to this threat was so given as to impress the audience with a sense of prophetic power, a feeling that the destiny of man is mysteriously linked with unseen and supernatural ranks of being:

"Thou liest, knave!
I am old, infirm, most feeble—but thou liest
Armand de Richelieu dies not by the hand
Of man. The stars have said it, and the voice
Of my own prophetic and oracular soul
Confirms the shining sibyls!"

A crowning glory of the impersonation of this great rôle by Forrest
was the august grandeur of the method by which he set the intrinsic
royalty of Richelieu over against the titular royalty of Louis. In many
nameless ways besides by his subtile irony, his air of inherent
command masked in studied courtesy of subordination, and the
continual contrast of the comprehensive measures and sublime visions
of the one with the petty personal spites and schemes of the other, he
made it ever clear that the crowned monarch was a sham, the
statesman the real one anointed and sealed by heaven itself. This true
and democratic idea of superiority, that he is the genuine king, not
who chances to hold the throne, but who knows how to govern,
received a splendid setting in all the interviews of the king and the
cardinal. When the conspirators had won Louis to turn his back on his
minister with the words,—

"Remember, he who made can unmake,"—

who that saw it could ever forget the dilating mien and burning
oratoric burst which instantly made the sovereign seem a menial
subject, and the subject a vindicated sovereign?

"Never! Your anger can recall your trust,
Annul my office, spoil me of my lands,
Rifle my coffers: but my name, my deeds,
Are royal in a land beyond your sceptre.
Pass sentence on me if you will. From kings,
Lo, I appeal to Time!"

Again, when Louis, with mere personal passion, had harshly rebuffed him with the words,—

"For our conference
This is no place nor season,"—

the narrow selfishness of the king makes him seem a pygmy and a plebeian in the light of the universal sentiment and expansive thought with which Richelieu overwhelmingly responds,—

"Good my liege, for justice
All place is a temple and all season summer.
Do you deny me justice?"

But the grandest exhibition of the superiority of democratic personal royalty of character and inspiration to the conventional royalty of title and place, the supreme dramatic moment of the play, was the protection of Julie from the polluting pursuit of the king. Folding the affrighted girl to his breast with his left arm, he lifted his loaded right hand, and, with visage of smouldering fire and clarion tone, cried,— "To those who sent you!

And say you found the virtue they would slay,
Here, couched upon this heart, as at an altar,
And sheltered by the wings of sacred Rome.
Begone!"

Baradas asserts that the king claims her. Then came such a climax of physical, moral, and artistic power as no man could witness without being electrified through and through. Forrest prepared and executed this climax with an exquisite skill that made it seem an unstudied inspiration. His intellect appeared to have the eager fire that burns and flashes along a train of thought, gathering speed and glory as it moves, till at last it strikes with irresistible momentum. At first with noble repression the low deep voice uttered the portentous words,—

"Ay, is it so? Then wakes the power which in the age of iron Burst
forth to curb the great and raise the low."

Here the surge of passion began to sweep cumulatively on. The eyes
grew wild, the outstretched hands quivered, the tones swelled and
rang, the expanded and erected figure looked like a transparent mass
of fire, and the climax fell as though the sky had burst with a broadside
of thunders.

"Mark where she stands! Around her form I draw
The awful circle of our solemn Church.
Set but a foot within that holy ground,
And on thy head, yea, though it wore a crown,
I launch the curse of Rome!"

The sudden passage of Richelieu from the extreme of tottering
feebleness to the extreme of towering strength, under the stimulus of
some impersonal passion, illustrated a deep and marvellous principle
of human nature. Forrest never forgot how startlingly he had once
seen this exemplified by Andrew Jackson when discussing the
expediency of the annexation of Texas to the United States. A
disinterested and universal sentiment suddenly admitted to the mind,
lifting the man out of egotism, sometimes seems to open the valves of
the brain, flood the organism with supernatural power, and transform
a shrivelled skeleton into a glowing athlete. Richelieu had fainted, and
was thought to be dying. The king repents, and restores his office,
saying,—

"Live, Richelieu, if not for me, for France!"

In one instant the might of his whole idolized country passes into his
withered frame.

"My own dear France, I have thee yet, I have saved thee.
All earth shall never pluck thee from my heart,
My mistress France, my wedded wife, sweet France!"

It was the colossal scale of intellect, imagination, passion, and energy exposed by Forrest in his representation of Richelieu that made the rôle to ordinary minds a new revelation of the capacities of human nature. When, with a tone and inflection whose sweet and long-drawn cadence almost made the audience hear the melody of the spheres clanging in endless space, he said,—

"No, let us own it, there is One above
Sways the harmonious mystery of the world

Even better than prime ministers,"—he produced on the stage a religious impression of which Bossuet might have been proud in the pulpit. And to hear him declaim, with a modest pomp and solemn glow of elocution befitting the thoughts and imagery, the following passage, was to receive an influence most ennobling while most pleasurable:

"I found France rent asunder;
The rich men despots, and the poor, banditti;
Sloth in the mart, and schism in the temple;
Brawls festering to rebellion, and weak laws
Rotting away with rust in antique sheaths.
I have re-created France, and from the ashes
Of the old feudal and decrepit carcass
Civilization, on her luminous wings,
Soars, phoenix-like, to Jove. What was my art?
Genius, some say; some, fortune; witchcraft, some.
Not so: my art was justice!"

It was no wonder that Charles Kean, after beholding this interpretation of Richelieu by Forrest, said to his wife, "Ellen, this is the greatest acting we have ever seen or ever shall see." It was but just that Henry Sedley, himself an accomplished actor and owned to be one of the best dramatic critics in the country, should write, "We can imagine a Richelieu more French than that of Mr. Forrest, but we cannot well conceive one more full of dramatic passion, of sustained power, or of the mysterious magnetism that takes captive and sways at will the average human imagination."

SHAKSPEAREAN CHARACTERS.

In all the last forty years of his life Forrest was an enthusiastic reader and student of Shakspeare. As his experience deepened and his observation enlarged and his familiarity with the works of this unrivalled genius became more thorough, his love and admiration rose into wondering reverence, and ended in boundless idolatry. His library teemed with books illustrative of the plays and poems of the immortal dramatist. He delighted to pore even over the commentators, and the original pages were his solace, his joy, and his worship. He relished the Comedies as much as he did the Tragedies, and in the Sonnets found inexhaustible beauties entwined with exquisite autobiographic revelations. Thus he came within the esoteric circle of readers. One of the latest schemes with which his heart pleased his fancy was a design to erect in some suitable place in his native city a group of statuary representing Shakspeare with Heminge and Condell, the two editors whose pious care collected and gave to posterity the matchless writings which otherwise might have been lost.

The personal feelings and the professional pride of Forrest were more bound up with his representations of Shakspearean characters than with any others. Of the eight Shakspearean roles which he played, those of Shylock and Iago were early dropped, on account of his extreme distaste for the parts, and his unwillingness to bear the ideal hate and loathing they awakened in the spectators. But to the remaining six parts—Macbeth, Richard, Hamlet, Coriolanus, Othello, and Lear—he gave the most unwearied study, and in their representation showed the extremest elaboration of his art. He spent an incredible amount of time and pains in striving to grasp the true types and attributes of these characters, and in perfecting his portrayals of them according to the intentions of the author and the realities of nature. And he actually attained conceptions of them far more comprehensive, accurate, and distinct than he received credit for. His playing of them, too, was marked not only by a bold sweep of power and truth, but also by a keenness of insight, a delicate perception of fitness, a just distribution of light and shade, a felicity of transition and contrast, which were lost on the average of an audience. The knowledge that his finest points were not appreciated by many was one of his trials. In spite of this, however, his own conviction of the minute truthfulness and merit of his acting of Shakspearean characters, based on indefatigable study of nature and honest reproduction of what he saw, was the sweetest satisfaction of his professional life. He always wished his fame to stand or fall with a fair estimate of his renderings of these rôles. And one thing is to be affirmed of him, which the carelessness of miscellaneous assemblies superficially seeking amusement generally failed to appreciate, namely, that he felt profoundly the solemn lessons with which those characters were charged, and conscientiously endeavored to emphasize and enforce them, making his performance a panorama of living instruction, an illuminated revelation of human nature and human destiny, and not a mere series of piques of curiosity or traps for sensation.

In the ordinary dramatist or novelist a character is manufactured out of a formula, but in Shakspeare every great character is so deeply true that it suggests many formulas. In the highest ancient art situations vary with characters; in average modern art characters vary with situations; in Shakspeare both these results are shown as they are in real life, where sometimes characters are moulds for shaping situations, and sometimes situations are furnaces for testing characters. Of old, when life was deeper because less complex, the dramatized legend was the channel of a force or fate; there its interest lay. In Shakspeare the interest is not to see the supernatural force reflected blazing on a character, but rather to see it broken up by the faculties of the character, to see it refracted on his idiosyncrasies. This makes the task of the player more difficult, because he must seize the unity of the character in its relations with the plot, and keep it clear, however modulated in variety of manifestations. This Forrest did in all his Shakspearean impersonations. Though few who saw him act appreciated it, the distinctness with which he kept this in view was his crowning merit as an artist.

MACBETH.

Many actors have represented Macbeth as a coward moulded and directed at will by his stronger wife,—a weakling caught like a leaf in an irresistible current and hurried helplessly on to his doom. Such is not the picture painted by Shakspeare. Such was not the interpretation given by Forrest. Macbeth is a broad, rich, powerful nature, with a poetic mind, a loving heart, a courageous will. He is also strongly ambitious, and prone to superstition. To gratify his ambition he is tempted to commit a dreadful crime, and the temptation is urged on him by what he holds to be supernatural agencies. After misgivings and struggles with himself, he yields. The horrid deed being perpetrated, the results disappoint him. The supernatural prophecies that led him on change to supernatural terrors, his soul is filled with remorse, his brain reels, and as the sequel of his guilt thickens darkly around him he rallies his desperate energies and meets his fate with superb defiance. The struggle of temptation in a soul richly furnished with good yet fatally susceptible to evil, the violation of conscience, the overwhelming retribution,—these points, softened with sunny touches of domestic love and poetic moral sentiment, compose the lurid substance and movement of the drama. And these points Forrest embodied in his portraiture with an emotional intensity and an intellectual clearness which enthralled his audience.

As he came over the hills at the back of the stage, accompanied by Banquo, in his Highland tartan, his plumed Scotch cap, his legs bare from the knee to the ankle, his pointed targe on his arm, with his free and commanding air, and his appearance of elastic strength and freshness, he was a picture of vigorous, breezy manhood. His first words were addressed to Banquo in an easy tone, such as one would naturally use in describing the weather:

"So foul and fair a day I have not seen."

The witches hailing him with new titles and a royal prophecy, he starts,—

"And seems to fear
Things that do sound so fair."

As they concluded, the manner in which, with subdued breathing eagerness, he said,—

"Stay, you imperfect speakers; tell me more,"—

showed what a deep and prepared chord in his soul their greeting had struck. And when they made themselves vapor and disappeared, he stood rapt in the wonder of it, and replied to the question of Banquo, "Whither have they vanished?" with a dissolving whispering voice, in an attitude of musing suspense and astonishment,—

"Into the air; and what seemed corporal melted
As breath into the wind. Would they had stayed!"

When the missives from the king saluted him Glamis and Cawdor, he attributed more than mortal knowledge to the weird sisters; and at once the terrible temptation to gratify his ambition by murder seized his soul, and conscience began to struggle with it. This struggle, in all its dread import, he pictured forth as he delivered the ensuing soliloquy with speaking features and in quick low tones of suppressed questioning eagerness:

"This supernatural soliciting
Cannot be ill; cannot be good. If ill,
Why hath it given me earnest of success,
Commencing in a truth? I am thane of Cawdor.
If good, why do I yield to that suggestion
Whose horrid image doth unfix my hair,
And make my seated heart knock at my ribs,
Against the use of nature?
My thought, whose murder yet is but fantastical,

Shakes so my single state of man that function
Is smothered in surmise, and nothing is,
But what is not."

In uttering these words he painted to eye and ear how temptation divides the soul into the desiring passion and the forbidding principle and sets them in deadly contention. Then the apologetic sympathy of his reply to the expostulation of Banquo,—

"Worthy Macbeth, we stay upon your leisure,"—
showed the gentle quality of his nature:
"Give me your favor: my dull brain was wrought
With things forgotten. Kind gentlemen, your pains
Are registered where every day I turn
The leaf to read them. Let us toward the king."

Macbeth was one originally full of the milk of human kindness, who would not play false, but would win holily what he wished highly: yet his ambition was so sharp that the sight of the coveted prize made him wild to snatch it the nearest way. This conflict Forrest continually indicated by alternations of geniality towards his comrades and of lowering gloom in himself, while his brain seemed heaving in the throes of a moral earthquake. Thus, when Duncan had indicated Malcolm as successor to the throne, Macbeth betrayed the depths of his soul by saying, with sinister mien, aside,—

"The Prince of Cumberland! That is a step
On which I must fall down, or else o'erleap,
For in my way it lies. Stars, hide your fires!
Let not light see my black and deep desires."

The earnest and tender warmth which Forrest made Macbeth put into his greeting of his wife after his absence, his dangers in battle, and his mysterious adventure with the witches, proved how deeply he loved her. And his first words,—

"My dearest love,
Duncan comes here to-night,"—

were spoken with an abstracted and concentrated air that fully revealed the awful scheme that loomed darkly far back in his mind. Left alone with himself, the temptation renewed the struggle between his better and his worse self. In the long and wonderful soliloquy, beginning—

"If it were done when 'tis done, then 'twere well,"—

he painted the gradual victory of reason, honor, conscience, and affection over the fell ambition that was spurring him to murder, and, as Lady Macbeth entered, he exclaimed, with a clearing and relieved look,—

"We will proceed no further in this business."

But the stinging taunts with which she upbraided him, and the frightful energy of her own resolution with which she eloquently infected him, worked so strongly on his susceptible nature that he reinstalled his discarded purpose, and went out saying firmly,—

"I am settled, and bend up
Each corporal agent to this terrible feat."

In this scene he so distinctly exhibited the operation of her influence on him, the slow change of his innocent determination into uncertain wavering, and then the change of the irresolute state into guilty determination, that the spectators could almost see the inspiring temptress pour her spirits into him, as with the valor of her tongue she chastised his hesitation away.

When he next appeared he looked oppressed, bowed, haggard, and pale, as if the fearful crisis had exerted on him the effect of years of misery. In half-undress, with semi-distraught air, his hushed and gliding manner of sinewy stealth, in conjunction with the silence and darkness of the hour, conveyed a mysterious impression of awe and terror to every soul. He said to the servant, with an absent look and tone, as if the words uttered themselves without his heed,—

"Go; bid thy mistress, when my drink is ready,
She strike upon the bell. Get thee to bed."

Then slowly came the appalling climax in the temptation whose influences had been progressively operating in the automatic strata of his being deeper than his free consciousness could reach. Those influences were now ready to produce an illusion, by a reversal of the normal action of the faculties unconscious ideas reporting themselves outwardly as objects. Buried in thought, he stands gazing on the floor. Lifting his head, at last, as if to speak, he sees a dagger floating in the air. He winks rapidly, then rubs his eyes, to clear his sight and dispel his doubt. The fatal vision stays. He reasons with himself, and acts the reasoning out, to decide whether it is a deception of fancy or a supernatural reality. First he thinks it real, but, failing in his attempt to clutch it, he holds it to be a false creation of the brain. Then its persistence drives him insane, and as he sees the blade and dudgeon covered with gouts of blood he shrieks in a frenzy of horror. Passing this crisis, he re-seizes possession of his mind, and, with an air of profound relief, sighs,—

"There's no such thing:
It is the bloody business which informs
Thus to mine eyes."

Then, changing his voice from a giant whisper to a full sombre vocality, the next words fell on the ear in their solemn music like thunder rolling mellowed and softened in the distance:

"Now o'er the one half world
Nature seems dead, and wicked dreams abuse
The curtained sleep."

Gathering his faculties and girding up his resolution for the final deed, as the bell rang he grasped his dagger and made his exit, saying,—

"Hear it not, Duncan; for it is a knell
That summons thee to heaven or to hell."

These words he spoke, not with the bellowing declamation many players had given them, but in a low, firm tone tinged with sadness, a tone expressive of melancholy mixed with determination. As he came out of the fatal chamber backwards, with his hands reeking, he did not see Lady Macbeth standing there in an attitude of intense listening, until he struck against her. They both started and gazed at each other in terror,—an action so true to nature that it always electrified the house.

Then at once began the dread reaction of sorrow, fear, and remorse. Forrest made the regret and lamentation of Macbeth over the crime and its irreparable consequences exquisitely piteous and mournful. The marvellous wail of his description of innocent sleep forfeited thenceforth, the panic surprise of his

"How is it with me when every noise appals me?"
the lacerating distress of his

"Wake Duncan with thy knocking: I would thou couldst!"
penetrated the heart of every hearer with commiseration.

Forrest gave Macbeth, in the first scene of the play, a cheerful and observant air; after the interview with the witches he was absorbed and abstracted; pending his direful crime he was agitated, moody, troubled,—

"Dark thoughts rolling to and fro in his mind
Like thunder-clouds darkening the lucid sky;"

after the murder he was restless, suspicious, terrified, at times insane. These alterations of mood and manner were distinctly marked with the evolution of the plot through its salient stages.

Of the pervasive remorse with which the moral nature of Macbeth afflicted and shook him, Forrest presented a picture fascinating in its fearful beauty and truth. When he spoke the following passage, the mournfulness of his voice was like the sighing of the November wind as it throws its low moan over the withered leaves:

"Better be with the dead,
Whom we to gain our peace have sent to peace,
Than on the torture of the mind to lie
In restless ecstasy. Duncan is in his grave:
After life's fitful fever he sleeps well:
Treason has done his worst; nor steel, nor poison,
Malice domestic, foreign levy, nothing
Can touch him farther."

Then, seeking sympathy and consolation, he turned to the partner of his bosom and his greatness with the agonizing outburst,—
"O, full of scorpions is my mind, dear wife."
Close on the awful remorse and on the pathetic tenderness, with consummate truth to nature the selfish instincts were shown hardening the man in his crime, making him resolve to strengthen with further ill things bad begun:

"I am in blood
Stept in so far, that, should I wade no more,
Returning were as tedious as go o'er."

So unstably poised was his disposition between his good affections and his wicked desires that the conflict was still repeated, and with each defeat of conscience the dominion of evil grew completer. As his remorseful fears translated themselves into outward spectres, Forrest vividly illustrated the curdling horror human nature experiences when guilt opens the supernatural world to its apprehension. He made Macbeth show a proud and lion-mettled courage in human relations, but seem cowed with abject terror by ghostly visitations. His criminal course collects momentum till it hurries him headlong to wholesale slaughters and to his own inevitable ruin. In his mad infatuation of self-entangling crime he says of his own proposed massacre of the family of Macduff,—

"No boasting like a fool:
This deed I'll do before this purpose cool."

Relying on the promise of the witches that none of woman born should harm him, and that he should never be vanquished till Birnam wood came to Dunsinane, he added crime to crime till the whole land was in arms for his overthrow. Then, despite his forced faith and bravery, a profound melancholy sank on him. His vital spirits failed. He grew sick of life and weary of the sun. To this phase of the character and career Forrest did conspicuous justice. Nothing of the kind could exceed the exquisite beauty of his readings of the three famous passages,—

"I have lived long enough; my way of life
Has fallen into the sere, the yellow leaf:"
"Canst thou not minister to a mind diseased,
Pluck from the memory a rooted sorrow?"
She should have died hereafter:
There would have been a time for such a word."

His voice lingered on the melodious melancholy of the words and every line of his face responded to their mournful and despairing significance.

When told that Birnam wood was moving, the sense of supernatural power turned against him. For a moment he stood, a solid dismay. Then he staggered as if his brain had received a blow from the words which smote to its reeling centre. So, when Macduff exposed to him the paltering of the fiends in a double sense, his boasted charm seemed visibly to melt from him, and he shrank back as though struck by a withering spell. His towering form contracted into itself, his knees shook, and his sword half dropped from his grasp. But the next instant, goaded by the taunts of his adversary, he rallied on his native heroism, braced himself for the struggle as if he resolved to rise superior to fate whether natural or demoniac, and fell at last like a ruined king, with all his blazing regalia on. The performance left on the mind of the appreciative beholder, stamped in terrible impress, the eternal moral of temptation and crime culminating in fatal success and followed by the inevitable swoop of retribution:

"Naught's had, all's spent,
Where our desire is got without content."

RICHARD.

Quite early in his histrionic career Forrest wrote to his friend Leggett, "My notions of the character of Richard the Third do not accord with those of the players I have seen personate it. They have not made him gay enough in the earlier scenes, but too sullen, frowning, and obvious a villain. He was an exulting and dashing, not a moody, villain. Success followed his schemes too rapidly and gave him too much elation to make appropriate the haggard and penthouse aspect he is usually made to wear. Contempt for mankind forms a stronger feature of his character than hatred; and he has a sort of reckless jollity, a joyous audacity, which has not been made conspicuous enough." In general accord with this conception he afterwards elaborated his portraiture of the deformed tyrant, the savage humorist, the murderous and brilliant villain. He set aside the stereotyped idea of Richard as a strutting, ranting, gloomy plotter, forever cynical and sarcastic and parading his crimes. Not excluding these traits, Forrest subordinated them to his cunning hypocrisy, his gleaming intellectuality, his jocose irony, his exulting self complacence and fiendish sportiveness. He represented him not only as ravenously ambitious, but also full of a subtle pride and vanity which delighted him with the constant display of his mental superiority to those about him. Above all he was shown to be possessed of a laughing devil, a witty and sardonic genius, which amused itself with playing on the faculties of the weaklings he wheedled, scoffing at what they thought holy, and bluntly utilizing the most sacred things for the most selfish ends. There can be no doubt that in removing the conventional stage Richard with this more dashing and versatile one Forrest restored the genuine conception of Shakspeare, who has painted him as rattling not brooding, exuberantly complacent even under his own dispraises, an endlessly inventive and triumphant hypocrite, master of a gorgeous eloquence whose splendid phrases adorn the ugliness of his schemes almost out of sight. His mental nature devours his moral nature, and, swallowing remorse, leaves him free to be gay. The character thus portrayed was hard, cruel, deceitful, mocking,—less melodramatically fiendish and electrical than the Richard of Kean, but more true to nature. The picture was a consistent one. The deformity of the man, reacting on his matchless intellect and courage and sensual passion, had made him a bitter cynic. But his genius was too rich to stagnate into an envenomed gloom of misanthropy. Its exuberance broke out in aspiring schemes and crimes gilded with philosophy, hypocrisy, laughter, and irony. Moving alone in a murky atmosphere of sin and sensuality, he knew himself to the bottom of his soul, and read everybody else through and through. He believed in no one, and scoffed at truth, because he was himself without conscience. But his insight and his solid understanding and glittering wit, making of everything a foil to display his self-satisfied powers, hid the degradation of his wickedness from his own eyes, and sometimes almost excused it in the eyes of others. Yet, so wondrous was the moral genius of Shakspeare, the devilish chuckling with which he hugged the notion of his own superiority in his exemption from the standards that rule other men, instead of infecting, shocked and warned and repelled the auditor:

"Come, this conscience is a convenient scarecrow;
It guards the fruit which priests and wise men taste,
Who never set it up to fright themselves."

Thus in the impersonation of him by Forrest Richard lost his perpetual scowl, and took on here and there touches of humor and grim comedy. He burst upon the stage, cloaked and capped, waving his glove in triumph over the downfall of the house of Lancaster. Not in frowning gutturals or with snarling complaint but merrily came the opening words,—

> "Now is the winter of our discontent
> Made glorious summer by this sun of York."

Gradually as he came to descant upon his own defects and unsuitedness for peace and love, the tone passed from glee to sarcasm, and ended with dissembling and vindictive earnestness in the apostrophe,—

> "Dive, thoughts, down to my soul. Here Clarence comes."

The scene with Lady Anne, where he overcomes every conceivable kind and degree of obstacles to her favor by the sheer fascination of his gifted tongue, was a masterpiece of nature and art. He gave his pleading just enough semblance of sincerity to make a plausible pathway to the feminine heart, but not enough to hide the sinister charm of a consummate hypocrisy availing itself of every secret of persuasion. It was a fearful unmasking of the weakness of ordinary woman under the siege of passion. No sermon was ever preached in any pulpit one-half so terrible in power for those prepared to appreciate all that it meant. When Lady Anne withdrew, the delighted vanity of Richard, the self-pampering exultation of the artist in dissimulation, shone out in the soliloquy wherewith he applauded and caressed himself:

> "Was ever woman in this humor wooed?
> Was ever woman in this humor won?
> I'll have her,—but I will not keep her long
> To take her in her heart's extremest hate,

With curses in her mouth, tears in her eyes,
The bleeding witness of my hatred by;
Having heaven, her conscience, and these bars against me!
And I no friends to back my suit withal,
But the plain devil, and dissembling looks!
And yet to win her,—all the world to nothing!"

In many places in the play his air of searching and sarcastic incredulity, and his rich vindictive chuckle of self-applause, were as artistically fine as they were morally repulsive. As Kean had done before him, he made an effective point in speaking the line,
"To shrink my arm up like a withered shrub:"
he looked at the limb for some time with a sort of bitter discontent, and struck it back with angry disgust. When the queenly women widowed by his murderous intervention began to upbraid him with his monstrous deeds, the cool audacity, the immense aplomb, the half-hidden enjoyment of the joke, with which he relieved himself from the situation by calling out,—

"A flourish, trumpets! strike alarums, drums!
Let not the heavens hear these tell-tale women
Rail on the Lord's Anointed!"—

were a bit of grotesque satire, a gigantic and serviceable absurdity, worthy of Rabelais.

The acting of Forrest in the tent-scene, where Richard in his broken sleep dreams he sees the successive victims of his murderous hand approach and threaten him, was original and effective in the highest degree. He struggled on his couch with horrible phantoms. Ghosts pursued him. Visions of battle, overthrow, despair, and death convulsed him. Acting his dreams out he dealt his blows around with frightful and aimless energy, and with an intense expression of remorse and vengeance on his face fell apparently cloven to the earth. He then arose like a man coming out of hell, dragging his dream with him, and, struggling fiercely to awake, rushed to the footlights, sank on his knee, and spoke these words, beginning with a shriek and softening down to a shuddering whisper:

"Give me another horse! Bind up my wounds!
Have mercy, Jesu! Soft; I did but dream.
O coward conscience, how dost thou afflict me!
The lights burn blue. It is now dead midnight.
Cold fearful drops stand on my trembling flesh."

The merely selfish individual instincts and passions of unregenerate human nature are kept from breaking out into the crimes which they would spontaneously commit, by an ethical regulation which consists of a set of ideal sympathies representing the rights and feelings of other men, representing the word of God or the collective principles of universal order. The criminal type of character embodied in Richard throws off or suppresses this restraining and retributive apparatus, and enthrones a lawless egotism masked in hypocrisy. Thus, Richard had so obscured, clogged, and deadened the moral action of conscience, that his egotistic passions held rampant supremacy, and success made him gay and exultant, unchecked by any touch of remorse or shame. In his own eyes he clothed himself in the glimmering mail of his triumphant deeds of wickedness, and dilated with pride like Lucifer in hell. He could not weep nor tremble, but he could shake with horrid laughter. In drawing this terrible outline Shakspeare showed that he knew what was in man. In painting the audacious picture Forrest proved himself a profound artist. And the moral for the spectators was complete when the hardened intellectual monster of depravity, in the culmination of the secret forces of destiny and his own organism, was stripped of his self-sufficiency, and, as the supernatural world broke on his vision, he stood aghast, with curdled blood and stiffened hair, shrieking with terror and despair.

Forrest was too large, with too much ingrained justice and heavy grandeur, to be really suited for this part. He needed, especially in its scolding contests of wit and spiteful invective, to be smaller, lighter, swifter, more vixenish. It was just the character for Kean and Booth, who in their way were unapproachable in it. Yet the conception of Forrest was far truer on the whole; and his performance was full of sterling merit.

HAMLET.

The clear good sense, the trained professional skill, and the deep personal experience of Forrest gave him an accurate perception of the general character of Hamlet. There will always be room for critical differences of judgment on the details. But he could not commit the gross blunders illustrated by so many noted actors who have exhibited the enigmatical prince either as a petulant, querulous egotist morbidly brooding over himself and irritable with everybody else, or as a robustious, periwig-pated fellow always in a roaring passion or on the verge of it. Forrest saw in the mind and heart of Hamlet sweet and noble elements of the courtier, the scholar, the philosopher, the poet, and the lover, but joined with a sensitive organization whose nerves were too exquisitely strung not to be a little jangled by the harsh contact of the circumstances into which he was flung. He regarded him as naturally wise, just, modest, and affectionate, but by his experience of wrong and fickleness in others, and of disturbed health in himself, led to an exaggerated self-consciousness profoundly tinged with mournfulness and easily provoke to sarcasm. In the melancholy young Dane was embodied the sad malady of the highest natures, the great spiritual disease of modern life,— an over-excited intellectuality dwelling with too much eagerness and persistence on the mysteries of things; allured, perplexed, baffled, vainly trying to solve the problems of existence, injustice, misery, death, and wearying itself out with the restless effort. Thus there is produced a tendency of blood to the head, which leaves the extremities cold, the centres congested, and the surface anæmic. The fevered and hungry brain devours the juices of the body, the exhausted organic and animal functions complainingly react on the spiritual nature or conscious essence with a wretched depression, everything within is sicklied over with a pale cast of thought, and everything without becomes a sterile and pestilent burden. The strong and gentle nature, finely touched for fine issues, but too delicately poised, is stricken with the disease of introspective inquiry, and, not content to accept things as they are and wholesomely make the best of them, keeps forever probing too curiously into the mysterious cause and import of events, until mental gloom sets in on the lowered physical tone. Then the opening of the supernatural world upon him, revealing the murder of his father and imposing the duty of vengeance, hurries him in his weakened and anxious condition to the edge of lunacy, over which he sometimes purposely affects to pass, and sometimes, in his sleepless care or sudden excitement, is really precipitated. Such was the conception which Forrest strove to represent in his portraiture of Hamlet. And in rendering it he did all he could to neutralize the ill-adaptedness of his stalwart person and abounding vigor for the philosophical and romantic sentimentality of the part by a subdued and pensive manner and a costume which made his figure appear more tall and slender. He laid aside the massive hauteur of his port, and walked the stage and conversed with the interlocutors as a thoughtful scholar would walk the floor of his library and talk with his friends. Even when he broke into passionate indignation or scorn a restraining power of culture and refinement curbed the violence. Still, the incongruity between his form and that of the ideal Hamlet was felt by the audience; and it abated from the admiration and enjoyment due to the sound intelligence, sincere feeling, beautiful elocution, and just acting which he displayed in the performance.

Most players of Hamlet, in the scene where he first appears among the courtiers before the king and queen, have taken a conspicuous position, drawing all eyes. Forrest, with a delicate perception that the deep melancholy and suspicion in which he was plunged would make him averse to ostentation, was seen in the rear, as if avoiding notice, and only came forward when the king called him by name with the title of son. He then betrayed his prophetic mislike of his uncle by the dark look and satirical inflection with which he said, aside,—

"A little more than kin and less than kind."

His reply to the expostulation of his mother against his grief seeming so particular and persistent,—

"Seems, madam: nay, it is: I know not seems.
'Tis not alone my inky cloak, good mother,
Nor customary suits of solemn black,"—

was given with a sincerity, naturalness, and beauty irresistible in effect. His grief and gloom appeared to embody themselves in a voice that wailed and quivered the weeping syllables like the tones of a bell swinging above a city stricken with the plague. The impression thus produced was continued, modified with new elements of emotion, and carried to a still higher pitch, when, left alone, he began to commune with himself and to utter his thoughts and feelings aloud. What an all-pervasive disheartenment possessed him, how sick he was of life, how tenderly he loved and mourned his father, how loathingly he shrank from the shameless speed and facility wherewith his widowed mother had transferred herself to a second husband,—these phases of his unhappiness were painted with an earnest truthfulness which seized and held the sympathies as with a spell.

"O that this too, too solid flesh would melt,
Thaw, and resolve itself into a dew:
Or that the Everlasting had not fixed
His canon 'gainst self-slaughter. O God! O God!
How weary, stale, flat, and unprofitable
Seem to me all the uses of this world!"

Hamlet had been a deep solitary self-communer, had penetrated the hollow forms and shows of the conventional world, and with his questioning spirit touched the very quick of the mystery of the universe. His soul must have vibrated at least with obscure presentiments of the invisible state and supernal ranges of being in hidden connection with the scenes in which he was playing his part. Forrest revealed this by his manner of listening to Horatio while he described how he and Marcellus and Bernardo had seen the ghost of the buried majesty of Denmark walking by them at midnight. This sense of a providential, retributive, supernatural scheme mysteriously interwoven with our human life was breathed yet more forcibly in his soliloquizing moods after agreeing to watch with them that night in hope that the ghost would walk again:

"My father's spirit in arms! All is not well;
I doubt some foul play: would the night were come!
Till then sit still, my soul. Foul deeds will rise,
Though all the earth o'erwhelm them, to men's eyes."

When Hamlet, with Horatio and Marcellus, came upon the platform at twelve to watch for the ghost, and said,—

"The air bites shrewdly: it is very cold,"—

he finely indicated by his absent and preoccupied manner that he was not thinking about the cold, but was full of the solemn expectation of something else. He took a position nigh to the entrance of the ghost, and continued his desultory talk about the custom of carousing in Denmark, till the spectral figure stalked in, almost touching him. Then Hamlet turned, with a violent start of amazement and a short cry, and, while the white face looked down into his own, uttered the most affecting invocation ever spoken by man, in a subdued and beseeching tone that seemed freighted with the very soul of bewildered awe and piteous pleading. His voice was in a high key but husky, the vocality half dissolved in mysterious breath. His look was that of startled amazement touched with love and eagerness. The remorseful Macbeth confronted the ghost of Banquo with petrifying terror. The thunderstruck Richard saw the ghosts of his victims with wild horror. But Hamlet was innocent; his spirit was that of truth and filial piety; and when the marble tomb yawned forth its messenger from the invisible world to revisit the glimpses of the moon, although his fleshly nature might tremble at recognizing the manifest supernatural, his soul would indeed be wonder-thrilled but not unhinged, feeling itself as immortal as that on which it looked. His figure perfectly still, leaning forward with intent face, his whole soul concentrated in eye and ear, breathed mute supplication. And when in reply to the pathetic words of the ghost,—

"My hour is almost come
When I to sulphurous and tormenting flames
Must render up myself,"—
he said,—
"Alas, poor ghost!"—his voice was so heart-brokenly expressive of commiseration that the hearers almost anticipated the response,—

"Pity me not: but lend thy serious hearing
To what I shall unfold."

The harrowing tale finished, the task of revenge enjoined, the ghost disappears, saying,—

"Adieu! adieu! Hamlet, remember me."

Nothing in dramatic art has ever been conceived more overwhelmingly affecting and appalling than this scene and speech. A withering spell seemed to have fallen on Hamlet and instantly aged him. He looked as pale and shrivelled as the frozen moonlight and the wintry landscape around him. He spoke the soliloquy that followed with a feeble and slow laboriousness expressive of terrible pain and anxiety:

"Hold, hold, my heart;
And you, my sinews, grow not instant old,
But bear me stiffly up! Remember thee?
Ay, thou poor ghost, while memory holds a sent
In this distracted globe. Remember thee?
Yea, from the table of my memory

I'll wipe away all trivial fond records,
All saws of books, all forms, all pressures past,
That youth and observation copied there,
And thy commandment all alone shall live
Within the book and volume of my brain."

To these words Forrest imparted an expression loaded with the whole darkening and dislocating effect which the vision and injunction of his father had exerted on him and was thenceforth to exert. For he was changed beyond the power of recovery. He now moves through the mysteries of the play, himself the densest mystery of all, at once shedding and absorbing night, his steady purpose drifting through his unstable plans, and his methodical madness hurrying king, queen, Polonius, Ophelia, Laertes, and himself to their tragic doom. The load of his supernatural mission darkens every prospect; yet his royal reason rifts the darkness with its flashes, the splendor of his imagination flings rainbows around him, and the native tenderness of his heart contrasts with his hard and lonely fate like an Alpine rose springing from the crags and pressing its fragrant petals against the very glacier. He was unhappy before, because his faculties transcended his conditions, his boundless soul chafed under the trifles of every-day experience, and his nobleness revolted from the hollow shams and frivolous routine which he saw so clearly. But now that the realm of the dead has opened on him, filling him with distressful doubts and burdening him with distasteful duty, revealing murder on the throne and making love and joy impossible, his miserable dejection becomes supreme. He seeks to escape from the pressure of his doom in thought, conversation, friendship sportive wit. Embittered by his knowledge, he turns on the shallow and treacherous praters about him with a sarcastic humor which seems not part of his character but elicited from him by accidents and glittering out of his gloom like lamplight reflected on an ebony caryatid, or like a scattered rosary of stars burning in a night of solid black.

Forrest endeavored to represent in their truth the rapid succession of transitory and contradictory moods of Hamlet and yet never to lose the central thread of unity on which they were strung. That unity was imaginative intellectuality, introspective skepticism, profound unhappiness, and a shrinking yet persistent determination to avenge the murder of his father. The great intelligence and skill of the actor were proved by his presenting both the variety and the unity, and never forgetting that his portraiture was of a refined and scholarly prince and a satirical humorist who loved solitude and secrecy and would rather be misunderstood than reveal himself to the crowd. Among the many delicate shadings of character exemplified in the impersonation one of the quietest and best was the contrast of his sharp lawyer-like manner of cross-examining Rosencrantz and Guildenstern and detecting that in the disguise of friends they were really spies, with the thoughtful and gracious kindness of his dealing with the players. Seated part of the time, he spoke to the poor actor like an old friend, and called him back, when he was retiring, to add another thought, and finally dismissed him with a sympathetic touch on his shoulder and a smile.

The closet scene with the queen-mother, as Forrest played it, was a model of justness. He began in a respectful and sorrowing tone. Gradually, as he dwelt on her faithlessness to his father, and her loathsome sensuality, his glowing memory and burning words wrought him up to vehement indignation, and he appeared on the point of offering violence, when the ghost reappeared with warning signal and message. The suddenness of change in his manner—pallor of face, shrunken shoulders, fixed dilatation of eyes—was electrifying. And when in response to the queen's

"O Hamlet, thou hast rent my heart in twain!"he said,—
"O throw away the worser part of it,
And live the purer with the other half.
Good-night: but go not to my uncle's bed:

Assume a virtue if you have it not,"—he compressed into his utterance, in one indescribable mixture, a world of entreaty, command, disgust, grief, deference, love, and mournfulness.

The scene in the church-yard was one full of felicitous design and execution. Entering slowly with Horatio, he seemed, as he looked about, invested with a religious reverence. Then he sat down on a tombstone, and entered easily into conversation in a humorous vein with the clown who was digging a grave. At the same time he kept up an even flow of understanding with Horatio. He so bore himself that the audience could reach no foregone conclusion to withdraw their absorbed attention from the strange funereal phantasmagoria on which the curtain was soon to sink like a pall. Over the skull of Yorick, in quick transition from the bantering with the clown, his reminiscences, not far from mirth, his profound yet simple moralizing, so heartfelt and natural, were naive and solemn and pathetic to the verge of smiles and awe and tears. When he learned that Ophelia was dead, and that this grave was for her, he staggered, and bent his head for a moment on the shoulder of his friend Horatio. Though so quickly done, it told the whole story of his love for her and his enforced renunciation.

Of all who have acted the part no one perhaps has ever done such complete justice to the genius of Hamlet as Forrest did in his noble delivery of the great speeches and soliloquies, with full observance of every requirement of measure, accent, inflection, and relative importance of thought. Some admired actors rattle the words off with no sense whatever of the fathomless depths of meaning in them. In the famous description by Hamlet of the disenchanting effect of his heavy-heartedness the voice of Forrest brought the very objects spoken of before the hearer,—the goodly frame, the earth; the most excellent canopy, the air; the brave overhanging firmament; the majestical roof fretted with golden fire. And when, turning from the beauty of the material universe to the greater glory and mystery of the divine foster-child and sovereign of the earth, man, he altered the tone of admiration to a tone of awe, his speech stirred the soul like the grandest chords in the Requiem of Mozart, thrilling it with sublime premonitions of its own infinity.

Forrest thoroughly understood from the combined lessons of experience and study the irremediable unhappiness and skepticism of the great, dark, tender, melancholy soul of Hamlet,—how sick he was at heart, how nauseated with the faithless shallowness of the hangers-on at court, how weary of life. He comprehended the misery of the affectionate nature that had lost all its illusions and was unable to reconcile itself to the loss,—the unrest of the ardent imagination that could not forego the search for happiness though constantly finding but emptiness and desolation. And he made all this so clear that he actually startled and spell-bound the audience by his interpretation of the wonderful soliloquy wherein Hamlet debates whether he had not better with his own hand seize that consummation of death so devoutly to be wished, and escape

"The whips and scorns of time,
The oppressor's wrong, the proud man's contumely,
The pangs of despised love, the law's delay,
The insolence of office, and the spurns
That patient merit of the unworthy takes."

The deep intuition that felt there were more things in heaven and earth than philosophy had ever dreamed, the sore resentment at the unjust discriminations of the world, the over-inquisitive intellect of the fool of nature, horridly shaking his disposition with thoughts beyond the reaches of his soul, the instinctive shrinking from the undiscovered country after death, the broken will forever hankering after action but forever baffled from it, the unfathomable desire for rest, the intense ennui raising sighs so piteous and profound that they seemed to shatter all the bulk,—all these were so brought out as to constitute a revelation of the history of genius diseased by excessive exercise within itself with no external outlets of wholesome activity. This lesson has the greatest significance for the present time, when so many gifted men allow their faculties to spin barrenly in their sockets, incessantly struggling with abstract desires and doubts, wasting the health and strength all away because the spiritual mechanism is not lubricated by outward fruition of its functions, till normal religious faith is made impossible, and at last, in their sterilized and irritable exhaustion, they apotheosize despair, like Schopenhauer, and perpetually toss between the two poles of pessimism and nihilism,— Everything is bad, Everything is nothing! The true moral of the revelation is, Shut off the wastes of an ambitious intellect and a rebellious will by humility and resignation, do the clear duties next your hand, enjoy the simple pleasures of the day with an innocent heart, trusting in the benignant order of the universe, and you shall at last find peace in such an optimistic faith as that illustrated by Leibnitz,—Everything is good, Everything in the infinite degrees of being from vacuity to plenum is centred in God!

It has always been felt that in Hamlet Shakspeare has embodied more of his own inner life than in any other of his characters. Certainly Hamlet is the literary father of the prolific modern brood of men of genius who fail of all satisfactory outward activity because wasting their spiritual peace and force in the friction of an inane cerebral strife and worry. Few appreciate the true teaching or importance of this portrayal. Hamlet said he lacked advancement, and that there was nothing good or bad but thinking made it so, and that were it not that he had bad dreams he could be bounded in a nutshell and count himself king of infinite space. His comments on others were usually contemptuous and satirical. He despised and mocked Polonius, and treated Osric, Rosencrantz, and Guildenstern with scorn and sarcasm. And yet, although he vilifies the general crowd and the drossy age, he is clearly sensitive to public opinion and really most anxious to appear well, and unwilling to bear a wounded name. In a word, he represents that class of select and unhappy spirits whose great imaginative sympathy is constantly showing to them themselves reflected in others and others reflected in themselves, the result of the comparisons being personal complacence and social irritability. For they form an estimate of their own superiority which they cannot by action justify to others and get them to ratify. The disparity of their inward power and their outward production annoys them, fixes itself in chronic consciousness, and in the consequent spiritual resistance and fret expends all the energy which if economized and fruitfully directed would remove the evil they resent and bless them with the good they desire. Then they react from the world into cynical bitterness and painful solitude. The empty struggle and misanthropic buzz within exhaust brain and nerves, and initiate a resentful, desponding, suicidal state made up of discordant aspiration and despair. Unable to fulfil themselves happily they madly seek to destroy themselves in order to end their misery. The remedy lies in a secret at once so deep and so transparent that hardly any of the victims ever see it. It is simply to think less pamperingly of themselves and more lovingly of others; cease from resistance, purify their ambition with humble faith, and in a quiet surrender to the Universal allow their drained and exasperated individuality leisure to be replenished and harmonized. Corresponding with a religious attunement of the soul, nervous tissues divinely filled with equalizing vitality and power are the physical ground of contentment with self, nature, mankind, destiny, and God. And the man of genius who has once lost it can gain this combined moral and physical condition only by a modest self-conquest, lowering his excessive exactions, and giving him a fair outlet for his inward desires in productive activity.

Forrest distinguished the wavering of his Hamlet from the indecision of his Macbeth and the promptitude of his Richard, and contrasted their deaths with a luminous marking both fine and bold. Richard, whose selfish intellect and stony heart had no conscience mediating between them, with solid equilibrium and ruthless decision swept directly to his object without pause or question. His death was characterized by convulsions of impotent rage that closed in paralyzing horror. The conscience of Macbeth made him hesitate, weigh, and vacillate until rising passion or foreign influence turned the scale. His death was one of climacteric bravery and frenzied exertion embraced in reckless despair. The intellect of Hamlet set his heart and his conscience at odds, and kept him ever balancing between opposed thoughts and solicitations. He had lost his stable poise, and was continually tipping from central sanity now towards dramatic madness, now towards substantial madness. He died with philosophic resignation and undemonstrative quietude. While all the mutes and audience to the act looked pale and trembled at the tragic chance, he bequeathed the justification of his memory to his dear Horatio, gave his dying voice for the election of Fortinbras, and slowly, as the potent poison quite o'ercrowed his spirit, let his head sink on the bosom of his one friend, and with a long breath faintly whispered,—

"The rest is silence;"—
and then all was done.
"Now cracks a noble heart. Good-night, sweet prince,
And flights of angels sing thee to thy rest."

In the few pages of this tragedy Shakspeare gives perhaps the supremest existing example of the richness and power of the dramatic art. It sums up the story of life,—the joy of lovers, the anguish of bereavement, the trial of friendship, hope and fear, plot and counterplot, lust, hatred, crime and the remorse that follows, hearty mirth contrasted with sublime despair, death, and the dark ignorance of what it all means which shuts around the horizon with impenetrable clouds. Here are expressed an intensity of passion, a bitter irony, a helpless doubt, a vain struggle, a saturating melancholy and a bewildered end which would be too repulsive for endurance were it not for the celestial poetry which plays over it and permeates it all and makes it appear like a strange and beautiful dream.

As to the interpretation by Forrest of the part of Hamlet in the play it is but fair to quote in close what was said by a severe and unfriendly anonymous critic who admitted that the intelligence shown was uncommon, the elocution perfect, the manner discreet, the light and shade impressive. "Mr. Forrest struggles continually with Mr. Forrest. Mind wrestles with muscle; and although intellect is manifest, it is plain that the body with great obstinacy refuses to fulfil the demands of thought. To conceive bright images is a different thing from portraying them on the canvas. And when Mr. Forrest, attempting with high ambition to do that which nature forbids him to do, makes of philosophy a physical exhibition and reduces mental supremacy to the dominion of corporeal authority, he must blame that fate which cast him in no common mould and gave to the body a preponderance which neither study nor inspiration can overcome." The critic here indicates the defect of the actor, unquestionably, but so exaggerated as to dwarf and obscure his greater merits.

CORIOLANUS.

Not many dramatic contrasts are wider than that between the complex imaginative character of the melancholy Hamlet, spontaneously betaking himself to speculation, and the simple passionate character of the proud Coriolanus, instinctively rushing to action. There was much in the build and soul of Forrest that closely resembled the haughty patrician, and he was drawn to the part by a liking for it accordant with his inherent fitness for it. For several years he played it a great deal and produced a strong sensation in it. So thoroughly suited were he and the part for each other, so pervasive and genuine was the identification of his personal quality with the ideal picture, that his most intimate friend, and the gifted artist chosen for the work, selected this as the most appropriate representative character for his portrait-statue in marble.

The features and contour of the honest, imperious, fiery, scornful, and heroic Coriolanus, as impersonated by Forrest with immense solidity and distinctness, were simple but grand in their colossal and unwavering relief. Kemble had been celebrated in this rôle. He played it as if he were a symmetrical statue cut out of cold steel and set in motion by some precise mechanical action. Forrest added to this a blood that seemed to flame through him and a voice whose ponderous syllables pulsated with fire. Stern virtue, ambition, deep tenderness, magnanimity, transcendent daring and pride and scorn,—the man as soldier and hero in uncorrupt sincerity and haughty defiance of everything wrong or mean,—these were the favorite attributes which Forrest met in Coriolanus, and absorbed as by an electric affinity, and made the people recognize with applauding enthusiasm. He might well utter as his own the words of his part to Volumnia,—

"Would you have me
False to my nature? Rather say, I play
The man I am."

What unconsciously delighted Forrest in Coriolanus, and what he represented with consummate felicity and force of nature, was that his aristocracy was of the true democratic type; that is, it rested on a consciousness of intrinsic personal worth and superiority, not on conventional privilege and prescription. He loathed and launched his scorching invectives against the commonalty not because they were plebeians and he was a patrician, but because of the revolting opposition of their baseness to his loftiness, of their sycophancy to his pride, of their treacherous fickleness to his adamantine steadfastness. As an antique Roman, he had the resentful haughtiness of his social caste, but morally as an individual his disdain and sarcasm were based on the contrast of intrinsically noble qualities in himself to the contemptible qualities he saw predominating in those beneath him. And although this is far removed from the beautiful bearing of a spiritually purified and perfected manhood, yet there is in it a certain relative historical justification, utility, and even glory, entirely congenial to the honest vernacular fervor of Forrest.

Coriolanus, in his utter loathing for the arts of the demagogue, goes to the other extreme, and makes the people hate him because, as they say, "For the services he has done he pays himself with being proud." At his first appearance in the play he cries to the citizens, with scathing contempt,—

"What's the matter, you dissentient rogues,
That, rubbing the poor itch of your opinion,
Make yourselves scabs?
He that trusts to you,
Where he should find you lions, finds you hares;
Where foxes, geese. You are no surer, no,
Than is the coal of fire upon the ice,
Or hailstone in the sun. Hang ye! Trust ye?

With every minute you do. change a mind;
And call him noble that was now your hate;
Him vile, that was your garland."

As his constancy despises their unstableness, so his audacious courage detests their cowardice:

"Now put your shields before your hearts, and fight
With hearts more proof than shields."
Seeing them driven back by the Volsces, he exclaims,—
"You souls of geese
That bear the shapes of men, how have you run
From slaves that apes would beat? Pluto and hell!
All hurt behind; backs red, and faces pale
With flight and agued fear! Mend, and charge home,
Or, by the fires of heaven, I'll leave the foe
And make my wars on you."

In all these speeches the measureless contempt, the blasting irony, the huge moral chasm separating the haughty speaker from the cowering rabble, were deeply relished by Forrest, and received an expression in his bearing, look, and tone, everyway befitting their intensity and their dimensions. Particularly in the reply to Sicinius,—

"Shall remain!
Hear you this Triton of the minnows? Mark you
His absolute 'shall'?"—

the width of the gamut of the ironical circumflexes gave one an enlarged idea of the capacity of the human voice to express contempt. And when his disdain to beg the votes of the people and his mocking gibes at them had aggravated them to pronounce his banishment, his superhuman expression of scornful wrath no witness could ever forget:

"You common cry of curs! whose breath I hate
As reek o' the rotten fens, whose loves I prize
As the dead carcasses of unburied men
That do corrupt my air, I banish you."

His eyes flashed, his form lifted to its loftiest altitude, and the words were driven home concentrated into hissing bolts. As the enraged mob pressed yelping at his heels, he turned, and with marvellous simplicity of purpose calmly looked them reeling backwards, his single sphere swallowing all theirs and swaying them helplessly at his magnetic will.

His farewell, when "the beast with many heads had butted him away," was a noble example of manly tenderness and dignity, all the more pathetic from the self-control which masked his pain in a smiling aspect:

"Thou old and true Menenius,
Thy tears are salter than a younger man's,
And venomous to thine eyes. I'll do well yet.
Come, my sweet wife, my dearest mother, and
My friends of noble touch, when I am forth,
Bid me farewell, and smile. I pray you, come.
While I remain above the ground, you shall
Hear from me still."

But his most charming and delightful piece of acting in the whole play was the interview with his family on his return with Aufidius and the conquering Volscians before the gates of Rome. The swift-recurring struggle and alternation of feeling between the opposite extremes of intense natural affection and revengeful tenacity of pride were painted in all the vivid lineaments of truth. Fixed in the frozen pomp of his power and his purpose, he soliloquizes,—

"My wife comes foremost, then the honored mould
Wherein this trunk was framed, and in her hand
The grandchild to her blood. But out, affection!

All bond and privilege of nature, break!
Let it be virtuous to be obstinate.
What is that curt'sy worth, or those doves' eyes,
Which can make gods forsworn? I melt and am not
Of stronger earth than others. My mother bows;
As if Olympus to a molehill should
In supplication nod; and my young boy
Hath an aspect of intercession, which
Great nature cries, 'Deny not.' Let the Volsces
Plough Rome and harrow Italy; I'll never
Be such a gosling to obey instinct; but stand
As if a man were author of himself
And knew no other kin."

But when Virgilia fixed her eyes on him and said, "My lord and husband!" his ice flowed quite away, and the exquisite thoughts which followed were vibrated on the vocal chords as if not his lungs but his heart supplied the voice:

"Like a dull actor now,
I have forgot my part, and I am out,
Even to a full disgrace. Best of my flesh,
Forgive my tyranny; but do not say,
For that, 'Forgive our Romans.' O, a kiss
Long as my exile, sweet as my revenge!
Now, by the jealous queen of heaven, that kiss
I carried from thee, dear; and my true lip
Hath virgined it e'er since. You gods! I prate,
And the most noble mother of the world
Leave unsaluted. Sink, my knee, i' the earth;
Of thy deep duty more impression show
Than that of common sons."

Yielding to the prayers of Volumnia, he took her hand with tender reverence, and said, with upturned look and deprecating tone,—

"O, mother, mother!
What have you done? Behold, the heavens do ope,
The gods look down, and this unnatural scene
They laugh at."

From the solemn reverence of this scene the change was wonderful
to the frenzied violence of untamable anger and scorn with which he
broke on Aufidius, who had called him "a boy of tears:"

"Measureless liar, thou hast made my heart
Too great for what contains it. Boy! O slave!
Cut me to pieces, Volsces; men and lads,
Stain all your edges on me. Boy! False hound!
If you have writ your annals true, 'tis there,
That, like an eagle in a dovecote, I
Fluttered your Volsces in Corioli:
Alone I did it. Boy!"

The signalizing memorable mark of the Coriolanus impersonated by
Forrest was the gigantic grandeur of his scale of being and
consciousness. He revealed this in his stand and port and moving and
look and voice. The manner in which he did it was no result of critical
analysis, but was intuitive with him, given to him by nature and
inspiration. He exhibited a gravitating solidity of person, a length of
lines, a slowness of curves, an immensity of orbit, a reverberating
sonority of tone, which illustrated the man who, as Menenius said,
"wanted nothing of a god but eternity, and a heaven to throne in." They
went far to justify the amazing descriptions given in the play itself of
the impressions produced by him on those who approached him.

"Being moved, he will not spare to gird the gods.
Marked you his lip, and eyes?"
"Who is yonder?
O gods! he has the stand of Marcius."
"The shepherd knows not thunder from a tabor

More than I know the sound of Marcius' tongue
From every meaner man."
"Marcius,
A carbuncle entire, as big as thou art,
Were not so rich a jewel. Thou art a soldier
Even to Cato's wish, not fierce and terrible
Only in strokes; but, with thy grim looks, and
The thunder-like percussion of thy sounds,
Thou mak'st thine enemies shake, as if the world
Were feverous and did tremble."
"The man I speak of cannot in the world
Be singly counterpoised."

When, after his peerless feats in battle, the army and its leaders would idolize him with praises, crown him with garlands, and load him with spoils, he felt his deeds to be their own sufficient pay, and waved all the rewards peremptorily aside with a mien as imposing as if some god

"Were slily crept into his human powers
And gave, him noble posture."

Entering the capital in triumph, the vast and steady imperiality of his attitude, the tremendous weight of his slightest inclination, as though the whole earth were the pedestal-slab on which he stood, drew and fascinated all gaze.

"Matrons flung gloves,
Ladies and maids their scarfs and handkerchiefs,
Upon him as he passed; the nobles bended
As to Jove's statue; and the commons made
A shower and thunder with their caps and shouts."

The rare and exalted use of such acting as this is that it invites the audience to lift their eyes above the vulgar pettinesses to which they are accustomed and extend their souls with a superior conception of the dignity of human nature and of the mysterious meanings latent in it.

The Coriolanus of Forrest was a marble apotheosis of heroic strength, pride, and scorn. His moral glory was that he asserted himself on the solid grounds of conscious truth, justice, and merit, and not, as popular demagogues and the selfish members of the patrician class do, on hollow grounds of assumption, trickery, and spoliating fraud. There was great beauty, too, in his reverential love for his mother, his tender love for his wife, his hearty love for his friend, and his magnanimous incapacity for any recognized littleness of soul or of deed. The weight and might of his spirit could give away victories and confer favors, but could not steal a laurel or endure flattery. His fatal defect was that he did not know the spirit of forgiveness, and was utterly incompetent to self-renunciation. He had the repulsive and fatal fault of a crude, harsh, revengeful temper, that clothed his gigantic indirect egotism in the glorifying disguise of justice and sacrificed even his country to his personal passion. Just and true at the roots, his virtues grew insane from pride. Wrath destroyed his equilibrium, and belched his grandeur and his life away in incontinent insolence of expression. Like all the favorite characters of Forrest, however, he was no starveling fed on verbality and ceremony, no pygmy imitator or empty conformist, but one who lived in rich power from his own original centres and let his qualities honestly out with democratic sincerity of self-assertion. There is indeed a royal lesson in what he says:

> "Should we in all things do what custom wills,
> The dust on antique time would lie unswept,
> And mountainous error be too highly heaped
> For truth to o'er-peer."

Still, self-will ought abnegatingly to give way in docile and disinterested devotion to the public good. The great, strong, fearless man should conquer himself, render his pride impersonal, renounce revenge for individual slights or wrongs, and, instead of despising and insulting the plebeian multitude, labor to abate their vices, remove their errors, guide their efforts, and build their virtues into a fabric of popular freedom and happiness. Then the selfish, passional ideal of the past would give way to the rational, social ideal which is to redeem the future. For, as a general rule thus far in the history of the world, power, both private and public, in the proportion of its degree, has been complacent instead of sympathetic despotic instead of helpful, indulging its own passions, despising the needs of others, filling civilization itself with the spirit of moral murder. The chief characters of Shakspeare embody this pagan ideal. Is there not a Christian ideal, long since divinely born, but still waiting to be nurtured to full growth, to be illustrated by dramatic genius, and to be glorified in universal realization?

OTHELLO.

There was no character in which Forrest appeared more frequently or with more effect on those who saw him than in that of Othello. He was pre-eminently suited to the part by his own nature and experience, as well as by unwearied-observation and study. The play turns on the most vital and popular of all the passions, love, and its revulsion into the most cruel and terrible one, jealousy. He devoted incredible pains to the perfecting of his representation of it; and undoubtedly it was, on the whole, the most true and powerful of all his performances, though in single particulars some others equalled and his Lear surpassed it. Unprejudiced and competent judges agreed that he portrayed Othello in the great phases of his character,—as a man dignified, clear, generous, and calm,—as a man ecstatically happy in an all-absorbing love,—as a man slowly wrought up through the successive degrees of jealousy,—as a man actually converted into a maniac by the frightful conflict and agony of his soul,—and, finally, as a man who in the frenzy of despair closes the scene with murder and suicide;—that he acted all this with an intensity, an accuracy, a varied naturalness and sweeping power very rarely paralleled in the history of the stage. The reason why the portraiture received so much censorious criticism amidst the abundant admiration it excited was because the scale and fervor of the passions bodied forth in it were so much beyond the experience of average natures. They were not exaggerated or false, but seemed so to the cold or petty souls who knew nothing of the lava-floods of bliss and avalanches of woe that ravage the sensibilities of the impassioned souls that find complete fulfilment and lose it. It is a most significant and interesting fact that when the matchless Salvini played Othello in the principal American cities to such enthusiastic applause, his conception and performance of the part were so identical with those of Forrest, and he himself so closely resembled his deceased compeer, that hundreds of witnesses in different portions of the country spontaneously exclaimed that it seemed as if Forrest had risen from the dead and reappeared in his favorite rôle. The old obstinate prejudices did not interfere; and although Salvini made the passion more raw and the force more shuddering and carried the climax one degree farther than the American tragedian had done, actually sinking the human maniac in the infuriated tiger, he was greeted with wondering acclaim. If his portraiture of the Moor was a true one,—as it unquestionably was,— then that of Forrest was equally true and better moderated.

In the first speech of Othello, referring to the purpose of Brabantio to injure him with the Duke, Forrest won all hearts by the impression he gave of the noble self-possession of a free and generous nature full of honest affection and manly potency. He alluded to Brabantio without any touch of anger or scorn, to himself with an air of quiet pride bottomed on conscious worth and not on any vanity or egotism, and to Desdemona with a softened tone of effusive warmth which betrayed the precious freight and direction of his heart:

"Let him do his spite;
My services, which I have done the seignory,
Shall out-tongue his complaints. My dements
May speak, unbonneted, to as proud a fortune

As this that I have reached. For know, Iago,
But that I love the gentle Desdemona,
I would not my unhoused, free condition
Put into circumscription and confine
For the sea's worth."

The easy frankness of his look and the rich flowing elocution of his delivery of these words indicated a nature so ingenuous and honorable that already the sympathies of every man and woman before him were won to the Moor. This impression was continued and enhanced when, in response to the abusive epithet of Brabantio and the threats of his armed followers, he said, in a tone of unruffled self-command, touched with a humorous playfulness and with a deprecating respect,—

"Keep up your bright swords, for the dew will rust them.—
Good seignior, you shall more command with years,
Than with your weapons."

There was an exquisite moral beauty in the whole attitude and carriage which Forrest gave Othello in the scene in the council-chamber, where he replied to the accusations of using spells and medicines to draw Desdemona to his arms. There was a combination of modest assurance and picturesque dignity in his bearing, and a simple eloquence in his pronouncing of the narrative of all his wooing, so artistic in its seeming artlessness, so full of breathing honesty straight from the heart of nature, that not a word could be doubted, nor could any hearer resist the conviction expressed by the Duke,—

"I think this tale would win my daughter too,
Good Brabantio."

To the bewitching power of simple sincerity and glowing truth he put into this marvellous speech hundreds of testimonies were given like that of the refined and lovely young lady who was heard saying to her companion, "If that is the way Moors look and talk and love, give me a Moor for my husband."

When Desdemona entered, while she stayed, as she spoke, as she departed, all the action of Othello towards her, his motions, looks, words, inflections, clearly betokened the nature and supremacy of his affection for her. Through the high and pure character of these signals it was made obvious that his love was an entrancing possession; not an animal love bred in the senses alone, but a love born in the soul and flooding the senses with its divineness. On the keen fires of his high-blooded organism and the poetic enchantments of his ardent imagination the exquisite sweetness of this surrendered and gentle Desdemona played a delicious intoxication, and the enthrallment of his passion made the very movement of existence a rapture. Everything else faded before the happiness he felt. Life was too short, the earth too dull, the stars too dim, for the blissful height of his consciousness. In contrast with this enchanted possession, day, night, joy, laughter, air, sea, the thrilling notes of war, victory, fame, and power, were but passing illusions. The voice of duty could rouse him from his dream, but the moment his task was done he sank again into its ecstatic depths. All this still saturation of delight and fulness of expanded being the Othello of Forrest revealed by his acting and speech on meeting Desdemona in Cyprus after their separation by his sudden departure to the wars. As, all eager loveliness, she came in sight, exclaiming, "My dear Othello!" the sudden brightness of his eyes, the rapturous smile that clothed his face, his parted lips, his heaving breast and outstretched arms, were so significant that they worked on the spectators like an incantation. And when he drew her passionately to his bosom, kissed her on the forehead and lips, and gazed into her face with unfathomable fondness, it was a picture not to be surpassed of the exquisite doting of the new-made husband while the honeymoon yet hung over them full-orbed in the silent and dewy heaven, its inundation undimmed by the breath of custom. Then he spoke:

"O, my soul's joy!
If after every tempest come such calms,
May the winds blow till they have wakened death;
And let the laboring bark climb hills of seas
Olympus-high, and duck again as low
As hell's from heaven! If it were now to die,
'Twere now to be most happy; for, I fear,
My soul hath her content so absolute,
That not another comfort like to this
Succeeds in unknown fate."

The last lines he uttered with a restrained, prolonged, murmuring music, a tremulous mellowness, as if the burden of emotion broke the vocal breath into quivers. It suggested a tenderness whose very excess made it timid and mystic with a pathetic presentiment of its own evanescence. The yearning, aching deliciousness of love filled his breast so more than full that even while he seemed to strive to hold back all verbal expression for fear of losing the emotional substance, it broke forth itself with melodious softness in the syllabled beats of the lingering words:

"I cannot speak enough of this content:
It stops me here: it is too much of joy.
Come, let us to the castle. O, my sweet,
I prattle out of fashion, and I dote
In mine own comforts."

In the scene of the drunken brawl in Cyprus most actors had made Othello rush in with drawn sword, crying, with extravagant pose and emphasis, "Hold, for your lives!" Forrest entered without sword, in haste, his night-mantle thrown over his shoulders as if just from his bed. He went through the scene, rebuking the brawlers and restoring order, with an admirable moderation combined with commanding moral authority. Only once, when answer to his inquiry was delayed, his volcanic heat burst out. He spoke rapidly, with surprise rather than anger, and bore down all with a personal weight that had neither pomp nor offence, yet was not to be resisted. Throughout the first and second acts Forrest played Othello as a man of beautiful human nature, noble in honor, rich in affection, gentle in manners, though, when justly roused, capable of a terrific headlong wrath:

"Now, by Heaven,
My blood begins nay safer guides to rule;
And passion, having my best judgment collied,
Assays to lead the way. If I once stir
Or do but lift this arm, the best of you
Shall sink in my rebuke."

In the third act the diabolical malignity and cunning of Iago begin to take effect, more and more insinuating poisonous suspicions and doubts into the naturally open and truthful mind of Othello. The process and advancement of the horrid struggle found in Forrest a man and an artist to whose experience of human nature and life no item in the whole dread catalogue of the courses, symptoms, and consequences of love encroached on and subdued by jealousy was foreign, and whose skill in expression was abundantly able to set every feature of the tragedy in distinct relief. As now the guileless Desdemona shone on him, and anon the devilish Iago distilled his venom, he was torn between his loving confidence in his wife and his confiding trust in his tempter:

"As if two hearts did in one body reign
And urge conflicting streams from vein to vein."

When he saw or thought of her a blessed reassurance tranquillized him; when he heeded the hideous suggestions of his treacherous servant a frozen shudder ran through him. The waves of tenderness and violence chased one another over the mimic scene. At one moment he said,—

"If she be false, O, then heaven mocks itself.
I'll not believe it."

At another moment he writhed in excruciating anguish under the
fearful innuendoes which Iago wound about him. The spectacle was
like that of an anaconda winding her tightening coils around a tiger
until one can hear the cracking of the bones in his lordly back.

When the fiendish suggestions of Iago first took thorough effect the
result startled even him, and he gazed on the awful convulsions in the
face of his victim as one might look into the crater of Vesuvius. That
which had seemed granite proved to be gunpowder. As with the prairie
fire: the traveller lets a spark fall, and the whole earth seems to be one
rushing flame. Then swiftly followed those lacerating alternations of
contradictory excitements which are the essence of jealousy,—the
mixture of intense opposites into an experience of infernal discord.
His love lingers on her and gloats over her, and will not believe any evil
of her. His suspicion makes him shrink into himself with horror:

"O curse of marriage,
That we can call these delicate creatures ours,
And not their appetites."

Now he seeks relief in loathing and hating her, trying to tear her dear
image out from among his heart-strings. From the crazing agony of
this effort he springs wildly into wrath against her traducer. Forrest
expressed these sudden and violent transitions from extreme to
extreme with exact truth to nature, by that constant interchanging of
intense muscles and languid eyes with intense eyes and languid
muscles which corresponds with the successive apprehension of a
blessing to be embraced and an evil to be abhorred. The change in his
appearance and moving too was commensurate with what he had
undergone. As he advanced to meet his wife on her arrival in Cyprus,
he walked like one inspired, weightless and illumined with joy:

"Treading on air each step the soul displays,
The looks all lighten and the limbs all blaze."

But after the dreadful doubt had ruined his peace, he grew so pale
and haggard, wore so startled and dismal a look, was so self-absorbed
in misery, that he appeared an incarnate comment on the descriptive
words,—

"Look where he comes! Not poppy nor mandragora,
Nor all the drowsy syrups of the world,
Shall ever medicine thee to that sweet sleep
Which thou ow'dst yesterday."

There was an imaginative vastness and unity in the soul of Othello
which aggrandized his experiences and allowed him to do nothing by
halves. Forrest so perceived and exemplified this as to make his
performance come before the audience as a new revelation to them of
the colossal and blazing extremes, the entrancing, maddening, and
fatal extremes, to which human passions can mount. His love, his
conflict with doubt, his melancholy, his wrath, his hate, his revenge, his
remorse, his despair, each in turn absorbingly possesses him and
floods the earth with heaven or hell.

The unrivalled speech of lamentation over his lost happiness he gave
not, as many a famous actor has, partly in a tone of complaining
vexation and partly with a noisy pomp of declamation. He began with
an exquisite quality of tearful regret and sorrow which was a breathing
requiem over the ruins of his past delights. The mournfulness of it was
so sweet and chill that it seemed perfumed with the roses and moss
growing over the tomb of all his love.

"I had been happy if the general camp,
Pioneers and all, had tasted her sweet body,
So I had nothing known."

Then the voice, still low and plaintive, swelled and quivered with the
glorious words that followed:

"O, now, forever,
Farewell the tranquil mind! farewell content!
Farewell the plumed troop, and the big wars,
That make ambition virtue! O, farewell!"
And as he ended with the line,
"Farewell! Othello's occupation's gone!"

his form and limbs drooping, his lips sunken and tremulous, his very life seemed going out with each word, as if everything had been taken from him and he was all gone. Suddenly, with one electrifying bound, he leaped the whole gamut from mortal exhaustion to gigantic rage, his eyeballs rolling and flashing and his muscles strung, seized the cowering Iago by the throat, and, with a startling transition of voice from mellow and mournfully lingering notes to crackling thunderbolts of articulation, shrieked,—

"If thou dost slander her, and torture me,
Never pray more; abandon all remorse;
On horror's head horrors accumulate;
Do deeds to make heaven weep, all earth amazed;—
For nothing canst thou to damnation add
Greater than that."

The wild inspiration subsided as swiftly as it had risen, and left him gazing in blank amazement at what he had done. Again his struggling emotions were carried to a kindred climax when Iago told him the pretended dream of Cassio. He uttered the sentence, "I will tear her all to pieces," in a manner whose force of pathos surprised every heart. His revenge began furiously, "I will tear her"—when his love came over it, and he suddenly ended with pitying softness—"all to pieces." It was as if an avalanche, sweeping along earth and rocks and trees, were met by a breath which turned it into a feather. In the next act he gave an instance just the reverse of this: first he says, with doting fondness, "O, the world hath not a sweeter creature;" then, the imaginative associations changing the picture, he screams ferociously, "I will chop her into messes!"

Thence onward Othello was painted in a more and more piteous plight. The great soul was conquered by the remorseless intellect of Iago, leagued with its own weakness and excess. He grew less massive and more petulant. He stooped to spies and plots, and compassed the assassination of Cassio. His misery sapped his mind and toppled down his chivalrous sentiments until he could unpack his sore and wretched heart in abusive words and treat Desdemona with unrelenting cruelty.

Finally his tossing convulsions passed away, and a fixed resolution to kill the woman who had been false to him settled down in gloomy calmness. The curtain rose and showed him seated at an open window looking out on the night sky. Desdemona was asleep in her bed. He sighed heavily, and in slow tones, loaded with thoughtful and resigned melancholy, soliloquized,—

> "It is the cause, it is the cause, my soul,—
> Let me not name it to you, you chaste stars!—
> It is the cause. Yet I'll not shed her blood,
> Nor scar that whiter skin of hers than snow,
> And smooth as monumental alabaster.
> Yet she must die, else she'll betray more men.
> Put out the light, and then put out the light.
> If I quench thee, thou flaming minister,
> I can again thy former light restore,
> Should I repent me. But once put out thy light,
> Thou cunning'st pattern of excelling nature,
> I know not where is that Promethean heat
> That can thy light relume."

He permitted the audience to see the vast dimension and intensity of his love, doubt, agony, sorrow, despair, vengeance,— and the revelation was appalling in its solemnity. Henceforth even his invective was moderated and quiet. He seemed to fancy himself not so much revenging his personal wrong as vindicating himself and executing justice. He did not make a horror of the killing, as Kean did. He drew the curtains apart,—a slight struggle,—a choking murmur,—and as Emilia knocked at the door, and he turned, with the pillow in his hand, his listening attitude and his bronze face and glistening eyes formed a dramatic picture not to be forgotten. Then came the final revulsion of his agonizing sorrow:

> "O, insupportable! O, heavy hour
> Methinks it should be now a huge eclipse
> Of sun and moon; and that the affrighted globe
> Should yawn at alteration."

His deadly distress and paralyzing bewilderment now illustrated what he had before said, that he loved her so with the entirety of his being that the loss of her, even in thought, brought back chaos:

> "Had she been true,
> If heaven would make me such another world
> Of one entire and perfect chrysolite,
> I'd not have sold her for it."

When Emilia revealed the plot by which he had been deceived, and convinced him of the innocence of his wife, an absolute desolation and horror of remorse, as if a thunderbolt had burst within his brain, smote him to the floor. Staggering to the fatal couch, his gaze was riveted on the marble face there, and a broken heart and a distracted conscience moaned and sobbed in the syllables,—

> "Now, how dost thou look now? O, ill-starred wench!
> Pale as thy smock! when we shall meet at compt,
> This look of thine will hurl my soul from heaven,
> And fiends will snatch at it Cold, cold, my girl?
> Even like thy chastity.
> O, cursed, cursed slave! Whip me, ye devils,
> From the possession of this heavenly sight!

Blow me about in winds I roast me in sulphur!
Wash me in steep-down gulfs of liquid fire!
O Desdemona! Desdemona! dead?"

The strain had been too great to be borne, and he was himself nearly dead. He wore the aspect of one who felt that to live was calamity, and to die the sole happiness left. Collecting himself, he spoke the calm words of appeal that justice might be done to his memory, nothing extenuated nor aught set down in malice. He turned towards the breathless form, once so dear, with a look of tenderness slowly dissolving and freezing into despair. Then, with one stroke of his dagger, he fell dead without a groan or a shudder.

"This did I fear, but thought he had no weapon;
For he was great of heart."

Some actors have made Othello feared and disliked; others have caused him to be regarded with moral curiosity or poetic interest. As Forrest impersonated him he was first warmly admired, then profoundly pitied. Of the tragedians most celebrated in the past, according to the best descriptions which have been given of their representations, it may be said that the Othello of Quin was a jealous plebeian; the Othello of Kean, in parts a jealous king, in parts a jealous savage; the Othello of Vandenhoff, a jealous general; the Othello of Macready, a jealous theatrical player; the Othello of Brooke, a jealous knight; the Othello of Salvini, a jealous lover transformed into a jealous tiger; but the Othello of Forrest was a jealous man carried truthfully through all the degrees of his passion. One of his predecessors in the rôle had veiled the woes of the man beneath the dignities of his rank and station as a martial commander; another had theatricized the part, with wondrous study and toil, elaborating posture, look, and emphasis, presenting a correctness of drawing which might secure admiring criticism but could never move feeling; yet another, fascinated with the romantic accessories and vicissitudes of the character, made a gorgeous picture of a gorgeous hero in a gorgeous time. Forrest analyzed away from his Othello all adventitious circumstances; took him from the picturesque scenes of Venice, stripped off his official robes, and placed him on the stage in the glories and tortures of his naked humanity, a living mirror to every one of the struggles of a master-passion tearing a great heart asunder, driving a powerful mind into the awful abyss of insanity, making a generous man a coward, an eavesdropper, a murderer, and a suicide.

The explicit contents and teaching of the part as Shakspeare wrote it and as Forrest acted it are the unspeakable privilege and preciousness of a supreme human love crowned with fulfilment, and the fearful nature and results of an ill-grounded jealousy. The deeper implicit meaning and lesson it bears is the animal degradation, the frightful ugliness and danger, the intrinsically immoral and murderous character of the passion of jealousy. This all-important revelation latent in the tragedy of Othello has not been illumined, emphasized, or brought into relief on the stage as yet. It ought to be done. The historical traditions of tyrannical selfishness, almost universally organized in the interests of the world, which make men feel that in sexual love the lover possesses the object of his love as an appanage and personal property, all whose free wishes are merged in his will and whose disloyalty is justly visited with merciless cruelty and even death itself, have blinded most persons to the inherent unworthiness and vulgarity, the inherent ferocity and peril, of the, passion of jealousy. It is common among brutes, and belongs to the brutish stage in man. It cannot be imagined in heaven among the cherubim and seraphim. Freedom, the self-possession of each one in equilibrium with all others and in harmony with universal order, belongs to the divine stage of developed humanity. There can be no certainty against madness, crime, and self-immolation so long as an automatic passion in the lower regions of the organism enslaves the royal reason meant to reign by right from God. Happen what may, self-poise and the steady aim at progress towards perfection should be kept. This cannot be when love is degraded to physical pleasure sought as an end, instead of being consecrated to the fruitful purposes for which it was ordained. The only absolute pledge of blessedness and peace between those who love and would hope to love always is an adjustment of conduct based not on mere feeling, whether low or high, but on feeling as itself subdued and disciplined by reason, justice, and truth, first developed in the thinking mind and constituted as it were into the science of the subject, then appropriated by the sentiments and made habitual in the individual character. What details of conduct will result, what innovations on the present social state will be made, when a scientific morality shall have mastered the subject and formulated its principles into practical rules, it is premature to say. But it is certain that the leading of one life in the light and another one in the dark will be forbidden. It is certain that the discords, the diseases, the distresses, the crimes, which are now so profuse in this region of experience will be no longer tolerated. And it is safe to prophesy that such delirious expressions of hate and revenge as have hitherto usually been thought tragic and terrible will come to be thought bombastic and ludicrous:

"O that the slave had forty thousand lives;
One is too poor, too weak for my. revenge!
Now do I see 'tis true. Look here, Iago;
All my fond love thus do I blow to heaven. 'Tis gone.—
Arise, black vengeance, from thy hollow cell!
Yield up, O love, thy crown, and hearted throne,
To tyrannous hate! swell, bosom, with thy fraught;
For 'tis of aspics' tongues! O blood, blood, blood!"

Othello, like most of the characters of Shakspeare, illustrates the historic actual, not the prophetic ideal. The present state of society is so ill adjusted, so full of painful evils, that things cannot always remain as temporary and local habits and mere empirical authority have seemingly settled them. To think they can is the sure mark of a narrow mind, a petty character, and a selfish heart. Nothing is more certain than continuous change. Nothing is, therefore, more characteristic of the genuine thinker than his ability to contemplate other modes of thought, other varieties of sentiment, than those to which he was bred. With the progress of social evolution the hitherto prevalent ideas of love and jealousy may undergo changes amounting in some instances, perhaps, to a reversal. Meanwhile, those who are not prepared to adopt any new opinions in detail should, with hospitable readiness impartially to investigate, consider within themselves which is better, an imperial delicacy and magnanimity in those who love causing them to refuse to know anything that occurs in absence so long as each preserves self-respecting personal fidelity to the ideal of progressive perfection? or as at present, spiritual mutilation and misery, treacherous concealment, espionage, detection, disgrace, frenzy, and death?

One thing at all events is sure, namely, that of him alone whose love for God, or the universal in himself and others, is superior to his love for the individual, or the egotistic in himself and others, can it ever be safely said, as it was once so mistakenly said of the unhappy Moor,—

"This is a man
Whom passion cannot shake; whose solid virtue
The shock of accident nor dart of chance
Can neither graze nor pierce."

LEAR.

Nearly every season for more than forty years Forrest played the part of Lear many times. He never ceased to study it and to improve his representation, adding new touches here and there, until at last it became, if not the most elaborately finished and perfect of all his performances, certainly the sublimest in spiritual power and tragic pathos. As he grew old, as his experience of the desolating miseries of the world deepened, as his perception was sharpened of the hollowness and irony of the pomps and pleasures of human power contrasted with the solemn drifting of destiny and death, as the massiveness of his physique was expanded in its mould and loosened in its fibre by the shocks of time and fate, he seemed ever better fitted, both in faculty and appearance, to meet the ideal demands of the rôle. He formed his conception of it directly from the pages of Shakspeare and the dictates of nature. His elaboration and acting of it were original, the result of his own inspiration and study. Heeding no traditional authority, copying no predecessor, but testing each particular by the standard of truth, he might have proudly protested, like the veritable Lear,—

"No, they cannot touch me for coining,—I am the king himself."

No person of common sensibility could witness his impersonation of the character during his latter years without paying it the tribute of tears and awe.

Lear appears in a shape of imposing majesty, but with the authentic signals of breaking sorrow and ruin already obvious. He is a king in the native build and furniture of his being, not merely by outward rank. His scale of passion is gigantic, and always exerted at the extremes. When deferred to and pleased, his magnanimity is boundless and his love most tender. But, once crossed, nothing can restrain his petulance, and his outbursts of anger are terrible to others and dangerously expensive to himself. His identity is always marked by greatness, like some huge landmark dwarfing everything near. There is a royal scope and altitude belonging to the structure of his soul which is never lost. It is seen, whether he be ruler, outcast, or madman, in the grandeur of his mien, in the majestic eloquence of his thought and expression, in the towering swell of his ambition. He is ever insistingly conscious of his kingliness, and must be bowed to and have his way, as much when with the poor fool he hides his nakedness from the pelting blast as when in august plenitude of power he divides his realm among his children. This central point of unity Forrest firmly seized, and made it everywhere in his representation abundantly prominent and impressive.

At the opening of the play Lear is a very old man. Moved by some secret premonition of failing reason or decay, he is about to abdicate his crown. He is seen to be an imperial spirit throned in an enfeebled nature, a power girdled with weakness. An exacting and unbridled spirit of authority, a splenetic assertion of his kingly will, with the incessant worries and frictions to which such a habit always gives rise, have undermined his poise and lowered his strength, and brought his mind into that state of unstable equilibrium which is the condition of an explosive irritability fated to issue in madness. He himself, in the organic strata below his free intelligence, has obscure premonitions of his crumbling state; but every intimation of it which reaches his consciousness fills him with an angry resentment that seeks some instant vent.

The task to indicate all this, so clearly, with such moving force, with such combination of overtopping power and piteous weakness, as to fix it all in the apprehending sympathies of the audience, was marvellously accomplished by Forrest in the opening scene. The vast frame whose motions were alternately ponderous and fretful, the pale massive face, the restless wild eyes, the rich deep voice magnificent in oratoric phrase and breaking in querulous anger,—these, skilfully managed, revealed at once the ruining greatness of the royal nature, dowered with imposing and gracious qualities but fatally cored with irritable self-love.

> "Know that we have divided
> In three our kingdom; and 'tis our fast intent
> To shake all cares and business from our age;
> Conferring them on younger strengths, while we,
> Unburthened, crawl toward death. Tell me, my daughters,
> Since now we will divest us, both of rule,
> Interest of territory, cares of state,
> Which of you, shall we say, doth love us most?
> That we our largest bounty may extend
> Where nature doth with merit challenge."

The treacherous Goneril and Regan, whose heartless natures their younger sister so well knew, made such fulsome protestations as shocked her into a dumb reliance on her own true affection; and when the yearning and testy monarch fondly asks what she can say, her whole being of love and sincerity is behind her words:

"Unhappy that I am, I cannot heave
My heart into my mouth. I love your majesty
According to my bond."

Then broke forth the insane pride and self-will, which, brooking no appearance of opposition or evasion, were stricken with judicial blindness and left to prefer evil to good, to embrace the selfishness which was as false and cruel as hell, and to reject the love which was as gentle and true as heaven. With a terrible look, and a deep intensely girded voice, whose rapid accents made his whole chest shake with muffled reverberations, like a throbbing drum, he cried,—

"Let it be so: thy truth then be thy dower;
For, by the sacred radiance of the sun,
The mysteries of Hecate, and the night;
By all the operations of the orbs,
From whom we do exist, and cease to be;
Here I disclaim all my paternal care,
Propinquity, and property of blood,
And as a stranger to my heart and me
Hold thee, from this, forever. The barbarous Scythian,
Or he that makes his generation messes
To gorge his appetite, shall to my bosom
Be as well neighbored, pitied, and relieved,
As thou, my sometime daughter."

And when the noble Kent would have interceded, his frenzied wrong-headedness peremptorily destroyed the last hope of remedy:
"Peace, Kent!
Come not between the dragon and his wrath."
Then, with the piteous side-revelation,—
"I loved her most, and thought to set my rest

On her kind nursery,"—he subscribed and sealed his hideous fault by harshly driving the poor, sweet Cordelia from his presence, and banishing from his dominions the best friend he ever had, honest Kent.

The disease in the nature of Lear, a morbid self-consciousness that prevented alike self-rule and self-knowledge, did not let his passion expire like flaming tinder, but kept it long smouldering. Forrest pictured to perfection its recurring swells and tardy subsidence. Each advancing step showed more completely the vice that had cloyed the kingly nobility and gradually prepared the retributive tempest about to burst. His injured vanity feeding itself with its own inflaming deception now made his fancy ascribe to the angelic Cordelia, dismantled from the folds of his old favor, such foul and ugly features of character that he called her,

"A wretch whom nature is ashamed

Almost to acknowledge hers,"—while, perversely investing the tiger-breasted Goneril and Regan with imaginary goodness and charm, he said to them,—

"Ourself, by monthly course
With reservation of an hundred knights,
By you to be sustained, shall our abode
Make with you by due turns. Only we will retain
The name and all the additions to a king."

So to combine in the representation of Lear the power and the weakness, the mental and physical grandeur and irritability, as to compose a consistent picture true to nature, and to make their manifestations accurate both in the whirlwinds of passion and in the periods of calm,—this is what few even of the greatest actors have been able to do. Forrest did it in a degree which made the most competent judges the most enthusiastic applauders. The nervous and tottering walk, with its sudden changes, the quick transitions of his voice from thundering fulness to querulous shrillness, the illuminated and commanding aspect passing into sunken pallor and recovering, the straightenings up of the figure into firm equilibrium, the palsying collapses,—all these he gave with a precision and entireness which were the transcript and epitome of a thousand original studies of himself and of grand old men whom he had watched in different lands, in the streets, in lunatic asylums.

But the deepest merit of this representation was not its exactness in mimetic simulation or reproduction of the visible peculiarities of shattered and irascible age. Its chief merit was the luminous revelation it gave of the inner history of the character impersonated. He made it a living exhibition of the justifying causes and the profound moral lessons of the tragedy of the aged monarch, who, self-hurled both from his outer and his inner kingdom, was left to gibber with the gales and the lightnings on the rain-swept and desolate moor. In every fibre of his frame and every crevice of his soul Forrest felt the tremendous teachings intrusted by Shakspeare to the tragedy of Lear. It is true the feeling did not lead him morally to master these teachings for a redemptive application to himself; and his own experience paid the bitter penalty of a personal pride too exacting in its ideal estimate of self and others. But the feeling did enable him dramatically to portray these lessons, with matchless vividness and power, and a rugged realism softened and tinted with art. Shakspeare's own notion of Lear is remarkably expressed by one of the characters in the play: "He hath ever but slenderly known himself. Then we must look from his age to receive not alone the imperfections of long-engrafted condition, but, therewithal, the unruly waywardness that infirm and choleric years bring with them."

The whole history of the world in every part of society abounds with correspondences to the cruel error, the awful wrong, committed by Lear in accepting Goneril and Regan and rejecting Cordelia. But there is a cause for everything that happens. These dread and lamentable injustices arise from vices in the characters that perpetrate them. Their blindness is the punishment for their sin. The most inherent and obstinate sin in every unregenerate soul is excess of egotistic self-love. The strongest and richest natures are most exposed to this evil disguised in shapes so subtile as to deceive the very elect, making them unconsciously desire to subdue the wills of others to their will. This is a proud and fearful historic inheritance in the automatic depth of man below his free consciousness. Overcoming it, he is divinely free and peaceful. Yielding to it, he wears his force away in unhappy repinings and resentments. Aggravated by indulgence, it blinds his instincts and perverts his perceptions, makes him praise and clasp the bad who yield and flatter, denounce and shun the good who faithfully resist and try to bless. This profound moral truth Shakspeare makes the dim background of the tragedy, whose foreground blazes with a dreadful example of the penalties visited on those who violate its commands. He teaches that those who, bound and blinded by wilful self-love, embrace the designing and corrupt instead of the honest and pure, are left to the natural consequences of their choice. These consequences are the avenging Nemesis of divine providence. The actor who, as Forrest did, worthily illustrates this conception, becomes for the time the sublimest of preachers; for his appalling sermon is not an exhortation verbally articulated, it is a demonstration vitally incarnated.

The monstrous mistake of Lear soon brought its results to sight. The poor old monarch, fast weakening, even-paced, in his wits and muscles, but not abating one jot of his arrogant self-estimate and royal requiring, was so scolded, thwarted, and badgered by Goneril that he was quite beside himself with indignation. Then, most pitiably in his distress, relenting memory turned his regards towards the faithful gentleness he had spurned:

"O, most small fault!
How ugly didst thou in Cordelia show,
Which, like an engine, wrenched my frame of nature
From the fixed place, drew from my heart all love,
And added to the gall. O Lear, Lear, Lear!
Beat at this gate, that let thy folly in,
And thy dear judgment out."

Uttering these remorseful words, striking his forehead, Forrest stood, for a moment, a picture of uncertainty, regret, self-deprecation, and woe. Then a sense of the insulting disrespect and ingratitude of Gorieril seemed to break on him afresh, and let loose the whole volcanic flood of his injured self-hood. Anguish, wrath, and helplessness drove him mad. The blood made path from his heart to his brow, and hung there, a red cloud, beneath his crown. His eyes flashed and faded and reflashed. He beat his breast as if not knowing what he did. His hands clutched wildly at the air as though struggling with something invisible. Then, sinking on his knees, with upturned look and hands straight outstretched towards his unnatural daughter, he poured out, in frenzied tones of mingled shriek and sob, his withering curse, half adjuration, half malediction. It was a terrible thing, almost too fearful to be gazed at as a work of art, yet true to the character, the words, and the situation furnished by Shakspeare. Drawing for the moral world comparisons from the material world, it was a maelstrom of the conscience, an earthquake of the mind, a hurricane of the soul, and an avalanche of the heart. By a perfect gradation his protruded and bloodshot eyeballs, his crimsoned and swollen features, and his trembling frame subsided from their convulsive exertion. And with a confidence touching in its groundlessness, he bethought him,—

"I have another daughter,
Who, I am sure, is kind and comfortable."
He went to her, and said, with a distraught air of sorrowful anger, more pathetic than mere words can describe,—
"Thy sister's naught: O Regan! She hath tied
Sharp-toothed unkindness, like a vulture, here:
I can scarce speak to thee; thou'lt not believe
With how depraved a quality,—O Regan!"

Told by her that he was old, that in him nature stood on the verge of her confine, that he needed guidance, and had best return to Goneril and ask her forgiveness, he stood an instant in blank amazement, as if not trusting his ears; a tremor of agony and rage shot through him, fixed itself in a scornful smile, and, throwing himself on his knees, he vented his heart with superhuman irony:

"Dear daughter, I confess that I am old:
Age is unnecessary; on my knees I beg
That you'll vouchsafe me raiment, bed, and food."

Goneril entered. Shrinking from her partly with loathing, partly with fear, he exclaimed, in a tone of mournful and pleading pain befitting the transcendent pathos of the imagery,—

"O Heavens!
If you do love old men, if your sweet sway
Allow obedience, if yourselves are old,
Make it your cause: send down, and take my part!"

As Regan and Goneril chaffered and haggled to reduce the cost of his entertainment, he revealed in his face and byplay the effect their conduct had on him. The rising thoughts and emotions suffused his features in advance of their expression. He stood before the audience like a stained window that burns with the light of the landscape it hides. He then began in a low tone of supplicating feebleness and gradually mounted to a climax of frenzy, where the voice, raised to screaming shrillness, broke in helplessness, exemplifying that degree of passion which is impotent from its very intensity. Those critics who blamed him for this excess as a fault were wrong, not he; for it belongs to a rage which unseats the reason to have no power of repression, and so to recoil on itself in exhaustion:

"You see me here, you gods, a poor old man,
As full of grief as age; wretched in both.
If it be you that stir these daughters' hearts
Against their father, fool me not so much
To bear it tamely; touch me with noble anger.

O, let not women's weapons, water-drops,
Stain my man's cheeks. No, you unnatural hags,
I will have such revenges on you both
That all the world shall—I will do such things—
What they are yet I know not—but they shall be
The terrors of the earth."

The elemental storm at that moment heard rumbling in the distance actually seemed an echo of the more terrible spiritual storm raging in him.

The scene by night on the heath, where Lear, discrowned of his reason, wanders in the tempest,—the earth his floor, the sky his roof, the elements his comrades,—was sustained by Forrest with a broad strength and intensity which left nothing wanting. Even the imagination was satisfied with the scale of acting when the old king was seen, colossal in his broken decay, exulting as the monarch of a new realm, pelted by tempests, shrilling with curses, and peopled with wicked daughters! His eyes aflame, his breast distended, his arms flying, his white hair all astream in the wind, his voice rolling and crashing like another thunder below, he seemed some wild spirit in command of the scene; and he called, as if to his conscious subjects,—

.

"Blow, winds, and crack your cheeks! rage! blow!
You cataracts and hurricanoes, spout,
Till you have drenched our steeples, drowned the cocks!
You sulphurous and thought-executing fires,
Vaunt-couriers to oak-cleaving thunderbolts,
Singe my white head! And thou, all-shaking thunder,
Strike flat the thick rotundity o' the world!
Nor rain, wind, thunder, fire, are my daughters.
I tax not you, ye elements, with unkindness:
I never gave you kingdom, called you children;
You owe me no subscription. Then let fall
Your horrible pleasure: here I stand, your slave,
A poor, infirm, weak, and despised old man.

But yet I call you servile ministers
That will with two pernicious daughters join
Your high-engendered battles 'gainst a head
So old and white as this. O, O, 'tis foul."

These last words, beginning with *"high-engendered battles,"* he delivered with a down-sweeping cadence as mighty in its swell as one of the great symphonic swings of Beethoven. The auditor seemed to hear the peal strike on the mountain-top and its slow reverberations roll through the valleys. The next speech, commencing with,—

"Let the great gods,
That keep this dreadful pother o'er our heads,
Find out their enemies now,"—

and ending with,—

"I am a man
More sinned against than sinning,"—

he pronounced in a way that emphasized the vast ethical meaning involved in it, and illustrated the strong humanity of Lear. He seemed to be saying, "These woes are just; I have been proud, rash, and cruel; but others have treated me worse than I have treated them." This unconscious effort at a halting justification this disguised appeal for kindly judgment, was profoundly natural and affecting. Then his brain reeled under its load of woe, and he sighed, with a piteous bewilderment," My wits begin to turn," bringing back with awful fulfilment his prophetic prayer long before, "O, let me not be mad, sweet heaven! keep me in temper: I would not be mad!"

There was something in the immense outspread of the sorrows of Lear and the enlacement of their gigantic portrayal with the elemental scenery of nature, the desolate heath, the blackness of night, the howling gale, the stabbing flashes of lightning, overwhelmingly pathetic and sublime. The passion of Othello pours along like a vast river turbulent and raging, yet with placid eddies. The passion of Lear is like the continual swell and moan of the ocean, whose limitless expanse, with no beacon of hope to meet the eye, baffles our comprehension and bewilders us with its awful mystery. This part of the play, as Forrest represented it in person and voice, gave one a new measure of the greatness of man in his glory and in his ruin. And in the subsequent scenes, where the disease of Lear had progressed and his faculties become more wrecked, he was so interpreted from the splendid might over which he had exulted to the mournful decay into which he had sunk, that when he said, in reply to a request to be allowed to kiss his hand, "Let me wipe it first; it smells of mortality," the whole audience felt like exclaiming with Gloster,—

"O ruined piece of nature! This great world
Shall so wear out to naught."

The acting of all the closing scenes with Cordelia was something to be treasured apart in the memories of all who saw it and who were capable of appreciating its exquisite beauty and its unfathomable pathos. When he was awakened out of the merciful sleep which had fallen on the soreness of his soul, and heard her whose voice was ever soft, gentle, and low, addressing him as she had been wont in happier days, his look of wondering weariness, his mistaking her for a spirit in bliss, his kneeling to her, his gradual recognition of her,—all these were executed with a unity of purpose, a simplicity of means, and an ineffable tenderness of affection, to which it is impossible for any verbal description to do justice. Who, that did not carry a stone in his breast in place of a heart, could refrain from tears when he heard the exhausted sufferer—his gaze fixed on hers, his hands moving in unpurposed benediction, a solemn calm wrapping him after the long tempest, passing from the old arrogance of self-assertion into a supreme sympathy—murmur,—

"Where have I been? Where am I?—Fair daylight?
I am mightily abused.—I should even die with pity
To see another thus."

Who that saw his instinctive action and heard his broken utterance when she was dead, and he stood trying with insane perseverance to restore her, fondling her with his paralyzed hands, can ever forget? With insistent eagerness he asked,—

"Why should a dog, a horse, a rat, have life,

And thou no breath at all?"
With complaining resignation he said,—
"Thou'lt come no more,
Never, never, never, never, never!—"
With wild surprise he exclaimed, while his lips parted and a weird
and shrivelling smile stole through his wearied face,—
"Do you see this?—Look on her,—look,—her lips,—
Look there, look there!"
He stood erect and still, gazing into vacancy. Not a rustle, not a
breath, could be heard in the house. Slowly the head nodded, the
muscles of the face relaxed, the hands opened, the eyes closed, one
long hollow gasp through the nostrils, then on the worn-out
king of grief and pain fell the last sleep, and his form sank upon the
stage, while the parting salvos of the storm rolled afar.

Such were the principal characters represented by Edwin Forrest. So,
as far as an incompetent pen can describe their portraiture, did he
represent them. The work was a dignified and useful one, moralizing
the scene not less than entertaining the crowd. It was full of noble
lessons openly taught. It was still richer, as all acting is, in yet deeper
latent lessons to be gathered and self-applied by the spectators who
were wise enough to pierce to them and earnest enough to profit from
them.

For every dramatic impersonation of a character in the unravelling of
a plot and the fulfilment of a fate is charged with implicit morals. This
is inevitable because every type of man, every grade of life, every kind
of conduct, every style of manners, embodies those laws of cause and
effect between the soul and its circumstances which constitute the
movement of human destiny, and illustrates the varying standards of
truth and beauty, or of error and sin, in charming examples to be
assimilated, or in repulsive ones to serve as warnings. Thus the stage is
potentially as much more instructive than the pulpit, as life is more
inclusive and contagious than words. The trouble is that its teaching is
so largely disguised and latent. It sorely needs an infusion of the
religious and academic spirit to explicate and drive home its morals.

For instance, when Coriolanus says, with action of immovable haughtiness,—

"Let them pull all about mine ears; present me
Death on the wheel, or at wild horses' heels;
Or pile ten hills on the Tarpeian rock,
That the precipitation might down stretch
Below the beam of sight, yet will I still
Be thus to them,—"

it is a huge and grand personality, filled to bursting with arrogant pride and indirect vanity, asserting itself obstinately against the mass of the people. As a piece of power it is imposing; but morally it is vulgar and odious. The single superior should not assert his egotistic will defiantly against the wills of the multitude of inferiors and hate them for their natural resistance. He should modestly modulate his self-will with the real claims of the collective many, or blend and assert it through universal right and good, thus representing God with the strength of truth and the suavity of love. That is the lesson of Coriolanus,—a great lesson if taught and learned. And, to take an exactly opposite example, what is it that so pleases and holds everybody who sees the exquisite Rip Van Winkle of Joseph Jefferson? Analyze the performance to the bottom, and it is clear that the charm consists in the absence of self-assertion, the abeyance of all egotistic will. Against the foil of his wife's tartar temper, who with arms akimbo and frowning brow and scolding acidity of voice opposes everything, and asserts her authority, and, despite her faithful virtues, is as disagreeable as an incarnated broomstick, Rip, lazy and worthless as he is, steals into every heart with his yielding movement, soft tones, and winsome look of unsuspicious innocence. He resists not evil or good, neither his appetite for drink nor his inclinations to reform. The spontaneity, the perfect surrender of the man, the unresisted sway of nature in him, plays on the unconscious sympathies of the spectators with a charm whose divine sweetness not all the vices of the vagabond can injure. It is, in this homely and almost unclean disguise, a moral music strangely wafted out of an unlost paradise of innocence into which drunkenness has strayed. But the real secret of the fascination is hidden from most of those who intuitively feel its delicious fascination. Did the audience but appreciate the graceful spirit of its spell, and for themselves catch from its influence the same unresisted spontaneousness of soul in unconscious abnegation of self-will, they would go home regenerated.

But beyond the special lessons in the parts played by Forrest, he was, through his whole professional course, constantly teaching the great lesson of the beauty and value of the practice of the dramatic art for the purposes of social life itself. Should the stage decline and disappear, the art so long practised on it will not cease, but will be transferred to the ordinary walks of social life. Nothing is so charming as a just and vivid play of the spiritual faculties through all the languages of their outer signs, in the friendly intercourse of real life. But in our day the tendency is to confine expression to the one language of articulate words. This suppression of the free play of the organism stiffens and sterilizes human nature, impoverishes the interchanges of souls makes existence formal and barren. The most precious relish of conversation and the divinest charm of manners is the living play of the spirit in the features, and the spontaneous modulation of the form by the passing experience. A man grooved in bigotry and glued in awkwardness, with no alert intelligence and sympathy, is a painful object and a repulsive companion. He moves like a puppet and talks like a galvanized corpse. But it is delightful and refreshing to associate with one thoroughly possessed by the dramatic spirit, who, his articulations all freed and his faculties all earnest, speaks like an angel and moves like a god. The theatre all the time offers society this inspiring lesson. For there are seen free and developed souls lightening and darkening through free and sensitive faces. If bodies did not answer to spirits nor faces reveal minds, nature would be a huge charnel-house and society a brotherhood of the dead. And if things go on unchecked as they have been going on, we bid fair to come to that. It is to be hoped, however, that the examples of universal, liberated expression given on the stage will more and more take effect in the daily intercourse of all classes. As a guiding hint and stimulus in that direction, the central law of dramatic expression may here be explicitly formulated. All emotions that betoken the exaltation of life, or the recognition of influences that tend to heighten life, confirm the face, but expand and brighten it. All emotions that indicate the sinking of life, or the recognition of influences that threaten to lower life, relax and vacate the face if these emotions are negative, contract and darken it if they are positive. In answer to the exalting influences the face either grasps what it has or opens and smiles to hail and receive what is offered; in answer to the depressing influences, it either droops under its load or shuts and frowns to oppose and exclude what is threatened. The eyes reveal the mental states; the muscles reveal the effects of those states in the body. In genial states active, the eyes and the muscles are both intense, but the eyes are smiling. In genial states passive, the eyes are intense; the muscles languid. In hostile states active, both eyes and muscles are intense, but the eyes are frowning. In hostile states passive, the eyes are languid, the muscles intense. In simple or harmonious states, the eyes and the muscles agree in their excitement or relaxation. In complex and inconsistent states, the eyes and the muscles are opposed in their expression. To expound the whole philosophy of these rules would take a volume. But they formulate with comprehensive brevity the central law of dramatic expression as a guide for observation in daily life.

In filling up the outlines of the majestic characters imperfectly limned in the preceding pages, exhibiting them in feature and proportion and color and tone as they were, setting in relief the full dimensions and quality of their intellect and their passion, living over again their experiences and laying bare for public appreciation the lessons of their fate, Forrest found the high and noble joy of his existence, the most satisfying employment for his faculties, and a deep, unselfish solace for his afflictions. He reposed on the grand moments of each drama, as if they were thrones which he was loath to abdicate. He dilated and glowed in the exciting situations, as if they were no mimic reflections of the crises of other souls but original and thrilling incarnations of his own. He lingered over the nobler utterances, as if he would have paused to repeat their music, and would willingly let the action wait that the thought might receive worthy emphasis. Every inspired conception of eloquence, every delicate beauty of sentiment, every aggrandizing attitude of man contained in the plays he lifted into a relief of light and warmth that gave it new attraction and more power. And to trace the thoughts and feelings that gained heightened expression through him, echoed and working with contagious sympathy in the hearts of the crowds who hung on his lips, was a divine pleasure which he would fain have indefinitely prolonged. But the movement on the stage, that affecting mirror of life, hurries forward, the business of the world breaks in upon philosophy, and the dreams of the poet and the player burst like painted bubbles.

Meanwhile, not only do the parts played and the scenes amidst which they are shown vanish and become the prey of oblivion, but those who played them disappear also, leaving the providential and prophetic Spirit of Humanity, a sublimer Prospero, to say,—

"These, our actors,
As I foretold you, were all spirits, and
Are melted into air, into thin air."

Chapter XXIII.
Closing Years and the Earthly Finale

When in the fullest glory of his strength and his fame Forrest bought a farm and quite made up his mind to retire from the stage forever. While under this impulse he played a parting engagement in New Orleans. Called out after the play, he said, among other things, "The bell which tolled the fall of the curtain also announced my final departure from among you. I have chosen a pursuit congenial to my feelings,—that pursuit which the immortal Washington pronounced one of the most noble and useful ever followed by man,—the tilling of the soil. And now, ladies and gentlemen, I have to say that little word which must so often be said in this sad, bright world,—farewell." The purpose however, passed away with its now forgotten cause. Again he seriously thought for a little time, when a nomination to Congress was pressed on him, of exchanging his dramatic career for a political one. This idea, too, on careful reflection he rejected. And once more, when depressed and embittered by his domestic trouble, and sick of appearing before the public, he was for a season strongly tempted to say he would never again enter the theatre as a player. With these three brief and fitful exceptions he never entertained any design of abandoning the practice of his profession, until a shattering illness in the spring of 1872 compelled him to take the step. Then he took the step quietly, with no public announcement.

Thus the dramatic seasons of the five years preceding his death found the veteran still in harness, working vigorously as of old in the art of which he had ever been so fond and so proud. His earnings during each of these seasons were between twenty-five and forty thousand dollars, and the applause given to his performances and the friendly and flattering personal attentions paid him were almost everywhere very marked. He had no reason to feel that he was lingering superfluous on the stage. Many, it is true, asked why, with his great wealth, his satiation of fame, his literary taste, his growing infirmity of lameness, he did not give up this drudgery and enjoy the luxury of his home in leisure and dignity. There were two chief reasons why he persisted in his vocation. No doubt the large sum of ready money he earned by it was welcome to him, because while his fortune was great it was mostly unproductive and a burden of taxes. No doubt, also, he well relished the admiration and applause he drew; for the habit of enjoying this had become a second nature with him. Neither of these considerations, however, was it which caused him to undergo the toil and hardship of his profession to the last. His real motives were stronger. The first was the sincere conviction that it was better for the preservation of his health and faculties, his interest and zest in life and the world, to keep at his wonted task. He feared that a withdrawal of this spur and stimulus would the sooner dull his powers, stagnate him, and break him down. He often asserted this. For example, in 1871 he wrote thus, after speaking of what he had suffered from severe journeyings, extreme cold, poor food, many vexations, and a fall over a balustrade so terrible that it would have killed him had it not been for his professional practice in falling: "This is very hard work; but it is best to do it, as it prevents both physical and mental rust, which is a sore decayer of body and soul."

But the most effectual motive in keeping him on the stage was a real professional enthusiasm, an intense love of his art for its own sake. He felt that he was still improving in his best parts, in everything except mere material power, giving expression to his refining conceptions with a greater delicacy and subtilty, a more minute truthfulness and finish. He keenly enjoyed his own applause of his own best performances. This was a satisfaction to him beyond anything which the critics or the public could bestow or withhold. It was a luxury he was not willing to forego. He was a great artist still delighting himself with touching and tinting his favorite pictures, still loyal to truth and nature, and feeling the joy of a devotee as he placed now a more delicate shade here or a more ethereal light there, producing a higher harmony of tone, a greater convergence of effects in a finer unity of the whole. Even had this been an illusion with him, it would have been touching and noble. But it was a reality. His Richelieu and Lear were never rendered by him with such entire artistic beauty and grandeur as the last times he played them. In the thoughts of those who knew that as he went over the country in his later years the plaudits of the audiences and the approvals of critics were insignificant to him in comparison with his own judgment and feeling, and that he deeply relished the minutely earnest and natural truth and power and rounded skill of his own chosen portrayals of human nature, the fact lent an extreme interest and dignity to his character. This unaffected enthusiasm of the old artist, this intrinsic delight in his work, was a sublime reward for his long-continued conscientious devotion, and an example which his professional followers in future time should thoughtfully heed. He wrote to a friend from Washington near the close of his career, "Last night I played Lear in a cold house, with a wretched support, and to a sparse and undemonstrative audience. But I think I never in my life more thoroughly enjoyed any performance of mine, because I really believed, and do believe so now, that I never before in my life played the part so well. For forty years I have studied and acted Lear. I have studied the part in the closet, in the street, on the stage, in lunatic asylums all over the world, and I hold that next to God, Shakspeare comprehended the mind of man. Now I would like to have had my representation of the character last night photographed to the minutest particular. Then next to the creation of the part I would not barter the fame of its representation." This, written to a bosom friend from whom he kept back nothing, when the shadow of the grave was approaching, was not egotism or vanity. It was truth and sincerity, and its meaning is glorious. What a man works for with downright and persevering honesty, that, and the satisfaction or the retribution of it, he shall at last have. And there is only one thing of which no artist can ever tire,—merit. The passion for mere fame grows weak and cold, and, under its prostituted accompaniments, dies out in disgust; but the zeal and the joy of a passion for excellence keep fresh and increase to the end.

   Aside from that self-rewarding love of his art and delight in exercising it and improving in it, of which no invidious influence could rob him, Forrest continued still to be followed by the same extremes of praise and abuse to which he had ever been accustomed. But one grateful form of compliment and eulogy became more frequent towards the close. He was in the frequent receipt of letters, drawn up and signed by large numbers of the leading citizens of important towns, urging him to pay them a visit and gratify them with another, perhaps a final, opportunity of witnessing some of his most celebrated impersonations. Among his papers were found, carefully labelled, autograph letters of this description from New Orleans, Savannah, Cincinnati, Louisville, Detroit, Troy, and other cities,— flattering testimonials to his celebrity and the interest felt in him. These dignified and disinterested demonstrations were fitted to offset and soothe the wounds continually inflicted on his proud sensibility by many vulgar persons who chanced to have access to newspapers for the expression of their frivolity, malignity, or envy. For detraction is the shadow flung before and behind as the sun of fame journeys through the empyrean. To illustrate the scurrilous treatment Forrest had to bear, even in his old age, from heartless ribalds, it is needful only to set a few characteristic examples in contrast with his real character. His professional and personal character, in the spirit and aim of his public life, is justly indicated in this brief newspaper editorial:

   "In the line of heroic characters—such as Brutus, Virginius, Tell—Mr. Forrest has had no rival in this country. He is himself rich in the generous, manly qualities fitted for such grand ideal parts. The old-time favorite plays of the heroic and romantic school, like Damon and Pythias, are wellnigh banished from the stage. The materialistic tendencies and aspirations of this intensely practical age disqualify most audiences for seeing with the zest of their fathers a play so purely poetic and imaginative as the immortal tale of the Pythagorean friends. That Mr. Forrest, almost alone among his contemporaries, should cling to this style of plays with such true enthusiasm is evidence of the fidelity with which he seeks purity rather than attractiveness in the models of his art. His name has never been identified with a single one of the meretricious innovations which have within the past two decades so lowered the dignity of the drama. Every play associated with his person has some noble hero as its central figure, and some sublime moral quality and lesson in the unravelling of its plot. And his unwavering seriousness of purpose in everything he plays cannot be questioned, whatever else may be questioned."

The above estimate is sustained by the unconscious betrayal, the latent implications, in the following speech made by Forrest himself when called out after a performance:

"Ladies and Gentlemen,—For this and for the many tokens of your kind approbation, I return you my sincere and heartfelt acknowledgments. It is a source of peculiar gratification to me to perceive that the drama is yet, with you, a subject of consideration. Permit me to express my conviction that it is, in one form or another, whether for good or for evil, intimately blended with our social institutions. It is for you, then, to give it the necessary and appropriate direction. If it be left in charge of the bad and the dissolute, the consequences will be deplorable; but if the fostering protection of the wise and the good be extended to it, the result cannot but tend to the advancement of morals and the intellectual improvement of the community. It is indeed the true province of the drama

'To wake the soul by tender strokes of art,
To raise the genius, and to mend the heart;
To make mankind in conscious virtue bold,
Live o'er each scene, and be what they behold;
For this, the tragic muse first trod the stage,
Commanding tears to stream through every age;
Tyrants no more their savage nature kept,
And foes to virtue wondered how they wept.'"

What a descent from the above level to the ridicule, insult, and misrepresentation in notices like the succeeding:

"Forrest reminded us of the Butcher of Chandos, and his rendition of the fifth act was reminiscent of the wild madness, the ungovernable bellowings and fierce snortings of a short-horned bull chased by a score of terriers. He raved, and rumbled, and snorted, and paused, gathering wind for a fresh start, as if the ghost of Shakspeare were whispering in his ear,

'Now crack thy lungs, and split thy brazen pipe;
Blow, actor, till thy sphered bias cheek
Outswell the colic of puffed Aquilon;
Come, stretch thy chest, and let thy eyes spout blood;
Thou blow'st for Hector.'

We are fearful that the more he studies and improves his part the worse it will be."

"Last night we went with great expectations to the Academy of Music to see Forrest. We were never so astonished as to witness there the most successful practical imposition ever played on the public. Manager Leake has got Old Brown the hatter there, with his white head blacked, playing Leading parts under the assumed name of Edwin Forrest.

"Mr. Forrest dragged his weary performances out to empty boxes last week. Save in his voice, which still soars, crackles, rumbles, grumbles, growls and hisses, as in his younger days, this great actor is but a dreary echo of his former self. Appropriately may he exclaim,—

'Othello's occupation's gone!'

and it would be well if, like the heroic Moor, he would bid farewell to the bustling world by an abrupt retirement from the stage, instead of inflicting nightly stabs upon his high reputation and wounding his old-time friends by his attempts to soar into the sublime regions of tragedy."

"The interest that still crowds the theatre whenever Mr. Forrest appears is less admiration of his present power than curiosity to see a gigantic ruin."

"The intellectual portion of the community never thoroughly appreciated the style of histrionic gymnastics which our great tragedian has introduced; the ponderous tenderness and gladiatorial grace of his conceptions, though excellent in their way, had never any charm for people of delicate nerves, who delight not in viewing experiments in spasmodic contortion, or delineations of violent death, evidently after studies from nature in the slaughterhouse I But lately the faithful themselves are tiring of it."

The man with a thin and acid nature who aspires to be an author or an artist, and cannot succeed, sometimes becomes a spiteful critic. The only pity is that he should usually find it so easy to get an organ for his spites. Would-be genius hates and criticises, actual genius loves and creates. The former enviously despises those who succeed where he has failed, the latter generously admires all true merit.

And now it will be a relief to turn from such criticisms to facts. The season of 1871 was marked by an experience altogether memorable in the professional history of Forrest, his last engagement in New York, where he played for twenty nights in February at the Fourteenth Street Theatre, sustaining only the two roles of Lear and Richelieu. These were his two best parts, and being characters of old men his cruel sciatica scarcely interfered with his rendering of them. One or two newspaper writers complained, as if it were a crime in the actor and a personal offence to them, that "when Forrest came this season to New York he neglected, and apparently with a purpose, the usual precautions of metropolitan managers, and seemed to avoid all the modern appliances of success, either from a contempt for the appliances or from indifference as to the result." They did not seem once to suspect that his scorn for every species of bribery or meretricious advertising, his frank and careless trust in simple truth, was, considering the corrupt custom of the times, in the highest degree honorable to him and exemplary for others. It was always his way to make a plain announcement of his appearance, and then let the verdict be what it might, with no interference of his.

There was no popular rush to see him now. In the crowd of new excitements and the quick forgetfulness belonging to our day, the curiosity about him and the interest in him had largely passed away. But the old friends who rallied at his name, and the respectable numbers of cultivated people who were glad of a chance to see the most historic celebrity of the American stage before it should be too late, were unanimous in their enthusiastic admiration. They declared with one voice that his playing was filled with wonderful power in general and with wonderful felicities in detail. That metropolitan press, too, from which he had so long received not only unjust depreciation, but wrong and contumely, spoke of him and his performances now in a very different tone. Its voice appeared a kindly response to what he had privately written to his friend Oakes: "Well, I am here, here in New York once more, and on Monday next begin again my professional labor,—labors begun more than forty years ago in the same city."

"What changes since then in men and things! Will any one of that great and enthusiastic audience which greeted my efforts as a boy, be here on Monday evening next to witness the matured performance of the man? If so, how I should like to hear from his own lips if the promises of spring-time have been entirely fulfilled by the fruits of the autumn of life!" Without any notable exception, extreme praise was lavished on his acting, and his name was treated with a tenderness and a respect akin to reverence. It seemed as though the writers felt some premonition of the near farewell and the endless exit, and were moved to be just and kind. The late amends touched the heart of the old player deeply. It was a comfort to him to be thus appreciated in the city of his greatest pride ere he ceased acting, and to have the estimates of his friends endorsed in elaborate critiques from the pens of the best dramatic censors, William Winter, Henry Sedley, John S. Moray, and others. It is due to him and to them that some specimens of these notices be preserved here. Space will allow but a few extracts from the leading articles:

"Edwin Forrest, the actor, who is identified with much that is intellectual, picturesque, and magnificently energetic in the history of the American stage, is again before the New York public. His reappearance is deeply interesting upon several accounts. His reputation, far from being confined to the United States, extends wherever the language of Shakspeare is spoken, and to a great many countries where translations have rendered that poet's meanings known. His name has grown with the name of the American people, and has greatened with the increasing greatness of the country. At home and abroad he is recognized as the superbly unique representative of several characters whose creators owe their inspiration to the genius of American history. No other actor has presented Americans with such powerful and original conceptions of King Lear, Coriolanus, and Macbeth. No other unites such grand physical forces with such intellectual vigor and delicacy. His hand has an infinity of tints at its command, and his tenderest touches are never weak. He is, therefore, deservedly and almost universally considered as the fair representative of what Americans have most reason to be proud of in the history of their stage. He is not a weak copyist of foreign originalities and of schools of the past. His virtues and his vices, dramatically speaking, are his own. His genius is thoroughly self-responsible, and his strong, conscious, and magnificent repose is resplendently suggestive of the degree in which the great actor rates, and has a right to rate himself."

"Mr. Forrest can indeed be now admired more than he ever was before; for his magnificent and picturesque energies are now chastened and restrained by great intellectual culture, and softened by the presence of that tender glow which varied experience is pretty sure to ultimately lend. One strives in vain to recall the name of any other actor, either in this country or in England, who possesses such immense physical energies under such perfect subservience to the intellect. We insist more particularly upon this point, because it is one upon which even the admirers of Mr. Forrest are not apt to dwell. There is a very large class of people who are so absorbed in the generous breadth, the brilliant coloring, and the large treatment of Mr.

Forrest's favorite themes, that they neglect to give him credit for intellectual niceties and delicate emotional distinctions. They vulgarly admire merely the large style and heroic presence of the man, and the rich reverberations of a voice that all the demands of the entire gamut of passion have not yet perceptibly worn, and they omit to give him that intellectual appreciation which is very decidedly his due. In no other character which he is fond of playing are all these qualifications so harmoniously united as in Lear. In no other character are the distinctive qualities of Mr. Forrest's genius so beautifully blended and played. Those who have been familiar with his rendering of this character in the days that are past will take a curious pleasure in accompanying him from scene to scene, and from act to act, and in remarking how true he remains to the ideal of his younger years, and how powerful he is in expressing that ideal. It is a rare thing for an actor to awaken in a later generation the same quality and degree of delight that he awoke in his own. It is a rare thing for him to be as youthful in his maturity as he was mature in his youth, and to thus succeed in delighting those who measure by a standard more exacting and severe than the standard was which the public, in an earlier age of American dramatic art, was fond of applying. Mr. Forrest has passed these tests. We do not care for the ignorant sarcasm of those who claim that the 'school' here presents is a 'physical' school. It is a school wherein Mr. Forrest is supreme master, and where an unrivalled voice and physique are made absolutely subservient to intellectual expression."

"Never were plaudits better deserved by any actor in any age than those which have been showered down upon Forrest during the past week. His conception and his rendering of King Lear were alike magnificent. In his prime, when theatres were crowded by the brightest and fairest of America, who listened spell-bound to the favorite of the hour, he never played this character half so well. The idiosyncrasy of his nature forbade it. The fierce ungovernable fire within him could not be restrained within the limits of the rôle. Forrest could never modulate the transport of his feelings. He leaped at once from a calm and even tenor to the full violence of frenzied anger.

There was no *crescendo*, no gradation. He was so fully possessed of his rôle that he threw aside every consideration of different circumstances which the case suggested. He was for the moment Lear, but not Shakspeare's old man: he was Forrest's Lear. Hence the fire of furious anger and the decrepitude of age were alike exaggerated. But these things have passed away. Age has tamed the lion-like excesses of the royal Forrest, and his impersonation of King Lear is now absolutely faultless. Seeing and hearing him under the disadvantages of a mangled text, a poor company, a miserable *mise en scène,* and a thin house, the visitor must still be impressed by the one grand central figure, so eloquent, so strong, so sweet in gentlest pathos. There is an unconscious reproach in the manner in which he bows his head to the shouts of applause. He is the King Lear of the American stage; he gave to his children, the public, all that he had, and now they have deserted him. They have crowned a new king before whom they bow, and the old man eloquent is cheered by few voices. The consciousness of his royal nature supports him. He knows that while he lives there can be no other head of the American stage; but still he is deserted and alone. That some such feeling overpowered him when the flats parted, and the audience, seeing the king on his throne, cheered him, there can be little doubt. He bowed his head slightly in response to the acclamations of those scantily-filled seats. But throughout the play there was an added dignity of sorrow, which showed that the neglect of the public had wounded him. He knew his fate. He recognized that he was a discrowned king, and that the fickle public had crowned another not worthy of sovereignty and having no sceptre of true genius. The play went on and he became absorbed in his rôle, forgetting in the delirium of his art that his house was nearly empty. Had there been but five there, he would have played it. For to him acting is existence, and the histrionic fire in his bosom can never be quenched save with life. Actors may come and actors may go, but it will be centuries before a Lear arises like unto this man Forrest, whom the public seems to have so nearly forgotten.

"The curtain rose a few minutes after eight, and the cold air issuing from the stage threw a chill over the audience. But when at last the scene opened and revealed Lear on his throne, the old form in its Jove-like grandeur, the quiet eye that spoke of worlds of reserved power, brought back the memories of old, and round after round of applause stopped the utterance of the opening words. There was such a heartiness of admiring welcome about the thing, so much of the old feeling of theatrical enthusiasm, that Forrest felt for once compelled to stand up, and, with a bend of his leonine head, acknowledge the welcome. He tested the love of his daughters; he gave away his kingdom, taking, as he gave it, the sympathies of the audience. He called on the eldest, and was taunted; he lost his ill-controlled temper, and finally, goaded till his whole frame seemed about to shatter, he invoked the curse of heaven. As he spoke, you could hear all over the house that hissing of breath drawn through the teeth which sudden pain causes, and when the curtain fell people looked into each other's eyes in silence. Then you would hear, 'That is acting.' 'It is awful!' Then suddenly rose bravos, not your petty clapping of hands, but shouts from boxes and orchestra, and they came in volleys. The old king tottered calmly out before the curtain, looked around slowly, and bowed back. But there was now in that quiet eye a suppressed gleam in which those nearest the stage could read as in a book the pride and gratification of genius enjoying the effect of its power.

"With the drawbacks of ordinary scenery and a wretched support, Forrest gives us a Richelieu which at the close of the fourth act nightly draws, forth a perfect whirlwind of applause, and brings the veteran before the curtain amidst a wild cry of enthusiasm which must stir old memories in his bosom. His genius spreads an electric glow through the house and carries the sympathies by storm.

"Mr. Forrest's reading of Richelieu is remarkable for its firmness and intelligibility of purpose, for its singular pathos, for its often unaffected melody of elocution, and—in this point approaching his Lear—for its revelation, at intervals, of unmistakable subtlety of thought. Like his Lear, too, the part is embroidered over with those swift touches of electricity that gild and enrich the underlying fabric which might otherwise appear too weighty and sombre.

"The actor who would vitalize this part has no common work to perform. It is incumbent upon him to make martial heroism visible through a veil of intellectual finesse, and to indicate the natural soldier-like qualities of the man projecting through that smoothness and dissimulation which the ambition of the statesman rendered expedient. It is necessary for him to develop so that they may be perceived by the audience those characteristics which Bulwer has unfolded in the play through the instrumentality of long soliloquies that are necessarily omitted upon the stage, and unless this is done by the actor the character is deprived of that subtlety and force and that human complexity of motive which Bulwer, in spite of his artificiality and conceits, contrives to make apparent.

"This, however, is the task which Mr. Forrest performs to perfection. Not being a purely intellectual character, Richelieu demands in the delineation all those aids which are desirable from Mr. Forrest's august physique and wonderfully rich voice. A just discrimination compels us to own that beside this representation that of Mr. Booth appears faint and pale. A film seems to cover it; whereas the representation of Mr. Forrest gathers color and strength from the contrast. As a piece of mere elocution Mr. Forrest's reading is exquisitely beautiful, the ear floating upon the profound and varied music of its cadences. But, flawlessly exquisite as are these graces of enunciation, they are, after all, merely channels in which the spirit of the entire interpretation runs. The most cultured man in the audience which last night filled the Fourteenth Street Theatre might have closely followed every line which the actor enunciated, without being able to perceive wherein it could be more heavily freighted with significance."

But perhaps the most gratifying testimony borne at this time to the natural power and artistic genius and skill of Forrest was the following eloquent article by Mr. Winter, whose repeated previous notices of the actor had been unfavorable and severe, but who, irresistibly moved, now showed himself as magnanimous as he was conscientious:

"Probably the public does not quite yet appreciate either the value of its opportunity or the importance of improving it. Two facts, therefore, ought to be strongly stated: one, that Mr. Forrest's personation of Lear is an extraordinary work of art; the other, that, in the natural order of things, it must soon pass forever away from the stage. Those who see it now will enjoy a luxury and a benefit. Those who miss seeing it now will sow the seed of a possible future regret. We have not in times past been accustomed to extol, without considerable qualification, the acting of Mr. Forrest. This was natural, and it was right. An unpleasant physical element—the substitution of muscle for brain and of force for feeling—has usually tainted his performances. That element has been substantially discarded from his Lear. We have seen him play the part when he was no more than a strong, resolute, robustious man in a state of inconsequent delirium. The form of the work, of course, was always definite. Strength of purpose in Mr. Forrest's acting always went hand in hand with strength of person. He was never vague. He knew his intent, and he was absolutely master of the means that were needful to fulfil it. Precision, directness, culminating movement, and physical magnetism were his weapons; and he used them with a firm hand. Self-distrust never depressed him. Vacillation never defeated his purpose. It was the triumph of enormous and overwhelming individuality. Lear could not be seen, because Mr. Forrest stood before him and eclipsed him.

"All that is greatly modified. Time and suffering seem to have done their work. It is no secret that Mr. Forrest has passed through a great deal of trouble. It is no secret that he is an old man. We do not touch upon these facts in a spirit of heartlessness or flippancy. But what we wish to indicate is that natural causes have wrought a remarkable change in Mr. Forrest's acting, judged, as we now have the opportunity of judging it, by his thrilling delineation of the tremendous agonies and the ineffably pathetic madness of Shakspeare's Lear. In form his performance is neither more nor less distinct than it was of old. Almost every condition of symmetry is satisfied in this respect. The port is kingly; the movement is grand; the transitions are natural; the delivery is resonant; the intellect is potential; the manifestations of madness are accurate; the method is precise. But, beyond all this, there is now a spiritual quality such as we have not seen before in this extremely familiar work. Here and there, indeed, the actor uses his ancient snort, or mouths a line for the sake of certain words that intoxicate his imagination by their sound and movement. Here and there, also, he becomes suddenly and inexplicably prosaic in his rendering of meanings. But these defects are slight in contrast with the numberless beauties that surround and overshadow them. We have paid to this personation the involuntary and sincere tribute of tears. We cannot, and would not desire to, withhold from it the merited recognition of critical praise. Description it can scarcely be said to require. Were we to describe it in detail, however, we should dwell, with some prolixity of remark, upon the altitude of imaginative abstraction which Mr. Forrest attains in the mad scenes. Shakspeare's Lear is a person with the most tremulously tender heart and the most delicately sensitive and poetical mind possible to mortal man, and his true grandeur appears in his overthrow, which is pathetic for that reason. The shattered fragments of the column reveal its past magnificence. No man can play Lear in these scenes so as to satisfy, even approximately, the ideal inspired by Shakspeare's text unless he knows, whether by intuition or by experience, the vanity, the mutability, the hollowness of this world. The deepest deep of philosophy is sounded here, and the loftiest height of pathos is attained. It is high praise to say that Mr. Forrest, whether consciously or unconsciously, interprets these portions of the tragedy in such a manner as frequently to enthrall the imagination and melt the heart. The miserable desolation of a noble and tender nature scathed and blasted by physical decay and by unnatural cruelty looks out of his eyes and speaks in his voice. This may be only the successful simulation of practised art; but, whatever it be, its power and beauty and emotional influence are signal and irresistible."

The New York "Courier" said, in a striking editorial, "The engagement of Edwin Forrest at the Fourteenth Street Theatre, and the praises lavished on him by the whole press of this city, afford us an opportunity to make a little contribution to the truth of history." The "Courier," after maintaining that Forrest had always been a great actor, and that the total change of tone in the press was not so much owing to his improvement as to the fact that time had softened and removed the prejudices of his judges, continues,—

"When Edwin Forrest, who might have been called at the time the American boy tragedian, was playing at the Old Bowery, and Edmund Kean at the Old Park, there was a little society of gentlemen in this city, who were passionate admirers of the drama. Young in years, they were already ripe in scholarship and profound as well as independent critics. Amongst them, and constantly associating together, were Anthony L. Robertson, afterwards Vice-Chancellor; John Nathan, afterwards law partner with Secretary Fish; John Lawrence; John K. Keese, better known as 'Kinney Keese,' the wittiest and most learned of book auctioneers, whose mind was a Bodleian Library and whose tongue a telegraph battery of joke and repartee, and a dozen others,— all since eminent at the bar, in literature, or in national politics. Their little semi-social, semi-literary society was known as 'The Column,' and subsisted for many years. During the rival engagements of Kean and Forrest these gentlemen went backwards and forwards between the 'Park' and the 'Bowery,' and after witnessing the 'Lear' of the greatest of English actors since Garrick, and the Lear of Forrest, unanimously decided, upon the most careful and critical discussion, that, great as Kean was, Forrest was the Lear. Unhappily he was only an American boy, and American actors were not then the fashion. It was in the days of Anglomania, and the fashion was to pooh-pooh everything that had not graduated at Covent Garden or Drury Lane and lacked the full diploma of cockney approbation. Forrest, both as man and actor, was a full-blooded American and a sturdy Democrat,—two fearful crimes at a time when art was measured wholly by an English standard and politics reduced criticism to almost as despicable servility as they do now. Happily for the impartiality of discussion in art we have outlived the period of Anglomania, and are rather virtuously proud than otherwise of anything genuinely American. And this Edwin Forrest is. His career, too, is a fine example at once of personal devotion to art, and of 'the sober second thought of the people,' which all the critics failed to alter. For, even when the latter were most mad against him, he always drew crowds, and we may say safely, by the power of native genius, supported only by an iron will, he has shone for fifty years, with increasing lustre, as a star in the dramatic firmament. William Leggett of the *Evening Post*, who was a power in New York politics and loved Forrest as a brother, tried to draw him, in his early manhood, into politics. Had the latter consented to abandon his profession, he might have commanded, at that time, any nomination in the gift of the New York Democracy, and risen to the highest political employments in the State. But he had chosen art as a mistress, and refused to abandon her for the colder but equally exacting idol of the mind,—political ambition. It is to this refusal we owe the fact that our stage is still graced by the greatest actor America has ever produced."

The dramatic season of 1871-72 gave an astonishing proof of the vital endurance and popular attractiveness of the veteran player, then in his sixty-sixth year. Between October 1st and April 4th he travelled over seven thousand miles, acted in fifty-two different places, one hundred and twenty-eight nights, and received the sum of $39,675.47. He began at the Walnut Street Theatre, Philadelphia, proceeded to Columbus and Cincinnati, and then appeared in regular succession at New Orleans, Galveston, Houston, Nashville, Omaha, and Kansas City. At Kansas City excursionists were brought by railroad from the distance of a hundred and fifty miles, at three dollars each the round trip. From this place his series of engagements took him to Saint Louis, Quincy, Pittsburg, Cleveland, Buffalo, Detroit, Rochester, Syracuse, Utica, Troy, and Albany. From Albany he journeyed to Boston, where he opened an engagement at the Globe Theatre with Lear, before an audience of great brilliancy completely crowding the house. He had a triumph in every way flattering, although the herculean toils of the season behind him had most severely taxed his strength. How he played may be imagined from the following report, made by a distinguished author in a private letter. "I went last night to see Forrest. I saw Lear himself; and never can I forget him, the poor, discrowned, wandering king, whose every look and tone went to the heart. Though mimic sorrows latterly have little power over me, I could not suppress my tears in the last scene. The tones of the heart-broken father linger in my ear like the echo of a distant strain of sad sweet music, inexpressibly mournful, yet sublime. The whole picture will stay in my memory so long as soul and body hang together."

On the Monday and Tuesday evenings of the second week, he appeared as Richelieu. He had taken a severe cold, and was suffering so badly from congestion and hoarseness that Oakes tried to persuade him not to act. He could not be induced, he said, to disappoint the audience by failing to keep his appointment. Oakes accompanied him to his dressing-room, helped him on with his costume, and, when the bell rang, led his tottering steps to the stage entrance. The instant the foot of the veteran touched the stage and his eye caught the footlights and the circling expanse of expectant faces, he straightened up as if from an electric shock and was all himself. At the end of each scene Oakes was waiting at the wing to receive him and almost carry him to a chair. Besought to take some stimulant, he replied, "No: if I die to-night, they shall find no liquor in me. My mind shall be clear." And so he struggled on, playing by sheer dint of will, with fully his wonted spirit and energy, but the moment he left the eyes of the audience seeming almost in a state of collapse. The play was drawing near its end. And this, though no one thought of it, this was to be the last appearance of Edwin Forrest on the stage. Debut, Rosalia de Borgia,— interval of fifty-five years with slow illumination of the continent by his fame,— exit, Richelieu! Oakes stood at the wing, all anxiety, peering in and listening intently. The characters were grouped in the final tableau. He stood central, resting on his left foot, his right slightly advanced and at ease, his right arm lifted and his venerable face upturned. Then his massive and solemn voice, breaking clear from any impediment, was heard articulating with a mournful beauty the last words of the play:

"There is one above
Sways the harmonious mystery of the world
Even better than prime ministers. Alas!
Our glories float between the earth and heaven
Like clouds that seem pavilions of the sun
And are the playthings of the casual wind.

Still, like the cloud which drops on unseen crags
The dews the wild-flower feeds on, our ambition
May from its airy height drop gladness down
On unsuspected virtue; and the flower
May bless the cloud when it hath passed away."

Then, instead of inclining for the rise of the audience and the fall of the curtain, he gazed for an instant musingly into vacancy, and, as if some strange intuition or prophetic spirit had raised the veil of fate, uttered from his own mind the significant words, "*And so it ends*."

He slept little that night, and, the next day, was clearly so much worse that Oakes insisted resolutely that he should not act at any rate. He was announced for Virginius, and was so set on going that his friend had almost to use force to restrain him. Dr. S. W. Langmaid, so justly eminent for his faithful skill, was called. He said, positively, "If you undertake to act to-night, Mr. Forrest, you will in all likelihood die upon the stage." He replied, pointing to Oakes, "Then I owe my life to that dear old fellow yonder; for if he had not obstinately resisted I should certainly have gone." Pneumonia set in, and for more than a week a fatal result was feared. During all this time Oakes was his constant nurse, catching a few moments of sleep when he could, but for the whole period of danger never taking off his clothes except for a daily bath. Unwearied and incessant in attentions, he left not his station until his friend was so far recovered as to be able to start for Philadelphia. The day after the convalescent reached home he wrote a letter of affectionate acknowledgment to Oakes for all the services rendered with such a loving fidelity. Here is an extract from it: "The air is sunny, warm, and delicious, and I am pervaded by a feeling of rest which belongs only to home. How marvellously I was spared from death's effacing fingers, and permitted for a little longer time to worship God in the glad sunshine of his eternal temple. To your tender care and solicitude during my illness I owe everything." And thus the old tie of friendship between the pair received another degree of depth and was cemented with a new seal.

Here it is fit to pause awhile in the narrative, go back a little to gather up a few interesting things not yet mentioned, and supplement the account previously given of his inner life by some further description of the kind of man he was in social intercourse and in the privacy of his home during his last years.

His home was always a charmed and happy place to him, although sorrowfully vacant of wife and children. He took great delight in the works of art he had collected. In his picture-gallery he had paintings of which he really made friends; and often of a night when he was restless he would rise, go to them, light the gas, and gaze on them as if they had a living sympathy to soothe and bless his spirit. But his library was the favorite haunt where he felt himself indeed at ease and supplied with just the ministration and companionship he craved. It opened in the rear upon a spacious garden. Mr. Rees once asked him why he did not clear up this garden and beautify it with more flower-beds. He answered, "I prefer the trees. When I sit here alone the whistling of the wind through their branches sounds like a voice from another world." He always went away with regret and came back with pleasure. Nor was his satisfaction altogether solitary. Writing to Oakes once he says, "Yes, my friend, I am indeed happy once more to reach this sweet haven of rest, my own dear home. My sisters received me with the greatest joy, the servants with unaffected gladness, and the two dogs actually went into ecstasies over me. It was a welcome fit for an emperor."

The loss of his three sisters one by one struck heavy blows on his heart, and left his house darker each time than it had been before. In 1863 he writes,—

"Dear Friend Oakes,—I cannot sufficiently thank you for the kind words of sympathy you have expressed for me in my late unhappy bereavement—the loss of my dear sister Henrietta, who on the death of my beloved mother devoted her whole life to me. Her wisdom was indeed a lamp to my feet, and her love a joy to my heart. Ah, my friend, we cannot but remember such things were that were most dear to us. Do we love our friends more as we advance in life, that our loss of them is so poignant, while in youth we see them fall around us like leaves in winter weather as though the next spring would once more restore them? I read your letter to my remaining sisters, and they thanked you with their tears. You may remember that once under a severe affliction of your own—the death of a loved friend—I endeavored to console you with the hope of immortality. That fails me now."

In 1869 he wrote again, "My sister Caroline died last night. We have a sad house. Why under such bereavements has God not given us some comforting reasonable hope in the future, where these severed ties of friendship and love may be again united? Man's vanity and self-love have betrayed him into such a belief; but who knows that the fact substantiates it?" And in 1871 once more he wrote, "My sister Eleanora is dead, and there is now no one on earth whose veins bear blood like mine. My heart is desolate." This obituary notice appeared at the time:

"The death of Eleanora Forrest, sister of Mr. Edwin Forrest the tragedian, has cast a gloom over the large circle of her acquaintances, which time alone can dispel; but the gloom which rests over the household in which her gentle sway and influence brought peace and happiness no change of time or season can ever remove. To one, at least, the light of home went out with her life. To one, now the last of his race, his splendid mansion will be as some stately hall deserted. Its light has gone out; the garlands which her hands twined are dead; 'the eyes that shone, now dimmed and gone,' will only appear again to him in memory. Memory, however,

"'Is but a gift
Within a ruined temple left,
Recalling what its beauties were
And then painting what they are.'

"There was something so mild, so pure, so Christian-like, in this lady, that her passing away from us is but a translation from earth to Heaven, like a flower blooming here for awhile to find eternal blossom there.

"Kind, gentle, with a hand open to charity, she did not remain at home awaiting the call of the destitute and suffering, but when the storms and the tempests of winter came and the poor were suffering, bearing their poverty and wretchedness in silence, she came forth unsolicited to aid them. We could name many instances of this; but she, who while living did not wish her charities known, receives her reward from One who reads the human heart and sways the destinies of mankind. The writer of this speaks feelingly of one whom it was a pleasure and a happiness to know. If ever a pure spirit left its earthly tenement to follow father, mother, brothers, and sisters to the 'home eternal in the skies,' it was that of Eleanora Forrest. There are many left to mourn her loss, but only one of kindred remains to grieve. To him the knowledge of her many virtues, sisterly affection, and the bright hereafter, must bring that peace no friendly aid can effect. Let us remember, in our hours of affliction, that

"'Life's a debtor to the grave,
Dark lattice, letting in eternal day.'"

The revolutions of his tempestuous blood, the resentful memory of wrongs, the keen perception of insincerity, shallowness, and evanescence, and the want of any grounded faith in a future life gave Forrest many hours of melancholy, of bitterness, and almost of despair. But he never, not even in the darkest hour, became a misanthrope or an atheist. In one of his commonplace books he had copied these lines which he was often heard to quote:

"The weariness, the wildness, the unrest,
Like an awakened tempest, would notecase;
And I said in my sorrow, Who is blessed?
What is good? What is truth? Where is peace?'

A few of his characteristic expressions in his depressed moods may have interest for the reader:

"Is there then no rest but in the grave? Rest without the consciousness of rest? The rest of annihilation?"

"I am very sad and disheartened at the iniquitous decisions of these juries and judges. I could willingly die now with an utter contempt for this world and a perfect indifference to my fate in the next."

"I wish the great Day of Doom were not a chimera. What a solace it would be to all those whom man has so deeply wronged!"

"This human life is a wretched failure, and the sooner annihilation comes to it the better."

While these impulsive phrases reveal his intense and unstable sensibility, they must be taken with great allowance, or they will do injustice to his better nature. They are transitory phases of experience betraying his weakness. In his deeper and clearer moods he felt a strange and profound presentiment of immortality, and surmised that this life was neither the first nor the last of us. But living as he did mostly for this material world and its prizes, he could not hold his mind steadily to the sublime height of belief in the eternal life of the soul. And so all sorts of doubts came in and were recklessly entertained. Had his spirituality equalled his sensibility and intelligence, and had he aimed at personal perfection as zealously as he aimed at professional excellence, his faith in immortality would have been as unshakable as was his faith in God. Also could he have filled his soul with the spirit of forgiveness and charity instead of harboring tenacious instincts of hate and disgust, he would have been a serene and benignant man. His complaining irritability would have vanished in a devout contentment; for he would have seen a plan of exact compensations everywhere threading the maze of human life.

But then he would not have been Edwin Forrest. Inconsistent extremes, unregulated impulsiveness, unsubdued passion, some moral incongruity of character and conduct, of intuition and thought, belonged to his type of being. It is only required that those who assume to judge him shall be just, and not be misled by any superficial or partial appearance of good or evil to give an unfair verdict. His defects were twofold, and he had to pay the full penalty for them. First, no man can lead a really happy and noble life, in the high and true sense of the words, who is infested with feelings of hate and loathing towards persons who have injured him or shown themselves detestable. He must refuse to entertain such emotions, and with a magnanimous and loving heart contemplate the fairer side of society. For almost all our experience, whether we know it or not, is strained through and tested and measured by our emotional estimates of our fellow-men. It is chiefly in them, or in ourselves as affected by our thoughts of them, that God reveals himself to us or hides himself from us. Second, Forrest not only dwelt too much on mean or hostile persons and on real or fancied wrongs, but he did not live chiefly for the only ends which are worthy to be the supreme aim of man. The genuine ends of a man in this world are to glorify God, to serve humanity, and to perfect himself. And these three are inseparably conjoined, a triune unity. The man who faithfully lives for these religious ends will surely attain peace of mind and unwavering faith in a Providence which orders everything and cannot err. The highest conscious ends of Forrest were not religious, but were to glorify his art, to perfect his strength and skill, and to win the ordinary prizes of society,— wealth, fame, and pleasure. Elements of the superior aims indeed entered largely into his spirit and conduct, but were not his proposed and consecrating aim. This, as now frankly set forth, was his failure, and the lesson it has for other men.

But, on the other hand, he had his praiseworthy success. If he was inferior to the best men, he was greatly superior to most men. For he was no hypocrite, parasite, profligate, squanderer of his own resources, or usurper of the rights of others. After every abatement it will be said of him, by all who knew the man through and through, that he was great and original in personality, honest in every fibre, truthful and upright according to the standard of his own conscience, tender and sweet and generous in the inmost impulses of his soul. On the other hand, it must be admitted that he was often the obstinate victim of injurious and unworthy prejudices, and abundantly capable of a profanity that was vulgar and of animosities that were ferocious. This is written in the very spirit which he himself inculcated on his biographer, to whom he addressed these words with his own hand in

1870: "Having revealed myself and my history to you without disguise or affectation, I say, Tell the blunt truth in every particular you touch, no matter where it hits or what effect it may have. To make it easier for you, I could well wish that my whole life, moral and mental professional and social, could have been photographed for your use in this biographical undertaking. And then, 'though all occasions should inform against me,' though I might have too much cause to sigh over my many weaknesses and follies, no single act of mine, I am sure, should ever make me blush with shame. I always admired the spirit of Cromwell, who said sternly, when an artist in taking his portrait would have omitted the disfiguring wart on his face, 'Paint me as I am!'"

Forrest was one of those elemental men who want always to live in direct contact with great realities, and cannot endure to accept petty substitutes for them, or pale phantoms of them at several removes. He craved to taste the substantial goods of the earth in their own freshness, and refused to be put off with mere social symbols of them. He loved the grass, the wind, the sun, the rain, the sky, the mountains, the thunder, the democracy. He loved his country earnestly, truth sincerely, his art profoundly, men and women passionately and made them love him passionately,—the last too often and too much. For these reasons he is an interesting and contagious character, and, as his figure is destined to loom in history, it is important that his best traits be appreciated at their full worth.

It is but justice, as an offset to his occasional fits of the blues and to the lugubrious sentiments he then expressed, some of which were quoted a page or two back, to affirm the truth that if he suffered more than most people he likewise enjoyed much more. Prevailingly he loved the world, and set a high value on life and took uncommon pains to secure longevity. As a general thing his spirit of enjoyment was sharp and strong. One illustration of this was the pronounced activity of the element of humor in him. This humor was sometimes grim, almost sardonic, and bordering on irony and satire, but often breathed itself out in a sunny playfulness. This lubricated the joints and sockets of the soul, so to speak, and made the mechanism of experience move smoothly when otherwise it would have gritted harshly with great frictional waste in unhappy resistances. It is difficult to give in words due illustration of this quality, of its genial manifestations in his manner, and of its happy influence on his inner life. But all his intimate friends know that the trait was prominent in him and of great importance. When on board the steamer bound for California, sick and wretched, he sent for the captain, and with great earnestness demanded, "For how much will you sell this ship and cargo?" After giving a rough estimate of the value, the captain asked, "But why do you wish to know this?" Forrest answered, "I want to scuttle her and end this detestable business by sinking the whole concern to the bottom of the sea!" A soft-spoken clergyman, who occupied the next state-room, overheard him giving energetic expression to his discontent, and called on him to expostulate on the duty of forbearance and patience, saying, "Our Saviour, you know, was always patient."

"Yes," retorted the actor, grimly, "but our Saviour went to sea only once, and then he disliked it so much that he got out and walked. Unfortunately, we cannot do that."

At another time a Calvinistic divine had been trying to convince him of the punitive character of death, arguing that death was not the original destiny of man, but a penalty imposed for sin. "What," said Forrest, "do you mean to say that if it had not been for that unlucky apple we should have seen old Adam hobbling around here still?"

Even to the end of his life he had the heart of a boy, and when with trusted friends it was ever and anon breaking forth in a playfulness and a jocosity which would have astonished those who deemed him so stern and lugubrious a recluse. One day he went into a druggist's shop where he was familiar, for some little article. The druggist chanced to be alone and stooping very low behind his counter pouring something from a jug. Forrest slipped up and leaning over him thundered in his ear with full pomp of declamation, "An ounce of civet, good apothecary!" The poor trader revealed his comic fright by a bound from the floor which would not have disgraced a gymnast.

On arriving at the places where he was to act he was often annoyed by strangers who pressed about him with pestering importunity merely from a vulgar curiosity. On these occasions he would sometimes, as he reached the hotel and saw the crowd, leap out of the carriage, say with a low bow to his agent, "Please keep your seat, Mr. Forrest, and I will inquire about a room," and then vanish, laughing in his sleeve, and leaving the embarrassed McArdle to sustain the situation as best he might.

His just and complacent pride in his work, too, kept him from being chronically any such disappointed and grouty complainer as he might sometimes appear. It is a sublime joy for a man of genius, a great artist, to feel, as the reward of heroic labor engrafted on great endowment, that his rank is at the top of the world that in some particulars he is superior to all the twelve hundred millions of men that are alive. There were passages in the acting of Forrest, besides the terrific burst of passion in the curse of Lear, which he might well believe no other man on earth could equal.

The knowledge and culture of Forrest were in no sense limited to the range of his profession. He was uncommonly well educated, not only by a wide acquaintance with books, but also by a remarkably varied observation and experience of the world. Whenever he spoke or wrote, some proof appeared of his reading and reflection. Speaking of Humboldt, he said, "Humboldt was a man open to truth without a prejudice. He was to the tangible and physical world what Shakspeare was to the mind and heart of man." Characterizing a religious discourse which much pleased him, he said, "Its logic is incontrovertible, its philosophy unexceptionable, and its humanity most admirable,—quite different from those homilies which people earth with demons, heaven with slaves, and hell with men." On one occasion, alluding to the facts that Shakspeare when over forty attended the funeral of his mother, and that his boy Hamnet died at the age of twelve, he regretted that the peerless poet had not written out what he must then have felt, and given it to the world. His genius under such an inspiration might have produced something which would have made thenceforth to the end of time all parents who read it treat their children more tenderly, all children love and honor their parents more religiously. But, he added, it seemed contrary to the genius of Shakspeare to utilize his own experience for any didactic purpose. At another time he said, "Shakspeare is the most eloquent preacher that ever taught humanity to man. The sermons he uttered will be repeated again and again with renewed and unceasing interest not only in his own immortal pages, but from the inspired lips of great tragedians through all the coming ages of the world."

A touching thing in Forrest in his last years was the unpurposed organic revelation in his voice of what he had suffered in the battle of life. What he had experienced of injustice and harshness, of selfishness and treachery, of beautiful things relentlessly snatched away by time and death, had left a permanent memorial in the unstudied tones and cadences of his speech. As he narrated or quoted or read, his utterance was varied in dose keeping with what was to be expressed. But the moment he fell back on himself, and gave spontaneous utterance from within, there was a perpetual recurrence of a minor cadence, a half-veiled sigh, a strangely plaintive tone, sweet and mournful as the wail of a dying wind in a hemlock grove.

A trait of Forrest, to which all his friends will testify, was the perfect freedom of his usual manner in private life from all theatricality or affectation. His bearing was natural and honest, varying truthfully with his impulses. With an actor so powerfully marked as he this is not common. Most great actors carry from their professional into their daily life some fixed strut of attitude or chronic stilt of elocution or pompous trick of quotation. It was not so with Forrest, and his detachment from all such habits, his straight-on simplicity, were an honor to him and a charm to those who could appreciate the suppression of the shop in the manly assertion of dignity and rectitude. He had no swagger, though he had a swing which belonged to his heavy equilibrium. His speech attracted attention only from its uncommon ease and finish, not from any ostentation. The actor, it has been justly said, is so far contemptible who keeps his mock grandeur on when his buskins are off, and orders a coffee-boy with the air of a Roman general commanding an army. He seems ever to say by his manner, It is easier to be a hero than to act one. Charles Lamb relates that a friend one day said to Elliston, "I like Wrench because he is the same natural easy creature on the stage that he is off." Elliston replied, with charming unconsciousness, "My case exactly. I am the same person off the stage that I am on." The inference instead of being identical was opposite. The one was never acting, the other always. Mrs. Siddons, it is said, used to stab the potatoes, and call for a teaspoon in a tone that curdled the blood of the waiter. Once when she was buying a piece of calico at a shop in Bath, she interrupted the voluble trader by inquiring, Will it wash? with an accent that made him start back from the counter. John Philip Kemble, dissatisfied with Sheridan's management and resolved to free himself from all engagements with him, rose in the greenroom like a slow pillar of state, and said to that astonished individual, "I am an eagle whose wings have long been bound down by frosts and snows; but now I shake my pinions and cleave into the general air unto which I am born." Sheridan looked into the heart of the eagle, and with a few wheedling words smoothed his ruffled plumage and made him coo like a dove in response to new proposals. Greatness of soul is necessary for a great actor, quick detachableness, and facility of transitions, with full understanding, sensibility, and fire; but cold counterfeits of these, empty forms of them swollen out with mechanic pomp, are as odious as they are frequent. Some are great only when inspired and set off by grand adjuncts; others are great by the native build of their being. Forrest was of this latter class. He knew how to act in the theatre, and to be simple and sincere in the parlor.

But, when all is said, the greatest quality and charm of Forrest, the deepest hiding of his magnetism, was his softness and truth of heart, the quickness, strength, and beauty of his affection. Bitter experience had taught him, before he was an old man, not to wear his heart on his sleeve for the heartless to peck at it. But how shallow the observation which, not seeing his heart on his sleeve, incontinently concluded that he had none! The reverential gratitude with which he delighted to dwell on the memory of his mother, the yearning fondness with which he was wont to recall the names of his early benefactors and dwell on the thought of the few living friends who had been ever kind and true to him, amply demonstrated the strong grasp of his affection. "My mother," he one day said to him who now copies his words, "was weeping on a certain occasion in my early childhood when she was hard pressed by poverty and care. My father, in his grave, almost awful way, said to her, 'Do not weep, Rebecca. It will do no good. I know it is very dark here. But it is all right. Above the clouds the sun is still shining.' I remember it made a great impression on my young mind; and many a time in afterlife it came up and was a comfort to me. Ah, what, what would I not give if I could really believe that when that dear good soul left the earth my father met her 'on a happier shore,' and said, 'Rebecca, you will weep no more now. Did I not tell you it was all right?'" After the death of Forrest, nigh a quarter of a century after it was written, was found among his papers a faded and tear-stained letter, enclosing two withered leaves, which read thus:

"Edwin Forrest, esq., Fonthill:

"These leaves were taken from your mother's grave, on Sunday, August 5th, 1849, and are presented as a humble but sacred memorial by your friend,

"W. H. M."

There is no surer proof of plentifulness of love within than is shown by its finding vent in endearments lavished on lower creatures and on inanimate things,—flowers, books, pictures, birds, dogs, horses. All these were copiously loved by Forrest. All his life he had some dog for a friend, and for the last twenty years he kept two or more. In the summer of 1870 a little turkey in his garden, only a week old, by some accident got its leg broken. He saw it, and commiserately picked up the poor thing, carefully set its leg, laid it in a basket of wool, hung it in a tree in the sunshine, and tenderly nursed and fed it till it was whole. This and the succeeding incidents occurred under the observation of his biographer, who was then paying him a visit.

He used to go into his stable and pat and fondle his horses and talk with them, looking in their eyes and smoothing their necks, as if they had full intelligence and sympathy with him. "Why, Brownie, poor

Brownie, handsome Brownie, are you not happy to come out to-day?" he said, as we rode along the Wissahickon, in a tone so tender and sad that it moistened the eyes of his human hearer. It was his custom to go up the river-side to a secluded place, and there get out and feed the horse with apples. One day he had forgotten his supply, and, as he dismounted and walked along in front of Brownie, he was touched to find the intelligent creature following him, smelling at his pockets and nudging him for her apples.

In one aspect it was beautiful, in another it was mournful, to see him going about his house, lonely, lonely, solacing himself for what was absent with humble substitutes. He had a mocking-bird wonderfully gifted and a great favorite with him and his sister. It bore the nickname of Bob. In moulting it fell sick, lost both voice and sight, and seemed to be dying. The great soft-hearted tragedian, thought by many to be so gruff and savage, was overheard, as he stood before the cage, talking to the sick bird, "Ah, poor Bob, poor Bob! Your myriad-voiced throat has filled my house with wondrous melodies these years past. Why must this cruel affliction come to you? You are a sinless creature. You cannot do any harm. It perplexes my philosophy to know why you should have to suffer in this way. Ah, little Bob, where now are all your sweet mockeries? Blind? Dumb? It cuts me to the very soul to think of it. Ah, well, well!" And he tottered slowly away, musing, quite as his Lear used to do on the stage when unkindness had broken the old royal heart.

Another characteristic incident is worth relating. He had a chamber at the Metropolitan Hotel fronting on Broadway. Oakes and the present writer were in a rear room. He sent for us to come to him and see the funeral-procession of Farragut pass. He sank on his knees at the open window as the sacred corse went by, and we saw the tears streaming down his cheeks. The bands played a dirge, and the soldiers and marines marched on, visible masses of music in blue and gold as the sailors proudly carried their dead admiral through the central artery of the nation, and every heart seemed vibrating with reverence and grief. "The grandest thing about this," said Forrest, "is that he was a good man, worthy of all the honor he receives. He whose modesty kept his bosom from ever swelling with complacency while he was alive may now well exult in death, as the sailors, unwilling to confide their commander to any catafalque, lovingly bear him on their shoulders to his grave."

The love which Forrest had for children was one of the deepest traits of his disposition. This tenderness was the same all through his career, except that it seemed to grow more profound and pensive in his age. Two anecdotes selected from among many will set this quality in an interesting light. When he was in the fullest strength of his manhood and was acting in Boston at the old National Theatre, there was at his hotel a very sick child whose mother was quite worn out with nursing it. Forrest begged permission to take care of the little sufferer through the succeeding night, that the mother might sleep. The mother, fearing that the terrible Metamora would prove rather a repulsive nurse for her darling, hesitated, but at length gave consent. At the close of the play he hurried back with so much haste that half the paint was left on one of his cheeks. Through the whole night, hour after hour, he paced up and down the room, tenderly soothing the fevered babe, which lay on his great chest with nothing but a silk shirt between its face and his skin. The mother slept, and so did the child. And when the doctor came in the morning, he said that the care of Forrest and the vitality the infant drew from his body during the long hours had saved its life.

All night long the baby-voice
Wailed pitiful and low;
All night long the mother paced
Wearily to and fro,
Striving to woo to those dim eyes
Health-giving slumbers deep;
Striving to stay the fluttering life
With heavenly balm of sleep.
Three nights have passed—the fourth has come:
O weary, weary feet!
That still must wander to and fro—
Relief and rest were sweet.

But still the pain-wrung, ceaseless moan
Breaks from the baby-breast,
And still the mother strives to soothe
The suffering child to rest.
Lo, at the door a giant form
Stands sullen, grand, and vast!
Over that broad brow every storm
Life's clouds can send has passed.
Those features of heroic mould
Can waken awe or fear;
Those eyes have known Othello's scowl,
The maniac glare of Lear.
The deep, full voice, whose tones can sweep
In thunder to the ear,
Has learned such softness that the babe
Can only smile to hear.
The strong arms fold the little form
Upon the massive breast.
"Go, mother, I will watch your child,"
He whispers; "go and rest!"
All night long the giant form
Treads gently to and fro;
All night long the deep voice speaks
In murmured soothings low,
Until the rose-light of the morn
Flushes the far-off skies:
In slumber sweet on Forrest's breast
At last the baby lies.
O Saviour, Thou didst bid one day
The children come to Thee!
He who has served Thy little ones,
Hath he not, too, served Thee?
Low lies the actor now at rest
Beneath the summer light;
Sweet be his sleep as that he gave

The suffering child that night!
Lucy H. Hooper.

The other anecdote, though less dramatic, is of still deeper
significance as a revelation of his soul. During the last ten or twelve
years of his life, when he was fulfilling his engagements in the different
cities, he used so to time and direct his walks that he might be near
some great public school at the hour when the children were
dismissed. There he would stand—the grim-looking, lonely old man,
whose surface might be hard, but whose heart was very soft—and gaze
with a thoughtful and loving regard on the throng of boys and girls as
they rushed out bubbling over with delight, variously sorting and
grouping themselves on their way home. This was a great enjoyment
to him, though not unmixed with an attractive pain. It soothed his
childless soul with ideal parentage, gave him a bright glad life in
reflected sympathy with the dancing shouters he saw, and stirred in his
imagination a thousand dreams, now of the irrevocable past, now of
the mysterious future.

Resuming the narrative with the opening of June, 1872, Forrest is
lying in his bed in a woeful state, brought on him by a nostrum called
"Jenkins's cure for gout." A doctor Jenkins of New Orleans told him if
he would take it, it would produce an excruciating attack of the
disease, but would then eradicate it from the system and effect a
permanent cure. He took it. He experienced the excruciating attack.
The permanent cure did not follow. As soon as Oakes learned of his
situation, body racked with torture, limbs palsied, mind at times
unhinged and wandering, he started for the scene. His own words will
best describe their meeting. "When I entered his chamber he was in a
doze, and I stood at his bedside until he awoke. Opening his eyes, he
gazed steadily into my face for about a minute. He knew me then, and
said, in the most touching manner, 'My friend, I am always glad to see
you, but never in my life so much so as now.' Again looking steadily at
me for about a minute, he said, ' Oakes, put my hand in yours: it is
paralyzed but true.' I took his hand tenderly from the bed and placed
it in mine. He could not move the fingers, but I felt his noble heart

throb through them. At once I began organizing my hospital. I had him washed, his flannel and the bed-linen changed, the doors and windows flung wide open, and gave him all he could take of the best of nourishment,—strawberries, fresh buttermilk, and beef tea strong enough to draw four hundred pounds the whole length of the house. Already he is greatly improved. I keep him perfectly quiet, allowing no one on any excuse whatever to see him." Under this style of doctoring and nursing, all impregnated with the magnetism of friendship, it was natural that in three weeks he should be comfortably about his house, as he was.

One morning in the midst of his illness, but when he had passed a night free from pain, and his mind was in a most serene state yet marked by great exaltation of thought and language, he began relating to Oakes, in the most eloquent manner, his recollections of old Joseph Jefferson, the great comedian. He told how when a boy he had visited that beautiful and gifted old man; what poverty and what purity and high morality were in his household; how he had educated his children; and how at last he had died among strangers, heart-broken by ingratitude. He told how he had seen him act Dogberry in a way that out-topped all comparison; how at a later time he had again seen him play the part of the Fool in Lear so as to set up an idol in the memory of the beholders, for he insinuated into the words such wonderful contrasts of the greatness and misery and mystery of life with the seeming ignorant and innocent simplicity of the comments on them, that comedy became wiser and stronger than tragedy.

His listener afterwards said, "We two were alone. Never had I seen him so deeply and so loftily stirred in his very soul as he was then about Jefferson. His eulogy had more moral dignity and intense religious feeling than any sermon I ever heard from the pulpit. It was as grand and fine as anything said by Cicero. This was especially true of his closing words. When he seemed to have emptied his heart in admiring praises on the old player, he ended thus, querying with himself as if soliloquizing: 'Is it possible that all of such a man can go into the ground and rot, and nothing of him at all be left forever? If he is not immortal, he ought to be. It must be that he is, though our philosophy cannot find it out."

It is a curious proof of how his moods shaped and colored his beliefs to read in connection with the above the following extract from a letter he wrote in 1866. "There is great consolation in the sincere belief of the immortality of the soul. If I could honestly and reasonably entertain such a faith, that the love and friendship of to-day will extend through all time with renewed devotion, death would have no sting and the grave no victory. I quite envied the closing hours of Senator Foote the other day. He was so serenely confident of seeing all his friends again, that by the perishing light of his fervid brain he seemed for a moment to realize the illusion of his earth-taught faith."

It was now September. The semi-paralyzed condition of his limbs forbade every thought of returning to the stage that season; though, with a self-flattery singular in one of so experienced and clear a head, he fondly hoped to recover in time, and to act for years yet His interest in everything connected with his profession knew no abatement, and he always took the most cheerful view of the future of the drama. He did not yield to that common fallacy which glorifies the past at the expense of the present and holds that everything glorious is always in decline and sure ere long to perish. Sheridan said, while surrounded by Johnson, Burke, Hume, Robertson, Gibbon, Pitt, and Fox, "The days of little men have arrived." The trouble is that we see the foibles and feel the faults of our contemporaries, but not those of our predecessors who sit, afar and still, aggrandized into Olympians in historic memory. Mrs. Siddons often saw before her, sitting together in the orchestra, all in tears, Burke, Reynolds, Fox, Gibbon, Windham, and Sheridan. Yet in her day as now the constant talk was of the failing glory of the theatre. Also in the time of Talma, in 1807, Cailhava presented a memoir to the Institute of France, "Sur les Causes de la Décadence du Théâtre." The fact is, the theatres of the world were never so numerous, so splendid, so largely attended, as now; the playing as a whole was never so good, the morality of the pieces never so high, and the behavior of the audiences never so orderly and refined. In spite of everything that can be said on the other side, this is the truth. The former advantage of the drama was simply that it stood out in more solitary and conspicuous relief, occupied a larger relative space, and made therefore a greater and more talked-of sensation. Its rule is now divided with a swarm of other claimants. Still, intrinsically its worth and rank must increase in the future, and not diminish. Forrest always clearly held to this faith, and was much cheered by it. His conviction that the drama was charged with a sacred and indestructible mission, and his enthusiastic love for the personal practice of its art,—these were thoughts and feelings

"In him which though all others should decay,
Would be the last that time could bear away."

Accordingly, he would withdraw from the worship of his life, if withdraw he must, only piecemeal and as compelled. His voice was unimpaired, and he had for years been solicited to give readings. And so he resolved, since he could not play Hamlet and Othello on the stage, he would read them in the lecture-room.

Therefore he read these two plays in Philadelphia, Wilmington, Brooklyn, New York, and Boston. Although the rich mellow fulness, ease, and force of his elocution were highly enjoyable, and there were many beauties of characterization in his readings, his physique was so deeply shattered, and his vital forces so depressed, that the vivacity, the magnetism, the spirited variety of power necessary to draw and to hold a miscellaneous crowd were wanting. The experiment was comparatively a failure. The large halls were so thinly seated that, though the marks of approval were strong, the result was not inspiring. He felt somewhat disheartened, much wearied, and sighed for a good long period of rest in his own quiet home. And so on Saturday afternoon, December 7, 1872, in Tremont Temple, Boston, he read Othello, and made unconsciously his last bow on earth to a public assembly, with the apt words of the unhappy Moor, whose character much resembled his own:

"I kissed thee ere I killed thee: no way but this,—
Killing myself, to die upon a kiss."

Oakes went with him to the train, saw him comfortably installed in the car, and bade him an affectionate good-bye. "Another parting, my friend!" said Forrest: "the last one must come some time. I shall probably be the first to die." Arriving at the hotel in New York, he ordered a room and a fire, and went to bed, "and lay there thinking," as he said, "what a pleasant time he was indebted to his friend for in Boston." He reached home safely on the 9th. Two days he passed in rest, lounging about his library, reading a little, and attending only to a few necessary matters of business. "The time glided away like an ecstatic dream, without any let or hindrance," he wrote on the 11th to Oakes,—the last letter he ever penned,—closing with the words, "God bless you ever, my dear and much valued friend."

The earthly finale was at hand. Twenty years before this, in 1852, he wrote to one of his early friends:

"I thank you for your kindness in drinking my health in company with my sisters to-day, the anniversary of my birth. The weather here is gloomy and wears an aspect in accordance with the color of my fate. There is a destiny in this strange world which often decrees an undeserved doom. The ways of Providence are truly mysterious. From boyhood to the present time I have endeavored to walk the paths of honor and honesty with a kindly and benevolent spirit towards all men. And I am not unwilling that my whole course of life should be scrutinized with justice and impartiality. When it shall be so all weighed together I have no fear of the result. And yet I have been fearfully wronged, maligned, and persecuted. I do not, however, lose my faith and trust in that God who will one day hold all men to a strict and sure account. Kind regards to all, and believe me,

"Ever yours,
"Edwin Forrest."

On the eighth recurrence of the same anniversary after the date of the above sombre epistle—that is, in 1860—he wrote these words:

"Friendship is as much prostituted as love. My heart is sick, and I grow aweary of life." And once more, on the 9th of March, 1871, he set down his feeling in the melancholy sentence, "This is my birthday, another funeral procession in my sad life, and the end not far off." These expressions reveal the gloomier side of a soul which had its sunny side as well, and the more painful aspect of a life which was also abundantly blessed with wealth, triumphs, and pleasures. But be the outward lot of any man what it may, unless he has communion with God, a love for his fellows that swallows up every hatred, and a firm faith in immortality, the burden of the song of his unsatisfied soul will ever be, "Vanity of vanities, all is vanity."

But sooner or later there is an hour for every earthly vanity to cease. Nothing mortal can escape or be denied the universal fate and boon of death. Its meaning is the same for all, however diverse its disguises or varied its forms. A slave and prisoner, starved and festered in his chains, groaned, as the sweet and strange release came, "How welcome is this deliverance! Farewell, painful world and cruel men!" A Sultan, stricken and sinking on his throne, cried, "O God, I am passing away in the hand of the wind!" A fool, in his painted costume, with his grinning bauble in his hand, said, as he too vanished into the hospitable Unknown, "Alackaday, poor Tom is a dying, and nobody cares. O me! was there ever such a pitiful to-do?" And a Pope, the crucifix lifted before his eyes and the tiara trembling from his brow, breathed his life out in the words, "Now I surrender my soul to Him who gave it!"

The death of a player is particularly suggestive and impressive from the sharp contrast of its perfect reality and sincerity with all the fictitious assumptions and scenery of his professional life. The last drop-scene is the lowering of the eyelid on that emptied ocular stage which in its time has held so many acts and actors. The deaths of many players have been marked by mysterious coincidences. Powell, starting from the bed on which he lay ill, cried, "Is this a dagger which I see before me? O God!"— and instantly expired. Peterson, playing the Duke in *Measure for Measure*, said,—

"Reason thus with life:
If I do lose thee, I do lose a thing
That none but fools would keep; a breath thou art"—

and fell into the arms of the Friar to whom he was speaking; and these were his last words. Cummings had just spoken the words of Dumont in Jane Shore—

"Be witness for me, ye celestial hosts,
Such mercy and such pardon as my soul
Accords to thee and begs of heaven to show thee,
May such befall me at my latest hour"—

when he suddenly gasped, and was dead. Palmer, while enacting the part of the Stranger, having uttered the sentence in his rôle, "There is another and a better world," dropped lifeless on the stage. In such instances Fate interpolates in the stereotyped performance a dread impromptu which must make us all feel what mysteries we are and by what mysteries enshrouded.

The morning of the 12th came, and the death of Edwin Forrest was at hand. In the early light, solitary in the privacy of his chamber, he who had no blood relative on earth, the last of his race, was summoned to give up his soul and take the unreturning road into the voiceless mystery. He who in the mimic scene had so often acted death was now to perform it in reality. Now he who in all his theatrical impersonations had been so democratic, was to be, in his closing and unwitnessed human impersonation, supremely democratic, both in the substance and in the manner of his performing. For this severing of the spirit from the flesh, this shrouded and mystic farewell of the soul to the world, is a part cast inevitably for every member of the family of man, and enacted under conditions essentially identical by all, from the emperor to the pauper. Perform or omit whatever else he may, every one must go through with this. Furthermore, in the enactment of it all artificial dialects of expression, all caste peculiarities of behavior, fall away; the profoundest vernacular language of universal nature alone comes to the surface, and the pallor of the face, the tremor of the limbs, the glazing of the eye, the gasp, the rattle, the long sigh, and the unbreakable silence,—are the same for all. Death knows neither politeness nor impoliteness, only truth. Now the hour was at hand whose coming and method had been foresignalled years ago, when, at Washington, an apoplectic clot hung the warning of its black flag in his brain. No visible spectators gathered to the sight, whatever invisible ones may have come. No lights were kindled, no music played, no bell rang, no curtain rose, no prompter spoke. But the august theatre of nature, crowded with the circulating ranks of existence, stood open for the performance of the most critical and solemn portion of a mortal destiny. And suddenly the startling command came. With a shudder of all the terrified instincts of the organism he sprang to the action. There was a sanguinary rush through the proscenium of the senses. The cerebral stage deluged in blood, the will instantly surrendered its private functions, all fleshly consciousness vanished, and that automatic procedure of nature, which, when not meddled with by individual volition, is infallible, took up the task. Then, step by step, point for point, phase on phase, he went through the enactment of his own death, in the minutest particulars from beginning to end, with a precision that was absolutely perfect, and a completeness that could never admit of a repetition. It was the greatest part, filled with the most boundless meaning, of all that he had ever sustained; and no critic could detect the slightest flaw in its representation.

The appalling performance was done, the actor disrobed, transformed, and vanished, when the servants, concerned at his delay to appear, and alarmed at obtaining no answer to their knocking, entered the chamber. The body, dressed excepting as to the outer coat, lay facing upwards on the bed, with the hands grasping a pair of light dumb-bells, and a livid streak across the right temple. A near friend and a physician were immediately called. But it was vain. The fatal acting was finished, and the player gone beyond recall.

The curtain falls. The drama of a life

Is ended. One who trod the mimic stage
As if the crown, the sceptre, and the robe
Were his by birthright—worn from youth to age—
"Ay, every inch a king," with voiceless lips,
Lies in the shadow of Death's cold eclipse.
Valete et plaudite! Well might he
Have used the Roman's language of farewell
Who was "the noblest Roman of them all;"
For Brutus spoke, and Coriolanus fell,
And Spartacus defied the she-wolf's power,
In the great actor's high meridian hour.
How as the noble Moor he wooed and wed
His bride of Venice; how his o'erwrought soul,
Tortured and racked and wildly passion-tossed,
Was whirled, resisting, to the fatal goal,
Doting, yet dooming! Every trait was true;
He lived the being that the poet drew.
Room for the aged Cardinal! Once more
The greatest statesman France has ever known
Waked from the grave and wove his subtle spells;
A power behind, but greater than, the throne.
Is Richelieu gone? It seems but yesterday
We heard his voice and watched his features' play.
Greatest of all in high creative skill
Was Lear, poor discrowned king and hapless sire.
What varied music in the actor's voice!
The sigh of grief, the trumpet-tone of ire.
Now both are hushed; we ne'er shall hear that strain
Of well-remembered melody again.
No fading laurels did his genius reap;
With Shakspeare's best interpreters full high
His name is graven on Fame's temple-front,
With Kean's and Kemble's, names that will not die

While memory venerates the poet's shrine
And holds his music more than half divine.
Francis A. Durivage.

Before noon Oakes received the shock of this portentous telegram
from Dougherty: "Forrest died this morning; nothing will be done
until you arrive." He started at once, and reached Philadelphia in the
bitter cold of the next morning at four o'clock. Describing the scene, at
a later period, he writes, "I went directly into his bedchamber. There he
lay, white and pulseless as a man of marble. For a few minutes it
seemed to me that my body was as cold as his and my heart as still. The
little while I stood at his side, speechless, almost lifeless, seemed an age.
No language can express the agony of that hour, and even now I
cannot bear to turn my mind back to it."

Arrangements were made for a simple and unostentatious funeral; a
modest card of invitation being sent to only about sixty of his nearest
friends or associates in private and professional life. But it was found
necessary to forego the design of a reserved and quiet burial on
account of the multitudes who felt so deep an interest in the occasion,
and expressed so strong a desire to be present at the last services that
they could not be refused admission. When the hour arrived, on that
dark and rainy December day, the heavens muffled in black and
weeping as if they felt with the human gloom below, the streets were
blocked with the crowd, all anxious to see once more, ere it was borne
forever from sight, the memorable form and face. The doors were
thrown open to them, and it was estimated that nearly two thousand
people in steady stream flowed in and out, each one in turn taking his
final gaze. The house was draped in mourning and profusely filled
with flowers. In a casket covered with a black cloth, silver mounted,
and with six silver handles, clothed in a black dress suit, reposed the
dead actor. Every trace of passion and of pain was gone from the firm
and fair countenance, looking startlingly like life, whose placid repose
nothing could ever disturb again. All over the body and the casket and
around it were heaped floral tributes in every form, sent from far and
near,—crosses, wreaths, crowns, and careless clusters. From four

actresses in four different cities came a cross of red and white roses, a basket of evergreens, a wreath of japonicas, and a crown of white camelias. Delegations from various dramatic associations were present. A large deputation of the Lotus Club came from New York with the mayor of that city at their head. All classes were there, from the most distinguished to the most humble. Many of the old steadfast friends of other days passed the coffin, and looked their last on its occupant, with dripping eyes. One, a life-long professional coadjutor, stooped and kissed the clay-cold brow. Several poor men and women who had been blessed by his silent charities touched every heart by the deep grief they showed. And the household servants wept aloud at parting from the old master who had made himself earnestly loved by them.

The only inscription on the coffin-lid was the words,

Edwin Forrest.
Born March 9, 1806. Died December 12, 1872.

The pall-bearers were James Oakes, James Lawson, Daniel Dougherty, John W. Forney, Jesse R. Burden, Samuel D. Gross, George W. Childs, and James Page. The funeral cortege, consisting of some sixty carriages, moved through throngs of people lining the sidewalk along the way to Saint Paul's Church, where the crowd was so great, notwithstanding the rain, as to cause some delay. It seemed as though the very reserve and retiracy of the man in his last years had increased the latent popular curiosity about him, investing him with a kind of mystery. A simple prayer was read; and then, in the family vault, with the coffined and mouldering forms of his father and mother and brother and sisters around him, loving hands placed all that was mortal of the greatest tragedian that ever lived in America.

The announcement of the sudden and solitary death of Forrest produced a marked sensation throughout the country. In the chief cities meetings of the members of the dramatic profession were called, and resolutions passed in honor and lamentation for the great man and player, "whose remarkable originality, indomitable will, and unswerving fidelity," they asserted, "made him an honor to the walk of life he had chosen," and "whose lasting monument will be the memory of his sublime delineations of the highest types of character on the modern stage."

For a long time the newspapers abounded with, biographic and obituary notices of him, with criticisms, anecdotes, personal reminiscences. In a very few instances the bitterness of ancient grudges still pursued him and spoke in unkindness and detraction. There are men in whose meanness so much malignity mixes that they cannot forgive or forget even the dead. But in nearly every case the tone of remark on him was highly honorable, appreciative, and even generous. Two brief examples of this style may be cited.

"One thing must be said of Edwin Forrest, now that he lies cold in the tomb—he never courted popularity; he never flattered power. Importuned a thousand times to enter society, he rather avoided it. The few friendships he had were sincere. He never boasted of his charities; and yet we think, when the secrets of his life are unsealed, this solitary man, who dies without leaving a single known person of his own blood, will prove that he had a heart that could throb for all humanity. Having known him and loved him through his tribulations and his triumphs for more than a generation, we feel that in what we say we speak the truth of one who was a sincere friend, an honest citizen, and a benevolent man."

"In our view Edwin Forrest was a great man; the one genius, perhaps, that the American stage has given to history. The conditions of his youth, the rough-and-tumble struggle of a life fired by a grand purpose, the loves, hates, triumphs, and failures that preceded the placing of the bays upon his brow, and the long reign that no new-comer ventured to disturb, all point to a nature that could do nothing by halves and bore the ineffaceable imprint of positive greatness. He was, essentially, a self-made man. All the angularities that result from a culture confined by the very conditions of its existence to a few of the many directions in which men need to grow were his. His genius developed itself irresistibly,—even as a spire of corn will shoot up despite encumbering stones,—gnarled, rugged, and perhaps disproportioned. His art was acquired not in the scholar's closet or under the careful eye of learned tradition, but from demonstrative American audiences. Therefore such errors of performance as jumped with the easily excited emotions of an unskilled auditory were made a part of his education and his creed by a law which not even genius can surmount. So Forrest grew to giant stature, a one-sided man. Experience and a liberal culture in later life worked for him all that opportunity can do for greatness. That these did not wholly remove the faults of his early training was inevitable, but they so broadened his life and power that men of wisest censure saw in him the greatest actor of his time, and a man who under favorable early conditions would have stood, perhaps, peerless in the history of his art. Such a man, bearing a life flooded with the sunshine of glory, but often clouded with storm and almost wrecked by the pain that is born of passion, needs from the nation that produced and honored him, not fulsome adulation or biased praise, but dispassionate analysis and intelligent appreciation."

One elaborate sketch of his life and character was published—by far the ablest and boldest that appeared—whose most condemnatory portion and moral gist ought to be quoted here, for two reasons. First, on account of its incisive power, honesty, and splendid eloquence. Second, that what is unjust in it may be seen and qualified:

"The death of this remarkable man is an incident which seems to prompt more of indefinite emotion than of definite thought. The sense that is uppermost is the sense that a great vitality, an enormous individuality of character, a boundless ambition, a tempestuous spirit, a life of rude warfare and often of harsh injustice, an embittered mind, and an age laden with disappointment and pain, are all at rest. Mr. Forrest, partly from natural bias to the wrong and partly from the force of circumstances and the inexorable action of time, had made shipwreck of his happiness; had cast away many golden opportunities; had outlived his fame; had outlived many of his friends and alienated others; had seen the fabric of his popularity begin to crumble; had seen the growth of new tastes and the rise of new idols; had found his claims as an actor, if accepted by many among the multitude, rejected by many among the judicious; and, in wintry age, broken in health, dejected in spirit, and thwarted in ambition, had come to the 'last scene of all' with great wealth, indeed, but with very little of either love or peace or hope. Death, at almost all times a blessing, must, in ending such an experience as this, be viewed as a tender mercy. His nature—which should have been noble, for it contained elements of greatness and beauty—was diseased with arrogance, passion, and cruelty. It warred with itself, and it made him desolate. He has long been a wreck. There was nothing before him here but an and waste of suffering; and, since we understand him thus, we cannot but think with a tender gratitude that at last he is beyond the reach of all trouble, and where neither care, sorrow, self-rebuke, unreasoning passion, resentment against the world, nor physical pain can any more torment him. His intellect was not broad enough to afford him consolation under the wounds that his vanity so often received. All his resource was to shut himself up in a kind of feudal retreat and grim seclusion, where he brooded upon himself as a great genius misunderstood and upon the rest of the world as a sort of animated scum. This was an unlovely nature; but, mingled in it, were the comprehension and the incipient love of goodness, sweetness, beauty, great imaginings, and beneficent ideas. He knew what he had missed, whether of intellectual grandeur, moral excellence, or the happiness of the affections, and in the solitude of his spirit he brooded upon his misery. The sense of this commended him to our sympathy when he was living, and it commends his memory to our respect in death."

The writer of the powerful article from which the above extract is taken, in another part of it, said of Forrest, "He was utterly selfish. He did not love dramatic art for itself, but because it was tributary to him."

Now, although the brave and sincere spirit of the article is as clear as its masterly ability something is to be said in protest against the sweeping verdict it gives and in vindication of the man so terribly censured. That there is some truth in the charges made is not denied. All of them—except the two last, which are wholly baseless—have been illustrated and commented on in this biography, but, as is hoped, in a tone and with a proportion and emphasis more accordant with the facts of the whole case. The charges, as above made, of sourness, ferocity, arrogance, cynicism, wretchedness, wreck, and despair, are greatly unjust in their overcharged statement of the sinister and sad, profoundly unfair in their omission of the sunny and smiling, features and qualities in the life and character with which they deal. The writer must have taken his cue either from inadequate and unfortunate personal knowledge of the man or from representations made by prejudiced parties. Ample data certainly are afforded in preceding pages of this volume to neutralize the extravagance in the accusations while leaving the truth that is also in them with its proper weight.

One fact alone scatters the entire theory that the social and moral condition of the tragedian was so fearfully dismal, forlorn, and execrable,—the fact that he had high and precious friendships with women, tenderly cherished and sacredly maintained. These were the foremost joy and solace of his life. They were kept up by unfailing attentions, epistolary and personal, to the last of his days. Into these relations he carried a fervor of affection, a poetry of sentiment, a considerate delicacy and refinement of speech and manner, which secured the amplest return for all he gave, and drew from the survivors, when he was gone, tributes which if they were published would cover him with the lustre of a romantic interest. But it is forbidden to spread such matters before the common gaze. They have a sacred right of privacy which must be no further violated than is needed to refute the absurd belief that the experience of Edwin Forrest was one of such unfathomable desolation and unhappiness.

No, a portrait in which he is shown as a man whose all-ruling motives were cruel egotism, pride, vanity, and avarice, a man "whose nature fulfilled itself, and for that reason made his life a half-ignominious and half-pathetic "failure," will be repudiated by his countrymen. At the same time his genuine portrait will reveal the truth that while he loved the good in this world well, he hated the evil too much,— the truth that while he sought success by honorable means, he too rancorously loathed those who opposed him with dishonorable means,—and the truth that while he won many of the solid prizes of existence and enjoyed them with a more than average measure of happiness, he missed the very highest and best prizes from lack of spirituality, serene equilibrium of soul, and religious consecration.

His literary agent for three years and intimate theatrical confrere for a much longer period, Mr. C. G. Rosenberg, moved by the injurious things said of him, published an article admitting his explosive irritability, but affirming his justice and kindness and fund of genial humor and denying the charges of an oppressive temper and arrogant selfishness. His business manager and constant companion for a great many years loved him as a brother, and always testified to his high rectitude of soul and his many endearing qualities. In one of his latest years, when this faithful servant lost a pocket-book containing over three thousand dollars of his money, and was in excessive distress about it, Forrest, without one sign of anger or peevishness or regret, simply said, in a gentle tone, "Do not blame yourself, McArdle. Accidents will happen. We can make it all up in a few nights. So let it go and never mind." John McCullough, who for six years had every condition requisite for reading his character to the very bottom, bore witness to his rare nobility and social charm, saying, "In heart he was a prince, and would do anything for a friend. A thorough student of human nature, gifted with intensity, he applied himself to the heart, and ever reached it. He was essentially an autocrat. His personal magnetism was great, and he could draw everything to him. Wherever he might be, men recognized him as king, and he reigned without resistance, also without imposition." For six years, after the close of the War, he gave a one-armed soldier, as a vegetable garden, the free use of a piece of land worth twenty-five thousand dollars. This is an extract from one of his letters: "Notice has been sent me that the price of the picture by Tom Gaylord is one hundred and fifty dollars, but that if I think this too much I may fix my own price. No doubt it is more than the painting is worth, but as the young man is just beginning, and needs to be cheered on, I shall gladly give it to encourage him for his long career of art." When a certain poor man of his acquaintance had died, and his widow knew not where to bury him, he gave her a space for this purpose in his own lot in the cemetery. And every winter he gave private orders to his grocer to supply such suffering, worthy families as he knew, with what they needed, and charge the bills to him. Surely these are not the kind of deeds done by, these not the kind of tributes paid to, a misanthropic old tyrant, discontented with himself, sick of the world, and breathing scorn and wrath against everybody who approached him.

The following letter, addressed by one of the oldest and choicest friends of Forrest to another one, speaks for itself:

"Newport, KY., December 30, 1872.

"S. S. Smith, esq.,—

"My Dear Friend,—Our old and distinguished friend is no more. It is a great sorrow to us and to his country. The papers show that all mourn his loss, for he and his fame belonged to the public. I knew Forrest well; except yourself, no man knew him better than I did. He was a man of genius, of great will and energy, and, without much education, by his own untiring efforts raised himself to the very highest pinnacle of fame in his profession. There was a grandeur in the man, in every thing he did and said, and hence the great admiration his friends had for him. He was a truly noble and generous man, one who loved his friends with devotion, and despised his enemies. I first made his acquaintance at Lexington, Kentucky, in the fall of 1822. He came there with Collins & Jones as one of their theatrical corps. He was then between sixteen and seventeen, and was the pet of us college boys. He made his first appearance as Young Norval, and the boys were so much taken with him that after the play was over we went to the greenroom, and took him, dressed as he was in character, to a supper. That night he slept with me in my boarding-house. We had breakfast in my room, and it was late before he left. I wanted to lend him a suit to go home in; but no, he would go in his Highland costume, a feather in his hat, straight down Main Street, with a crowd of boys following him to his hotel. He played all that winter in Lexington, and when the Medical and Law Colleges broke up in the spring he went to Cincinnati. That was in March or April, and he boarded at Mrs. Bryson's, on Main Street. In the summer of 1823 he came to Newport with Mrs. Riddle and her daughter and two or three actors, and rented a house on the bank of the river. I assisted him in fixing up a small theatre in the old frame buildings of the United States barracks at the Point of Licking, and we had plays there until October. My brother-in-law, Major Harris, played Iago to his Othello. I was to have played Damon to his Pythias, but some difficulty occurred which prevented it. Forrest was then very poor, but kept up his spirits, and spent many nights with me in my father's old office. His great delight was to get in a boat and sail for hours on the river when the wind was high. In the fall of 1823 he returned with Collins & Jones to Lexington, the Drakes, I think, uniting, and played the winter of 1823-24. He played with Pelby and his wife, and Pemberton, an actor from Nashville. He improved rapidly in his profession, and had always one of the most prominent characters cast to him. In fact, he would play second to no man. I was very intimate with him that whole winter, and on the first day of January, 1824, Tom Clay and several of us gave a fine dinner at Ayers's Hotel, and he was the *distinguished guest*. We all made speeches and recitations, and before we had finished the entertainment we had an extensive audience. Forrest had many intimate friends among the students, and he often attended the college declamations. He had a great admiration for the eloquence of Doctor Holley, our President, and has often told me of the benefit he derived from the style of this remarkable orator. In March of 1824 I returned home, after the breaking up of the Law School, and played Zanga, in Young's Revenge, at the Columbia Street Theatre. for the benefit pf old Colonel John Cleve Symmes. We had a crowded house. Sallie Riddle played in the same piece. It was to enable Mr. Symmes to get to his Hole at the North Pole; but, poor man, he never got further than New York. I think Mr. Forrest went that spring to New Orleans. I am very certain he was not in Cincinnati when I played in the Revenge, otherwise he would have performed in the same play. It has been published in the papers that Forrest was once a circus rider and tumbler. No such thing. The only time he was ever connected with a circus was when with the circus company in Lexington he played Timour the Tartar. Mrs. Pelby and others were in the same piece. He looked Grandeur itself when mounted on Pepin's famous cream-colored horse. After March, 1824, I did not meet Mr. Forrest again until the spring of 1828. He was then playing in New York, and I saw him in his great character of Othello. His star had then begun to rise, and it continued to rise until it reached its zenith, and there it continued to shine until the last hour of his life. His place cannot be filled in this country. Great actors are born, and not made. To be a great tragedian a man must possess the soul, the passion, and the eloquence to delineate the character he represents. Forrest had that beyond most men.

"I thank you for the paper containing his will and other reminiscences of him. My wife has been since his death clipping from the newspapers all that has been written about him, and has put the notices in her scrap-book. Some of the journals have done him justice, others have not; but posterity will cherish his memory and feel proud of the man. In 1870 I had a copy made of my portrait of George Frederick Cooke by Sully, and sent it to him. I think you saw it. He wrote me at Fire Island, New York, a long and affectionate letter acknowledging the receipt of the portrait and pressing me to spend a week with him at his house. My daughter, Mrs. Jones, has the letter, and has copied it in her book of original letters written to my father by Henry Clay and many other distinguished men of our country. The last time Mr. Forrest was in Cincinnati he walked over one morning to see me and the family. We took him back in my carriage to his hotel, and as he parted from my daughter Martha and myself his eyes were filled with tears, and he exclaimed, 'God bless you!' and left us. This was the last time I ever saw our distinguished and much beloved friend. My daughter, only last night, was speaking of this event of our parting, and how much affected Mr. Forrest seemed to be.

"Forrest was a great favorite with my wife. She knew him in 1823 and 1824, and, before our marriage, had often witnessed his performances at Lexington when a girl. She well knew the great friendship that united us: hence in referring to our boy and girl days in Lexington, Kentucky, she often speaks of Forrest, and how much he was respected and his company sought by the college boys at Old Transylvania. I have a very fine daguerreotype picture of our friend, and two quite large photographs he sent me through you several years ago. They will be faithfully preserved and handed down to my children and to their children as the picture of a man concerning whom it may well be said, 'Take him for all in all, we shall not look upon his like again.'

"All we have left to us, my friend, is to meet and talk over the pleasure we once enjoyed in the company of our friend. He was so full of wit and humor! And how well he told a story! I remember the day, some years back, he and you spent at my house. All my family were present, together with several friends, and he fascinated us all at dinner by his eloquence, and his incidents of foreign travel. How heartily we laughed at the anecdotes which he told with such fine effect! Then we had music at night, and he recited the ' Idiot Boy,' to the delight of every one, and it was the 'witching time of night' when the company broke up.

"I am very truly your friend and obedient servant,

"James Taylor."

Alas, how easy it is, and how congenial it seems to be to many, to let down and tarnish the memory of a great man by an estimate in which his vices are magnified and his virtues omitted! So did old Macklin say of David Garrick, "He had a narrow mind, bounded on one side by suspicion, by envy on the other, by avarice in front, by fear in the rear, and with self in the centre." But against every unkind or demeaning word spoken of the departed Forrest a multitude of facts protest. Two of these may be cited to show the genius he had to make himself loved and admired and remembered.

On receiving intelligence of the death of his benefactor, a literary gentleman who had been tried by severe misfortunes of poverty and blindness and paralysis, and had experienced extreme kindness as well as generous aid at the hands of Forrest, wrote to Oakes a long letter, eloquent with gratitude and admiration, and closing with the poetic acrostic which follows. The writer thoroughly knew and loved the actor both personally and professionally,—a fact that adds value to his eulogistic appreciation:

Ever foremost in histrionic fame,
Death cannot dim the lustre of thy name.
Wondrously bright the record of thy life,
In spit? of wrongs that drove thee into strife.
Nobler by far than titled lord or peer!
Friend of thy race, philanthropist sincere,
On earth esteemed for charms of intellect,
Renowned as well for manhood most erect;
Reserved, but kind, from ostentation free,
Envying no one of high or low degree,
Scorning all tricks of meretricious kind,
Thy course is run, thy glory left behind!
Louis Frasistro.

On the first anniversary of his death a company of gentlemen, actuated by purely disinterested motives, met in New York and organized the Edwin Forrest Club, with a president, vice-president, and seven directors. "The primary object of the club shall be to foster the memory of the great actor, to erect a statue of him in the Central Park, and to collect criticisms, pictures, and all things relating to him, for the purpose of forming a Forrest Museum." After the memory of Forrest had been drunk standing, Mr. G. W. Metlar, a friend from his earliest boyhood, paid an affectionate eulogy to his worth. Others offered similar tributes. And the corresponding secretary of the club, Mr. Harrison, said, "Gentlemen, however well the world may know Mr. Forrest as an actor, it knows comparatively nothing of him as a man. A kinder heart never beat in the bosom of a human being. In the finer sympathies of our nature he was more like a child than one who had felt an undue share of the rude buffets of ingratitude. When speaking with him of the troubles of others I have often seen his eyes suffused with tears. The beggar never knocked at his door and went away unladen. And many is the charity that fell from his manly hand and the relieved knew not whence it came; but

'Like the song of the lone nightingale,

Which answereth with her most soothing song
Out of the ivy bower, it came and blessed.'

And I may say with conscientious pride that however much any of
the great actors may have done for their national stage, Mr. Forrest,
equal to any of them, has done as much for the theatre of his country,
and will remain a recognized peer in the everlasting group.

'He stands serene amid the actors old,
Like Chimborazo when the setting sun
Has left his hundred mountains dark and dun.
Sole object visible, the imperial one
In purple robe and diadem of gold.
Immortal Forrest, who can hope to tell,
With tongue less gifted, of the pleasing sadness
Wrought in your deepest scenes of woe and madness?
Who hope by words to paint your Damon and your Lear?
Their noble forms before me pass,
Like breathing things of a living class.'

The longer I allude to the tragedian the stronger becomes the sadness
that tinctures my feelings to think that he is no more, and that the
existence of the gifts Nature had so liberally bestowed on him had to
cease with the cessation of his pulse.

Everything set down by the biographer in this volume has been
stated in the simple spirit of truth. And if the pen that writes has
distilled along the pages such a spirit of love for their subject as makes
the reader suspect the writer possessed with a fond partiality, he asks,
Why is it so? His love is but a response to the love he received, and to
the grand and beautiful qualities he saw. A dried-up and malignant
heart does not breathe such effusive words in such a sincere tone as
those which, in 1869, Forrest wrote to Oakes: "The good news you
send of the restored health of our dear friend Alger gives me
inexpressible relief. Now I go into the country with abounding joy."

The fortune Forrest had laboriously amassed would amount, it was thought, when it should all be made available, to upwards of a million dollars. It was found that in his will he had left the whole of it—excepting a few personal bequests—to found, on his beautiful estate of "Spring Brook," about eight miles from the heart of Philadelphia, the Edwin Forrest home, for the support of actors and actresses decayed by age or disabled by infirmity.

The trustees and executors have arranged the grounds and prepared the buildings, removed thither all the relics of the testator, his books, pictures, and statues, and made public announcement that the home is ready for occupation. Thus the greatest charity ever bequeathed in the sole interest of his own profession by any actor since the world began is already in active operation, and promises to carry the name it wears through unlimited ages. It pleasantly allies its American founder with the old tragedian Edward Alleyn, the friend of Shakspeare, who two hundred and fifty years ago established munificent institutions of knowledge and mercy, which have been growing ever since and are now one of the princeliest endowments in England.

Those who loved Forrest best had hoped for him that, reposing on his laurels, pointed out in the streets as the veteran of a hundred battles, the vexations and resentments of earlier years outgrown and forgotten, enjoying the calls of his friends, luxuriating in bookish leisure, overseeing with paternal fondness the progress of the home he had planned for the aged and needy of his profession, taking a proud joy in the prosperity and glory of his country and in the belief that his idolized art has before it here amidst the democratic institutions of America a destiny whose splendor and usefulness shall surpass everything it has yet known,—the days of his mellow and vigorous old age should glide pleasantly towards the end where waits the strange Shadow with the key and the seal. Then, they trusted, nothing in his life should have become him better than the leaving of it would. For, receding step by step from the stage and the struggle, he should fade out in a broadening illumination from behind the scenes, the murmur of applause reaching him until his ear closed to every sound of earth.

It would have been so had he been all that he should have been. It was ordained not to be so. Shattered and bowed, he was snatched untimely from his not properly perfected career.

But all that he was and did will not be forgotten in consequence of what he was not and did not do.

He will live as a great tradition in the history of the stage. He will live as a personal image in the magnificent Coriolanus statue. He will live as a learned and versatile histrionist in the exact photographic embodiments of his costumed and breathing characters. He will live as a diffused presence in the retreat he has founded for his less fortunate brethren. Perhaps he will live, in some degree, as a friend in the hearts of those who perusing these pages shall appreciate the story of his toils, his trials, his triumphs, and his disappearance from the eyes of men. He will certainly live in the innumerable and untraceable but momentous influences of his deeds and effluences of his powerful personality and exhibitions caught up by sensitive organisms and transmitted in their posterity to the end of our race. And, still further, if, as Swedenborg teaches, there are theatres in heaven, and all sorts of plays represented there, those who in succeeding ages shall recall his memory amidst the shades of time may think of him still as acting some better part before angelic spectators within the unknown scenery of eternity.

Here the pen of the writer drops from his hand in the conclusion of its task, and, with the same words with which it began, ends the story of Edwin Forrest.

Accept my best wishes.

Horatio Alger, Jr.

Appendix I.
The Will of Edwin Forrest

I, Edwin Forrest, of the city of Philadelphia, State of Pennsylvania, do make and publish this my last Will and Testament.

I give, bequeath and devise unto my friends james oakes, Esquire, of Boston, james lawson, Esquire, of New York, and daniel dougherty, Esquire, of Philadelphia, all my property and estate, real and personal, of whatsoever description and wheresoever situated, upon the trusts and confidences hereinafter expressed; and I also appoint them my executors to administer my personal estate and bring it into the hands of said trustees; that is to say, upon trust.

First. That they the said trustees, the survivors and survivor of them, shall be authorized to sell all my real estate, at public or private sale, at such times as in their judgment shall appear to be for the best advantage of my estate, excepting from this power my country place, in the Twenty-third Ward of the city of Philadelphia, called "Springbrook," and to convey to purchasers thereof a good title, in fee simple, discharged of all trusts and obligation to see to the application of the purchase moneys; and such purchase moneys, and the proceeds of all the personal estate, shall be invested in such securities and loans as are made lawful investments by the laws of Pennsylvania, and shall be in the joint names of the trustees under my Will. The investments which I shall have made my executors or trustees may retain or change as they may think for the best advantage of my estate.

Secondly. Upon trust, to pay to my two sisters, Caroline and Eleanora, jointly, while both remain single, and to the survivor of them until her marriage or death, which shall first happen, an annuity of six thousand dollars, in equal quarterly payments, in advance, from the date of my decease; and should one marry, then to pay the said annuity of six thousand dollars unto the other until marriage or death, whichever the drama, and cause it to subserve its true and great mission to mankind, as their prufoundest teacher of virtue and morality.

Article 9th. The "Edwin Forrest Home" shall also be made to promote the love of liberty, our country and her institutions, to hold in honor the name of the great Dramatic Bard, as well as to cultivate a taste and afford opportunity for the enjoyment of social rural pleasures. Therefore there shall be read therein, to the inmates and public, by an inmate or pupil thereof, the immortal Declaration of Independence, as written by Thomas Jefferson, without expurgation, on every Fourth day of July, to be followed by an oration under the folds of our National flag. There shall be prepared and read therein before the like assemblage, on the birthday of Shakspeare, the twenty-third of April in every year, an eulogy upon his character and writings, and one of his plays, or scenes from his plays, shall, on that day, be represented in the theatre. And on the first Mondays of every June and October the "Edwin Forrest Home" and grounds shall be opened for the admission of ladies and gentlemen of the theatrical profession, and their friends, in the manner of social picnics, when all shall provide their own entertainments.

The foregoing general outline of my plan of the Institution I desire to establish, has been sketched during my preparations for a long voyage by sea and land, and should God spare my life, it is my purpose to be more full and definite; but should I leave no later Will or Codicil, my friends, who sympathize in my purposes, will execute them in the best and fullest manner possible, understanding that they have been long meditated by me and are very dear to my heart.

They will also remember that my professional brothers and sisters are often unfortunate, and that little has been done for them either to elevate them in their profession or to provide for their necessities under sickness or other misfortunes. God has favored my efforts and given me great success, and I would make my fortune the means to elevate the education of others, and promote their success and to alleviate their sufferings, and smooth the pillows of the unfortunate in sickness, or other disability, or the decay of declining years.

These are the grounds upon which I would appeal to the Legislature of my Native State, to the Chief Magistrate of my Native City, to the Courts and my Fellow-Citizens to assist my purposes, which I believe to be demanded by the just claims of humanity, and by that civilization and refinement which spring from intellectual and moral culture.

I, therefore, lay it as a duty on my Trustees to frame a bill which the Legislature may enact as and for the Charter of said Institution, which shall ratify the Articles in said Outline of Plan, shall authorize the Mayor of the City to act as one of its Managers, and the said Court to exercise the visitatorial jurisdiction invoked; and prevent streets from being run through so much of the Springbrook grounds as shall include the buildings and sixty acres of ground. Such a Charter being obtained, the corporation shall be authorized, at a future period, to sell the grounds outside said space, the proceeds to be applied to increase the endowment and usefulness of the Home. And so far as I shall not have built to carry out my views, I authorize the said Managers, with consent of my sisters, or survivor of them, having a right to reside at Springbrook, to proceed to erect and build the buildings required by my outline of plan, and towards their erection apply the income, accumulated or current, of my estate. And should my sisters consent, or the survivor of them consent, in case of readiness to open the Home, to remove therefrom, a comfortable house shall be procured for them elsewhere, furnished, and rent and taxes paid, as required in respect to Springbrook, at the cost and charge of my estate, or of the said corporation, if then in possession thereof. Whensoever the requisite Charter shall be obtained, and the corporation be organized and ready to proceed to carry out its design, then it shall be the duty of said Trustees to assign and convey all my said property and estate unto the said "Edwin Forrest Home," their successors and assigns forever; and for the latter to execute and deliver, under the corporate seal, a full and absolute discharge and acquittance forever, with or without auditing of accounts by an auditor of the court as they may think proper, unto the said Executors and Trustees.

In testimony whereof, I have hereunto set my hand and seal, this fifth day of April, eighteen hundred and sixty-six.

EDWIN FORREST, [SEAL.]

Signed, sealed, declared and published as and for his last Will and Testament by Edwin Forrest, in our presence, who at his request and in his presence, and in presence of each other, have hereunto set our hands as witnesses thereto.

Eli K. Price,

H. C. Townsend,

J. Sergeant Price.

Whereas I, Edwin Forrest, of the city of Philadelphia, State of Pennsylvania, having made and duly executed my last Will and Testament in writing, bearing date the fifth day of April, eighteen hundred and sixty-six. Now I do hereby declare this present writing to be as a Codicil to my said Will, and direct the same to be annexed thereto, and taken as a part therof.

And I do hereby give and bequeath unto my friend James Lawson, Esq., of the city of New York, the sum of five thousand dollars.

And, also, to my beloved friend Miss Elizabeth, sometimes called Lillie Welsh, eldest daughter of John R. Welsh, broker, of Philadelphia, the sum of five thousand dollars.

And, also, to my friend S.S. Smith, Esq., of Cincinnati, Ohio, the sum of two thousand dollars.

And, also, to the benevolent society called the actors' Order of Friendship, "the first one of that name established in Philadelphia," I will and bequeath the like sum of two thousand dollars.

In witness whereof, I, the said Edwin Forrest, have to this Codicil set my hand and seal, this fifth day of April, eighteen hundred and sixty six.

EDWIN FIRREST, [SEAL]

Published and declared as a Codicil to his Will in our presence, by E. Forrest, who in his presence and at his request have signed as witnesses in presence of each other.

Eli K. Price,

H. C. Townsend,

J. Sergeant Price.

Whereas I have this day, October 18th, 1871, provided my friend James Oakes with an annuity of twenty-five hundred dollars' legacy to him, and now do bequeath the said sum of five thousand dollars intended for James Oakes, to my beloved friend Miss Elizabeth, sometimes called Lillie Welsh, eldest daughter of John R. Welsh, broker, of Philadelphia. This five thousand dollars already bequeathed to the said Miss Welsh, making in all to her the gift of ten thousand dollars ($10,000).

In witness hereof I set my hand and seal.

EDWIN FORREST, [SEAL]

Witnesses present at signing:

Geo C. Thomas,

J. Paul Diver.

Appendix II.
The Forrest Medals

The duplicate of the first medal in gold was presented by Mr. Forrest to the New York Historical Society, at a meeting held June 22d, 1868, through the hands of James Lawson. It was accepted, with a vote of thanks to the donor, and placed in the archives of the Society.

The legend or motto on the second medal is from a sonnet by James Lawson "To Andrew Jackson," which may be found in Duyckinck's Cyclopædia of American Literature, vol. ii. p. 280, New York edition, 1855.

The tokens were issued by tradesmen as a mode of advertisement. They are an interesting proof of the great popularity of the tragedian.

I

Ob.—A profile head of Forrest, facing to the left. Below the head engraver's initials, "C. C. W., Sc."

Leg.—"Histrioni optimo Eduino Forrest, viro præstanti, MDCCC. XXXIV."

Rev.—The muse of Tragedy seated, holding in one hand a wreath, the other holding a dagger, and resting on her lap. A mask resting beside her.

Leg.—"Great in mouths of wisest censure."

Ex.—"C. INGHAM, Del."

Metal, silver; size, 1 11/16 inch; edge plain. Two struck in gold, twenty-six in silver.

II.

Ob.—A profile bust of Forrest, facing to the left.

Leg.—"Edwin Forrest."

Ex.—In small letters, "*A. W. Jones, Del.* F. B. Smith & Hartmann, N. Y., fecit."

Rev.—A wreath bound with a ribbon, on which are inscribed the names of Mr. Forrest's celebrated characters. Within the wreath, "Born in the City of Philadelphia, Pa., March 9, 1806." "Just to opposers, and to friends sincere."

Metal, copper; size, 3 inches; edge plain. Two struck in silver; also struck in tin.

III.

Ob.—A profile head of Forrest, facing to the left. Below the head the engraver's name, "Merriam, Boston."

Leg.—"Edwin Forrest, born March 9, 1806."

Rev.—An olive wreath, enclosing the words, "Rose by his own efforts," also engraver's name, "Merriam, Boston." Outside of the wreath, "Just to opposers, and to friends sincere."

Metal, copper; size, 1 1/5 inch; edge plain. Also struck in tin.

THE FORREST TOKENS.

Ob. — A profile bust of Forrest enclosed with laurel branches, and facing to the right.

Rev.—" E. Hill, Dealer in Coins, Medals, Minerals, Autographs, Engravings, Old Curiosities, &c., No. 6 Bleecker St., N. York, 1860."

Metal, tin; edge plain; size, 1 1/8 inch.

II.

Ob. —Same as last.

Rev.—Half-length figure of a man smoking. Legend, "No pleasure can exceed the smoking of the weed."

Metal, tin; edge milled; size, 1 1/8 inch.

III.

Ob.—Same as No. I.

Rev.—A box of cigars (regalias), two pipes crossed above the box. Legend, "Levick, 904 Broadway, New York, 1860."

Metal, tin; edge milled; size, 1 1/8 inch.

IV.

Ob. — Same as No. I.

Rev. — "F. C. Key & Sons, Die Sinkers and Medalists, 123 Arch St., Phila.," enclosed within a circle of thirty-two stars.

Metal, tin; edge plain; size, 1 1/8 inch.

V.

Ob.— A profile bust of Forrest, facing to the right. Legend, "Edwin Forrest."

Rev.—Same as Rev. IX., last.

Metal, tin; edge plain; size, 1 1/8 inch.

VI.

Ob. — Same as No. v.

Rev.—Profile bust of Webster, facing to the right. Legend, "Daniel Webster."

Metal, tin; edge plain; size, 1 1/8 inch.

VII.

Ob. —Same as No. v.

Rev.—"Dedicated to Coin and Medal Collectors," enclosed by two palm branches crossed. Ex., "1860."

Metal, tin; edge plain; size, 1 1/8 inch.

VIII.

Ob. — Same as No. v.

Rev.—A race-horse standing, and facing to the left. "Mobile Jockey Club." "Member's Medal."

Metal, tin; edge plain; size, 1 1/8 inch.

IX.

Ob.—Same as No. v.

Rev.—A witch riding on a broom-stick. "We all have our hobbies." "G. H. L."

Metal, tin; edge plain; size, 1 1/8 inch.

x.

Ob. —Same as No. v.

Rev.—The name "Key" in large letters occupying the entire centre of the field; within the name are enclosed in small letters the following, "Ornamental Medal and Seal Die Sinkers, &c., &c., 329 Arch St., Phila." The whole surrounded by a constellation of stars.

Metal, tin; edge plain; size, 1 1/8 inch.

XI.

Ob.—Same as No, v.

Rev.—"Not transferable, 1853."

Metal, tin; edge plain; size, 1 1/8 inch.

XII.

Ob.—Same as No. v.

Rev.—Cupid on a dolphin. Ex., "1860."

Metal, tin; edge plain; size, 1 1/8 inch.

XIII.

Ob.— Same as No. v.

Rev.—" F. C. Key & Sons, Die Sinkers and Medalists, 123 Arch St., Philadelphia."

Metal, tin; edge plain; size, 1 1/8 inch.

Titles in Alphabetical Order
Original Publisher and Date of Publication

Abraham Lincoln: The Backwoods Boy; or, How a Young Rail-Splitter became President.
JOHN R. ANDERSON AND HENRY S. ALLEN, 1883.

Adrift in New York: or, Tom and Florence Braving the World.
STREET & SMITH, 1904.

Adrift in the City; or, Oliver Conrad's Plucky Fight.
PORTER & COATES, 1895.

Andy Grant's Pluck
HENRY T. COATES & CO., 1902.

Ben Bruce. Scenes in the Life of a Bowery Newsboy.
A.L. BURT, 1901.

Ben Logan's Triumph; or, The Boys of Boxwood Academy.
Cupples & Leon, 1908.

Ben's Nugget; or, A Boy's Search for Fortune.
PORTER & COATES, 1882.

Ben, the Luggage Boy; or, Among the Wharves.
LORING, 1870.

Bernard Brooks' Adventures. The Story of a Brave Boy's Trials.
A.L. BURT, 1903.

Bertha's Christmas Vision: An Autumn Sheaf.
BROWN, BAZIN, & CO, 1856.

Bob Burton; or, The Young Ranchman of the Missouri.
PORTER & COATES, 1888.

Bound to Rise; or, Harry Walton's Motto.
LORING, 1873.

A Boy's Fortune; or, The Strange Adventures of Ben Baker.
HENRY T. COATES & CO., 1898.

Brave and Bold; or, The Fortunes of a Factory Boy.
LORING, 1874.

Cast Upon the Breakers.
DOUBLEDAY & COMPANY, 1974.

Charlie Codman's Cruise. A Story for Boys.
LORING, 1866.

Chester Rand; or, A New Path to Fortune.
HENRY T. COATES & CO., 1903.

Dan, the Detective.
G.W. CARLETON & CO/STREET & SMITH, 1884.

Dean Dunham; or, The Waterford Mystery.
U.S. BOOK COMPANY, 1891.

A Debt of Honor. The Story of Gerald Lane's Success in the Far West.
A.L. BURT, 1900.

Digging For Gold. A Story of California.
PORTER & COATES, 1892.

The Disagreeable Woman; A Social Mystery. (Julian Starr)
G.W. DILLINGHAM, 1895.

Do and Dare; or A Brave Boy's Fight for Fortune.
PORTER & COATES, 1884.

The Erie Train Boy.
U.S. BOOK COMPANY, 1890.

The Errand Boy; or, How Phil Brent Won Success.
A.L. BURT, 1888.

Facing the World; or, The Haps and Mishaps of Harry Vane.
PORTER & COATES, 1893.

Falling in With Fortune; or, The Experiences of a Young Secretary.
THE MERSHON COMPANY, 1900.

Fame and Fortune; or, The Progress of Richard Hunter.
LORING, 1868.

Finding a Fortune.
PENN PUBLISHING CO., 1904.

$500; or, Jacob Marlowe's Secret.
U.S. BOOK COMPANY, 1890.

Forging Ahead.
PENN PUBLISHING CO., 1903.

Frank and Fearless; or, The Fortunes of Jasper Kent.
HENRY T. COATES & CO., 1897.

Frank Fowler, The Cash Boy.
A.L. BURT, 1887.

Frank Hunter's Peril.
HENRY T. COATES & CO., 1896.

Frank's Campaign; or, What Boys can do on the Farm for the Camp.
LORING, 1864.

From Canal Boy to President; or, The Boyhood and Manhood of James A. Garfield.
JOHN R. ANDERSON & CO., 1881.

From Farm Boy to Senator: Being the History of the Boyhood and Manhood of Daniel Webster.
J.S. OGILVIE & CO., 1882.

From Farm to Fortune; or Nat Nason's Strange Experience.
STITT PUBLISHING COMPANY, 1905.

Grand'ther Baldwin's Thanksgiving with Other Ballads and Poems.
LORING, 1875.

Hector's Inheritance; or, The Boys of Smith Institute.
PORTER & COATES, 1885.

Helen Ford.
LORING, 1866.

Helping Himself; or, Grant Thornton's Ambition.
PORTER & COATES, 1886.

Herbert Carter's Legacy; or, The Inventor's Son.
LORING, 1875.

Herbert Selden, The Poor Lawyer's Son.
NEW YORK SUN, 1859.

Hugo, the Deformed.
GILBERT K. WESTGARD II, 1978.

In a New World; or, Among the Gold-Fields of Australia.
PORTER & COATES, 1893.

In Search of Treasure. The Story of Guy's Eventful Voyage.
A.L. BURT, 1907.

Jack's Ward; or, The Boy Guardian.
LORING, 1875.

Jed, The Poorhouse Boy.
HENRY T. COATES & CO., 1899.

Jerry the Backwoods Boy; or, The Parkhurst Treasure.
THE MERSHON COMPANY, 1904.

Joe's Luck; or, A Boy's Adventures in California.
A.L. BURT, 1887.

Joe the Hotel Boy; or, Winning Out By Pluck.
CUPPLES & LEON, 1906.

Julius; or, The Street Boy out West.
LORING, 1874.

Lester's Luck.
HENRY T. COATES & CO., 1901.

Life of Edwin Forrest, with William Rounseville Alger.
J.B. LIPPINCOTT & CO., 1877.

Lost at Sea; or, Robert Roscoe's Strange Cruise.
THE MERSHON COMPANY, 1904.

Luck and Pluck; or, John Oakley's Inheritance.
LORING, 1869.

Luke Walton; or, The Chicago Newsboy.
PORTER & COATES, 1889.

Madeline, The Temptress. A Tale of Two Continents.
NEW YORK SUN, 1857.

The Mad Heiress.
NEW YORK SUN, 1860.

Making His Mark
PENN PUBLISHING CO., 1901.

Marie Bertrand; or, The Felon's Daughter.
NEW YORK WEEKLY, 1864.

Mark Manning's Mission. The Story of a Shoe Factory Boy.
A.L. BURT, 1905.

Mark Mason's Victory; or, The Trials and Triumphs of a Telegraph Boy.
A.L. BURT, 1899.

Mark Stanton.
U.S. BOOK COMPANY, 1890.

Mark The Match Boy; or, Richard Hunter's Ward.
LORING, 1869.

Ned Newton; or, The Fortunes of a New York Bootblack.
U.S. BOOK COMPANY, 1890.

Nelson the Newsboy; or, Afloat in New York.
THE MERSHON COMPANY, 1901.

The New Schoolma'am; or, A Summer in North Sparta.
LORING, 1877.

A New York Boy.
U.S. BOOK COMPANY, 1890.

Nothing To Do: A Tilt at Our Best Society.
JAMES FRENCH & CO., 1857.

Number 91; or, The Adventures of a New York Telegraph Boy. (Arthur Lee Putnam)
FRANK A. MUNSEY, 1887.

The Odds Against Him; or, Carl Crawford's Experience.
PENN PUBLISHING CO., 1890.

Only an Irish Boy; or, Andy Burke's Fortunes and Misfortunes.
PORTER & COATES, 1894.

Out for Business; or, Robert Frost's Strange Career.
THE MERSHON COMPANY, 1900.

Paul Prescott's Charge. A Story For Boys.
LORING, 1865.

Paul the Peddler; or, The Adventures of a Young Street Merchant.
LORING, 1871.

Phil the Fiddler; or, The Story of a Young Street Musician.
LORING, 1872.

Ragged Dick; or, Street Life in New York With the Bootblacks.
LORING, 1868.

Ralph Raymond's Heir; or, The Merchant's Crime (Arthur Hamilton)
FREDERICK GLEASON, 1869.

Randy of the River; or, The Adventures of a Young Deckhand.
CHATTERTON-PECK COMPANY, 1906.

Risen from the Ranks; or, Harry Walton's Success.
LORING, 1874.

Robert Coverdale's Struggle; or, On the Wave of Success.
STREET & SMITH, 1910.

A Rolling Stone; or, The Adventures of a Wanderer.
THOMPSON & THOMAS, 1902.

Rough and Ready; or, Life Among the New York Newsboys.
LORING, 1869.

Rufus and Rose; or, The Fortunes of Rough and Ready.
LORING, 1870.

Rupert's Ambition.
HENRY T. COATES & CO., 1899.

Sam's Chance; and How He Improved It.
LORING, 1876.

The Secret Drawer; or, The Story of the Missing Will.
NEW YORK SUN, 1858.

Seeking His Fortune, And Other Dialogues, with O. Augusta Cheney□
LORING, 1875.

Shifting for Himself; or, Gilbert Greyson's Fortune's.
LORING, 1876.

Silas Snobden's Office Boy.
J.S. OGILVIE & COMPANY, 1899.

Sink or Swim; or, Harry Raymond's Resolve.
LORING, 1870.

Slow and Sure; or, From the Street to the Shop.
LORING, 1872.

The Store Boy; or, The Fortunes of Ben Barclay.
PORTER & COATES, 1887.

Strive and Succeed; or, The Progress of Walter Conrad.
LORING, 1872.

Striving for Fortune; or, Walter Griffith's Trials and Successes.
STREET & SMITH, 1902.

Strong and Steady; or, Paddle Your Own Canoe.
LORING, 1871.

Struggling Upward; or, Luke Larkin's Luck.
PORTER & COATES, 1890.

Tattered Tom; or, The Story of a Street Arab.
LORING, 1871.

The Telegraph Boy.
LORING, 1879.

Timothy Crump's Ward; or, The New Years Loan, And What Became of It.
LORING, 1866.

Tom Brace: Who He Was and How He Fared.
STREET & SMITH, 1901.

Tom Temple's Career.
A.L. BURT, 1888.

Tom Thatcher's Fortune.
A.L. BURT, 1888.

Tom Tracy; or; The Trials of a New York Newsboy.
FRANK A. MUNSEY, 1888.

Tom Turner's Legacy, The Story of How He Secured It.
A.L. BURT, 1902.

Tony the Hero.
J.S. OGILVIE & CO., 1880.

The Train Boy.
G.W. CARLETON & CO/STREET & SMITH, 1883.

Try and Trust; or, The Story of a Bound Boy.
LORING, 1873.

Victor Vane, The Young Secretary.
PORTER & COATES, 1894.

Wait and Hope; or, Ben Bradford's Motto.
LORING, 1877.

Wait and Win. The Story of Jack Drummond's Pluck.
A.L. BURT, 1908.

Walter Sherwood's Probation.
HENRY T. COATES & CO., 1897.

The Western Boy; or, The Road to Success.
G.W. CARLETON & CO/STREET & SMITH, 1878.

The World Before Him.
PENN PUBLISHING CO., 1902.

The Young Acrobat of the Great North American Circus.
FRANK A. MUNSEY, 1888.

The Young Adventurer; or, Tom's Trip Across the Plains.
LORING, 1878.

The Young Bank Messenger.
HENRY T. COATES & CO., 1898.

The Young Boatman of Pine Point.
PENN PUBLISHING CO., 1892.

The Young Book Agent; or, Frank Hardy's Road to Success.
STITT PUBLISHING CO., 1905.

Young Captain Jack; or, The Son of a Soldier.
THE MERSHON COMPANY, 1901.

The Young Circus Rider; or, The Mystery of Robert Rudd.
PORTER & COATES, 1883.

The Young Explorer; or, Among the Sierras.
LORING, 1880.

The Young Miner; or, Tom Nelson in California.
LORING, 1879.

The Young Musician.
PENN PUBLISHING CO., 1906.

The Young Outlaw; or, Adrift In The Streets.
LORING, 1875.

The Young Salesman.
HENRY T. COATES & CO., 1896.

Polyglot
Press

Polyglot Press offers comprehensive collections by well-known authors in a specially designed, easy-to-read typeface.

This book is set in 11-point Minion Pro, an Adobe original typeface designed by Robert Slimbach. Minion Pro is inspired by classical, old style typefaces of the late Renaissance, a period of elegant, beautiful, and highly readable type designs. Minion Pro combines the aesthetic and functional qualities that make text type highly readable with the versatility of modern digital technology.

***

Polyglot Press titles are available in Large Print.

***

Polyglot Press collections include rare as well as scarce titles.

For a complete list of authors, titles, special offers, discounts and future products visit

www.polyglotpress.com.